Santa Fe, Taos & Albuquerque

STEVEN HORAK

Santa Rosa Lake State Park
Pecos River
Santa Rosa
84
54
60
Villanueva State Park
285
40
3
41
Moriarty
Edgewood
Estancia
14
SANDIA PEAK SKI AREA
CORONADO HISTORIC SITE
Bernalillo
TINKERTOWN MUSEUM
TIJERAS PUEBLO ARCHAEOLOGICAL SITE
Sandia
Albuquerque
347
Rio Rancho
South Valley
VOLCANOES DAY USE AREA
Petroglyph National Monument
45
47
Isleta
Peralta
Rio Communities
47
25
Belen
Los Lunas
Rio Puerco
6
Laguna
Navajo Nation
Rio San Jose
Laguna
Laguna
Acoma
Acoma
Navajo Nation
40
Acoma
ACOMA PUEBLO
117
Milan
Grants
El Malpais National Monument

RANCHO BONITO

Manzano Mountains State Park
60

QUEBRADAS BACKCOUNTRY BYWAY

380
Bosque del Apache National Wildlife Refuge
Rio Grande
Rio Salado
25
60
12

54
37

Inset map (MAP AREA):
OK
64
40
Clovis
Roswell
70
Hobbs
180
COLORADO
NEW MEXICO
Taos
Santa Fe
25
Los Alamos
Albuquerque
285
Las Cruces
TEXAS
550
Rio Rancho
Farmington
25
491
40
10
MAP AREA
ARIZONA
MEXICO
380
42

30 mi
30 km
0
0

© MOON.COM

Contents

Santuario de Chimayó

Santa Fe, Taos & Albuquerque

Breathtakingly beautiful, culturally rich, and heaving with history, this landscape holds an unmistakable cinematic quality. It's easy to feel as if you're stepping onto a grand stage, about to be swept up into a time-less epic—a feeling not lost on New Mexico's burgeoning film industry. There are good reasons for this, of course, not the least of which are the numerous Native American pueblos, cliff dwellings, and petroglyphs that speak to an unbroken heritage that dates back hundreds of years.

With its signature adobe buildings and dusty lanes set against the imposing backdrop of the Sangre de Cristo Mountains, Santa Fe looks every bit the country's oldest state capital. Its identity, like much of New Mexico, is shaped in equal measure by centuries-long Spanish Ameri-can and Native American influences, yet this is also a city that has been forged by the artists who continue to be drawn to and inspired by its elemental and otherworldly beauty. Taos, too, is a mecca for creative types, yet its greater isolation makes it feel off the grid; its free-spirited residents are proudly self-reliant. Far to the south, the old Route 66 slices through the physical heart of Albuquerque, in some ways a literal reminder of the city's strong connection to its past, as its forward-think-ing efforts to attract tech startups continue apace.

Make no mistake: This is the high desert, and forgiveness is not in its nature. That said, come prepared for outdoor adventures and you'll be rewarded. From Class IV rafting trips buoyed by snowmelt in the spring to perspective-shifting balloon rides in the fall and hair-raising black diamond ski runs in the winter, the choices before you could oc-cupy a lifetime.

It's this boundlessness—be it in terms of time, vistas, or options—that is perhaps this region's greatest appeal. It's not a place easily con-tained or defined, and it's all the better for it. So, settle back and sample what you can at your own pace. Chances are you will be back for more.

Taos Pueblo

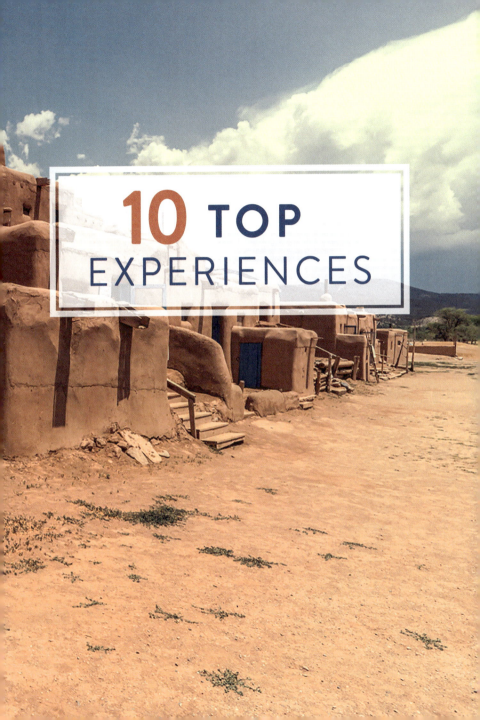

10 TOP
EXPERIENCES

1 Touring **Acoma Pueblo,** the Sky City that has persevered for centuries (page 232).

2 Admiring the stepped adobe buildings at **Taos Pueblo,** home to the oldest continually inhabited community in the United States (page 137).

3 Visiting **Ghost Ranch**—the house where **Georgia O'Keeffe** created her art—and the surrounding landscape that inspired it (page 115).

6   **Ballooning** across New Mexico's endless blue sky (page 205).

7 Appreciating art in Santa Fe at its beating heart, **Canyon Road** (page 51).

Ewe and Me by Kevin Box and Beth Johnson (left) and *Conversation Peace* by Kevin Box (right) in front of Kay Contemporary Art

8 Seeking out **Native American Culture** (page 32), including taking in ceremonial dances (page 31).

Planning Your Trip

WHERE TO GO

Santa Fe

Marked by winding streets and thick-walled adobe homes, New Mexico's picturesque capital is intimate in scale and exudes a golden glow. Scores of **galleries**—including those lining fabled **Canyon Road**—are a major draw, as are **museums** for state history, Native American and folk art, and more. Scenic **hiking** trails are just a few minutes' drive—not far beyond are the cliff dwellings at **Bandelier National Monument,** as well as the landscape that inspired painter Georgia O'Keeffe at **Abiquiu,** and the birthplace of the atomic bomb at **Los Alamos.**

Taos

A small town of about 6,500, Taos is home to **artists,** trust-fund **hippies, spiritual seekers,** and ski bums—in addition to the Spanish and American Indian families who've called the place home for centuries. There are memorable sights, most notably the ancient **Taos Pueblo,** the iconic **San Francisco de Asis Church,** and a handful of small museums, while the **Taos Ski Valley** continues to cement its world-class status. But its atmosphere, cultivated in mellow coffee shops, understated but exceptional restaurants, and **hidden hot springs,** is the real attraction. Spend a day driving around the **Enchanted Circle,** a loop of two-lane roads through high valleys and historic wilderness gateways.

Albuquerque

A modern Western city, and the state's biggest, Albuquerque sprawls at the base of the

Canyon Road, sculptures *Aria* (left) and *Breeze* (right) by Gilberto Romero

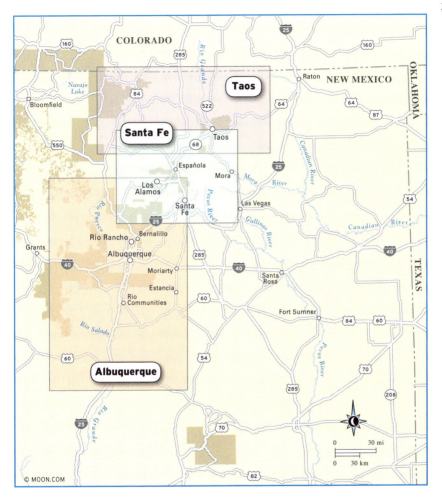

Sandia Mountains. It's proud of its **Route 66** heritage, but it's also preserving **farmland** along the **Rio Grande** and enlivening its downtown core. To the west, the breathtaking **Acoma Pueblo** sits atop a monolithic mesa, while the wetlands of the **Bosque del Apache** **National Wildlife Refuge** to the south attract thousands of migratory birds. Head north to Santa Fe through the former mining towns of the **Turquoise Trail** or alongside the **Jemez Mountains** and the red rocks of **Jemez Pueblo.**

KNOW BEFORE YOU GO

Seasons

About 300 days of sunshine annually mean just about anytime is the right time to visit. **High season** for tourism is mid-May to mid-September, but the early summer can be hot, windy, and dry, with a risk of forest fires. The weather is far more pleasant from **July** on, when the day's heat is usually tamed with a strong, brief rainstorm in the afternoon, and the landscape is shrouded in green hues. **Summer** is the only time to hike at higher elevations, as many trails are still snow covered as late as May. If you want to go **rafting,** plan on late May-early June, when the snowmelt makes the rivers run high and wild. **Winter** sees a surge of visitors heading straight to the slopes, and traditional celebrations preceding Christmas are wonderful; many sights are closed or have limited hours, however.

The **shoulder seasons** have their own appeal and can be cheaper, particularly in **April,** when ski season has wound down, and in **November,** when it hasn't gotten started. Note that **Taos Pueblo closes** to visitors for about 10 weeks February-April. **Spring** weather brings the most

Light Among the Ruins at the Jemez Historic Site

If You Have . . .

- **THREE DAYS:** Pick one city to explore.

- **FIVE DAYS:** Visit Santa Fe, with a night in Taos; or do Albuquerque, with a night in Santa Fe.

- **ONE WEEK:** From Santa Fe, add a day in Abiquiu and Bandelier; from Albuquerque, visit Acoma and the Bosque.

- **TWO WEEKS:** Do it all, including heading north to Chama and driving the scenic Turquoise Trail.

variables, with chances of snowfall or ceaseless hot winds—and roads can be bogged down with mud. In the **fall,** the crowds disperse, leaving crisp temperatures and generally clear skies through late October—great **hiking** weather, especially among the aspen trees, which turn a brilliant yellow.

Advance Reservations

New Mexico is a just-show-up kind of place, but a few special events and activities require some forethought.

If you're planning a visit between **Christmas** and **New Year's,** during Santa Fe's **Spanish Market** (July) or **Indian Market** (August), or Albuquerque's **Balloon Fiesta** (October), book a hotel **6-8 months in advance.**

Attending a **ceremonial dance** is worth planning a trip around. They occur several times a year at every pueblo, on village feast days, Catholic holidays, and around seasonal turning points. Check the schedules for **Taos Pueblo** (page 152), as well as pueblos around **Santa Fe** (page 102) and **Albuquerque** (pages 215 and 234).

The **Georgia O'Keeffe Home** (page 113) in Abiquiu is open to guided tours that can fill up fast; book at least a month in advance.

Online ticket sales for the **Santa Fe Opera**

(page 72) start in October for the July and August summer season. Book in the winter for the best seat selection.

Accommodations in the **Taos Ski Valley** can be hard to come by during the winter months. Reserve your stay a couple of months out if you plan on hitting the slopes.

New Mexico CulturePass

The New Mexico CulturePass ($30) is good for 12 months and grants onetime access to all 15 state-run museums and historic sites. This includes four Santa Fe institutions—the New Mexico Museum of Art, the New Mexico History Museum, the Museum of Indian Arts & Culture, and the Museum of International Folk Art—as well as two in Albuquerque (the National Hispanic Cultural Center and the Museum of Natural History and Science), and the Coronado and Jemez historic sites. It also covers attractions farther afield, in Las Cruces, Alamogordo, and

Taos Ski Valley village

more—great if you're a state resident or you're already planning a longer return visit within the year. Purchase the pass at any of the state's museums and historic sites.

the Rio Grande Gorge Bridge

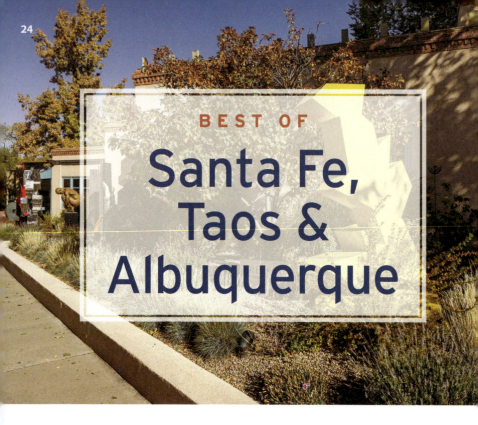

BEST OF

Santa Fe, Taos & Albuquerque

While you could conceivably explore Santa Fe, Taos, and Albuquerque for months on end, seeking out ever more remote hiking trails and sweeping vistas, six days gives just enough time to appreciate the distinct character of each community.

Day 1

Arrive at Albuquerque's Sunport airport; make your way directly to **Santa Fe.** For old-school style, stay at **La Fonda**—it's a short stroll to **The Shed** for dinner, and you can cap the evening with a margarita in the lively hotel lobby bar.

Day 2

Start with a breakfast burrito at **Tia Sophia's,** then stroll around the plaza. Depending on your interests, visit the history museum at the **Palace of the Governors** or the **New Mexico Museum of Art.** Pop in to see the winding staircase at the **Loretto Chapel,** then cruise the galleries on **Canyon Road,** finishing up with drinks and tapas, and maybe even dancing at **El Farol.**

Day 3

Get an early start to **Bandelier National Monument,** followed by lunch at **La Cocina** in Española. In midafternoon, return to Santa Fe to explore the **House of Eternal Return** at **Meow Wolf Santa Fe,** followed by happy hour drinks in the **Railyard** at **Cowgirl BBQ.** Settle in for dinner at **Joseph's** or **Radish & Rye.**

A Landscape that Inspires

Santa Fe and Taos have long histories of fostering creative output, much of it inspired by the surrounding landscape. Tour northern New Mexico with a creative eye, and you'll find art of all sorts in the cities and towns and along the dusty roads in between. What really makes the region special are the numerous opportunities it presents to learn about the inspiration behind the art—often from the artists themselves.

SANTA FE

- Art lovers need not spend all their time in museums (though there are some great ones). It can be just as rewarding to visit studios, talk with artists, and see how their creations come to life. No place in the state—and perhaps the country—exemplifies this quite like **Canyon Road** (page 51).

- Drive the **High Road to Taos** (page 119) to see woodworkers' studios and weavers' workshops.

- Northwest of Santa Fe lies Abiquiu, turf that painter Georgia O'Keeffe called her own, even if she had only a small house in town and a studio at **Ghost Ranch** (page 115). Everything under the sway of flat-topped Pedernal Peak, so often depicted in her work, was grist for her creativity.

TAOS

- Taos is the best place to see where and how local artists lived: At the **Mabel Dodge Luhan House** (page 135), now an inn, Mabel's own bed is still in place in her sunlit room with views of Taos Mountain. Elsewhere in town, the **E. L. Blumenschein Home** (page 131) and **Taos Art Museum at Fechin House** (page 135) both show how artists adapted their residences to their personal styles.

- Perhaps the most illuminating spot is Dorothy Brett's miniscule cabin at the **D. H. Lawrence Ranch** (page 181). Across the yard, in front of Lawrence's only slightly larger home, is the towering pine depicted in Georgia O'Keeffe's *The Lawrence Tree*. Get her perspective, and the curving lines of the painting come into focus.

Above: Dorothy Brett's cabin at the D. H. Lawrence Ranch

Day 4

Drive to **Taos** via the low road, detouring to the pilgrimage site of **Chimayó**. Stop for lunch at **Zuly's** in Dixon. In Taos, head straight to **Taos Pueblo.** Admire the sunset at the **Rio Grande Gorge,** then stop at the **Adobe Bar** at the **Taos Inn** for a margarita and head up the road for dinner at **The Love Apple** or **Orlando's.**

Day 5

In the morning, have breakfast at **Gutiz** or **Michael's Kitchen,** and, on your way out of town, stop by **San Francisco de Asis Church.** Drive back to **Albuquerque** via the high road past Truchas and Las Trampas, then along the **Turquoise Trail,** stopping for lunch in **Cerrillos** or **Madrid** before visiting the **Tinkertown Museum.** In Albuquerque, take a sunset ride up the **Sandia Peak Tramway.** Enjoy dinner and drinks downtown at **505 Central**.

Day 6

Have a big breakfast at **The Frontier** and, if time allows, stroll around **Nob Hill** before catching your plane out of the Albuquerque airport.

Top to bottom: Santuario de Chimayó; historic buildings lining Santa Fe Plaza; Sandia Peak Tramway.

High Desert Adventure

Stark, unforgiving, rugged—all are words used to describe New Mexico's high desert, where Santa Fe, Taos, and Albuquerque are located. Marked by jagged mountains, endless and impossibly blue skies, and flora that endures against all odds, this landscape has a primal beauty that can impact you to your core. The sheer vastness is intoxicating; the adventures that await are suitably epic.

- **Valles Caldera National Preserve:** With mountain streams, thick alpine forests, and herds of elk grazing seemingly endless lush meadows, this pristine 13-mile-wide preserve beckons backcountry **hikers, mountain bikers,** and **cross-country skiers** (page 109).

- **Taos Box:** Steep canyon walls loom alongside the 16 miles of surging waters of the Taos Box; the only way out is **rafting** the increasingly wild rapids that provide thrills and gasps in equal measure (page 147).

- **Taos Ski Valley: Skiers** and **snowboarders** take to the slopes at this world-class resort that has it all—including stunning scenery and a German beer garden (page 148).

- **Hot-Air Ballooning:** As you drift silently over Albuquerque, unmatched views open up in all directions—there's simply no better way to take in the Sandia Mountains and the Rio Grande than from a balloon (page 205).

Weekend Getaways

Just an hour from the Albuquerque airport, Santa Fe lends itself perfectly to a romantic weekend. Settle in at one of the many remarkable hotels and make reservations at a couple of the city's best restaurants (those mentioned here are just a few possibilities). With planning, you could also spend an evening at the Santa Fe Opera in the summer. Isolated, countercultural Taos is worth the extra 90-minute drive if you're really looking to get off the map and off the grid, while Albuquerque offers a fun and funky city break, along with great outdoor activities.

Santa Fe
Day 1
Fly into Albuquerque. Head to Santa Fe via the scenic **Turquoise Trail** and check in to your hotel: **La Fonda** for a touch of history or **Inn of the Governors.** If it's summertime, head to **Canyon Road** for the gallery crawl, which gets started around 5pm. In winter, have a cocktail at **Secreto Lounge,** then walk over to dinner at **Joseph's.**

Day 2
Grab breakfast in a booth at the **Plaza Café.**

Traditionalists can spend the morning at the **New Mexico Museum of Art** and **Georgia O'Keeffe Museum.** Quirkier tastes? Head for the **House of Eternal Return** and **Museum of International Folk Art.** In the afternoon, soak in a private hot tub at **Ten Thousand Waves,** followed by a massage, then dinner at the spa's restaurant, **Izanami.** Hit the late-night movie at **Violet Crown.**

1: Alebrije by Pedro Linares at the Museum of International Folk Art **2:** the House of Eternal Return at Meow Wolf Santa Fe **3:** New Mexico Museum of Art

1

2

3

Day 3

Take an early morning stroll around the **Santa Fe Canyon Preserve.** Treat yourself to brunch at **Harry's Roadhouse** or **Café Fina,** a little south of town, for high-end diner-style goodies and one last great view, then drive back down I-25 to catch your flight out.

Taos
Day 1

Fly into Albuquerque. Head to Taos via I-25 and the **low road.** Pick a prime plaza-view room at **Hotel La Fonda de Taos** or luxuriate in a suite at **Palacio de Marquesa.** Stroll the **plaza** and visit the **E. L. Blumenschein Home** and the galleries on Ledoux Street. Have a gourmet burger for dinner at **The Burger Stand,** then check out **The Alley Cantina.**

Day 2

Visit **Taos Pueblo** in the morning. In the afternoon, tour the **Taos Art Museum at Fechin House** and the **Millicent Rogers Museum.** If you'd rather hike, head for **Williams Lake** in the **Taos Ski Valley**—it's a steep hike, but fairly short. Be dazzled by dinner at **Medley** in **Arroyo Seco.**

Day 3

Drop by **San Francisco de Asis Church** in the morning, then prepare for the drive back south with breakfast at **Ranchos Plaza Grill.** Head out along the **high road** to Santa Fe and then I-25 to the airport, which takes about four hours without much dawdling; a straight shot back down the low road will shave about 40 minutes off the trip.

Albuquerque
Day 1

Arrive at **Albuquerque International Sunport (ABQ)** and transfer to your hotel: Try **Los Poblanos Historic Inn** for rural quiet, or the **Hotel Andaluz** downtown if you want to be in the middle of the action. Stroll around downtown and peek in the **KiMo Theatre,** then have sunset drinks at the **Apothecary**

New Mexico's Cultural Mix

New Mexicans have particular ways of identifying themselves and the elements of the state's unique cultural mix. The people who have lived in the highlands and along the Rio Grande for millennia usually refer to themselves as "Indians," or "American Indians" in formal situations; or they will call themselves by their pueblo's specific name—Jemez or Santa Clara, for instance. The term "Native American" appears occasionally, but most New Mexican Indians see it as just another inaccurate label.

Those who trace their roots to the conquistadors call themselves "Spanish" or "Hispano." The latter is not to be confused with "Hispanic," which refers to Spanish speakers regardless of background. "Hispano" is also distinct from "Mexican" and "Latino."

The third category is the catchall term "Anglo," which really just means "none of the above"— whether you're white, Asian, or even African American, you could be considered Anglo, a relative latecomer to the state of New Mexico.

Lounge, followed by dinner down the street at **Farina Pizzeria.**

Day 2

Stroll around Old Town and take the **ABQ Trolley Co.** tour. Have lunch at **Duran Central Pharmacy,** then check out the **Indian Pueblo Cultural Center.** Spend the evening in **Nob Hill** with dinner at **Frenchish.**

Day 3

Get up early (again) for a **hot-air balloon ride,** overlooking the city from the Rio Grande to the mountains. Head to **The Grove** for a late breakfast, then cruise Route 66 and up to the East Mountains to see the **Tinkertown Museum** and **Madrid.** Optional: Cut west on dirt roads to **Kasha-Katuwe Tent Rocks National Monument** and get a last dose of chile at the **Pueblo Restaurant.**

What to Expect at Ceremonial Dances

Visiting a pueblo for a ceremonial dance or feast-day celebration is one of the most memorable parts of a trip to New Mexico. But it's important to remember that a pueblo dance is not at all for the benefit of tourists. It is a ceremony and a religious ritual, not a performance—you are a guest, not an audience member.

Keep this in mind as a guide to your own behavior. Applause is not appropriate, nor is conversation during the dance. Queries about the meaning of the dances are generally not appreciated. Never walk in the dance area, and try not to block the view of pueblo residents. The kivas, as holy spaces, are always off-limits to outsiders. During feast days, some pueblo residents may open their doors to visitors, perhaps for a snack or drink—but be considerate of others who may also want to visit, and don't stay too long. Photography is strictly forbidden at dances (sometimes with the exception of Los Matachines, which is not a religious ritual). Don't even think about trying to sneak a shot with your smartphone, as tribal police will be more than happy to confiscate it.

On a practical level, be prepared for a lot of waiting around. Start times are always approximate, and everything depends on when the dancers are done with their kiva rituals. There will usually be a main, seasonal dance—such as the corn dance at the summer solstice—followed by several others. If you go in the winter, dress warmly, but in layers. Ceremonies often start inside the close-packed, overheated church, and then dances often proceed outside in the cold.

You can learn more about ceremonial dances in the following areas:

- Santa Fe (page 102)

- Taos (page 152)

- Albuquerque (page 215 and page 234)

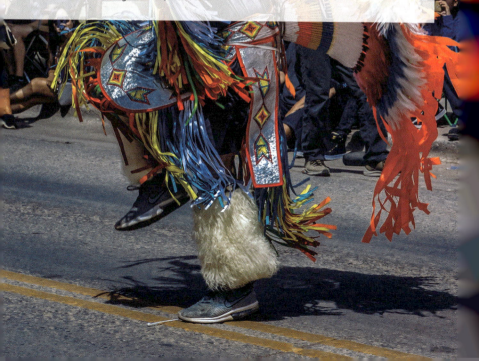

American Indian Heritage

The culture that developed before the Spanish conquest in the 16th century is visible in the pueblos (both ruined and inhabited) and in excellent museums that hold some of the region's finest works. Even if you're visiting only one city on your trip, there's a lot of Native history to see in and around each place—but definitely try to schedule a visit around a dance ceremony, as this will give you the most memorable impression of the living culture.

If you're serious about buying art and jewelry, you could time your visit with the **Santa Fe Indian Market** in August, which showcases more than 1,200 Native American artisans. Otherwise, visit the gift shops at the Museum of Contemporary Native Arts in Santa Fe or the Indian Pueblo Cultural Center in Albuquerque to get an idea of prices and quality; you can also buy directly from craftspeople at the pueblos.

Santa Fe

On **Museum Hill,** visit the **Wheelwright Museum of the American Indian** and the **Museum of Indian Arts & Culture,** two fascinating exhibitions of arts and crafts. Then see what current work is on display at the **Museum of Contemporary Native Arts,** perhaps picking up some craftwork at the gift shop or from the vendors at the **Palace of the Governors.** Even **Hotel Santa Fe,** co-owned by Picurís Pueblo, showcases tribal art.

The pueblos north of the city offer more in the way of casinos than they do in traditional sightseeing, but the **Poeh Museum** at Pojoaque is worth a stop, and collectors will want to make the drive to **San Ildefonso Pueblo** for its stunning black-on-black pottery. Finally, visit the **Puyé Cliff Dwellings** or **Bandelier National Monument** to see the homes inhabited by the ancestors of today's Pueblo people.

Taos

Head straight to **Taos Pueblo**—one of the most beautiful spots in the state, the organic adobe structures seemingly untouched by time (only *seemingly*—in fact, they get a fresh coat of mud nearly every year). Have a meal at **Tiwa Kitchen,** or at least sample the fry bread and chokecherry syrup. Don't miss the excellent weaving and pottery collections at the **Millicent Rogers Museum.**

Albuquerque

Start with a visit to the **Indian Pueblo Cultural Center,** with its excellent museum and café. Then head to the edge of town: to the West Mesa, where **Petroglyph National Monument** has trails past hundreds of ancient rock carvings, and to Bernalillo, north of the city, where you can climb down into a ceremonial kiva at **Coronado State Monument.**

Mesa-top **Acoma Pueblo** is well worth the drive west of the city—along with Taos Pueblo,

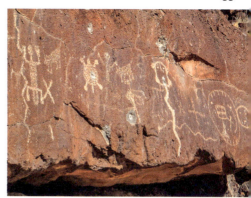

Petroglyph National Monument

it's the most scenic (and oldest) in New Mexico. You can break up the trip with a stop at **Laguna Pueblo** to see its mission church. South and east through the Manzano Mountains are the **Salinas Pueblo Missions,** ruined villages that didn't survive the Spanish conquest. North of the city, the **Jemez Mountain Trail** runs through **Jemez Pueblo**—the red-rock scenery is beautiful, and don't miss the **fry bread** from the vendors set up in front of the **Walatowa Visitor Center.**

Rest up from your road trips at the **Hyatt Regency Tamaya** resort, owned by Santa Ana Pueblo.

Bandelier National Monument

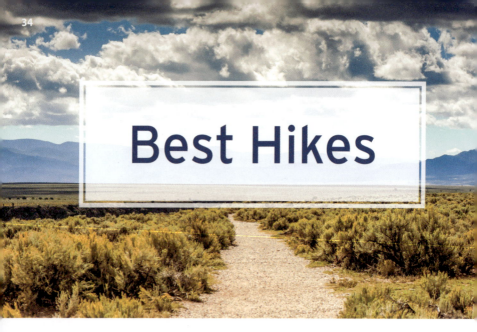

Best Hikes

Not only is New Mexico's mountain scenery stunning, but also the population is sparse, so it's easy to get out of town, hit a trail, and have the natural splendor all to yourself. Bear in mind that hiking is not advisable until at least mid-May; even then you will encounter snowpack at higher elevations. Visiting in the fall may be colder, but the glowing yellow aspen groves that stud the mountains are a major attraction. Hiking distances and times given below are round-trip approximations.

Williams Lake

Santa Fe

- **Atalaya Mountain (6 miles, 4 hours):** This hike, which sets off from a college parking lot and ends at a 9,121-foot peak, is a prime example of the bounty that trails near Santa Fe offer (page 61).

- **Aspen Vista (11.5 miles, 6-8 hours):** Although grueling at times for its relentless ascent on the first leg, this hike offers views—particularly when the aspens change color in the fall—that will keep you pushing onward. The first 2.5 miles are the most aspen-intense, so if you don't have a full day to spare, you can do a shorter out-and-back hike (page 61).

- **Rio en Medio (7 miles, 4-5 hours):** Waterfalls and wildflowers make this trail a perennial favorite among locals. That it's fairly flat for northern New Mexico is a bonus (page 63).

Taos

- **Devisadero Trail (6 miles, 3-4 hours):** Some of the best views of Taos can be had from this trail's many overlooks (page 144).

- **West Rim Trail (9 miles, 3-4 hours one-way):** Take a hike along the state's most famous gorge and keep an eye out for bighorn sheep along the way (page 144).

- **Williams Lake Trail (4 miles, 3 hours):** A pretty alpine lake, cut out of the mountain like a bowl, awaits you on this well-traveled trail in the Taos Ski Valley (page 146).

Albuquerque

- **Embudito Canyon Trail (12 miles, 7-8 hours):** Hike through a canyon dotted with cholla and chamisa at the lower elevations before passing through a forest of pines on your way up to the 9,768-foot South Sandia Peak (page 206).

- **Crest Trail (3.2 miles, 2 hours):** Whether you arrive by the Sandia Peak Tramway or the scenic Sandia Crest Road, this teaser of a hike, with its stunning views, will whet your appetite for more (page 206).

Aspen Vista trail

Best Mountain Biking

While mountain bikers can take advantage of many of the same trails as hikers, those listed below are held in special regard among northern New Mexico's off-road riders.

Santa Fe

- **La Tierra Trails:** Sample a variety of single- and double-track routes on this 25-mile network of trails just outside the city (page 64).
- **Winsor Trail:** With downhill sections, technical challenges, and a dirt road, this 9.25-mile (one-way) trail has it all (page 64).

Taos

- **Alpine Wildflower Loop:** Not too challenging, this 10.3-mile loop trail is one to ride for the mountain scenery, with numerous overlooks (page 146).

- **South Boundary Trail:** Start this classic 20-mile (one-way) tour of the Sangre de Cristos at the Angel Fire Resort, and be prepared for an exhilarating ride with a bit of everything (page 173).

Albuquerque

- **Sandia Peak Ski Area:** In the summer months, head up to this 30-mile network of cross-country trails (page 208).
- **Trail 365:** This popular and varied 16-mile single-track trail is a great introduction to the many rides close at hand in the Sandia foothills (page 209).

The Best of New Mexican Cuisine

Given the region's distinctive cuisine—from only-in-New-Mexico hot chile to gourmet creativity—it would be easy to plan a vacation entirely around eating.

BEST TRADITIONAL NEW MEXICAN

"Red or green?" is the official state question, the dilemma diners face when they order anything that can be drowned in an earthy red-chile sauce or a chunky, vegetal green one (Hint: if you can't decide, choose "Christmas").

- **Tia Sophia's:** History was made in this old-school spot near the Santa Fe Plaza: It's allegedly where the breakfast burrito was invented (page 82).

- **Rancho de Chimayó:** An essential stop after visiting the nearby Santuario, this inviting inn has a menu full of immensely satisfying dishes such as sopaipilla relleno (page 121).

- **Orlando's:** The Taos favorite is known for its green-chile sauce, deceptively smooth and velvety, considering the heat it packs (page 157).

- **Mary & Tito's Café:** This family restaurant in Albuquerque has been named a James Beard American Classic, thanks to its carne adovada (page 223).

BEST GREEN-CHILE CHEESEBURGERS

This greasy treat is so genius, it has been immortalized in the official **New Mexico Green Chile Cheeseburger Trail** (www.newmexico.org). A few GCCB options:

- **Bang Bite:** The signature roasted five-chile-blend burger at this orange food truck draws long lines. The wait is more than worth it (page 83).

- **Santa Fe Bite:** This casual restaurant grinds its own meat and shapes the enormous patties by hand (page 89).

- **The Frontier:** With a pot of green-chile stew at the condiment counter, you can ladle on as much heat as you want (page 221).

- **Laguna Burger:** Unfussy spots—two locations are at gas stations—with exceedingly flavorful patties stuffed inside grilled buns (page 232).

BEST FRESH AND LOCAL

New Mexico's extreme climate makes farming difficult—locally grown produce is justifiably treasured.

- **Café Pasqual's:** At this Santa Fe legend, open since 1979, Chef Katharine Kagel went organic before organic was cool (page 81).

- **Joseph's:** Chef Joseph Wrede, formerly a Taos icon, moved to Santa Fe to teach this glitzy town what New Mexican terroir really is—and even elevates the GCCB (page 84).

- **Vinaigrette:** This "salad bistro" in Santa Fe grows its own greens on a nearby farm and can vouch for every ingredient on its menu (page 84).

- **The Love Apple:** This candlelit bistro proudly lists the source of all of its fresh ingredients, from its beef to its cornmeal (page 155).

- **Campo:** Guests at Los Poblanos Historic Inn in Los Ranchos de Albuquerque enjoy fresh eggs for breakfast, and sublime salads and ribeye steaks at dinner (page 224).

Santa Fe

More than 400 years after its founding as a remote Spanish outpost, Santa Fe remains proudly and blissfully quite unlike anywhere else in the country.

Indeed, this small cluster of mud-colored buildings in the mountains of northern New Mexico seems to subsist on dreams alone, as this city of 70,000 has a larger proportion of writers and artists than any other community in the United States. Art galleries are ubiquitous—one famous half-mile stretch of road alone has more than 80—and lots packed with film crews are increasingly common sights. In all, nearly half the city is employed in the larger arts industry. (Cynics would lump the state legislature, which convenes in the capitol here, into this category as well.)

Highlights

Look for ★ to find recommended sights, activities, dining, and lodging.

★ **Canyon Road Galleries:** Along this road are more than 80 galleries comprising the heart of Santa Fe's art scene (page 51).

★ **Museum of International Folk Art:** In the main exhibition hall, all the world's crafts, from Appalachian quilts to Zulu masks, are jumbled together in an inspiring display of human creativity (page 55).

★ **Meow Wolf Santa Fe:** Meow Wolf's immersive House of Eternal Return expands the mind—and the definition of art—in Santa Fe (page 58).

★ **Sky Railway:** Take a train to solve a murder mystery, or simply gaze upon a star-filled sky (page 60).

★ **Ten Thousand Waves:** As much a part of Santa Fe's identity as a centuries-old adobe, this Japanese-styled spa is the ultimate mountain getaway (page 67).

★ **Santa Fe Indian Market:** The amount and quality of Native American artwork on display during this late-summer celebration is staggering (page 74).

★ **Bandelier National Monument:** Spend a day exploring the once-hidden valley of Frijoles Canyon, where ancestors of today's Pueblo people constructed an elaborate city complex with cliffside cave homes (page 106).

★ **Valles Caldera National Preserve:** You're more likely to spot elk herds than groups of hikers in the lush meadows and pristine backcountry of this massive crater, where you can also mountain bike and snowshoe under the stars (page 109).

★ **Ghost Ranch:** This landscape's dramatic red cliffs and windblown pinnacles inspired Georgia O'Keeffe. Take in the scenery on a horseback ride or hike to Chimney Rock for sweeping views of Abiquiu and the Pedernal (page 115).

★ **Santuario de Chimayó:** Faith is palpable in this village church north of Santa Fe, known as "the Lourdes of America," thanks to the healing powers attributed to the holy dirt found here (page 119).

Santa Fe

To La Tierra Trails

Veterans Memorial Highway

Buckman Rd

West Frontage Rd

Rio Grande

Arroyo de las Trampas

Frank S Ortiz Park

Arroyo Torreon

Solana Laundromat

Bicentennial Alto Park

Camino Alire

Saint Francis Dr

Ras Rody

Tune-Up Café

Avenida Cristobal Colon

14

West Alameda St

Santa Fe River

Frenchy's Field Park

Agua Fria St

Counter Culture

Ashbaugh Park

Iconik Red

Broken Spoke

Santa Fe International Hostel

Pacheco St

Saint Francis Dr

Siler Rd

Tumbleroot

2nd St

Iconik

The Pantry

La Reina

El Rey Court

San Mateo Rd

Cerrillos Rd

Jambo

Saint Michaels Dr

Rufina St

Kokopelli Rafting Adventures

Santa Fe Bite

Llano St

5th St

Calle Lorca

Photo-Eye Gallery

Second Street Brewery

The Mystic

Jackalope

Lu Lu's

General Franklin E Miles Park

Alumni St

Meow Wolf Santa Fe

Taqueria Gracias Madre

Santa Fe Climbing Center

Siringo Rd

Camino Carlos Rey

84

285

14

Herb Martinez Park

Yucca St

Arroyo de los Chamisos

Zia Rd

599

To ⊕ **TEN THOUSAND WAVES**

Rio Grande

Old Fort Marcy Park

HYDE PARK RD

475

THE REEL LIFE

PASEO DE PERALTA

475

DOLINA ▼

BUMBLE BEE'S BAJA GRILL ▼

Santa Fe

PALACE AVE

Historic Fort Marcy Park

Arroyo Sais

SEE "DOWNTOWN SANTA FE" MAP

Santa Fe River

AGUA FRIA ST

GUADALUPE ST

⊕ **SANTA FE INDIAN MARKET**

ALEMEDA ST

NEW MEXICO STATE CAPITOL

SAN MIGUEL CHAPEL

GERALD PETERS GALLERY

Santa Fe

River State Park

Arroyo Cañada Ancha

Santa Fe River

PASEO DE PERALTA

CANYON RD

EL ZAGUAN

★

CANYON ROAD GALLERIES ⊕

4KINSHIP

CRAFT DONUTS & COFFEE

KAKAWA CHOCOLATE HOUSE

NÚART GALLERY

GERONIMO

EL FAROL

NEDRA MATTEUCCI GALLERIES

THE TEAHOUSE

DOWNTOWN SUBSCRIPTION

JOHNNIE'S CASH STORE

CRISTO REY CATHOLIC CHURCH

SEE "GUADALUPE AND THE RAILYARD" MAP

Railyard Park

NEW MEXICO MILITARY MUSEUM

MARIA'S

ALPINE SPORTS

DON GASPAR AVE

CCA CINEMA

CAMINO DEL MONTE SOL

BIKE N SPORT

CLAFOUTIS

Salvador Perez Park

BODY OF SANTA FE

SANTA FE CHILDREN'S MUSEUM

ALTA VISTA ST

CORDOVA RD

GALISTEO ST

Arroyo de los Pinos

SANTA FE BOTANICAL GARDEN

MUSEUM OF SPANISH COLONIAL ART

SAN MATEO RD

MUSEUM OF INTERNATIONAL FOLK ART ⊕

MUSEUM OF INDIAN ARTS & CULTURE

WHEELWRIGHT MUSEUM OF THE AMERICAN INDIAN

SUN MOUNTAIN

OLD PECOS TR

466

Arroyo de los Chamisos

OLD PECOS TR

OLD SANTA FE TR

SANTA FE MOUNTAIN ADVENTURES

To ⊕ **SKY RAILWAY**

PECOS TRAIL INN

0   500 yds
0   500 m

© MOON.COM

The city fabric itself is a by-product of this creativity—many of the "adobe" buildings in the distinctive downtown area are in fact plaster and stucco, built in the early 20th century to satisfy an official vision of how Santa Fe should present itself to tourists. And the mix of old-guard Spanish, Pueblo Indians, groovy Anglos, and international jet-setters of all stripes has even developed a soft but distinct accent—a vaguely continental intonation, with a vocabulary drawn from the 1960s counterculture and alternative healing.

What keeps Santa Fe grounded is its location, tucked in the foothills of the Sangre de Cristos. The mountains are never far, even if you're just admiring the view from your massage table at a Japanese-style spa or dining at an elegant restaurant on mushrooms sourced from secret high meadows. You can be out of town and at a trailhead in 10 minutes, skiing down a precipitous slope in 30, or wandering among the ochre-colored hills you've seen in Georgia O'Keeffe's paintings of Abiquiu in 60. East of the city is the Pecos Wilderness Area, a couple hundred thousand acres studded with summits such as the 12,600-foot Santa Fe Baldy and 13,100-foot Truchas Peak.

Santa Fe's history is intrinsic to that of the Southwest; what took place here echoed across the region and farther east, too. It's the second-oldest city in the United States (after St. Augustine, Florida), and it's surrounded by pueblos that have been inhabited since well before the Spanish arrived, alongside remnants of older settlements, such as the cliff dwellings in Bandelier National Monument. As the capital of the Spanish territory of Nuevo México, Santa Fe was a far-flung outpost, a gateway to the wilder, emptier lands to the north. And it still is, with two scenic routes running north to Taos: The high road winds along mountain ridges, while the low road follows the Rio Grande.

PLANNING YOUR TIME

Santa Fe is an ideal destination for a **three-day weekend.** Add another day or two to take a day hike outside of town or make the drive to Taos, Los Alamos, or Abiquiu. **Summer** is high season, no more so than during Spanish Market and Indian Market, in July and August, respectively. This is also when the gallery scene is in full swing; plan to be in the city on a Friday night, when the Canyon Road galleries have their convivial openings.

In **fall,** the city is much calmer and offers beautiful hiking; the hills are greener, and dense groves of aspen trees on the Sangre de Cristo Mountains turn bright yellow. As in the rest of New Mexico, **spring** and **early summer** can be hot and windy, but the city is still pleasant, as lilacs bloom in May, tumbling over adobe walls and filling the air with scent. **Winter** is cold and occasionally snowy, but cloudy days are few. Late December in Santa Fe is a special time, as houses and hotels are decked with farolitos (paper-bag lanterns) and Canyon Road is alight with bonfires on Christmas Eve. After this, in January and February, hotel prices tend to drop dramatically, as the few tourists in town are here only to ski.

HISTORY

Around 1609, La Villa Real de la Santa Fé (The Royal City of the Holy Faith) was established as the capital of Spain's northernmost territory in the New World. The Camino Real, the route that connected the outpost with Mexico, ended in the newly built plaza. Mexico's independence from Spain in 1821 marked a shift in the city's fortunes, as the new government opened up its northernmost territory to outside trade, via the Santa Fe Trail, from Missouri.

When the railroad arrived in nearby Lamy in 1880, it spurred what's still Santa

---

Previous: Canyon Road, statue *Earth Mother* by Estella Loretto; Bandelier National Monument; Santuario de Chimayó.

Fe's lifeblood: tourism. Loads of curious Easterners flocked in. In 1912, a council of city planners decided to promote Santa Fe as a tourist destination and preserve its distinctive architecture. By 1917, the Museum of Fine Arts (now the New Mexico Museum of Art) had opened, and the first Indian Market was held in 1922, in response to the trend of Anglos collecting local arts and crafts.

Decades later, Santa Fe played a minor part in events that would shape the future of humanity. In 1943, the building at 109 East Palace Avenue became the "front office" and only known address for Los Alamos, where the country's greatest scientists were developing the atomic bomb under a cloud of confidentiality. But the rational scientists left little mark. Right-brain thinking has continued to flourish, and the city is a modern, evolving version of its old self, an outpost of melding cultures that still draws artists and an increasing number of adventurers looking to explore the mountainous landscape.

ORIENTATION

Santa Fe is compact, with many of its major sights within walking distance from Santa Fe Plaza. You're likely to spend much of your time within the oval formed by **Paseo de Peralta,** the main road that almost completely encircles the city's **downtown.** On its east side, it connects with **Canyon Road,** the center of the city's art scene, and Old Santa Fe Trail, which leads to **Museum Hill** and some of the city's finest museums. Southwest of the plaza, around the intersection of Paseo de Peralta and **Guadalupe Street,** is the city's mixed-use **Railyard** district. The Railyard is bounded on its southeastern edge by **Cerrillos Road,** a wide avenue lined with motel courts, shopping plazas, and chain restaurants. Compared with the central historic district, it's unsightly, but there are some great local places to eat here, as well as the few inexpensive hotels in town. About five miles southwest of the plaza, the **Siler-Rufina** neighborhood has a more youthful feel than much of the city and is home to Meow Wolf Santa Fe. If you venture out to the broader **Santa Fe metro area,** you'll find a smattering of diverse sights that are all easily reached via a quick outing from the city center.

Sights

DOWNTOWN
Santa Fe Plaza

Bordered by Lincoln Ave to the west, E. San Francisco St. to the south, Cathedral Pl. to the east, and W. Palace Ave. to the north

When Santa Fe was established around 1609, its layout was based on Spanish laws governing town planning in the colonies—hence the central plaza fronted by the Casas Reales (Palace of the Governors) on its north side. The pretty Santa Fe Plaza, its radial walkways shrouded in shade, is still the city's social hub, and the blocks surrounding it are rich with history. Along the north side, under the portal of the **Palace of the Governors,** is one of the more iconic sights of Santa Fe: American Indians from all over New Mexico selling their craft work as they've been doing since the 1930s. More than 500 vendors are licensed to sell here after going through a strict application process that evaluates their technical skills. Every morning the 69 spots, each 12 bricks wide, are doled out by lottery. Expect anything from silver bracelets to pottery to heishi (shell bead) necklaces to freshly harvested piñon nuts. It's a great opportunity to buy directly from a skilled artisan and learn about the work that went into a specific piece.

The controversial **Soldiers' Monument** (known locally as "the obelisk"), which had occupied the center of the plaza since 1867—and was dedicated to those who died in "battles with savage Indians in the territory of New Mexico"—was pulled down by demonstrators in 2020.

New Mexico History Museum

113 Lincoln Ave.; 505/476-5200; www.nmhistorymuseum.org; 10am-5pm daily May-Oct., 10am-5pm Tues.-Sun. Nov.-Apr.; $12

Opened in 2009, the New Mexico History Museum was intended to give a little breathing room for a collection that had been in storage for decades. Oddly, though, it feels like few actual objects are on display. The permanent exhibits give a good overview, but if you're already familiar with the state's storied past, you might not find much new here.

The museum has **free admission** every Friday (5pm-8pm) May-October, and the first Friday (5pm-7pm) of the month in winter. **Walking tours** depart from the blue gate on the Lincoln Avenue side of the New Mexico History Museum at 10:15am (Wed.-Sat. mid-Apr.-mid-Oct.; $25), covering all the plaza-area highlights in about two hours.

Palace of the Governors

105 W. Palace Ave.; 505/476-5100; 10am-5pm Mon.-Thurs. and Sat.-Sun., 10am-7pm Fri.; $12

Your ticket also admits you to the adjacent Palace of the Governors, the former seat of Santa Fe's government, and a generally more compelling display. An unimposing building constructed in 1610, it's been the site of several city-defining events. Diego de Vargas fought the Indian rebels here room by room when he retook the city in 1693; ill-fated Mexican governor Albino Pérez was beheaded in his office in 1837; and Governor Lew Wallace penned *Ben Hur* here in the late 1870s. The exhibits showcase some of the most beautiful items in the state's collection: trinkets and photos from the 19th century, as well as the beautiful 18th-century Segesser hide paintings, two wall-size panels of buffalo skin. These works, along with the room they're in (trimmed with 1909 murals of the Puyé cliffs) are worth the price of admission. In a couple of the restored furnished rooms, you can compare the living conditions of the Mexican leadership circa 1845 to the relative comfort the U.S. governor enjoyed in 1893.

New Mexico Museum of Art

107 W. Palace Ave.; 505/476-5072; www.nmartmuseum.org; 10am-4pm Tues.-Sun.; $12

Famed as much for its facade as for what it contains, the New Mexico Museum of Art is dedicated to work by New Mexican artists. Built in 1917, it is a beautiful example of Pueblo Revival architecture, originally designed as the New Mexico pavilion for a world expo in San Diego, California, two years prior. The curvaceous stucco-clad building combines elements from the most iconic pueblo mission churches—the bell towers, for instance, mimic those found at San Felipe. Inside, the collection starts with Gerald Cassidy's oil painting *Cui Bono?*, on display since the museum's opening in 1917 and still relevant, as it questions the benefits of pueblo tourism. Look out for an excellent collection of Awa Tsireh's meticulous watercolors of ceremonial dances at **San Ildefonso Pueblo,** alongside works by other local American Indian artists.

On your way out, don't miss the adjacent **St. Francis Auditorium,** where three artists adorned the walls with art nouveau murals depicting the life of Santa Fe's patron saint. It's rare to see a secular style—usually reserved for languorous ladies in flowing togas—used to render such scenes as the apotheosis of Saint Francis and Santa Clara's renunciation, and the effect is beautiful.

As at the history museum, Friday evenings (5pm-7pm) are **free admission** in summer; November-April, only the first Friday of the month is free. Free docent-led **tours** around the museum run daily; call for the latest times. The museum also runs art-themed **walking tours** ($10) around the city center at 10am Monday; June-August, they also run at 10am Friday.

Supply shortages and increased costs have delayed the opening of the museum's new contemporary art annex, Vladem Contemporary, scheduled to open in 2023 in a sleek Railyard building at the corner of Guadalupe Street and Montezuma Avenue.

La Fonda

100 E. San Francisco St.; 505/982-5511;
www.lafondasantafe.com

La Fonda, at the corner of East San Francisco Street and Old Santa Fe Trail, has been offering respite to travelers in some form or another since 1607, and it still hums with history—even though the stacked Pueblo Revival place you see today dates from 1920. "The Inn at the End of the Trail" boomed in the early years of the trade route across the West, and also in the later gold-digging era, with a casino and saloon. It hosted the victory ball following General Stephen Watts Kearny's takeover of New Mexico in the Mexican-American War. During the Civil War it housed Confederate general Henry Hopkins Sibley. Lynchings and shootings took place in the lobby. In the 1920s, La Fonda got a bit safer for the average tourist, as it joined the chain of Harvey Houses along the country's railways, and architect Mary Jane Colter (best known for designing the hotels at the Grand Canyon) redesigned the interior. Since the 1960s, it has been a family-owned hotel.

Something about the waxed tile floors, painted glass, and heavy furniture convey the pleasant clamor of hotel life the way many more modern lobbies do not. Guests pick up their keys at an old wood reception desk, drop their letters in an Indian-drum-turned-mailbox, and chat with the concierge below a poster for Harvey's Indian Detour car trips. Also look around—including up on the mezzanine level—at the great art collection. **La Plazuela** restaurant, in the skylight center courtyard, is a beautiful place for a meal (with good brunches), and the bar is timeless, with live country music many nights.

Cathedral Basilica of St. Francis of Assisi

131 Cathedral Pl.; 505/982-5619; www.cbsfa.org;
9:30am-4:30pm Mon.-Sat.; free

Santa Fe's showpiece, Cathedral Basilica of St. Francis of Assisi, towering at the end of East San Francisco Street, was built over some 15 years in the late 19th century by domineering Bishop Jean-Baptiste Lamy. For more than three decades, the Frenchman struggled to "elevate" the city to European standards, and his folly is exemplified in this grandiose cathedral.

Lamy looked down on the locals' religious practices, as the cult of the Virgin of Guadalupe was already well established, and the Penitente brotherhood was performing public self-flagellation. He also disliked their aesthetics. How could a person possibly reach heaven while praying on a dirt floor inside a building made of mud? Lamy assessed the tiny adobe church dedicated to St. Francis of Assisi, which had stood for 170 years, and decided he could do better. Construction on his Romanesque revival St. Francis Cathedral began in 1869, under the direction of architects and craftsmen from Europe. They used the old church as a frame for the new stone structure, and then demolished all of the adobe, save for a small side chapel. Lamy ran short of cash, however—hence the stumpy aspect of the cathedral's facade, which should be topped with domed towers.

Inside is all Gothic-inspired light and space and glowing stained-glass windows, with a gilt altar screen installed in 1987 for the centennial of the building's dedication. It features primarily New World saints, such as Kateri Tekakwitha, a 17th-century Mohawk woman beatified in 1980 and canonized in 2012 (her statue also stands outside the cathedral). She is depicted with a turtle, representing her membership in the Turtle Clan.

The salvaged adobe chapel is to the left of the altar. It is dedicated to the figure of La Conquistadora, a statue brought to Santa Fe from Mexico in 1625, carried away by the retreating Spanish during the Pueblo Revolt, then proudly reinstated in 1693 and honored ever since. She glows in her shimmering robes, under a heavy viga ceiling. Lamy, who died in 1888, probably shudders in his crypt in front of the main altar.

Downtown Santa Fe

POST OFFICE

SOUTH FEDERAL PL.

GRIFFIN ST

STAAB ST

GRANT AVE

← To Dolina
and Bumble Bee's
Baja Grill

SANTA FE CONVENTION
& VISITORS BUREAU

MCKENZIE ST.

WEST MARCY ST.

COMMUNITY
GALLERY

CHAPELLE ST

TOKO
SANTA FE

LA BOCA

GEORGIA
O'KEEFFE MUSEUM

GLORIANNA'S
BEADS

JOHNSON ST.

SHERIDAN AVE

LINCOLN AVE

TOYOPOLIS

ALLAN
HOUSER
GALLERY

SANDOVAL ST.

TUMBLEROOT
POTTERY PUB

NEW MEXICO
MUSEUM OF ART

NEW MEXICO
HISTORY MUSEUM

WEST PALACE AVE.

WEST SAN FRANCISCO ST.

PALACE OF
THE GOVERNORS

**SEE
"GUADALUPE AND
THE RAILYARD"
MAP**

LENSIC PERFORMING
ARTS CENTER

JAMES
JOHNSON
BUILDING

Santa Fe
Plaza

EVANGELO'S

PLAZA CAFÉ

SANTA FE
DRY GOODS

TIA SOPHIA'S

THUNDERBIRD

MATADOR

SANTA FE
INDIAN MARKET

WEST WATER ST.

FIVE & DIME
GENERAL STORE

SEÑOR
MURPHY

FRENCH
PASTRY
SHOP

35° NORTH

COLLECTED
WORKS

DOODLET'S

CAFÉ PASQUAL'S
TONIC

LA
PLAZUELA

LA FONDA

COYOTE
CANTINA

SANDOVAL ST.

WEST ALAMEDA ST.

GALISTEO ST

ORTIZ ST

SECRETO
LOUNGE

DON GASPAR AVE

SHELBY ST

OLD SANTA FE TRAIL

SERET & SONS

Santa Fe River State Park

THE
PANTRY
RIO

INN OF THE
GOVERNORS

Santa Fe River
State Park

Santa Fe River

To New Mexico State
Capitol and
San Miguel Chapel

© MOON.COM

CAMPANILLA
COMPOUND

PASEO DE PERALTA

OTERO ST

WASHINGTON AVE

Historic Fort

Marcy Park

★
CROSS OF
THE MARTYRS

EAST MARCY ST

CASTILLO PL

Girls Club

ECCO

■ MELLOW VELO

NUSBAUM ST

● HOTEL
CHIMAYÓ

OTERO ST

*Thomas
MacAione
Park*

HILLSIDE AVE

EAST MARCY ST

CIENEGA ST

LA VIDA SPA ■

▼ THE SHED

EAST PALACE AVE

LA CASA SENA
▼

★
MUSEUM OF
CONTEMPORARY
NATIVE ARTS

Cathedral Park

EAST FAITHWAY ST

✝ CATHEDRAL BASILICA
OF ST. FRANCIS OF ASSISI

DRURY PLAZA
SANTA FE ●

LA POSADA ●

EAST PALACE AVE

EAST WATER ST

PASEO DE PERALTA

● LORETTO
CHAPEL

CATHEDRAL PL

TRAVEL BUG ■

0   100 yds
0   100 m

INN ON THE
ALAMEDA ■

EAST ALAMEDA ST

*Santa Fe River
State Park*

On your way out, check the great cast-bronze doors—they're usually propped open, so you'll have to peer behind to see the images depicting the history of Catholicism in New Mexico. One plaque shows the Italian stoneworkers constructing the cathedral, and another shows families fleeing from attack in 1680—a rare depiction of the Pueblo Revolt that's sympathetic to the Spanish.

Museum of Contemporary Native Arts

108 Cathedral Pl.; 505/428-5912; www.iaia.edu; 10am-5pm Mon. and Wed.-Sat., 11am-4pm Sun.; $10

Occupying two floors in the city's former post office, the Museum of Contemporary Native Arts is the showcase for students, professors, and alumni of the prestigious Institute of American Indian Arts. The shows can be hit or miss; if your time is limited, the **Museum of Indian Arts & Culture** on Museum Hill is a better bet. The gift shop stocks items with a good blend of modern and traditional styles.

Loretto Chapel

207 Old Santa Fe Tr.; 505/982-0092; www.lorettochapel.com; 9:30am-4:30pm daily; $5

Initiated by Bishop Lamy in 1873, the Loretto Chapel was the first Gothic structure built west of the Mississippi. Its beautiful interior has a great story to match, although the recording broadcast inside (the place was desanctified in 1971) explaining all this on an endless loop is slightly maddening.

The chapel's decorative elements reflect Lamy's fondness for all things European: the stations of the cross rendered by Italian masons, the harmonium and stained glass windows imported from France. Even the stone from which it was built was hauled at great expense from quarries 200 miles south.

What draws the eye is the elegant spiral staircase leading to the choir loft. Made entirely of wood, it makes two complete turns without a central support pole. It was built in 1878 by a mysterious carpenter who appeared seemingly at the spiritual behest of the resident Sisters of Loretto. The carpenter toiled in silence for six months, the story goes, then disappeared, without taking any payment. He was never heard from again—though some historians claim to have tracked him down to Las Cruces, where he met his end in a bar fight.

San Miguel Chapel

401 Old Santa Fe Tr.; 505/983-3974; www.sanmiguelchapel.org; 1pm-3pm Mon., 10am-3pm Tues.-Sat., docent history talks 11am and 2pm Tues.-Sat.; donations accepted

The San Miguel Chapel is a sturdy adobe building where Mass is still said in Latin at 2pm on Sunday. It is the oldest church structure in the United States, and it's set in Barrio de Analco, the city's oldest residential neighborhood, at the head of De Vargas, the oldest street. The church was built starting in 1610, and then partially reconstructed a century later, after it was set aflame in the Pueblo Revolt. Its stone buttresses are the product of a desperate attempt to shore up the sagging walls in the late 19th century.

The interior is snug and whitewashed, with a restored altar screen that had been covered over in house paint for decades. The late 18th-century work is attributed to the anonymous Laguna Santero, a Mexican artist who earned his name from the intricately carved and painted screen at the Laguna Pueblo church, near Albuquerque. The screen functions as an enormous picture frame, with both oil paintings and bultos (painted wood statues of saints) inserted in the openings. In front of the altar, cutouts in the floor reveal the building's original foundations.

The old church bell, set at the back of the church, is said to have been cast in Spain in 1356. It was brought to the New World and installed at San Miguel in the early 19th century, and it hums beautifully even when tapped.

New Mexico State Capitol

491 Old Santa Fe Tr.

A round building with an entrance at each

1: Cathedral Basilica of St. Francis of Assisi **2:** San Miguel Chapel **3:** New Mexico State Capitol of the cardinal points, the 1966 New Mexico State Capitol mimics the zia sun symbol used on the state flag. In the center of the rotunda is a mosaic rendition of the state seal: the Mexican brown eagle grasping a snake and shielded by the American bald eagle. Don't forget to look up at the stained-glass skylight, with its intricate Indian basket-weave pattern.

But the real attraction of the Roundhouse, as the building is commonly known, is its excellent but often overlooked **art collection** (505/986-4614; www.nmcapitolart.com; 8am-5pm Mon.-Fri.; free), with works by the state's best-known creatives. You'll find paintings and photographs in the halls on every floor, in the upstairs balcony area of the senate, and in the 4th-floor Governor's Gallery.

Oh, and the building is used for legislating—though not particularly often (beginning on the third Tuesday in January, for 30 days in even-numbered years, and 60 days in odd). When house and senate meetings are in session, visitors are welcome to sit in the galleries and watch the proceedings.

Georgia O'Keeffe Museum

217 Johnson St.; 505/946-1000; www.okeeffemuseum. org; 10am-5pm Thurs.-Mon.; $20
Opened in 1997, the Georgia O'Keeffe Museum, northwest of the plaza, honors the artist whose name is inextricably bound with New Mexico. The contrarian member of the New York avant-garde ("Nothing is less real than realism," she famously said) started making regular visits to the state in the 1920s, and then moved to Abiquiu full-time in 1949, a few years after the death of her husband, photographer Alfred Stieglitz.

Many of O'Keeffe's finest works—her signature sensuous, near-abstract flower blossoms, for instance—have already been ensconced in other famous museums, so it's best to temper expectations accordingly. That said, the exhibits provide an intimate look at the artist's life not easily seen elsewhere, as they draw on the work that she kept, plus

ephemera and other work her foundation has amassed since her death in 1986. Often the space is given over to exhibitions on her contemporaries or those whose work she influenced or admired.

The museum offers a variety of **tours,** most notably an in-depth look at O'Keeffe's home and studio at Ghost Ranch in Abiquiu ($60-200).

Construction of a new campus slated to replace the museum, one block east of the current site, is expected to start in 2024. Upon its completion, the new museum will display more of its collection, host more educational initiatives, and provide public access to a one-acre green space.

Cross of the Martyrs and Historic Fort Marcy Park

Sitting at the top of a hill overlooking downtown Santa Fe, the white Cross of the Martyrs is a memorial to the Spanish settlers who were killed in the Pueblo Revolt. It's not a strenuous walk, and the bird's-eye view from the hilltop is excellent.

Behind the cross is Historic Fort Marcy Park, site of the first U.S. fort in the Southwest, though today there are no signs of it remaining. Built in 1846 by General Kearny, the fort was then abandoned in 1894, and the land was disused for several decades. The path up to the cross begins on Paseo de Peralta just east of Otero Street.

CANYON ROAD AND THE EASTSIDE

This narrow mostly one-way street southeast of the plaza epitomizes "Santa Fe style," or at least the ritzy side of it. The galleries are the primary draw, but it's worth heading a bit off the main drag, too. There's a city **parking** lot at the east (upper) end of the road and public parking near the bottom just north off **Canyon Road** on Delgado Street. Public **restrooms** (9:30am-5:30pm daily) are near the west end, in the complex at 225 Canyon Road, behind Meyer Gallery.

★ Canyon Road Galleries

Canyon Road, from Paseo de Peralta to East Palace Ave.

The intersection of Paseo de Peralta and Canyon Road is ground zero for the city's **art market.** This is the beginning of a 0.5-mile strip that contains more than 80 galleries. In the summer, Canyon Road is a solid mass of strolling art lovers—pro collectors and amateurs alike. It's especially thronged on summer Fridays, when most galleries have an open house or an exhibition opening, from around 5pm until 7pm or 8pm.

Hard to believe, but the street wasn't always chockablock with thousand-dollar canvases. Long ago, it was farmland, irrigated by the "Mother Ditch," Acequia Madre, which still runs parallel one block to the south. Starting in the 1920s, transplant artists settled on this muddy dirt road, and the area gradually came to be associated with creative exploits. Eventually the art market really boomed in the 1980s. While those days have long since passed and many of the road's galleries seem to be in the throes of a never-ending game of musical chairs, it remains an enthralling stretch with some real gems.

El Zaguán

545 Canyon Rd.; 505/983-2567; www.historicsantafe.org; 9am-5pm Mon.-Fri.; free

In addition to the galleries and a few of the city's best restaurants, you'll also pass the mid-19th-century house El Zaguán, which contains the offices of the **Historic Santa Fe Foundation.** Named for its long internal hallway (zaguán), the building was the home of a local merchant, James L. Johnson, from 1854, and then occupied by several other city bigwigs after he lost his fortune in 1881. Its **garden** (9am-5pm Mon.-Sat.), laid out in the late 19th century, is a lovely place to rest in the summer.

Camino del Monte Sol

To get some sense of what the neighborhood was like before the gallery era, walk south on Camino del Monte Sol, which is still residential—though decidedly tonier now than in centuries past. Turning off Canyon Road, you'll cross Acequia Madre, shaded by cottonwoods and channeling water through the neighborhood. Farther up the road, starting at No. 558, is a clutch of homes first inhabited in the 1920s by Los Cinco Pintores, the band of young realist painters who called themselves the "five little nuts in five mud huts."

the view at the Cross of the Martyrs

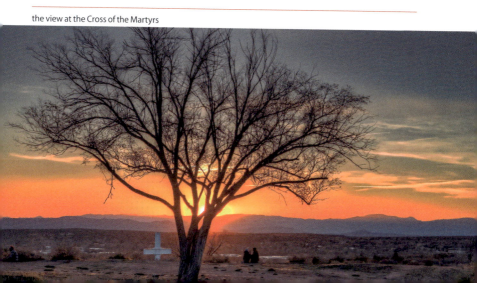

(Will Shuster is the best known of the five today, in part because he started the Zozobra tradition; Walter Mruk, Fremont Ellis, Joseph Bakos, and Willard Nash were the other four.)

Johnnie's Cash Store

420 Camino Don Miguel; 505/982-9506; 9am-3pm Mon.-Sat.; cash only

Cut east on Camino Santander, then north on Camino San Acacio and northwest on Camino Don Miguel to find the several-decades-old Johnnie's Cash Store, a little relic of a corner store, complete with a swinging screen door and a steamer full of famous homemade tamales.

Cristo Rey Catholic Church

1120 Canyon Rd.; 505/983-8528

Head beyond the shops and through a residential stretch to the far north end of Canyon Road to see John Gaw Meem's enormous Cristo Rey Catholic Church. Built of 180,000 adobe bricks around a steel frame, the church opened in 1940 but looks as if it could be much older. Inside is a dramatic mid-18th-century baroque stone altarpiece, salvaged from La Castrense, the military chapel that used to occupy the south side of the plaza.

New Mexico Military Museum

1050 Old Pecos Tr.; 505/476-1477; newmexicomilitarymuseumfoundation.org; 10am-3pm Mon., Wed. and Fri.; free

One of three small museums in a single complex a bit out of the center, the New Mexico Military Museum began as a homegrown memorial for soldiers in the Bataan Death March of World War II. It was a particular tragedy in New Mexico because most of the state's national guardsmen, drafted as the 200th Coast Artillery, were among the more than 70,000 U.S. and Filipino soldiers subject to torture, malnourishment, random execution, and three years' imprisonment. Of the 1,800 who started in the regiment, fewer than 900 came home, and a full one-third of those men died in the first year back.

The troops' experience is recalled with newspaper clippings, maps, and testimonials. The museum also contains Civil War memorabilia and exhibits on Native American contributions in U.S. wars, such as the Choctaw and Navajo code talkers of World War I.

Santa Fe Children's Museum

1050 Old Pecos Tr.; 505/989-8359; www.santafechildrensmuseum.org; 10am-6pm Wed.-Sat., noon-5pm Sun.; $5

Kids can have tons of hands-on fun at the Santa Fe Children's Museum. Fitting for New Mexico, pint-size looms give kids a chance to learn to weave. Then there are the globally appealing bits: a giant soap-bubble pool, face painting, fun-house mirrors, and a dazzling collection of bugs. On Thursdays after 4pm, admission is free.

MUSEUM HILL

These museums on the southeast side merit the trip from the plaza area. It's a short drive, or you can take the "M" route bus or the free Santa Fe Pick-Up shuttle, optionally strolling back downhill to the center, about a 30-minute walk via Camino Lejo and Old Santa Fe Trail.

Museum of Spanish Colonial Art

750 Camino Lejo; 505/982-2226; www.spanishcolonial.org; 1-4pm Wed.-Fri.; $10

The museum of the **Spanish Colonial Arts Society** exhibits a strong collection of folk art and historical objects dating from the earliest Spanish contact. One-of-a-kind treasures—such as the only signed retablo (altarpiece) by the 19th-century santero Rafael Aragón—are shown alongside more utilitarian items from the colonial past, such as silk mantas, wool rugs, and decorative tin. The museum features an extensive collection of Peruvian art, and new work by contemporary artisans is also on display.

1: Santuario de Guadalupe **2:** Standing Skeleton Figure with Animals and Flowers by Felipe Linares at the Museum of International Folk Art **3:** Canyon Road

52 SANTA FE SIGHTS

1

2

3

It's Not *All* Adobe

New Mexico Museum of Art

Santa Fe's distinctive look is the product of stringent building codes that define and maintain "old Santa Fe style," from the thickness of walls (at least eight inches) to the shade of stucco finish, in only "brown, tan, or local earth tones." But look closely, and you'll see some variations.

COLONIAL

Colonial is the term applied to adobe (or adobe-look) buildings, usually one story, with their typical rounded edges and flat roofs supported by vigas, the long crossbeams made of single tree trunks. The style mimics one developed by the Spanish colonists in the 16th, 17th, and 18th centuries, based on their previous experience with adobe architecture and forms they saw in the pueblos. The **Museum of Spanish Colonial Art** (750 Camino Lejo) is one of many such styled buildings throughout the city.

TERRITORIAL

In the 19th century, when New Mexico became a U.S. territory and the railroad could carry new building materials, timber-frame houses came into fashion. These so-called territorial buildings were often two stories tall, with balconies, and trimmed with brick cornices and Greek revival details, such as fluted wood columns and pediments above windows. The **James Johnson Building** (62 Lincoln Ave.), on the northeast corner of the plaza, is a fine example of the style developed in this period.

PUEBLO REVIVAL

In the early part of the 20th century, the Pueblo Revival style was the product of architects like John Gaw Meem and Isaac Rapp, who admired the pueblo mission churches and Spanish colonial adobes for their clean-lined minimalism. Because they used frame construction, Pueblo Revival buildings could be taller: Rapp's **New Mexico Museum of Art** (107 W. Palace Ave.) towers on the northwest corner of the plaza, and Meem's additions to the **La Fonda Hotel** (100 E. San Francisco St.) make it five stories. The trend coincided with an aggressive tourism campaign and the development of a comprehensive look for the city, and in the process many territorial houses were simply covered over in a thick layer of faux-adobe plaster. The result is not really true to history, but the city planners achieved their goal: Santa Fe looks like no other city in the United States.

Museum of Indian Arts & Culture

710 Camino Lejo; 505/476-1250;
www.miaclab.org; 10am-5pm daily May-Oct.,
10am-5pm Tues.-Sun. Nov.-Apr.; $12

The excellent Museum of Indian Arts & Culture is devoted to Native American culture from across the country. Cornerstone exhibit *Here, Now and Always* traces the New Mexican Indians from their ancestors on the mesas and plains up to their present-day efforts at preserving their culture. It displays inventive spaces (looking into a Housing and Urban Development-house kitchen on the reservation, or sitting at desks in a public schoolroom), sound clips, and stories. Another wing is devoted to contemporary art, while the halls of craft work display gorgeous beaded moccasins, elaborate headdresses, and more. The gift shop has beautiful jewelry and other tidbits from local artisans.

★ Museum of International Folk Art

708 Camino Lejo; 505/476-1200;
www.internationalfolkart.org; 10am-5pm daily
May-Oct., 10am-5pm Tues.-Sun. Nov.-Apr.; $12

A marvelous hodgepodge, the Museum of International Folk Art is one of Santa Fe's biggest treats—if you can handle visual overload. In the main exhibition space, some 10,000 folk-art pieces from more than 100 countries are on permanent display, hung on walls, set in cases, even dangling from the ceiling, juxtaposed to show off similar themes, colors, and materials. The approach initially seems jumbled but in fact underscores the universality of certain concepts and preoccupations. Join a guided **tour** (10:30am, 11:30am, and 2pm) to learn all the details.

A separate wing is dedicated to northern New Mexican Hispano crafts (a good complement to the Museum of Spanish Colonial Art) and a lab area where you can see how pieces are preserved. Temporary exhibits take up the rest of the space, usually with colorful interactive shows. Don't skip the gift shop, which stocks some smaller versions of the items in the galleries.

Wheelwright Museum of the American Indian

704 Camino Lejo; 505/982-4636;
www.wheelwright.org; 10am-4pm daily; $10

In the early 1920s, Mary Cabot Wheelwright, an adventurous East Coast heiress, made her way to New Mexico, where she met a Navajo medicine man named Hastiin Klah. Together they devised the Wheelwright Museum of the American Indian, which opened in 1937 as the House of Navajo Religion. The mission has since incorporated all Native American cultures, with exhibits of new work by individual artists rotating every few months. The building is modeled after a traditional Navajo hogan, with huge timbers supporting the eight-sided structure. Another wing, added later, is dedicated to Southwestern jewelry. The basement gift shop is a re-creation of a 19th-century trading post, which would feel like a tourist trap if it weren't for the authentically creaky wood floors and the beautiful antique crafts on display. The museum offers **guided tours** (upon request Tues., Thurs., and Sat.).

Santa Fe Botanical Garden

715 Camino Lejo; 505/471-9103;
https://santafebotanicalgarden.org; 9am-5pm daily
Apr.-Oct., 10am-4pm Fri.-Sun. Nov.-Mar.; $12

The 19-acre Santa Fe Botanical Garden features three distinct areas, with a garden thriving on zero irrigation and an orchard containing peach, apple, and cherry trees, and an annually updated art trail featuring sculptures thoughtfully incorporated into the landscape among the highlights. Note that the art trail is not wheelchair accessible.

GUADALUPE AND THE RAILYARD

The neighborhood southwest of the plaza developed around the depot for the rail spur from the main line at Lamy. Now it's the terminus for the Rail Runner from Albuquerque.

The clutch of cafés and shops here are more casual and local, and generally lighter on the adobe look, as Guadalupe Street falls just outside the historic zone's most stringently enforced building codes.

South of the train depot, the focus of much of the city's efforts at enlivening its downtown core is the Railyard (www.railyardsantafe.com), a mixed-use district where former warehouses and workshops have been adapted to new businesses and residences. As well as holding the city's excellent farmers market, it's also home to two of the best cinemas in the state. The south side of this area is the green space of **Railyard Park,** nicely landscaped with local grasses and fruit trees.

Santuario de Guadalupe

417 Agua Fria St.; 505/983-8868; 9am-noon and 1pm-4pm Mon.-Sat.; free

Built 1776-1796, the Santuario de Guadalupe is the oldest shrine to the Virgin of Guadalupe in the United States. The interior is spare, in front of a Mexican baroque oil-on-canvas altar painting from 1783. Mass is still said regularly, and a museum in the small anteroom displays relics from earlier incarnations of the building, such as Greek-style columns carved in wood. In winter, the church is closed on Saturday.

SITE Santa Fe

1606 Paseo de Peralta; 505/989-1199; http://sitesantafe.org; 10am-5pm Mon., Thurs., Sat.-Sun., 10am-7pm Fri.; free

Fronted by a striking, angular facade, the modern exhibition space of SITE Santa Fe shows edgy art year-round, with installations often taking over the whole interior (and sometimes exterior). In July and August, it's also open on Wednesday, and entrance is free on Friday and Saturday until noon, when the farmers market is on, kitty-corner across the train tracks. A renovation and expansion dramatically increased its footprint and its visual impact, as well as adding a 200-seat auditorium, gift shop, and coffee bar.

El Museo Cultural de Santa Fe

555 Camino de la Familia; 505/992-0591; www.elmuseocultural.org; hours vary; donation

Dedicated to Hispanic culture in New Mexico and beyond, El Museo Cultural de Santa Fe is a grassroots effort in a surprisingly massive warehouse space that has room for installations, live theater, and more. It often

Santa Fe Botanical Garden

Guadalupe and the Railyard

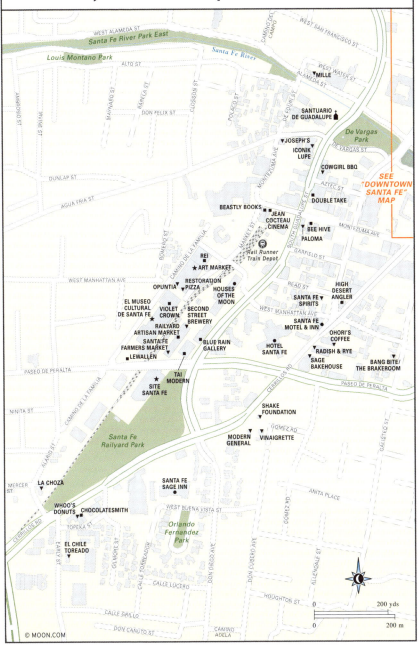

WEST ALAMEDA ST
Santa Fe River Park East
Louis Montano Park
Santa Fe River
ALTO ST
WEST SAN FRANCISCO ST
CAMINO DEL CAMPO
WEST WATER ST
ALAMEDA ST
▼ MILLE
AMBROSO ST
IRVINE ST
MAYNARD ST
BARELA ST
CLOSSON ST
DON FELIX ST
POLACO ST
DE FOURI ST
SANTUARIO DE GUADALUPE ◆
De Vargas Park
DUNLAP ST
AGUA FRIA ST
▼ JOSEPH'S
ICONIK
LUPE
DE VARGAS ST
COWGIRL BBQ
SEE "DOWNTOWN SANTA FE" MAP
AZTEC ST
DOUBLE TAKE
BEASTLY BOOKS
MARKET ST
MONTEZUMA AVE
SOUTH GUADALUPE ST
JEAN COCTEAU CINEMA
BEE HIVE
PALOMA
MONTEZUMA AVE
Rail Runner Train Depot
GARFIELD ST
ROMERO ST
CAMINO DE LA FAMILIA
★ REI
★ ART MARKET
RESTORATION
OPUNTIA ▼ PIZZA
READ ST
WEST MANHATTAN AVE
HOUSES OF THE MOON
HIGH DESERT ANGLER
EL MUSEO CULTURAL DE SANTA FE
VIOLET CROWN
SECOND STREET BREWERY
SANTA FE SPIRITS
WEST MANHATTAN AVE
SANTA FE MOTEL & INN
RAILYARD ARTISAN MARKET
SANTA FE FARMERS MARKET
■ LEWALLEN
▪ BLUE RAIN GALLERY
OHORI'S COFFEE
HOTEL SANTA FE
RADISH & RYE
SAGE BAKEHOUSE
BANG BITE/ THE BRAKEROOM
PASEO DE PERALTA
CERRILLOS RD
PASEO DE PERALTA
★ TAI MODERN
★ SITE SANTA FE
NINITA ST
CAMINO DE LA FAMILIA
Santa Fe Railyard Park
SHAKE FOUNDATION
GOMEZ RD
MODERN GENERAL
VINAIGRETTE
GALISTEO ST
ALARID ST
MERCER ST
LA CHOZA
SANTA FE SAGE INN
ANITA PLACE
WHOO'S DONUTS
CHOCOLATESMITH
WEST BUENA VISTA ST
Orlando Fernandez Park
GOMEZ RD
DON DIEGO AVE
DON CUBERO AVE
ALLENDALE ST
CERRILLOS RD
TOPEKA ST
EL CHILE TOREADO
EARLY ST
GILMORE ST
CALLE TORREAOR
CALLE LUCERO
HOUGHTON ST
N
CALLE GRILLO
DON CANUTO ST
CAMINO ADELA

© MOON.COM

0   200 yds
0   200 m

hosts special events outside of normal museum hours.

SANTA FE METRO AREA
★ Meow Wolf Santa Fe

1352 Rufina Circle; 505/395-6369;
http://meowwolf.com; 10am-8pm Sun.-Thurs.,
10am-10pm Fri.-Sat.; $39-45

The anchor of the thriving Siler-Rufina neighborhood, Meow Wolf Santa Fe features an ethereal permanent exhibition dreamed up by a Santa Fe-based art collective. Giving life to a massive and long-shuttered space once occupied by a bowling alley, the 20,000-foot multilevel **House of Eternal Return** consists of a bewildering mix of kaleidoscopic rooms and nooks, each loosely building on an evolving narrative of the melding of real and otherworldly dimensions. Equally immersive and ambitious, the Victorian house holds the kinds of unexpected and multilayered surprises that reward multiple visits. It's great for both kids and adults, and you'll want to block out at least two hours, if not four; lines can be quite long during peak hours.

In addition to the permanent exhibit, the complex also contains the **David Loughridge Learning Center,** used by Meow Wolf's nonprofit educational outreach program, a gallery space that features the works of local artists, and a music venue that quickly established itself as one of the best spots in town to catch live acts. The art collective has broadened its reach, with fantastical exhibitions in Denver and Las Vegas.

Rancho de las Golondrinas

334 Los Pinos Rd.; 505/471-2261; www.golondrinas.org;
10am-4pm Wed.-Sun. June-Sept.; $6

About a 15-minute drive southeast, Rancho de las Golondrinas, the "Ranch of the Swallows," is Santa Fe's equivalent of Colonial Williamsburg, a 200-acre museum where staff members in period costumes demonstrate crafts and other aspects of early New Mexican history. The core of it is a restored Spanish colonial paraje, a way station on the Camino Real, and outbuildings contain a blacksmith shop, a schoolhouse, mills, and even a rebuilt Penitente morada (dwelling). The docent who works here is a Penitente himself and may sing some of the group's hymns.

The ranch hosts big to-dos (entrance fees typically $10-15), including a wine festival in early July, a celebration of Mexican culture in late July, a lively renaissance fair in September, and a harvest festival in October. It's a good idea to pack your own picnic; there's a basic café at the ranch, but it's open only on weekends. Allow a few hours to see the whole place. In April, May, and October, the museum is open on weekdays for guided tours by appointment; call 505/471-2261 to make arrangements. In these shoulder months, the ranch is also occasionally open for special theme weekends.

Lamy

151 Old Lamy Tr.; 505/466-1650

Although little more than a depot—purchased in 2020 by local author George R. R. Martin, who plans to restore it and make it available for film shoots—with a brewery, restaurant, and several disused train cars, Lamy is a mighty fine place to step off Amtrak's Southwest Chief. Across the road, the **Lamy Railroad & History Museum** is a sprawling Old West saloon and dining room (known as Legal Tender) that doubles as a treasure trove of old railroading days; there's even a model train set. The place has a spotty record of opening, so call ahead if you plan to make the trip.

Take Old Las Vegas Highway (or I-25) southeast out of Santa Fe; six miles out of town, turn south on U.S. 285. After six miles, turn left for the last bumpy mile to Lamy. Note that the brewery and Legal Tender have sporadic hours at best and are typically only open during the summer.

1: Meow Wolf Santa Fe **2:** Sky Railway **3:** SITE Santa Fe **4:** Rancho de las Golondrinas

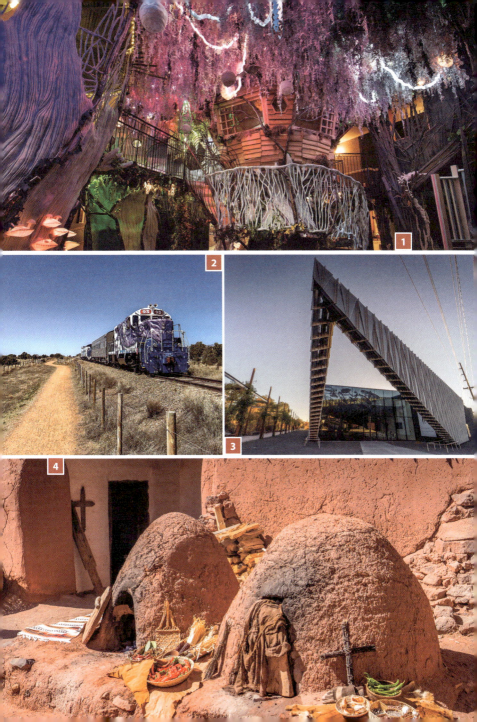

★ **Sky Railway**

430 W. Manhattan Ave.; 844-743-3759;
https://skyrailway.com; 2-3 hours, trains run
year-round; from $109

The most memorable way to reach Lamy is on the Sky Railway, which departs from Santa Fe's train depot and provides a bewildering range of experiences that belie the train's—and the route's—small size. Taking place on a handful of colorfully painted passenger cars, the ride to Lamy and back can feature a sunset burlesque show, flamenco performance, jazz, stargazing, and even a murder mystery. It's all very well put together and the attention to detail promises a trip not soon forgotten. Of course, the scenery is pretty spectacular, too, and you can step outside and take it all in on one of the open cars.

Recreation

It's no accident *Outside* magazine has its offices here. After work and on weekends, Santa Feans leave the town to the tourists and scatter into the surrounding mountains and rivers on foot, bike, and raft—and in winter, on skis and snowboards. You'll find something to do all four seasons, though hikes above the foothills shouldn't be attempted until mid-May at least (and not until you're acclimated to the altitude). If you're in town in the fall, don't miss the aspen leaves turning, usually in early to mid-October. The access route for activities in the Sangre de Cristos is winding Highway 475—it starts out from the north side of Santa Fe as Artists Road, then the name changes to Hyde Park Road, and farther north it's Ski Basin Road.

Information, Guides, and Gear
Public Lands Information Center

301 Dinosaur Tr.; 505/954-2002;
www.publiclands.org; 8am-4pm Mon.-Fri.

Just off Highway 14, immediately south of I-25, the Public Lands Information Center is the best starting point for any planning. The staff will also know the latest status on areas affected by wildfires or floods.

Outspire!

505/660-0394; www.outspire.com; from $190

Outspire! runs guided full- and half-day outings—hiking in summer, snowshoeing in winter. They also offer a two-hour guided hike through the Tsankawi Mesa section of Bandelier National Monument.

Santa Fe Mountain Adventures

505/988-4000; www.santafemountainadventures.com

Santa Fe Mountain Adventures offers guided mountain biking trips (from $240) of varying difficulty levels between 4-6 hours in and around Santa Fe; they also lead guided hikes (from $192) and 4x4 outings (from $150).

REI

500 Market St.; 505/982-3557; 10am-8pm Mon.-Fri.,
10am-7pm Sat., 11am-6pm Sun.

For gear, visit REI in the Railyard district, which has everything from bikes and tents to coolers and coats.

Alpine Sports

541 W. Cordova Rd.; 505/983-5155; 10am-6pm
Tues.-Sat.

The locally owned Alpine Sports, on Cordova Road, focuses mainly on skiing and snowboarding gear and apparel.

HIKING

Some of the best hiking trails in the state can be reached by just a short drive or bike ride from the center of Santa Fe. Even in the height of summer, none of them feels particularly overcrowded, meaning you can enjoy some seriously gorgeous scenery in relative solitude. The trails in this section are ordered based on their distance from downtown.

Santa Fe Canyon Preserve

Distance: *1.5 mi loop*
Time: *1 hour*
Trailhead: *Cerro Gordo Rd., just north of intersection with Upper Canyon Rd.*

For an easy saunter in town, head for Santa Fe Canyon Preserve, a 190-acre patch of the foothills managed by **The Nature Conservancy** (505/988-3867). The preserve covers the canyon formed by the now-diverted Santa Fe River. An easy interpretive loop trail leads around the marshy area, passing the remnants of the dam and winding through dense stands of cottonwoods and willows. The area is open only to people on foot—no mountain bikes and no pets.

From the plaza, it's a 3.5-mile drive along Canyon Road and Upper Canyon Road.

Randall Davey Audubon Center & Sanctuary

Distance: *0.5 mi for loop trail, 0.25 mi for haiku trail*
Time: *15 minutes for loop trail, 10 minutes for haiku trail*
Trailhead: *1800 Upper Canyon Rd.*

Birders will definitely want to start a hike here, but even general visitors will be intrigued by the house of artist Randall Davey (505/983-4609; http://randalldavey.audubon.org; 8am-4pm Mon.-Sat.; $2 suggested donation) and a pretty loop trail that leads into the forest and canyons behind and a short haiku-themed trail around the center. The beautifully painted back rooms of the house are open for a guided **tour** ($5) at 2pm every Friday, and a free guided bird walk departs from the parking lot at 8am every Saturday.

Sun Mountain

Distance: *2 mi round-trip*
Time: *1.5 hours*
Trailhead: *on Old Santa Fe Trail, 2.2 mi southeast of Paseo de Peralto*

The trail up solitary Sun Mountain (elev. 7,920 feet) starts off fairly flat, passing through shaded woods, before beginning a sharp ascent. After 0.25 mile, the trail emerges on Sun Mountain's exposed western flank, where a series of switchbacks pass by yucca, cholla, and prickly pear. From the top, a little over 900 feet from the trailhead, sweeping panoramas take in the city's orderly grid below and an arc of jagged Sangre de Cristo summits to the east.

Atalaya Mountain

Distance: *6 mi round-trip*
Time: *4 hours*
Trailhead: *on the campus of St. John's College*

One of the most accessible trails in the Santa Fe area (you can take the M city bus to the trailhead) is also one of the more challenging. The mostly shaded hike heads up to a 9,121-foot peak, starting out as a gentle stroll along the city's edge, then becoming increasingly steep.

Aspen Vista

Distance: *11.5 mi round-trip*
Time: *6-8 hours*
Trailhead: *parking area on right of Ski Basin Rd. (Hwy. 475), just under 13 mi from town*

The most popular trail in the Sangre de Cristos is probably Aspen Vista. It is well traveled in fall, as the promised views of golden aspen groves are spectacular. In the densest spots, when the sun is shining through the leaves, the air itself feels yellow. Though at a high elevation, the hike is reasonably easy, on a service road with a gradual slope. The first 2.5 miles are the most aspen-intense, and a little under 4 miles in, you get a great view of Santa Fe below; this makes a good turnaround point for a 2-hour hike.

Raven's Ridge

Distance: *7-10.5 mi*
Time: *4-6 hours*
Trailhead: *Winsor trailhead (no. 254) in the Santa Fe ski area parking lot*

This is another local favorite, though not too heavily traveled, with great views of Santa Fe Baldy (elev. 12,622 feet). After leaving the trailhead, the path heads to the right along the outside of the fence. The trail shows up on only one local map (Drake Mountain Maps'

Scenic Drives: Fall Foliage

along Highway 475 in fall

With its evergreens and scrub trees, New Mexico doesn't seem a likely spot for a vivid display of fall colors. But the deciduous trees that flourish here—aspen, maple, cottonwood—are wild pockets of color against the rocky landscape, often bright gold against red rocks. You don't have to drive far to see the colors, which are usually at their peak in **mid-October.**

FROM SANTA FE

From Santa Fe, just drive up **Highway 475** (the road to the ski basin), where pullouts are positioned for the best vistas of the many colorful aspen stands; the pullout at the aptly named Aspen Vista trailhead is one of the best. Abiquiu's dramatic rock formations are also a good backdrop for cottonwoods.

FROM ALBUQUERQUE

From Albuquerque, head to the east face of the **Sandia Mountains** and up the road to the peak, stopping off at Cienega Picnic Area and Las Huertas Picnic Area, about midway up the mountain. Or head southeast to the Manzano Mountains, where **Fourth of July Canyon,** with maple leaves turning shades of pink and crimson, is a beautiful color show. The area around Jemez is especially nice, with the cottonwoods contrasting with red canyon walls, though when you get close to Valles Caldera National Preserve, you hit wildfire damage.

FROM TAOS

From Taos, the entire **Enchanted Circle** drive passes through various patches of color.

Map of the Mountains of Santa Fe), but it's easy to follow once you're up there. When in doubt, just head uphill: You'll bag Deception, Lake, and Tesuque peaks in a total of seven miles, with a top elevation of 12,409 feet, returning to the ski area parking lot by walking down along the Tesuque chairlift. But this final stretch isn't particularly scenic, so you may want to take in only one or two of the peaks (Lake Peak, the second you reach, is the highest) and then retrace your steps.

Rio en Medio

Distance: *7 mi round-trip*
Time: *4-5 hours*
Trailhead: *parking area off Pacheco Canyon Rd.; check with U.S. Forest Service for new trailhead location*

The serene Rio en Medio trail (no. 163) begins north of Tesuque and parallels a clear stream to a series of waterfalls and then up some rather strenuous switchbacks to a large meadow that's filled with wildflowers in springtime. From the trailhead to the first cascade is 1.7 miles. The meadow is at the 3.5-mile mark, where you'll probably want to turn around, for a hike that will take a total of 4-5 hours.

To reach the trailhead, drive north out of Santa Fe on Washington Avenue, which becomes Bishops Lodge Road (Highway 590). Drive straight through the village of Tesuque and then turn right in less than a mile onto Highway 592, passing the Four Seasons along the way. After about 1.5 miles, turn right on Pacheco Canyon Road. Note: The old trailhead off Country Road 78-D has been permanently closed due to heavy rains; check with the U.S. Forest Service for the new trailhead location.

BIKING

Mountain bikers have fantastic outlets close to Santa Fe, while those who prefer the open road will love the challenges in the winding highways through the mountains north of the city. There are several reliable bike shops in and around town.

Outfitters
Broken Spoke

1426 Cerrillos Rd.; 505/992-3102; 10am-6pm Mon.-Fri., 10-5pm Sat.; rentals from $60/day

Broken Spoke provides a full range of bike services, including tune-ups and repairs—all at very reasonable rates. They have a small selection of rentals available by the day as well.

Bike N Sport

524 W. Cordova Rd.; 505/820-0809; 10am-6pm Mon.-Fri., 10-5pm Sat.

On the city's south side, Bike N Sport provides the usual bike services and also offers bike rentals (from $45 per day), including e-bikes, hybrids, and gravel bikes.

Mellow Velo

132 E. Marcy St.; 505/995-8356; 10am-6pm Mon.-Fri., 10am-5pm Sat., 10am-3pm Sun.; from $30/day

For bike rentals just off the plaza, Mellow Velo stocks cruisers for around town as well as deluxe mountain and road bikes. It's also an excellent resource for information on area rides.

Mountain Biking
Santa Fe Rail Trail

A local classic and the gentlest introduction to mountain biking around Santa Fe, the Santa Fe Rail Trail starts as a paved path in the Railyard Park, then turns to dirt south of Rabbit Road, following a relatively easy and wide track along the railroad line to Lamy. The trail is about 12.5 miles one-way. Except for a grade near I-25, it's fairly level.

Dale Ball Trails

The Dale Ball Trails are the heart of the city's mountain biking scene: 22 miles of single-track routes for both hikers and mountain bikers, winding through stands of piñon and juniper in the Sangre de Cristo foothills. Two trailheads give access to the North, Central, and South Sections of the trail. From the northern trailhead, on Sierra del Norte (immediately off Highway 475 after mile marker 3), the North Section trails vary a bit in elevation, but the Central Section (south from the parking area) is more fun because it's a longer chunk of trails. The southern trailhead, on Cerro Gordo just north of its intersection with Canyon Road, gives access to the Central Section and the South Section, which is for advanced riders only. Note that the trail that starts at the southern trailhead lot, part of the Santa Fe Canyon Preserve, is for foot traffic only—ride your bike 0.1 mile down Cerro Gordo to the start of the Dale Ball system.

La Tierra Trails

In the rolling hills west of the city, La Tierra Trails are for biking, hiking, and horseback riding—though it's the two-wheel crew who makes the most use of them, especially after work, when the day is cooler (there's not much shade out here). There are three trailheads, all interconnected by various loops; the more technical ones are clearly marked. Take Highway 599, the bypass road around the city, north out of the city for about 3.5 miles and turn right onto Camino La Tierra. The parking lot for the trailhead is a quarter of a mile down on the right.

Winsor Trail

A bit farther out of town is the immensely popular Winsor Trail (no. 254), a catchall that covers a great range of scenery and terrain and presents a few challenges, too. Heading up, there are few deadly steep ascents, so it's tiring but not impossible, and you'll rarely have to hike-a-bike; you're rewarded with a long, joyful downhill run. The trailhead is in Tesuque: Take Washington Avenue north out of the center of Santa Fe, continuing as it becomes Bishops Lodge Road (Highway 590). After not quite four miles, turn right onto County Road 72-A, also signed as Big Tesuque Canyon. There are two small pullout areas for parallel parking, and the trail starts about 0.1 mile up the road from the second parking area—the first 0.5 mile is through private land.

Road Biking

Make sure you're acclimated to the altitude before you set out on any lengthy trip and stay hydrated—road biking typically means little shade and long distances in between resupply points. Shoulders aren't a given; it's especially important to ride single file.

High Road to Taos

The area's best tour, along the High Road to Taos, will take you through some of the area's highest elevations. Starting in Chimayó

shaves some not-so-scenic miles off the ride and gives you a reasonable 45-mile jaunt to Taos.

To Tesuque Village and Beyond

A less taxing ride can be had by taking Washington Avenue north from downtown. After 0.25 miles it becomes Bishops Lodge Road (Highway 590) and descends into the shady village of Tesuque. Past Tesuque the road continues as Highway 591 before turning into Frontage Road, just past the Highway 285 overpass. The stretch along Frontage Road before it ends in Pojoaque is not as scenic as the earlier portion, but it is generally flat and blissfully free of traffic.

Santa Fe Century

www.santafecentury.com

The annual Santa Fe Century is the biggest organized riding event in the state, taking place mid-May. The course runs a 104-mile loop south down the Turquoise Trail and back north via the old farm towns in the Galisteo Basin, southeast of Santa Fe. There's also a Gran Fondo version that pits you against the clock and other riders, as well as more manageable 25- and 50-mile rides and gravel options as well.

ROCK CLIMBING
Santa Fe Climbing Center

3008 Cielo Court; 505/986-8944; www.climbsantafe.com; 9am-9pm Mon.-Fri., noon-8pm Sat., 10am-6pm Sun.

To polish your rock climbing skills or get tips on nearby routes, talk to the experts at Santa Fe Climbing Center. You can play around on the walls at the gym ($20 for a day pass), participate in clinics (from $25), and sign up for private instruction (from $60).

RAFTING
Rio Grande

With the Rio Grande within easy reach of

1: the view from Sun Mountain **2:** the view from the Aspen Vista trailhead

Santa Fe, some of the best rafting opportunities in the country are close at hand. Snowmelt runoff determines the peak spring times for many of the runs, though it has much less of an impact throughout the summer months, when the water levels are more constant.

Taos Box
Just west of Taos, the 17-mile-long Taos Box features the longest and some of the most challenging stretches of whitewater in the state. Dotted with rapids with names like The Trench and the Boat Reamer, this is not a trip for the faint-hearted, particularly in a season that follows heavy snowmelt. Going with a guide is advised.

Racecourse
One of the more popular trips is the Racecourse, an adrenaline-packed half-day adventure near Pilar. A succession of Class III rapids with names such as The Maze and The Narrows provide plenty of white-knuckle moments. Going with a guide is advised.

Lower Gorge and the Orilla Verde Recreation Area
There are more mellow trips on the Rio Grande, too, particularly in the Lower Gorge and the Orilla Verde Recreation Area, where it's easy to float carefree for several miles.

Rio Chama
The Rio Chama offers mostly gentle outings through the heart of O'Keeffe Country, with some Class III rapids as well. The entire stretch is about 30 miles long.

Kokopelli Rafting Adventures
1164 Parkway Dr., Unit A; 505/983-3734; http://kokopelliraft.com; Apr.-Sept.; from $64
Half-day and full-day trips on both rivers are offered by longtime outfitters Kokopelli Rafting Adventures.

FISHING
Trout teem in the **Rio Chama,** northwest of Santa Fe, in the streams of **Valles Caldera**

National Preserve, and in pockets of a few lesser-known rivers north of the city, such as the **Vallecitos River** off Highway 64, about 30 minutes east of Tierra Amarilla. Both outfitters listed below can suggest the best current spots.

High Desert Angler
460 Cerrillos Rd.; 505/988-7688; www.highdesertangler.com; 9am-6pm Mon.-Sat., 11am-4pm Sun.
The High Desert Angler fly shop is a locals' favorite, providing guiding services (from $425 for two), stream reports, and a full slate of fly-fishing gear.

The Reel Life
526 N. Guadalupe St.; 505/995-8114; www.thereellife.com; 9am-5pm Mon.-Sat., 10am-5pm Sun.
In the DeVargas Center, The Reel Life sells gear and can arrange guided day trips to nearby waters (from $395 for two).

GOLF
Marty Sanchez Links de Santa Fe
205 Caja del Rio Rd.; 505/955-4400; www.linksdesantafe.com; from $25
Marty Sanchez Links de Santa Fe is a "water-aware" course that uses indigenous grasses and other plants to minimize water use. It offers great views of the mountains as you tour the 18 holes designed by Baxter Spann; there's also "The Great 28," an additional par-3 nine-holer that's exceptionally challenging. With five sets of tees, the course is good for both beginners and experts. Greens fees start at $25 for nine holes, and there are discounts after 2pm.

WINTER SPORTS
Ski Santa Fe
Hwy. 475; 505/982-4429; www.skisantafe.com; $92 full-day lift ticket, $45 full equipment rentals
Sixteen miles northeast of town in the Santa Fe National Forest, Ski Santa Fe is a well-used day area with over 80 trails of varying difficulty, including quite a few challenging runs. Along with its impressive cross-section of

trails, another major selling point is that there are virtually no lines on any of the seven lifts.

Exclusively for cross-country skiers, the groomed **Norski Trail** (also known as Trail #255) starts about 0.25 mile before the Ski Santa Fe parking lot, off the west side of Highway 475. The standard route is about 2 miles, winding through the trees and along a ridgeline, and you can shorten or lengthen the tour by taking various loops and shortcuts, as long as you follow the directional arrows counterclockwise.

Hyde Memorial State Park

740 Hyde Park Rd.; 505/983-7175;
www.emnrd.state.nm.us

Just seven miles out of town along the road to the ski basin, Hyde Memorial State Park has a couple of nicely maintained sledding runs, and some shorter cross-country ski and snowshoeing routes.

Cottam's Ski Shop

740 Hyde Park Rd.; 505/982-0495;
from 7:30am daily in ski season

For gear, Cottam's Ski Shop is the biggest rental operation in the area, handily located at the entrance to Hyde Memorial State Park.

Alpine Sports

541 W. Cordova Rd.; 505/983-5155;
10am-6pm Tues.-Sun.

In a more spacious location on Cordova Road, the knowledgeable and family-run Alpine Sports specializes in winter apparel and equipment, with a good selection of the latest in skiing and snowboarding.

SPAS

★ Ten Thousand Waves

3451 Hyde Park Rd.; 505/982-9304;
www.tenthousandwaves.com; 9am-9pm daily

A Santa Fe institution, Ten Thousand Waves is a traditional Japanese-style bathhouse that melds seamlessly into the mountainside above town. Featuring two big communal pools, it also has five smaller private ones tucked among the trees; many have adjoining cold plunges and saunas. The place also offers full day-spa services, with intense massages and luxe facials and body scrubs. Prices are no longer quite the bargain they once were, starting at $58 for 90 minutes in the community soaking hot tub (Mon.-Thurs. at 7:30 p.m. reservations required) and $219 for 80-minute massages. Opening hours can vary seasonally; call ahead to confirm hours and for reservations.

Body of Santa Fe

333 W. Cordova Rd.; 505/986-0362;
www.bodyofsantafe.com; 8:30am-7pm daily

The relaxed and welcoming atmosphere of Body of Santa Fe has helped it earn a devoted following—and its affordable treatments (massages from $130/80 mins) help, too. An understated renovation has added to its appeal, with certified green materials used throughout. There's also an on-site studio offering a wide range of yoga classes (from $18) daily.

La Vida Spa

106 Faithway St.; 505/930-5430;
http://lavidasantafe.com; 10am-6pm daily

In town, La Vida Spa has an elegant Southwestern style and a wide range of massages and facials (from $135/hr). Afterward, you can relax in the gardens with a cup of tea and some organic sweets from the adjacent tearoom.

Ojo Santa Fe

242 Los Pinos Rd.; 505/977-8212;
http://ojosparesorts.com; 10am-8pm daily

South of the city and down the road from Rancho de Las Golondrinas, Ojo Santa Fe is suited for those looking to truly get away. Under the same ownership as Ojo Caliente, the spa spreads over 70 idyllic acres and includes yoga and fitness studios, outdoor pools, soaking tubs, hot tubs, and an art studio. A comprehensive list of services and packages is offered, including hot stone massages ($160 for 50 minutes) and various forms of bodywork.

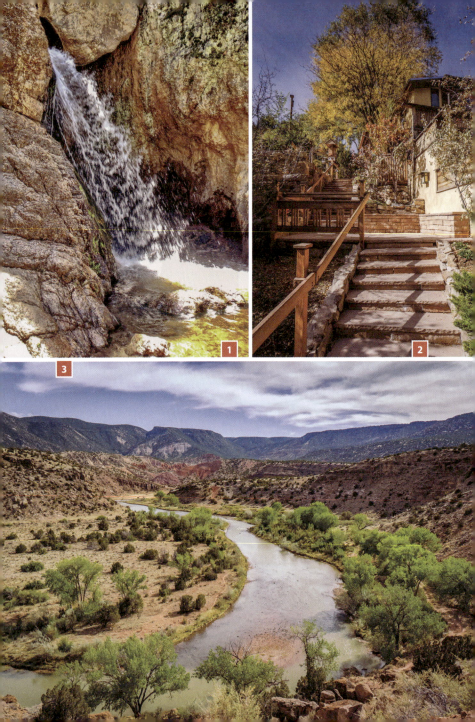

1

2

3

SPECTATOR SPORTS
Fort Marcy Park
490 Bishops Lodge Rd.; $9 tickets

The **Santa Fe Fuego** (www.santafefuego.com), a baseball team that puts the minor in minor league, plays at Fort Marcy Park, just north of the plaza area, mid-May–early August. It's part of the incredibly scrappy Pecos League (www.pecosleague.com), which fields 16 teams from around the Southwest, California, Texas, and Kansas.

Entertainment

NIGHTLIFE
With breezy summer evenings and a populace that always seems to be able to knock off work a little early, Santa Fe typically favors happy hour over late-night carousing.

Bars and Clubs
Dragon Room Lounge
406 Old Santa Fe Tr.; 505/983-7712;
4pm-11pm Tues.-Sun.

Longtime city haunt the Dragon Room Lounge is so dim you might not notice at first the huge tree growing up from the left side of the bar. Guys in cowboy hats chat with mountain bikers and dressed-up cocktail drinkers. There's live music Tuesday, Thursday, and Saturday.

Maria's
555 W. Cordova Rd.; 505/983-7929;
11:30am-9pm daily

South of the city center, Maria's has gained a devoted following by serving impeccably balanced margaritas, with fresh lime and nearly any brand of tequila you can imagine.

La Reina
1862 Cerrillos Rd.; 505/982-1931; 5pm-11pm daily

About 1.5 miles to the south on Cerrillos Road and inside El Rey Court, hip and unpretentious La Reina is the place to go for mezcal and tequila-tinged cocktails; there's also a good selection of draft beers, wines, and sakes for good measure.

Evangelo's
200 W. San Francisco St.; 505/982-9014; 3pm-2am Mon.-Fri., 2:30pm-2am Sat., 2pm-midnight Sun.

The grungier side of Santa Fe is on display at Evangelo's, where soul and blues bands take the small stage at the back. When there's no band, there's room at the pool tables, plus no shortage of crusty characters.

Matador
116 W. San Francisco St., entrance on Galisteo St.; 505/984-5050; 5pm-2am Mon.-Sat., 5pm-midnight Sun.

Those who descend the stairs to the basement-level Matador will find a good cross section of Santa Fe's younger artists, among other renowned drinkers, in the bar's dark and decidedly grungy environs. If there's not a live band, there's punk rock on the stereo to match the concert posters on the walls.

Coyote Cantina
132 Water St.; 505/983-1615; 11:30am-11pm daily

A few downtown restaurants have standout bars and merit a visit alone, even if you're not looking for a meal. The upscale rooftop Coyote Cantina of the Coyote Café has one of the liveliest scenes around the plaza.

Geronimo
724 Canyon Rd.; 505/982-1500; 5:30pm-9:30pm daily

The handsome and intimate bar at Geronimo is a good place to put your feet up after a Canyon Road cruise. With just over a handful of seats, soft lighting, and attentive bar staff, you'll likely want to settle in for a while

1: a waterfall on the Rio en Medio trail **2:** Ten Thousand Waves **3:** the Chama River

Open-Air Bars

Cowgirl BBQ

Framed by the Sangre de Cristos to the east and the Jemez Mountains to the west and with historic adobe architecture wherever you look, Santa Fe is an ideal spot to savor a drink outside. Along with **Coyote Cantina** (page 69), these are the best spots in town to take it all in.

- For a perfectly perched sunset drink, get to the **Bell Tower Bar** (100 E. San Francisco St.; 505/982-5511; 11am-sunset daily May-Oct.) early if you can, as this spot on the rooftop at La Fonda fills up fast. It's usually packed with tourists, but the view over the plaza is inspiring.

- If there's no room at the Bell Tower, the next best spot for plaza views is **Thunderbird** (50 Lincoln Ave.; 505/490-6550; 11:30am-9pm daily), which has a 2nd-floor porch and 20 beers on tap. At happy hour (4pm-6pm), margaritas are $6.

- The mellow patio scene at **Cowgirl BBQ** (319 S. Guadalupe St.; 505/982-2565; 11:30am-9pm Sun.-Thurs., 11:30am-10pm Fri.-Sat.) gets started early, with happy hour kicking off at 3pm and lasting until 6pm, with two-for-one apps and $4 margaritas. It's good later, too, with live music many nights.

- On Canyon Road, stalwart **El Farol** (808 Canyon Rd.; 505/983-9912; 3pm-9pm Wed.-Sun.) is the gallerists' post-work hangout, with outside seating on a creaky wooden portal and a large back patio.

- A strong selection of over 30 craft ales is on tap at the **Violet Crown** (1606 Alcaldesa St.; 505/216-5678; 10:30am-11pm daily), which offers one of the more scenic views in the Railyard and a great starting point to a night out in the district.

and enjoy the memorable scene, which feels like having a piece of old Santa Fe all to yourself.

La Casa Sena
125 E. Palace Ave.; 505/988-9232; 11am-9pm daily
La Casa Sena is set in a truly dreamy garden

courtyard; order a cocktail and an appetizer and enjoy the eye candy.

Breweries
Second Street Brewery

Railyard district: 7 Paseo de Peralta; 505/989-3278; 3pm-9pm Mon.-Thurs., noon-9pm Fri.-Sun; Siler-Rufina: 2920 Rufina St.; 505/954-1068; noon-9pm daily

Local operation Second Street Brewery brews stouts, bitters, IPAs, and other beers on tap in a chummy, semi-industrial atmosphere, sometimes backed up by a band. With the original location now closed, two outposts remain: the more central spot in the Railyard with a patio area and another much larger option in the heart of the Siler-Rufina neighborhood. Happy hour is 4pm-6:30pm daily.

Tumbleroot

2791 Agua Fria St.; 505/780-5730; 5pm-10pm Fri.-Sun.

At Tumbleroot, a 10-minute drive west of the plaza, you can choose from IPAs, pale ales, lagers, stouts, and quite a few others. Where this locals' favorite really stands out, however, is with its selection of spirits—it's also a distillery—and its shaded outdoor patio set in a semicircle around a koi pond. There's live music most nights and a couple of food trucks parked outside.

Just a couple of blocks from the plaza, its **Tumbleroot Pottery Pub** (135 W. Palace Ave., Ste. 100; 11am-9pm daily) offshoot is equal parts cocktail bar and ceramics studio and gallery. If you're feeling particularly inspired, you can sample a home-brewed beer, take a seat at a community table, and try your hand at making your own mug.

Santa Fe Brewing Company

35 Fire Pl.; 505/424-3333; 11:30am-9pm Mon.-Tues., 11:30am-10pm Wed.-Thurs., noon-10pm Sat., noon-9pm Sun.

On the southern outskirts of the city, venerable Santa Fe Brewing Company, which opened in 1988, is the oldest brewery in New Mexico. The new expansive beer hall offers more than two dozen craft beers and ciders, including its popular Happy Camper IPA and Santa Fe Gold lager, as well as seasonal varieties. Tours (noon Sat.) provide an excellent glimpse behind the scenes of the on-site brewery.

The Brakeroom

510 Galisteo St.; 505/780-8648; 3pm-10pm Mon.-Thurs., noon-10pm Fri.-Sat., 3pm-9pm Sun.

The Brakeroom, Santa Fe Brewing Company's intimate downtown location, is set inside a building that once provided respite for railroad brakemen on their travels. There's a small patio in the back where food trucks, including Bang Bite, frequently set up.

Cocktail Lounges
Secreto Lounge

210 Don Gaspar Ave.; 505/983-5700; 4pm-10pm Tues.-Thurs., 1pm-10pm Fri.-Sat., 4pm-9pm Sun.

While most Santa Fe bars stick to margaritas, Secreto Lounge is up on the cutting edge of cocktail culture. Its "garden to glass" menu uses only fresh herbs and other seasonal ingredients in such drinks as the Ginny Juice: a lemonade, orange juice, and vodka concoction with a serious kick. Of course, it still does a margarita or two: Its Agave Way is a pseudo-margarita that's spicy and sweet, with black grapes. Happy hour (4pm-7pm Mon.-Fri.) is worth planning around, as it knocks the price down to $7 or so, and you can sit out in the loggia of the Hotel St. Francis and watch the passing parade.

Tonic

103 E. Water St.; 505/982-1189;
www.tonicsantafe.com; 4:30pm-midnight Tues.-Sat.

Intimate and ornately designed, Tonic unabashedly evokes a bygone era. Sip on sophisticated cocktails—several of which are fairly elaborate—and enjoy the art deco flourishes steps from a jazz quartet.

Santa Fe Spirits

308 Read St.; 505/780-5906; 3pm-10pm Tues.-Sat., noon-6pm Sun.

Boozehounds will also want to drop by the tasting room of Santa Fe Spirits, a relaxed place to sample all the local distiller's products. Order a full flight, or enjoy a show-case drink such as the Whiskeyrita, which features the distiller's un-aged Silver Coyote whiskey, or a simple gin and tonic with its aromatic, sage-infused gin.

Live Music
The Bridge
37 Fire Pl.; 505/557-6182; https://santafebrewing.com
The Bridge, Santa Fe Brewing Company's indoor and larger outdoor performance spaces, hosts touring bands and local acts across the lot from the taproom.

Meow Wolf
1352 Rufina Circle; 505/395-6369; www.meowwolf.com
Intimate and otherworldly, Meow Wolf is the antithesis of a standard concert venue. It hosts shows year-round in a colorful "portal"—the name for the many idiosyncratic rooms in the complex's House of Eternal Return—often featuring acts that you wouldn't expect to see making a detour to Santa Fe.

THE ARTS
Performing Arts
Lensic Performing Arts Center
211 W. San Francisco St.; 505/988-1234; www.lensic.com
Set in a 1931 Moorish curlicue palace, the Lensic Performing Arts Center is Santa Fe's showpiece venue, with 820 seats and an eclectic wide-ranging schedule. The six-week-long summer **Santa Fe Chamber Music Festival** (505/983-2075; www.santafechambermusic.com) holds events here, with performances nearly every day mid-July-mid-August. The chamber orchestra **Santa Fe Pro Musica** (505/988-4640; http://sfpromusica.org) also performs at the Lensic, fall-spring, as well as in Loretto Chapel and other intimate venues.

Santa Fe Opera
U.S. 84/285; 505/986-5900; www.santafeopera.org
If you think opera is all about tuxes, plush seats, and too-long arias, give the Santa Fe

Opera a chance. Half the fun is arriving early to "tailgate" in the parking lot, which involves gourmet goodies, lots of champagne, and time to mill around and check out other attendees' bolo ties. Then there's the show itself, featuring the country's best singers, who treat this as their "summer camp" July-August. The elegant 2,000-plus-seat open amphitheater is beautiful at sunset; pack blankets to ward off the chill later on. If you have kids to entertain, time your visit for bargain-priced "family nights" or a special dress rehearsal with extra info to introduce young ones to the art form.

Cinema
Violet Crown
1606 Alcaldesa St.; 505/216-5678; http://santafe.violetcrown.com
Santa Fe's take on the Austin, Texas, beloved cinema and the Railyard's biggest draw, the Violet Crown offers the most well-rounded and enjoyable movie-watching experience around. Select from a full snack and dinner menu and an extensive beer and wine list and settle into cushy seats to watch the latest blockbusters, handpicked indies, and one-night-only showings of film classics.

Jean Cocteau Cinema
418 Montezuma Ave.; 505/466-5528; www.jeancocteaucinema.com
The delightful Jean Cocteau Cinema gets press because of its owner, resident author George R. R. Martin, but it's a real treat on its own. The 120-seat theater oozes art-house charm and shows eclectic offerings and hosts readings for an appreciative local audience. It also holds a small bar area where you can order a pint, and cocktails such as a Jon Snow Cone, and splurge on signed Game of Thrones merchandise.

CCA Cinema
1050 Old Pecos Tr.; 505/982-1338; www.ccasantafe.org
The CCA Cinema has an extensive film program with an emphasis on international titles and music documentaries.

George R. R. Martin in Santa Fe

Eclectic films await at the Jean Cocteau Cinema.

Santa Fe has been home to the wildly celebrated author George R. R. Martin since long before readers and HBO viewers were devouring his epic tales of warring nobles, zombie armies, and dragons in a land called Westeros. The author is quick to profess his love for the city—and green chile—and that affection is writ large around town. He restored and reopened the **Jean Cocteau Cinema,** giving Santa Fe its most eclectic theater—the kind of place where obscure 1970s horror movies can be seen on the big screen alongside Italian film classics. Part of the impetus behind the theater was to provide "The City Different" with something different—a compelling late-night diversion unlike anything else in town. That desire was likely also a contributing factor in his decision to back **Meow Wolf Santa Fe.** Now a runaway success, the complex was anything but a surefire hit when the idea to fund it was presented to Martin by its directors. It's hard to imagine the project getting off the ground without his support.

Martin continues to give back to Santa Fe. In 2017, he formed the **Stagecoach Foundation** (www.stagecoachfdn.org), a nonprofit that supports Santa Fe's growing presence in the film industry as well as in the fields of education and technology. Its headquarters include space for film productions. Perhaps the White Walkers will someday come to the high desert.…

More recently, Martin opened **Beastly Books**—next door to the Jean Cocteau Cinema—which sells a number of titles signed by well-known and up-and-coming science fiction and fantasy authors, including many who have made appearances at the cinema over the years. In 2020, Martin further committed to the local industry when he bought the historic **Lamy train depot,** just south of Santa Fe, plus nearby railroad tracks and several train cars and locomotives along with it. Some of the trains now even ply people to Lamy and back for earthly and otherworldly adventures on the **Sky Railway.**

Lectures

Lannan Foundation Lecture Series

505/986-8160; www.lannan.org

The Lannan Foundation Lecture Series is run by a Santa Fe-based organization funding international writers and socially active artists. The program brings major writers and intellectuals to the Lensic Performing Arts Center for fascinating interviews and conversation. Events usually sell out quickly—check the schedule a couple of months before your visit.

Southwest Seminars Series

1501 Paseo de Peralta; www.southwestseminars.org; 505/466-2775

The Southwest Seminars Series runs weekly year-round. Speakers are anthropologists, archaeologists, and other researchers with a special interest in the history and people of the region. Talks take place nearly every Monday (50 weeks a year) at 6pm at the Hotel Santa Fe.

FESTIVALS AND EVENTS

International Folk Art Market

Railyard Park; 505/992-7600;
http://folkartmarket.org; July

One weekend in early to mid-July, the International Folk Art Market showcases traditional crafts from all over the globe, often from the artists in person. It's now set up in the Railyard Park; arrive early for parking and be prepared to walk a bit. On Sunday, tickets are cheaper than Friday and Saturday, and vendors are ready to make deals.

Spanish Market

505/982-2226; www.spanishcolonial.org; late July

The Spanish Market takes over the plaza with traditional New Mexican woodwork (especially santos), weaving, and furniture.

★ Santa Fe Indian Market

505/983-5220; www.swaia.org; late Aug.

The city's biggest annual event, the Santa Fe Indian Market, welcomes 100,000 visitors. Centered on the plaza, the massive showcase of Native American art features more than 1,200 artisans selling jewelry, pottery, weaving, and more. It's the opportunity to interact with some of the Southwest's most seminal artists that makes this event truly special. The biggest crowds wander among the numerous stalls over the weekend, though there are celebratory events leading up to it.

If you're in town the first weekend in December, check out its much smaller **Winter Indian Market,** which showcases more than

Santa Fe Indian Market

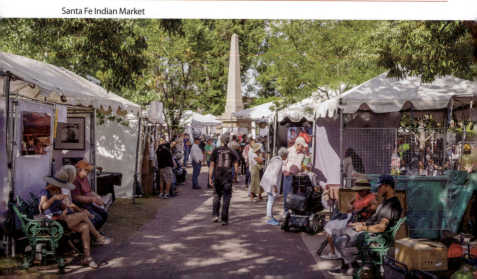

The Burning of Zozobra

Every fall a raucous chant fills the air in Santa Fe's Fort Marcy Park: "Burn him! Burn him! Burn him!" It's the ritual torching of Zozobra, a 50-foot-tall marionette with long, grasping arms, glowering eyes, and a moaning voice. In the weeks before the event, Old Man Gloom, as he's commonly known, is stuffed with divorce papers, pictures of his ex, hospital gowns, and other anxiety-inducing scraps. Setting Old Man Gloom aflame is intended to purge these troubles, clearing the way for a fresh start.

This Santa Fe tradition sounds like a medieval rite, but it dates only from the 1920s, when artist Will Shuster—a bit of a local legend who's also credited with inventing piñon-juniper incense and starting the tradition of city-wide bonfires on Christmas Eve—wanted to lighten up the heavily Catholic Fiesta de Santa Fe. Shuster, who had moved to Santa Fe in 1920 to treat his tuberculosis, was inspired by the Mummers Parade from his native Phila-delphia, as well as the Yaqui Indians in Tucson, Arizona, who burn Judas in effigy in the week before Easter. A 1926 *Santa Fe New Mexican* article describes the spec-tacle Shuster developed, with the help of the Kiwanis Club:

the burning of Zozobra

> Zozobra … stood in ghastly silence illuminated by weird green fires. While the band played a funeral march, a group of Kiwanians in black robes and hoods stole around the figure.… [Then] red fires blazed at the foot … and leaped into a col-umn of many colored flames.… And throwing off their black robes the specta-tors emerged in gala costume, joining an invading army of bright-hued harlequins with torches in a dance around the fires as the band struck up "La Cucaracha."

Shuster oversaw Zozobra nearly every year until 1964. In the late 1930s, actor Errol Flynn, in town with Olivia de Havilland and Ronald Reagan to film *The Santa Fe Trail,* set Zozobra aflame. A few years later, during World War II, the puppet was dubbed Hirohitlomus, a stringing together of abbreviated names of the enemy leaders. In 1950, Zozobra appeared on the New Mexico state float in the New Year's Day Rose Bowl parade and won the national trophy.

Although Zozobra now has a Twitter account and accepts worries-to-burn online, the spectacle is roughly unchanged, with dozens of white-clad children playing "glooms," followed by a "fire dancer" who taunts Zozo until he bursts into flame; fireworks cap off the event. It's a raucous spectacle, attended by a great cross section of New Mexicans. But anyone leery of crowds may prefer to watch from outside the perimeter of the ball field; the streets above and to the east of Fort Marcy Park provide a great vantage point and a less intense experience.

150 Native American artists in the conven-tion center.

Fiesta de Santa Fe

505/204-1598; www.santafefiesta.org; early fall

After the bustle of summer tourism, locals celebrate the arrival of fall with the weeklong Fiesta de Santa Fe, which has been celebrated in some form since 1712. It begins with a reen-actment of Diego de Vargas's entrada into the city, then a whole slew of balls and parades, including the Historical/Hysterical Parade and a children's pet parade—eccentric Santa Fe at its finest. The kickoff event is usually the Burning of Zozobra (855/969-6272; www. burnzozobra.com), a neo-pagan bonfire; the schedule has fluctuated a bit but typically falls on the Friday before Labor Day. Some downtown businesses close for some fiestas, particularly on Zozobra day.

Green Chile Cheeseburger Smackdown

35 Santa Fe Pl.; https://ediblesmackdown.com; early Sept.; from $35

Held at Santa Fe Brewing Company's beer hall, the Green Chile Cheeseburger Smackdown is the definitive showcase for all things green-chile cheeseburger. Judges and the public take on the tough task of tasting and choosing the best green-chile cheeseburger around—perhaps not surprisingly, it's a hugely popular event.

Santa Fe Wine and Chile Festival

505/438-8060; www.santafewineandchile.org; late Sept.; from $25

Foodies flock to the city for the Santa Fe Wine and Chile Festival, five days of tastings and special dinners at various venues around town.

InterPlanetary Festival

Railyard Park; interplanetaryfest.org; mid-Oct.; from $10

One of the last events in Santa Fe's festival season and a relative newcomer, the InterPlanetary Festival takes place in and around the Railyard Park over a weekend in mid-October and features screenings of science fiction classics and documentaries, panel discussions and podcasts on all manner of extraterrestrial and more earthbound subjects—and book signings, too.

Shopping

Even people who clutch their purse strings tight may be a little undone by the treasures for sale in Santa Fe. The rational approach would be to consider the most expensive shops more as free museums. (The cheapest, on the other hand, are stocked with made-in-China junk and are eternally on the brink of "going out of business" and should be avoided.) Several souvenir shops and a few influential galleries are clustered around the plaza. Canyon Road is lined with a bewildering number of galleries, though there can be a certain sameness to many of them. South Guadalupe Street and surrounding blocks have more funky and fun boutiques. If you buy too much to carry, **Pak Mail** (369 Montezuma Ave.; 505/989-7380) can ship your treasures home safely; it even offers free pickup from hotels.

ART GALLERIES

The densest concentration of artwork is on Canyon Road, though it can seem a bit crowded with Southwestern kitsch. The Siler-Rufina neighborhood has emerged as one of the city's best spots to see modern art, with a proliferation of independent galleries. Summer hours are given here; in the winter, most galleries are closed at least Monday and Tuesday.

Local Artists
Community Gallery

201 W. Marcy St.; 505/955-6707; 10am-3pm Wed.-Fri.

In the convention center, the Community Gallery is run by the Santa Fe Arts Commission and always has a wide mix of works by local artists on display.

Contemporary
LewAllen

1613 Paseo de Peralta; 505/988-3250; 10am-6pm Mon.-Fri., 10am-5pm Sat.

Santa Fe's contemporary scene isn't always easy to find, with the notable exception being LewAllen, fittingly across the street from SITE Santa Fe. One of the Railyard's longtime draws, the vast industrial space holds a strong collection of well-conceived exhibitions.

TAI Modern

1601 Paseo de Peralta; 505/984-1387; 10am-5pm Tues.-Sun.

A couple of doors down, TAI Modern showcases colorful abstract and pop art, though they particularly stand out with their extensive collection of Japanese bamboo art.

Nüart Gallery

670 Canyon Rd.; 505/988-3888; 10am-5pm daily

A rare spot for abstraction on Canyon Road, Nüart Gallery also showcases a wide variety of international artists, with a focus on magic realism.

photo-eye Gallery

1300 Rufina Circle, Ste. A3; 505/988-5152; 10am-5:30pm Mon.-Sat.

In the Siler-Rufina neighborhood, photo-eye Gallery, both a bookstore and a gallery, features fine art photo prints and photography books, with rotating exhibits by influential photographers from the last few decades.

Tesuque Glassworks

1510 Bishops Lodge Rd.; 505/988-2165; 9am-5pm daily

Tesuque Glassworks functions as a co-op with a range of glass artists using the furnace and displaying their work. To get to Tesuque, head north out of Santa Fe on Washington Avenue, which becomes Bishops Lodge Road; Shidoni is on the left side of the road.

Native American and Southwestern

4Kinship

812 Canyon Rd.; 11am-5pm Wed.-Sun.

Navajo-owned 4Kinship sells a variety of pieces made exclusively by both established and up-and-coming Native American artists, including ceramics, rugs, and wall art, with a focus on Indigenous fashion, such as brightly colored dresses, jewelry, and hats.

Gerald Peters Gallery

1005 Paseo de Peralta; 505/954-5700; 10am-5pm Tues.-Sat.

Near Canyon Road, Gerald Peters Gallery is an icon of the Santa Fe arts scene, both as a champion of groundbreaking artists but also as a gallery long intertwined with Southwestern art.

Nedra Matteucci Galleries

1075 Paseo de Peralta; 505/982-4631; 9am-5pm Mon.-Sat.

Nedra Matteucci Galleries is one of the biggies when it comes to Taos Society of Artists and other Western art, though it has contemporary artists, too. Even if nothing inside hits the spot, the one-acre sculpture garden and ponds in back are a treat.

Allan Houser Gallery

125 Lincoln Ave.; 505/982-4705; 10am-5pm Mon.-Sat.

Near the plaza, Allan Houser Gallery showcases the work of the Southwest's best-known Native sculptor; it also maintains a sculpture garden south of the city near Cerrillos, with visits by appointment.

Blue Rain Gallery

544 S. Guadalupe St.; 505/954-9902; 10am-6pm Mon.-Fri., 9am-5pm Sat.

In the Railyard, Blue Rain Gallery showcases work from many pueblo residents, such as Tammy Garcia's modern takes on traditional Santa Clara pottery forms—she sometimes renders bowls in blown glass or applies the geometric decoration to jewelry.

CLOTHING AND JEWELRY

Santa Fe Dry Goods

53-55 Old Santa Fe Tr.; 505/982-6192; 11am-5pm Mon.-Sat.

On the plaza, Santa Fe Dry Goods has a wide-ranging collection of high-end women's clothing and accessories, including jewelry, bags, and shawls; it also sells stylish home items.

TOKo Santa Fe

101 W. Marcy St.; 505/470-4425; 10am-5pm Tues.-Sat.

Nearby, TOKo Santa Fe has a collection of Asian-inspired women's and men's clothing and accessories by several hip designers.

Glorianna's Beads

55 W. Marcy St.; 505/982-0353; 10am-4:30pm Mon.-Tues. and Thurs.-Sat., often closed for lunch 1pm-2pm

Just down the block, Glorianna's Beads is packed to bursting with veritable eggs of raw turquoise, trays of glittering Czech glass, and ropes of African trade beads.

Double Take

321 S. Guadalupe St.; 505/989-8886; 11am-5pm Wed.-Sat., 12:30pm-4:30pm Sun.

The city's best consignment shop is Double Take, a sprawling two-story space with an excellent selection of boots, belts, and cowboy hats, as well as cool clothing, rodeo-themed 1950s sofas, Fiestaware, and plenty more.

GIFT AND HOME

Seret & Sons

224 Galisteo St.; 505/988-9151; 9am-5pm Mon.-Fri., 9am-6pm Sat., 9:30am-5pm Sun.

Santa Fe icon Seret & Sons deals in finely woven rugs, antique doors and chests, and large-scale wooden creations from its cavernous warehouse just south of the plaza.

Jackalope

2820 Cerrillos Rd.; 505/471-8539; 9am-5pm daily

For funky folk art that won't break the bank, head for the equally gigantic Jackalope, crammed with mosaic-topped tables, wooden chickens, Mexican pottery vases, and inexpensive souvenirs. Sharing the space is a community of prairie dogs—a good distraction for children while adults cruise the breakables.

Doodlet's

120 Don Gaspar St.; 505/983-3771; 10am-5:30pm Mon.-Sat., 10am-5pm Sun.

A totally absorbing corner shop filled with bits and bobs for kids and adults, Doodlet's is the kind of place where you can find toy accordions to kitchen tchotchkes.

Toyopolis

150 Washington Ave.; 505/988-5422; 10am-5:30pm Mon.-Sat., 11am-5pm Sun.

Toyopolis is stocked with colorful and well-curated collection of toys that often aren't on the shelves of the big department stores.

BOOKSTORES

Beastly Books

418 Montezuma Ave.; 505/466-5528; noon-7pm Wed.-Sat., noon-4pm Sun.

For the latest fantasy and sci-fi releases and quite a few George R. R. Martin collectibles—the writer owns the store—visit Beastly Books. There's an on-site café, a few comfy seats to savor your signed hardback, and a (human-sized) Iron Giant to keep you company.

Travel Bug

839 Paseo de Peralta; 505/992-0418; 10am-6pm Mon.-Sat., noon-4pm Sun.

Travel Bug specializes in getting you ready to get out in the world—from guidebooks and a huge selection of maps to luggage locks and water bottles. It also hosts language classes and has good coffee and baked goods to munch on while you plan your next adventure.

Collected Works

202 Galisteo St.; 505/988-4226; 9am-5pm daily

For a general selection of books, Collected Works is the place to go for a trove of local-interest titles.

Bee Hive

328 Montezuma Ave.; 505/780-8051; 10:30am-5:30pm Mon.-Sat., noon-4pm Sun.

A lovingly curated bookstore primarily aimed at kids, Bee Hive often has story time on Saturdays. The selection for adults is thoughtfully compiled, too.

1: Doodlet's **2:** Double Take consignment shop **3:** 4Kinship on Canyon Road

OPEN-AIR MARKETS
Santa Fe Flea
7 Caliente Rd.; 505/585-1803

As much a quirky fashion show and social scene as a shopping event, the Santa Fe Flea convenes vintage aficionados, fine artists, crafty folks, and "tailgate traders" of miscellaneous oddities. In recent years the market has moved annually for the warmer months; call first to confirm the current location. In winter, many of the vendors move indoors to **El Museo Cultural** (555 Camino de la Familia; 8am-3pm Sat.-Sun. late Nov.-Apr.) at the Railyard complex.

Railyard Artisan Market
1607 Paseo de Peralta; www.artmarketsantafe.com; 10am-3pm Sun.

In the Santa Fe Farmer's Market Pavilion, the Railyard Artisan Market showcases locally crafted goods, such as blown glass, ceramics, blankets, jewelry, and clothing. The selection is better in the shoulder seasons, when fewer competing craft fairs siphon off vendors.

SWEET TREATS
Chocolatesmith
851-A Cerrillos Rd.; 505/473-2111; 10am-5:30pm Mon.-Fri., 10am-5pm Sat.; $2

Intense hand-dipped truffles and dark chocolate bark are the specialty at Chocolatesmith, a small spot bursting with exquisite chocolates and displays to match.

Señor Murphy
100 E. San Francisco St.; 505/982-0461; 10am-5pm daily

If you prefer nuts and chews, head to longtime candy vendor Señor Murphy for some "caramales" (chewy balls of caramel and piñon nuts wrapped up in little corn husks) and other New Mexico-inspired sweets, including several infused with chile.

Food

Dining out is one of Santa Fe's great pleasures. For its size, the city supports a dazzling range of excellent restaurants, some nationally recognized and others simply revered by locals. Sure, you can get a cheese-smothered, crazy-hot plate of green-chile-and-chicken enchiladas, but there's so much more from across the globe to choose from. Top-notch Southwestern, Italian, French, Mediterranean, and—of course—New Mexican fare can all be had within walking distance of the plaza; drive a little farther out and the options open up exponentially.

DOWNTOWN
The ring formed by Alameda Street and Paseo de Peralta contains some classic Santa Fe spots, plus a few hidden treats. On the plaza itself, the carnitas and fajitas carts are institutions—and there are usually a few carts serving other cuisines, too.

New Mexican
The Shed
113½ E. Palace Ave.; 505/982-9030; 11am-2:30pm and 5pm-9pm Mon.-Sat.; $17

The Shed has been serving up platters of enchiladas since 1953—bizarrely, with a side of garlic bread. But that's just part of the tradition at this colorful, comfortable, marginally fancy place that's as popular with tourists as it is with longtime residents. There are perfectly decent distractions like lemon-garlic shrimp and fish tacos on the menu, but it's the red chile you should focus on. Reservations are essential throughout the summer.

Mexican
Bumble Bee's Baja Grill
301 Jefferson St.; 505/820-2862; 11am-8pm daily; $4.50

The specialty at Bumble Bee's Baja Grill is Baja-style shrimp tacos, garnished with shredded cabbage and a creamy sauce, plus a spritz of lime and your choice of house-made salsas. There are several delectable vegetarian options, including a sizeable veggie especial burrito with grilled peppers and onions. The seafood stew is also delicious, as are the fried-fresh tortilla chips and that Tijuana classic, Caesar salad. Don't leave without indulging in the flan. Bumble Bee's also boasts a rare perk so near the plaza: a drive-thru.

Fresh and Local
★ Café Pasqual's

121 Don Gaspar St.; 505/983-9340; 8am-3pm and 5:30pm-10pm daily; $29

Open since the late 1970s, Café Pasqual's has defined its own culinary category, relying almost entirely on organic ingredients. Its breakfasts are legendary, but the food is delicious any time of day. Expect nearly anything on the menu, such as smoked-trout hash or Yucatán-style huevos motuleños for breakfast and pan-seared ribeye with a single malt Scotch and creme fraiche sauce or mole enchiladas for dinner. Call ahead for a reservation or brace yourself for the inevitable line, as the brightly painted dining room seats only 50.

Spanish
La Boca

72 W. Marcy St.; 505/982-3433; 11:30am-9pm daily; little plates $7-16

Cozy, creative-tapas joint La Boca tempts with a strong selection of Spanish staples, such as olives stuffed with jamón serrano, grilled octopus, and bruschetta; the wine list, heavy on South American and Mediterranean vintages, is stellar as well. The little plates can add up fast, unless you're at La Boca 3pm-5pm, when there's a selection for half price. Reserve, ideally, and go early if you're sensitive to noise.

Italian
Upper Crust Pizza

329 Old Santa Fe Tr.; 505/982-0000; 11am-10pm daily; $14

Off the plaza, next to Mission San Miguel, Upper Crust Pizza is a slice of old-school Santa Fe, with a nice, creaky front porch, often with a live country crooner. Choose from regular, whole-wheat, or gluten-free crust and several specialty pizzas, or build your own. Piping-hot calzones, subs, and generously sized fresh salads round out the menu.

French
French Pastry Shop

100 E. San Francisco St.; 505/983-6697; 6:30am-5pm daily; $5-15

The French Pastry Shop has been doling out sweet crepes, buttery pastries, croques monsieurs, and chewy baguette sandwiches for more than 40 years. Early mornings attract a fascinating crew of Santa Fe regulars.

Cafés
★ Dolina

402 N. Guadalupe St.; 505/982-9394; 8am-2pm daily; $9-19

With its white walls, cozy furnishings, and tempting pastry case, it's easy to imagine strolling upon Dolina in the Slovakian countryside, which is not surprising given it's where the café's owner was born. In addition to a truly mouthwatering selection of baked goods, the menu focuses on a mix of Eastern European and New Mexican breakfast and lunch staples such as paprikash, stuffed schnitzel, and breakfast burritos. The soups—including Hungarian goulash—and salads are top-notch, too.

35º North

60 E. San Francisco St.; 505/983-6138; 7:30am-3:30pm Mon.-Fri., 8:30am-2:30pm Sat.-Sun.

Adorned with handsome maps denoting international coffee trade routes, 35º North, on the second floor of The Arcade and overlooking Water Street, serves up some of the best espressos around the plaza as well as a filling and energizing "Latitude Adjustment"—coffee blended with grass-fed butter, coconut oil, and MCT oil.

Ecco

128 E. Marcy St.; 505/986-9778; 7am-9:30pm Mon.-Thurs., 7am-10pm Fri., 8am-10pm Sat., 8am-8pm Sun.

Ecco is packed with coffee junkies in the mornings, giving way to gelato lovers later in the day; choose from nearly 100 flavors of the cold treat, including banana rum, fig and walnut, and chocolate cabernet.

Diners
Five & Dime General Store

58 E. San Francisco St.; 505/992-1800; 9am-9pm daily; $4-8

For just about the most casual lunch around, stop in at the Five & Dime General Store, on the plaza. In this former Woolworth's where, allegedly, the Frito pie was invented (Frito-Lay historians beg to differ), the knickknack shop has maintained its lunch counter and still serves the deadly combo of corn chips, homemade red chile, onions, and shredded cheese, all composed directly in the Fritos bag. Eat in, or, better still, lounge on the plaza grass—and don't forget the napkins.

★ Tia Sophia's

210 W. San Francisco St.; 505/983-9880; 7am-2pm Mon.-Sat., 8am-1pm Sun.; $6-11

Tia Sophia's is one of the last places around the plaza that feels untouched by time and tourists, serving New Mexican plates to a slew of regulars without a touch of fuss or fusion—so authentic, in fact, the kitchen claims to have invented the breakfast burrito decades back.

Plaza Café

54 Lincoln Ave.; 505/982-1664; 7am-9pm daily; $9-29

Plaza Café may look shiny and new, but it's a city institution where residents have long come to read the paper and load up on coffee and great renditions of New Mexican and American diner favorites. This is no greasy spoon, though—the piñon blue-corn pancakes are fluffy and fresh, the posole is perfectly toothsome, and the chicken-fried steak is a plateful of comforting goodness. There's another, far larger and livelier outpost on the

southside (3466 Zafarano Dr.; 505/424-0755; 10am-9pm Mon.-Thurs., 8am-9pm Fri.-Sun.).

GUADALUPE AND THE RAILYARD

An easy walk from the plaza, the Railyard and a few surrounding blocks hold some of the better, quirkier dining options in town.

New Mexican
La Choza

905 Alarid St.; 505/982-0909; 11am-2:30pm and 4:30pm-9pm Mon.-Sat.; $12-20

The cousin of downtown's The Shed, La Choza has a similar creative New Mexican menu but is more of a local's hangout and has a livelier atmosphere; in the summer months, it's especially packed after the workday ends. Count on well-executed New Mexican fare, such as a posole stew and a filling chile relleno. The location in the Railyard district makes it a handy destination if you're coming to Santa Fe by train—just walk back along the tracks a few blocks.

Mexican
★ Paloma

401 S. Guadalupe St.; 505/467-8624; 5pm-9pm Tues.-Thurs. and Sun., 5pm-10pm Fri.-Sat.; $8-28

Find fresh and flavorful Mexican dishes at Paloma, which has built a reputation for creative meals at reasonable prices as well as its agave-tinged cocktails. Tacos are featured for dinner—think red chile-braised beef with romaine lettuce—but there are several other options to choose from, including squash blossom enmoladas (like enchiladas, with a mole instead of chile sauce) and a roasted half-chicken with mole poblano. For dessert, look no further than the excellent and perfectly crispy churros with sea salt caramel.

Pizza
Restoration Pizza

1607 Alcadesa St.; 505/582-2720; 11am-9pm Mon.-Thurs., 11am-10pm Fri., 10:30am-10pm Sat., 10:30am-9pm Sun.; $8-26.25

In the Railyard, Restoration Pizza is the

Food Trucks

Bang Bite

Santa Fe's food trucks can be counted on for some of the tastiest meals in the city. Many pull up at the same spot throughout the week, and food trucks are also fixtures at major events around town. Of course, as they're mobile by nature, it's good to call ahead to confirm current locations.

- For mouthwateringly good burgers, including one with sharp cheddar, bacon, and maple bacon jam, stop by the neon orange ★ **Bang Bite** (510 Galisteo St.; 505/469-2345), on the southside of downtown in the parking lot of The Brakeroom.

- **Craft Donuts & Coffee** (502 Old Santa Fe Tr.; 505/490-9171) prepares an impressive selection of fresh and irresistible donuts. Classics such as glazed and plain cake might sound straightforward but they are anything but, while their signature recipes—like s'mores and maple bacon—are all uniformly excellent.

- **El Chile Toreado** (807 Early St.; 505/500-0033), just east of Cerrillos Road, delivers a cilantro-tinged green salsa that is a near-mystical experience. The carnitas may be the best in town; it also serves excellent breakfast burritos—get one with Mexican chorizo.

- ★ **Ras Rody** (1320 Agua Fria St.; 505/385-3011), with its hearty Jamaican meals, is all the reason you need to venture a little farther out from the center of the city. The vegetarian-exclusive menu changes daily, but count on a comforting combo plate, soup, and dessert.

- **Santafamous** (502 Old Santa Fe Tr.; 505/269-2858) focuses mainly on tacos—try one stuffed with sweet potatoes and dates and topped with a honey chipotle cream, and you might forsake all others.

- One of the city's longest-running food trucks remains one of its best: At **Santa Fe Barbecue** (502 Old Santa Fe Tr.; 505/603-9051), you'll need a bib and a big appetite to handle pulled pork, beef brisket, and baby back pork ribs slathered with a barbecue sauce not soon forgotten.

- Meow Wolf is a reliable draw for food trucks, particularly for **Taqueria Gracias Madre** (505/795-6397), which serves chicken, beef and fish tacos.

first outpost in the city for the longtime Albuquerque pizzeria. Choose from signature pizzas such as the Roadrunner, which is smothered with grilled chicken, pine nuts, red onions, roasted red peppers, mozzarella, and a basil pesto sauce, or create your own combination. You can wash it all down with a familiar selection of Bosque Brewing Co. ales, including its excellent Riverwalker IPA. There's patio seating, too.

Fine Dining
★ Joseph's
428 Agua Fria St.; 505/982-1272; 5pm-9pm Wed.-Sun.; $16-44

Whether you want hearty bar food or an ethereal creation that will take your taste buds in new directions, Chef Joseph Wrede delivers at his lovely, candlelit space Joseph's. Wrede's best dishes are vegetable-centric, though not necessarily vegetarian, such as a root vegetable Napoleon. But he's also into local meats, so carnivores will find a beef tenderloin, green chile, and potato stew, and a seemingly simple lamb patty that may be the state's best green-chile cheeseburger. Book ahead if you can, or try for a seat at the bar. And whatever happens, don't miss the duck-fat ice cream.

★ Radish & Rye
505 Cerrillos Rd.; 505/930-5325; 5pm-close daily; $32-46

Superlatives come easy when speaking of Radish & Rye, an unpretentious farm-to-table restaurant that is so much more than what that concept suggests. It's a beautiful and inviting space with service that is at once impeccable and never overbearing, with the best selection of bourbons, ryes, and American whiskeys in town. For all that, the food is what makes the place so singular. The menu is American with a decidedly Southern feel, with flavorful dishes such as chicken-fried quail with a buttermilk waffles and beef ribeye with fingerlings cooked in duck

fat. The produce is predominantly sourced locally—as much as the seasons allow—and the freshness comes through, particularly in the strong selection of starters. For dessert, a bourbon pecan pie with crème anglaise awaits.

Fresh and Local
Modern General
637 Cerrillos Rd.; 505/930-5462; 8am-4pm daily; $8-13

Next door, you'll first see the same owner's faux farm shop and café, Modern General, which is also good, with its simple menu of juices, avocado toast, a few other breakfasts all day, and exquisite Czech kolaches—pastries with all manner of sweet and savory fillings. Vinaigrette is in the building behind that.

★ Tune-Up Café
1115 Hickox St.; 505/983-7060; 7am-10pm Mon.-Fri., 8am-10pm Sat.-Sun.; $8-18

Just outside the Paseo de Peralta loop, the Tune-Up Café is a homey joint that locals love, whether for fish tacos or a suitably Santa Fe-ish brown-rice-and-nut burger. The place is especially packed during weekend brunches, when early morning outdoor adventures are recapped over heaping plates of fruit compote-stuffed French toast and steak and eggs.

★ Vinaigrette
709 Don Cubero Alley; 505/820-9205; 11am-9pm Mon.-Sat.; $10-20

If you're on green-chile-and-cheese overload, head to Vinaigrette and dig into a big pile of fresh greens. This self-proclaimed "salad bistro" uses largely organic ingredients, from its farm in Nambé, in imaginative combos, such as a highbrow taco salad with chorizo and honey-lime dressing. The setting is pure homey Santa Fe, with tea towels for napkins, iced tea served in canning jars, and local art on the whitewashed walls. There's a shaded patio, too.

1: Santa Fe Farmers Market **2:** Restoration Pizza **3:** The Teahouse **4:** chicken fried steak at the Plaza Café Southside

★ Santa Fe Farmers Market

1607 Paseo de Peralta, 505/983-4098;
www.santafefarmersmarket.com; 7am-1pm Tues.
and Sat. late May-Nov., 8am-1pm Tues. and Sat.
Dec.-late May

The popular Santa Fe Farmers Market is a buzzing social scene and a great place to pick up fresh local produce and treats as well as souvenir chile ristras. It's in a market hall in the Railyard complex, off Paseo de Peralta near Guadalupe Street; from late May to November the stalls spill out along the nearby train tracks and the landmark water tower.

Burgers and Barbecue
Shake Foundation

631 Cerrillos Rd.; 505/988-8992; 11am-7pm Mon.-
Thurs., 11am-8pm Fri.-Sat., 11am-6pm Sun.; $4-7.50

An outdoor burger joint that's so good people flock to it even in winter, Shake Foundation serves undersized beef, lamb, and turkey burgers (order a double if in doubt) on lavishly buttered buns; there's also a melt-in-your-mouth fried oyster sandwich with red-chile mayo. The eatery's dense, namesake drinks come in "adobe mud shakes," with ice cream made from New Mexico dairy. Seats in the shade are in short supply; plan accordingly in the heat of a summer afternoon.

Cowgirl BBQ

319 S. Guadalupe St.; 505/982-2565; 11:30am-9pm
Sun.-Thurs., 11:30am-10pm Fri.-Sat.; $9-19

All things Texan are the specialty at Cowgirl BBQ—think mesquite-smoked baby back ribs, chile with cheese and jalapeño cornbread, and barbecued chicken. It's a kitsch-filled spot that's as friendly to kids as it is to margarita-guzzling, barbecued-rib-gnawing adults. For non-meat-eaters, there are more options than you might expect, including an ooey-gooey butternut squash casserole that comes with a salad on the side. Both carnivores and vegetarians can agree on the flourless chocolate cake with red chile and the ice cream "baked potato."

French
★ Mille

451 W. Alameda St.; 505/930-5492; 7:30am-2pm
Wed.-Sun.; $6.50-19.75

Mille has a mouthwatering collection of French breakfast and lunch classics, including croque madame, quiche Florentine, duck confit, and an assortment of baguette sandwiches and savory crepes. A selection of colorful macarons, chocolate croissants, and eclairs practically guarantee you'll leave with your sweet tooth satiated. There's also an outside seating area.

Cafés
★ Sage Bakehouse

535 Cerrillos Rd.; 505/820-7243; 7:30am-2pm
Mon.-Sat.; $5

Make room in your morning for an almond croissant from Sage Bakehouse. Washed down with a mug of coffee, these butter-soaked pastries will have you set for hours. Before you leave, pick up some sandwiches for later—classics such as egg salad on sourdough, and smoked turkey and cheddar on the bakery's excellent homemade whole wheat crust. And maybe a pecan-raisin wreath. And a chocolate-chip cookie, too.

Whoo's Donuts

851-B Cerrillos Rd.; 505/629-1678; 7am-3pm daily;
$2-9

Choose from rich donuts such as organic maple bacon, orange cardamom cream, blue corn blueberry lavender, and cherry coconut at this Santa Fe institution, which also prepares burritos to go, including a satisfying one made with Impossible meat crumbles. Be sure to get there before they sell out, which they sometimes do.

★ Opuntia

1607 Alcadelsa St.; 505/780-5796; 10am-3pm
Mon.-Tues., 10am-3pm and 5pm-9pm Wed.-Fri.,
9am-3pm and 5pm-9pm Sat.-Sun.; $9-16

Catering to green-tea drinkers and green thumbs alike, and occupying airy digs in the Railyard, Opuntia tempts with healthy food and drinks to nosh on as well as potted plants and ceramics to take home. Breakfast dishes include items like an omelet featuring seasonal ingredients. Later in the day you can choose from a bewildering array of flavorful bowls and tasty toasts—the one with sautéed mushrooms, roasted garlic, kale, and reggiano cheese is especially savory.

Ohori's Coffee
505 Cerrillos Rd.; 505/988-9692; 7am-6pm Mon.-Sat., 8am-5pm Sun.

Ohori's Coffee is Santa Fe's small-batch coffee epicure; its dark-as-night brew makes Starbucks seem weak. With few seats, it's not so much a place to linger as one where you'll appreciate the clear attention to detail.

CANYON ROAD AND THE EASTSIDE

Gallery hopping on Canyon Road can make you hungry—and it's all uphill from the road's terminus at Paseo de Peralta. Fortunately, there are a few places where you can fill up on caffeine to get you going and find a satisfying meal at the day's end.

Fine Dining
★ Geronimo
724 Canyon Rd.; 505/982-1500; 5pm-close daily; $27-52

Elegant Geronimo is consistently rated one of Santa Fe's—and the country's—best restaurants, and it's easy to see why. Standouts on the menu include an elk tenderloin with an applewood-smoked bacon and brandied mushroom sauce, grilled rack of lamb, and a pan-seared salmon with gnocchi. The service is impeccable, too.

Spanish
El Farol
808 Canyon Rd.; 505/983-9912; 3pm-9pm Wed.-Sun.; $8-36

One of the oldest restaurants in the country, El Farol is Canyon Road's liveliest nightspot. There's usually lots of action in the bar area, including frequent live flamenco,

but it's the outside seating, under a creaky wooden portal and on a back patio, that really makes this historic adobe one of the better places in town to settle in for an evening. Pair drinks with numerous hot and cold tapas, such as patatas bravas and Spanish olives with anchovies and roasted peppers, or opt for larger plates, including its popular house paella.

Cafés
★ Kakawa Chocolate House
1050 E. Paseo de Peralta; 505/982-0388; 11am-6pm Mon.-Sat., noon-6pm Sun.; $4

Chocolate devotees should consider Kakawa Chocolate House an essential—and educational—stop. It elevates hot chocolate to an art form, specializing in historically accurate drinks based on Mesoamerican and medieval European recipes. Complete your indulgence with decadent bite-size chocolates as well as dense dark-chocolate brownies. It's in a tiny adobe house with a kiva fireplace; when the temperature drops in winter, there's no place better to settle in.

The Teahouse
821 Canyon Rd.; 505/992-0972; 9am-3pm Mon.-Thurs., 9am-5pm Fri.-Sun.; $12

Located near the top end of Canyon Road, The Teahouse is the ideal place to put your feet up after a long art crawl. Choose from an incredibly long list of teas from around the world, many of which are prepared in a variety of ways. There are also vittles such as mixed greens with cranberries, pecans, and feta and a deliciously hearty bowl of oats, black rice, buckwheat groats, and maple cream for breakfast. The service could be described as "very Santa Fe" (i.e., forget about a quick meal), but the teas and food are unquestionably worth it.

Downtown Subscription
376 Garcia St.; 505/983-3085; 7am-6pm daily

For a morning brew, stroll over to Downtown Subscription, an airy coffee shop buzzing with locals and stocked with a bewildering selection of magazines. In the warmer months, enjoy your drink in the shaded garden in the back.

CERRILLOS ROAD

This commercial strip south of the plaza isn't Santa Fe's most scenic stretch, but you'll find some great culinary gems down this way and along various side streets.

New Mexican
Maria's
555 W. Cordova Rd.; 505/983-7929; 11:30am-9pm daily; $11-18

Long appreciated for its dazzling list of margaritas, Maria's is well worth settling into for a meal of hearty New Mexican classics, starting with a genuinely spicy table salsa and chips. Both red and green are sold here, and the tamales are exceptionally rich and creamy (even the vegetarian ones!).

The Pantry
1820 Cerrillos Rd.; 505/986-0022; 7am-8:30pm daily; $8.75-24

A welcoming, no-frills family diner, The Pantry has been slinging eggs, pancakes, and chile since 1948; breakfast is served all day. There's a lunch counter up front, but regulars request the back room. **The Pantry Rio** (229 Galisteo St.; 505/989-1919; 7:30am-8:30pm daily), its newer location across from the Santa Fe River, has much the same menu and is conveniently near the plaza.

French
★ Clafoutis
333 W. Cordova St.; 505/988-1809; 7am-3pm Mon.-Sat.; $5-12.50

In an incongruous location adjacent to Body of Santa Fe, Clafoutis oozes laid-back Parisian charm and tempts with the sweet smells of crepes, bruschettas, and croissants. The croque madame is delectable and the beignets can be ordered by the bagful. The salads, including one with smoked salmon and toasted almonds, don't disappoint either.

African
★ Jambo
2010 Cerrillos Rd.; 505/473-1269; 11am-9pm Mon.-Sat.; $10-25

Situated unassumingly in a strip mall, Jambo offers spicy, earthy East African dishes that are well priced and consistently satisfying. There's a heavy Indian influence—lentil stew spiked with chile and softened with coconut, for instance—as well as Caribbean- and Moroccan-inspired meals. Be mindful of the strong selection of starters—it's easy to fill up fast on the coconut shrimp, cinnamon-dusted plantains, and paprika hummus, among other savory choices.

Asian
Lu Lu's
3011 Cerrillos Rd.; 505/473-1688; 11am-9pm Mon.-Thurs. and Sun., 11am-9:30pm Fri.-Sat.; $8-17

Attached to a Quality Inn, Lu Lu's serves some of the most satisfying Chinese food around. Count on familiar pleasures such as sweet and sour chicken and kung pao, but don't overlook several standout house specialties, including a generous Royal Seafood Pot—scallops, crabmeat, shrimp, fish, and vegetables in a white-wine sauce.

Cafés
Counter Culture
930 Baca St.; 505/995-1105; 8am-3pm daily; $12

Counter Culture is generally a locals-only scene, well liked for its catchall menu (including carne asada, Vietnamese banh mi sandwiches, and tire-size cinnamon buns), its casual-industrial vibe, and its large outdoor patio where kids can run around.

★ Iconik
1600 Lena St.; 505/428-0669; 7:30am-5pm daily

In the heart of Lena Street's industrial lofts, airy Iconik is worth seeking out for its heady mix of top-notch pour-overs and drips, bagel sandwiches, and smart decor. It's a large communal space with comfy couches set against a backdrop of coffee-roasting equipment and features occasional live music. The company also operates the **Iconik Lupe** (314 S. Guadalupe St.; 505/428-0669; 7:30am-5pm daily), a sun-kissed spot with a shaded patio off Agua Fria, and **Iconik Red** (1366 Cerrillos Rd.; 505/428-0669; 7:30am-5pm daily), a roomy location across from the Santa Fe Indian School.

Diners
★ Santa Fe Bite

1616 St. Michael's Dr.; 505/438-0328; 9am-8pm Tues.-Sat.; $11-24

Longtime burger connoisseurs may remember Bobcat Bite, just outside the city. It closed in 2013, becoming Santa Fe Bite—an even better incarnation, now in a more spacious locale off Cerrillos. The 10-ounce green-chile cheeseburgers, made from beef ground fresh every day and served on a home-baked bun, remain worthy of a pilgrimage. There's plenty more now, too, including a bulging patty melt, big salads, and, on Friday, fish-and-chips.

SANTA FE METRO AREA
New Mexican
★ Horseman's Haven Café

4354 Cerrillos Rd.; 505/471-5420; 8am-7pm Tues.-Fri., 8:30am-7pm Sat., 8:30am-2pm Sun.; $8-20

The decision of which chile to slather your breakfast burrito with is not one to be taken lightly at the Horseman's Haven Café, home to some of the hottest green chile in Santa Fe. It picks and mixes chile varieties to offer a couple of consistent grades that are doled out generously with filling plates of old-school New Mexican fare. Like all good chile purveyors, the café is in an unassuming box of a building next to a gas station, and it takes cash only.

Classic American
Harry's Roadhouse

96 Old Las Vegas Hwy.; 505/989-4629; 11am-9pm Wed.-Thurs., 8am-9pm Fri.-Sun.; $10-25

On the frontage road for I-25, Harry's Roadhouse is an easy detour off the freeway (exit at Old Santa Fe Tr.). The pretty patio is usually buzzing, there's a full bar, and the diner-style menu includes everything from fried catfish with grits to turkey meat loaf to pizza, plus coconut cream pie. Expect a line and a packed parking lot; reserve ahead, if possible.

Fresh and Local
Café Fina

624 Old Las Vegas Hwy.; 505/466-3886; 8am-3pm Tues.-Sun.; $8-13.50

For a calmer, more wholesome vibe, keep driving down the road to Café Fina, also easily

Horseman's Haven Café

accessible at exit 290 off I-25. This is a casual order-at-the-counter place, with a short but flavor-packed menu (including ricotta pancakes, migas, and grilled salmon tacos) from mostly locally grown ingredients.

Italian
★ El Nido
1577 Bishop's Lodge Rd.; 505/954-1272;
4:30pm-8:30pm Wed.-Sat.; $18-39

Handsome and welcoming El Nido serves up refined and hearty fare in a historical Tesuque adobe. The seasonal menus are smorgasbords of roasted and grilled creations, such as roasted half chicken, grilled Scottish salmon, and roasted poblano; there are also exquisite pasta dishes and several wood-fired pizzas to choose from. Though portions are substantial, think twice about skipping dessert.

Asian
Izanami
3451 Hyde Park Rd.; 505/982-9304; noon-9pm
Wed.-Mon., 5pm-9pm Tues.; $4-22

The restaurant at Ten Thousand Waves, Izanami, melds old Japan and new without feeling like you've stepped into a theme park. On the menu, there's pickled burdock root and grilled avocado, as well as wagyu-beef burgers and sake-braised mushrooms in a butter sauce, served in small plates to share. The dining room has a rustic mountain-lodge feel, with an optional shoes-off tatami-mat seating area. Throw in arguably the most extensive sake menu in the Southwest and surprisingly reasonable prices, and it's one of Santa Fe's cooler places to eat, whether you make the drive up for dinner or just wander over after your bath.

Accommodations

Santa Fe offers some great places to stay, but few are particularly cheap and rates have gone up exponentially in recent years. Prices quoted for the bigger hotels are standard rack rates; chances are, you'll find substantially lower ones by calling or booking online, at least at the higher-end properties. Prices spike in July and August, often up to holiday rates. If you're coming for Indian Market or Christmas, try to book several months in advance. On the other hand, despite ski season, rates are often quite low in early December, January, and February.

DOWNTOWN
$150-200
Inn of the Governors
101 W. Alameda St.; 505/982-4333;
www.innofthegovernors.com; from $199 d

The 100-room Inn of the Governors isn't flashy on the outside, but inside it has a personable only-in-Santa-Fe feel, starting with the afternoon "tea and sherry hour," when guests are plied with free drinks and bizco-chitos. The inn's unique profit-sharing system may account for the exceptionally nice staff. Breakfast is generous, parking is free (unheard-of elsewhere downtown), and there's even a tiny pool. Rooms in the Governors Wing are quietest. The attached Del Charro Saloon serves the best-value meals and margaritas around the plaza.

$200-250
Drury Plaza Santa Fe
828 Paseo de Peralta; 505/424-2175;
www.druryhotels.com; $239 d

Downtown's largest property, Drury Plaza Santa Fe has a somewhat corporate feel, but it occupies a sprawling historic hospital complex behind the St. Francis Cathedral—a convenient location at a good price for amenities that include a rooftop pool and bar, full breakfast, and free afternoon drinks. Rooms are a little small but comfortably furnished.

La Posada

330 E Palace Ave.; 505/986-0000;
www.laposadadesantafe.com; $244 d

A short walk from the plaza, the handsome La Posada offers a full range of high-end amenities, including an outdoor pool, a fitness center, and a popular spa. The decor is decidedly Southwestern throughout but not over the top, with earth tones and vigas beams in common areas and guest rooms, the latter of which can vary in size. Some rooms have kiva fireplaces and face out on to the pool; all exude an understated elegance.

Hotel Chimayó

125 Washington Ave.; 505/988-4900;
www.hotelchimayo.com; from $249 d

Not quite the great budget option it once was, Hotel Chimayó is still a good value, though not everyone will like its folksy style, done up with wooden crosses and striped rugs from its namesake village. Upstairs rooms have private balconies, and some suites have fireplaces. Free downtown walking tours are included in the rate.

Over $250

Campanilla Compound

334 Otero St.; 800/828-9700;
www.campanillacompound.com; $270

A rental condo is a great option if you have a family or group, and those at Campanilla Compound are especially nice, with white-washed walls, fireplaces, and Mexican-tiled kitchens. Each one- and two-bedroom unit has plenty of space inside and out, with a private patio or porch, and, thanks to the location on a hill, some have excellent views of the city and the sunset. There's a three-night minimum in summer, and two nights the rest of the year.

Inn on the Alameda

303 E. Alameda St.; 505/984-2121;
www.innonthealameda.com; from $275 d

Inn on the Alameda is an ideal choice for those who want adobe style *and* space, and its location near Canyon Road is handy for gallery-hoppers. The big rooms have triple-sheeted beds, wireless Internet access, and overstuffed armchairs that are only lightly dusted with Southwestern flair; most also have a patio or balcony. Gas fireplaces are usually an additional $20. The continental breakfast spread is generous, and there's a wine-and-cheese hour every afternoon.

La Fonda

100 E. San Francisco St.; 505/982-5511;
www.lafondasantafe.com; $299 d

The iconic, family-owned La Fonda has been offering respite to travelers in some form or another since 1607. A renovation has lightened up its guest rooms considerably but also spoiled the impeccable historic feeling in the public areas. The whole place feels more generic and modern as a result, though many rooms do have original folk art, and a few have latilla ceilings and kiva fireplaces—along with all the necessary luxuries, such as pillow-top beds. You can soak up most of the place's atmosphere in the public areas, of course, but the location couldn't be better. It helps to have flexible dates—in periods of high demand, the rates can spike to exorbitant levels. Even if you don't stay here, do at least take a spin through the lobby and the mezzanine—there are still traces of the 1920 designs by Mary Colter (best known for the hotels at the Grand Canyon), and some great paintings.

The Inn of the Five Graces

150 E. De Vargas St.; 505/992-0957;
www.fivegraces.com; from $715 d

The singular Relais & Chateaux property The Inn of the Five Graces can transport you to exotic lands—for at least slightly less than a plane ticket. Outside, it looks like a typical historic Southwestern lodge, a collection of interconnected adobe casitas on Santa Fe's oldest street. But inside, the 24 sumptuous suites are done in the style of an opium dream: antique Turkish kilims, heavy wooden doors, mosaics, and handcrafted furnishings—all courtesy of the boho-style dealers Seret & Sons. Amenities include a Tibetan-themed spa and the most stylish fitness center around. Rates include full breakfast, delivered to your room, if you like.

GUADALUPE AND THE RAILYARD
$100-150
Santa Fe Motel & Inn
510 Cerrillos Rd.; 505/982-1039;
www.santafemotel.com; $129 d

Santa Fe Motel & Inn is a good budget option close to the center, with rooms done up in simple, bright decor that avoids motel sameness despite the generic layout. A few kitchenettes are available, along with more-private casitas with fireplaces. Lots of nice touches—such as bread from the Sage Bakehouse across the street along with the full breakfast—give the place a homey feel without the tight quarters of a typical bed-and-breakfast.

Santa Fe Sage Inn
725 Cerrillos Rd.; 505/982-5952;
www.santafesageinn.com; $135 d

The bones of Santa Fe Sage Inn are standard highway motel, but the super-clean rooms are done in sharp, modern red and black, with Southwestern rugs hung on the walls. Little touches such as free Wi-Fi, plush beds,

and an above-average breakfast (fresh bagels, fruit, yogurt, and more) make this an excellent deal. The place even has a swimming pool. It's still walking distance to the center, and it's right across the street from the Railyard Park and the farmers market. The on-site restaurant, Social Kitchen, is a good spot for a drink and a casual meal after a day out.

Over $250
★ Hotel Santa Fe
1501 Paseo de Peralta; 800/825-9876;
http://hotelsantafe.com; from $274 d

Operated by Picurís Pueblo, Hotel Santa Fe is the only Native American-owned hotel in the city. A thoroughly enjoyable place to stay, it incorporates a successful amalgam of Native American cultural touchstones and Southwestern decor. The standard rooms are a bit small—it's worth upgrading to the junior suite. If you book online, rates for the exceedingly high-end Hacienda wing—where the huge rooms all have fireplaces and butler service—are a steal compared to other luxury options in town. Amenities include a large outdoor pool, spa, and the contemporary Amaya restaurant, which serves mostly New Mexican dishes.

The Inn of the Five Graces

★ Houses of the Moon

3451 Hyde Park Rd.; 505/992-5003;
www.tenthousandwaves.com; $395 d

Secluded and wonderfully restful, Houses of the Moon, the guest cottages at the Ten Thousand Waves spa, are real gems. Some have more of a local feel, with viga ceilings and kiva fireplaces, while others feel straight out of Japan, both samurai era and contemporary anime. Some larger suites have kitchens. Rates include a suitably organic granola breakfast and Japanese teas, as well as free access to the communal and women's tubs. There is a two-night minimum stay.

CERRILLOS ROAD
Under $100
Santa Fe International Hostel

1412 Cerrillos Rd.; 505/988-1153;
www.hostelsantafe.org; $25 dorm, $40 s, $55 d

As hostels go, Santa Fe International Hostel is best appreciated with rose-colored glasses firmly in place, viewed as an old-school hippie project (it is run as a nonprofit). The dorms are dim, and cleanliness can be spotty, as you're relying on the previous guests' efforts as part of the required daily chores. Cash only.

$150-200
★ El Rey Court

1862 Cerrillos Rd.; 505/982-1931;
www.elreycourt.com; $195 d

Built around a 1936 motor court, the renovated El Rey Court counts as one of the more charming motels in Santa Fe. Though it has been expanded over the years, its character remains intact, and it has been meticulously kept up and adjusted for modern standards of comfort, with beautiful gardens, a big swimming pool, hot tub, sauna, and the chic cocktail lounge La Reina. The 86 rooms, spread over 5 acres, vary considerably in style (and in price), from the oldest section with snug adobe walls and heavy viga ceilings to airier rooms with balconies. The only drawback is

that the plaza is too far to walk, but a city bus stops right outside.

The Mystic

2810 Cerrillos Rd.; 505/471-7663;
http://themysticsantafe.com; $199 d

Wedged in among the chain hotels on Cerrillos, The Mystic has largely moved beyond the retro charm of its long-running previous incarnation, the Silver Saddle. In its place are understated breezy rooms adorned with modern art and sleek furnishings, with rates to match. In an ode to the place's history, a handful of older rooms have retained a more vintage look.

SANTA FE METRO AREA
$100-150
★ Pecos Trail Inn

2239 Old Pecos Tr.; 505/982-1943;
www.thepecostrailinn.com; from $149

Another standout motel dating back to the 1950s, cheerful Pecos Trail Inn has a range of tidy and comfortable rooms, including one with a kitchenette and a two-bedroom casita. There are nice touches throughout, including storage for bikes and gear in some of the rooms, and there's an onsite café and outdoor swimming pool.

Camping
Hyde Memorial State Park

Hwy. 475; 505/983-7175; www.emnrd.nm.gov; from $10

For camping, the closest tent sites to the center are at Hyde Memorial State Park, about eight miles northeast of the city, with primitive ($10) and developed sites with electricity ($14) as well as a few yurts ($150).

Santa Fe Skies RV Park

14 Browncastle Ranch Rd.; 505/473-5946;
www.santafeskiesrvpark.com; $70

On the southern edge of the city, with quick access to the plaza thanks to nearby I-25, Santa Fe Skies RV Park has nearly 100 back-in and pull-through RV sites with full hook-ups. Some have large patios with shaded areas.

Information and Services

TOURIST INFORMATION

The **Santa Fe Convention and Visitors Bureau** (800/777-2489; www.santafe.org) hands out its visitors guide and other brochures from offices at the **convention center** (201 W. Marcy St.; 8am-5pm Mon.-Fri.), at the small **plaza kiosk** next to the First National Bank (66 E. San Francisco St.; 10am-6pm daily) and at the **Rail Runner depot** (401 S. Guadalupe St.; 9am-5pm Mon.-Sat.); the depot office is also open for the same hours Sunday May-October. The New Mexico Tourism Department runs a **visitors center** (491 Old Santa Fe Tr.; 505/827-7336; www.newmexico.org; 8am-5pm Mon.-Fri.) near San Miguel Mission.

For info on the outdoors, head to the Bureau of Land Management's comprehensive **Public Lands Information Center** (301 Dinosaur Tr.; 505/954-2002; www.publiclands.org; 8am-4:30pm Mon.-Fri.), just off Highway 14 (follow Cerrillos Road until it passes under I-25). You can pick up detailed route descriptions for area day hikes, as well as guidebooks, topo maps, and hunting and fishing licenses.

SERVICES
Banks

First National Santa Fe (62 Lincoln Ave.; 505/992-2000; 8am-5pm Mon.-Fri.) is on the west side of the plaza, while a **Wells Fargo** (241 Washington Ave.; 505/984-0500; 9am-5pm Mon.-Fri.) branch a couple of blocks to the northeast has a drive-thru ATM.

Post Office

Santa Fe's **main post office** (120 S. Federal Pl.; 505/988-2239; 8am-5:30pm Mon.-Fri., 9am-4pm Sat.) is conveniently just north of the plaza, near the district courthouse.

Laundry

Most self-service laundries are on or near Cerrillos Road. Nearer to the center is **Solana Laundromat** (949 W. Alameda; 505/982-9877; 7am-8pm daily). It also has drop-off service.

Getting There and Around

GETTING THERE
Air

Santa Fe Municipal Airport (SAF, 121 Aviation Dr.; 505/955-2900; http://flysantafe.com), west of the city, receives direct flights from Dallas and Phoenix with American Airlines, and from Denver with United. Typically, fares are better to the Albuquerque airport (ABQ), an hour's drive away.

Groome Transportation (505/474-5696; www.groometransportation.com), formerly Sandia Shuttle, does pickups every 1.25 hours from the Albuquerque airport 5:15am-12:30am and will deliver to any hotel or B&B ($39 one-way) or drop off passengers at 269 W. Water Street.

Train

The **Rail Runner** (866/795-7245; www.riometro.org) goes from Albuquerque to downtown Santa Fe—the final stop is at the rail yard in the Guadalupe district (410 S. Guadalupe St.). The ride takes a little over 90 minutes and costs $10, or $11 for a day pass, and the last train back to Albuquerque leaves at 9pm weekdays, 10:14pm Saturday, and 8:10pm Sunday.

Amtrak (800/872-7245; www.amtrak.com) runs the Southwest Chief once a day through

Lamy, 18 miles south of Santa Fe. It's a dramatic place to step off the train—with little visible civilization for miles around, it feels like entering a Wild West movie set. Trains arrive from Chicago and Los Angeles in the afternoon, and Amtrak provides a shuttle van to the city.

Car

From Albuquerque to Santa Fe, it's a straight shot north on I-25 for 65 miles; you'll reach Santa Fe in about an hour.

Coming from Taos, allow 1.5-2.5 hours, depending on whether you come on the low road (on Hwy. 68 and U.S. 84/285, via Española), via Ojo Caliente (mostly on U.S. 285), or on the high road (mostly on Hwy. 76, via Truchas).

GETTING AROUND

If you're staying on the plaza or nearby, you can see plenty of Santa Fe on foot and the area encircling the plaza is welcomely flat, including the walkable Railyard District to the southwest. Bear in mind, however, that the sight that best lends itself to being seen on foot—Canyon Road—climbs steadily the farther along it you go.

Bus and Shuttle

Santa Fe Pick-Up (505/231-2573; www.santafenm.gov; every 10 minutes 6:30am-5:30pm Mon.-Fri., 8:30am-5:30pm Sat., 10am-5:30pm Sun.; free) is a service for tourists, with two routes covering all the main sights. It's free and runs more frequently than the regular city bus. The main circuit starts and ends in front of Jean Cocteau Cinema, on Montezuma Avenue just north of the Rail Runner depot, and it stops at the capitol, the St. Francis Cathedral, four points on Canyon Road, Museum Hill, and a few other tourist-friendly spots around town. From the capitol, the second route runs a loop up Canyon Road and out to Museum Hill.

For Cerrillos Road, you can use Route 2 on the city bus system, **Santa Fe Trails** (505/955-2001; www.santafenm.gov), from the handy central depot on Sheridan Street northwest of the plaza. Buses on all routes are not terribly frequent, every 20 minutes at the most. Fare is $1, or you can buy a day pass for $2, payable on board with exact change.

Car

Having a car in Santa Fe itself is not necessary, though with a car day trips become that much more feasible. Bear in mind that street and garage parking is limited and expensive in the city's center. **Hertz, Budget, Avis,** and **Enterprise** all have branches on or just off Cerrillos Road.

Outside Santa Fe

Less than an hour's drive from Santa Fe are six-century-old ruins of Ancestral Puebloan culture at Bandelier National Monument, and the 20th-century atomic developments in Los Alamos, home of the Manhattan Project. Abiquiu, best known as O'Keeffe Country, is a landscape of rich red rocks bisected by the tree-lined Rio Chama, while green is the predominate color of the endless valleys of the Valles Caldera National Preserve, an hour to the northwest of Santa Fe.

The most popular outing from the city is to Taos—and even the route there is filled with compelling diversions. The main options are the low road along the Rio Grande or the high road that passes through tiny mountain villages. You can also take a more roundabout route through Ojo Caliente, a village built around hot springs.

PECOS

Santa Fe backs up against the 223,000 acres of the **Pecos Wilderness,** the second-largest nature reserve in New Mexico (after the Gila,

Outside Santa Fe

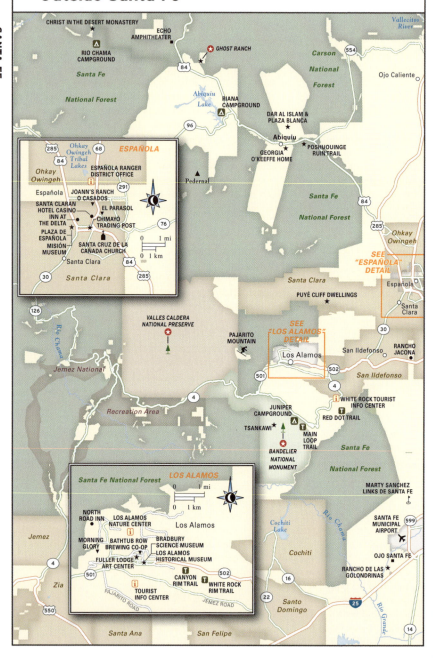

CHRIST IN THE DESERT MONASTERY
ECHO AMPHITHEATER
RIO CHAMA CAMPGROUND
GHOST RANCH
554
Carson National Forest
Ojo Caliente
84
Santa Fe National Forest
Abiquiu Lake
RIANA CAMPGROUND
DAR AL ISLAM & PLAZA BLANCA
96
Abiquiu
GEORGIA O'KEEFFE HOME
POSHUOUINGE RUIN TRAIL
Pedernal
Santa Fe National Forest
84
285
Ohkay Owingeh

ESPAÑOLA

285
68
Ohkay Owingeh Tribal Lakes
84
ESPAÑOLA RANGER DISTRICT OFFICE
Ohkay Owingeh
291
JOANN'S RANCH O CASADOS
EL PARASOL
Española
SANTA CLARAN HOTEL CASINO INN AT THE DELTA
CHIMAYÓ TRADING POST
76
PLAZA DE ESPAÑOLA
MISIÓN MUSEUM
SANTA CRUZ DE LA CAÑADA CHURCH
0   1 mi
0   1 km
Santa Clara
84
30
Santa Clara
285

Santa Clara
PUYÉ CLIFF DWELLINGS

SEE "ESPAÑOLA" DETAIL
Española
Santa Clara

126
Rio Chama

VALLES CALDERA NATIONAL PRESERVE
PAJARITO MOUNTAIN
SEE "LOS ALAMOS" DETAIL
Los Alamos
San Ildefonso
RANCHO JACONA
30
502
501
4
San Ildefonso

Jemez National
4
JUNIPER CAMPGROUND
WHITE ROCK TOURIST INFO CENTER
RED DOT TRAIL
Recreation Area
TSANKAWI
MAIN LOOP TRAIL
Santa Fe National Forest
BANDELIER NATIONAL MONUMENT
MARTY SANCHEZ LINKS DE SANTA FE

LOS ALAMOS
Santa Fe National Forest
0   1 mi
0   1 km
NORTH ROAD INN
LOS ALAMOS NATURE CENTER
Los Alamos
Jemez
MORNING GLORY
BATHTUB ROW BREWING CO-OP
BRADBURY SCIENCE MUSEUM
LOS ALAMOS HISTORICAL MUSEUM
FULLER LODGE ART CENTER
4
501
CANYON RIM TRAIL
WHITE ROCK RIM TRAIL
502
TOURIST INFO CENTER
Zia
PAJARITO ROAD
JEMEZ ROAD
550
Santa Ana
San Felipe

Cochiti Lake
Rio Chama
SANTA FE MUNICIPAL AIRPORT
599
Cochiti
OJO SANTA FE
RANCHO DE LAS GOLONDRINAS
16
22
25
Santa Domingo
14

Vallecitos River

in the southwestern part of the state). The mountain streams seethe with trout, and elk ramble through emerald-green meadows. The heart of the wilderness is slowly recovering from the 2011 Pacheco Fire, but day visitors will find plenty to enjoy. The wilderness's gateway is the former logging town of Pecos, where mountain men rub shoulders with alternative healers and monks; south of town are the ruins of **Pecos Pueblo,** the regional power before the Spanish arrived.

On the drive out on I-25, near exit 295, you pass the site of the westernmost Civil War battle in the United States, the **Battle of Glorieta Pass.** It raged March 26-28, 1862, part of a Confederate plan to invade the West with a force of Texans—a plan that was foiled in this decisive rout. The fight is reenacted here annually, and the property owner maintains a makeshift memorial and exhibit on the side of the highway.

Pecos National Historical Park

Hwy. 63, 505/757-7241; www.nps.gov/peco; 8am-6pm daily June-Aug., 8am-4:30pm Sept.-May; free

When the Spanish made first contact with local people in 1540, Pecos was the largest pueblo in the region, with a population of 2,000 living in and around four- and five-story stone buildings sealed with mud. In Pecos National Historical Park, the ruins of this complex community are accessible to visitors via a 1.5-mile interpretive trail that winds through the remnants of the Pecos Pueblo walls, a few restored kivas, and, most striking, the shell of a Franciscan mission. A free **guided walking tour** around the site runs Friday-Sunday in spring and daily at 10am in summer. Additional free **van tours** cover different aspects of local history; check the website for schedules. For a history of the pueblo, set aside twelve minutes for the video that runs on demand in the visitors center.

On a ridge looking out onto the plains to the northeast and the mountains behind, the park provides a beautiful view today; around AD 1100, when the area was being settled into the first villages, it also provided a livelihood. The ridge was part of a natural trade path between the Rio Grande farmers and the buffalo hunters of the Great Plains. Both groups met in Pecos, itself an agricultural community, to barter. What began as a series of small villages consolidated in the 14th century into a city, with a layout so orderly it appears to have been centrally planned, and by 1450, the fortress

Pecos National Historical Park

Perhaps it was the city's trading culture and relative worldliness that made the Pecos Indians welcome Spaniard Francisco Vásquez de Coronado and his men in 1540 with music and dancing rather than bows and arrows. Nearly 60 years later, Don Juan de Oñate visited the area and ordered a mission church built—a giant structure with six bell towers and buttresses 22 feet thick in some spots. The building was destroyed during the Pueblo Revolt, however, and the Pecos people dug a kiva smack in the middle of the ruined convent area—symbolic architecture, to say the least.

But the Spanish returned, and they were even welcomed and aided at Pecos. When they built a new church in the early 1700s, it was noticeably smaller, maybe as a form of compromise. But even as a hybrid Pueblo-Spanish culture developed, the Indian population was falling victim to disease and drought. When the Santa Fe Trail opened up in 1821, Pecos was all but empty, and in 1838, the last city dwellers marched to live with fellow Towa speakers at Jemez Pueblo, 80 miles west; their descendants still reside there today.

Pecos Canyon State Park

505/670-8196; www.emnrd.nm.gov; $5/car

A committed push by locals led to the establishment in 2019 of the Pecos Canyon State Park, which incorporates much of the area's best hiking, trout fishing, and camping and is set within the larger Pecos Wilderness. The park consists of three sections spread along the Pecos River and Highway 63, with the main one bordering the small community of Terrero, about 14 miles north of Pecos. The other two—the Willow Creek Recreation Area and Mora Recreation area—are farther north along Highway 63.

Stop in at the **Pecos ranger station** (Hwy. 63; 505/757-6121; 8am-4:30pm Mon.-Fri.) on the south end of Pecos town to get maps and information on trail conditions as well as the park's campgrounds; there are no ranger stations within the park itself. At this high elevation—much of the park is around 8,000 feet—summer temperatures are usually below 75°F and can dip below freezing at night, so pack accordingly.

Hamilton Mesa Trail

Distance: 7.6 mi round-trip
Time: 3 hours
Trailhead: Iron Gate Campground

About a mile after Mora campground on Highway 63 is the right turn for Forest Road 223, a rough road (ideally, for high-clearance cars only; proceed slowly) that leads 4.5 miles up to Iron Gate Campground and Hamilton Mesa Trail (no. 249), a fairly gentle 3.8-mile hike to a wide-open meadow on an elevated plateau—look for strawberries among the wildflowers.

Cave Creek Trail

Distance: 5 mi round-trip
Time: 2.5-3 hours
Trailhead: Panchuela Campground

At Cowles Ponds, a developed fishing area where a mining camp once stood, you can turn left off Highway 63 on Windsor Road to follow a paved one-lane road 1.5 miles to Panchuela campground, the start of Cave Creek Trail (no. 288). It's an easy walk that follows a small waterway up to some caves that have been carved out of the white limestone by the stream's flow. If you go past the caves, up a steep hillside, you reach an area burned in the 2013 Jaroso Fire, but hiking here is not recommended, due to the danger of falling trees.

Jack's Creek Trail

Distance: 13.5 mi round-trip
Time: 7 hours
Trailhead: 0.5 mi south of Jack's Creek
Campground at the Jack's Creek Horse Camp

Continuing straight past Cowles on Highway 63 brings you in about three more miles to the scenic Jack's Creek Campground and two minutes farther to the Jack's Creek Trail (no.

Farther Afield: Highway 3 to Villanueva

Villanueva State Park

From exit 323 off I-25, 14 miles southeast of Pecos, **Highway 3** is a beautiful drive south. The two-lane road meanders through a narrow valley with rich red earth cut into small farm plots, dotted by villages such as Ribera and El Pueblo dating to the late 18th century. Stop in **Villanueva,** the largest settlement along the road, at the area institution that is the family-run **Villanueva General Store** (1225 Hwy. 3; 575/421-2265; 8am-6:30pm Mon.-Sat., noon-5:30pm Sun.) for everything from Frito Pies to camping supplies, and then visit the small but beautiful **Villanueva State Park** (575/421-2957; www.emnrd.nm.gov; $5/car), which occupies a bend in the Pecos River against 400-foot-tall sandstone cliffs. It's rarely crowded—you'll probably have the 2.5-mile Canyon Trail to yourself. Spring comes early, filling trails with wildflowers by late April; fall is a burst of red scrub oak and yellow cottonwood leaves, in sharp contrast to the evergreens.

257), which ascends sharply at times to the Pecos Baldy Lake. All trails in this area require a $2 trailhead parking fee; additional fees apply for camping or picnicking, depending on the spot.

Food and Accommodations
Frankie's at the Casanova
12 Main St.; 505/757-3322; 8am-2pm daily,
5:30pm-8:15pm Fri.-Sat.; $9
At the main crossroads in Pecos, where Highway 50 meets Highway 63, Frankie's at the Casanova is the town social center, set in an old adobe dance hall. The food, mainly filling New Mexican fare and diner staples, isn't always a hit, but it's worth a stop just to see the murals over the bar.

Our Lady of Guadalupe Monastery
Hwy. 63; 505/757-6415; www.pecosmonastery.org;
$105 d
Our Lady of Guadalupe Monastery, about 1.5 miles north of the town center, maintains simple rooms with beautiful views; the rate is a suggested donation and includes continental breakfast and dinner.

Los Pinos Ranch
32 Panchuela Rd.; 505/757-6213;
www.lospinosranch.com; $150 pp
Several mountain lodges deeper in the forest, such as Los Pinos Ranch in the village of Cowles and about 6.5 miles north of Terrero off Highway 63, are typically open only in summer and offer multiday packages with

all meals included and a variety of outdoor activities, including horseback riding (from $90).

Terrero Campground

West of Hwy. 63, just south of Terrero; $10
Tucked into a canyon along the Pecos River, the Terrero campground has nine tranquil and well-maintained sites, all of which can be reserved in advance. Aim for one of the two more removed sites along the river.

Jack's Creek Campground

Forest Rd. 555 off Hwy. 63; 505/438-5300;
www.fs.usda.gov; $10
Set amid towering conifers 21 miles north of Pecos, Jack's Creek Campground has more than 35 spacious and exceedingly pretty campsites. The first-come, first-served sites can accommodate tents as well as RVs.

THE PUEBLOS

Between Santa Fe and Taos lie seven pueblos, each occupying its own patch of land with its own tribal governments. Unlike scenic Taos Pueblo, these are not notable for their ancient architecture and, with a few small exceptions, do not have any tourist attractions. Some pueblos are closed to visitors all or part of the year, but do make the trip on feast days or for other ceremonial dances if you can.

Tesuque and Pojoaque

Just north of Santa Fe, the highway overpasses are decorated with the original Tewa names of the pueblos. Tesuque (Te Tesugeh Owingeh, "village of the cottonwood trees") is marked by **Camel Rock,** a piece of sandstone on the west side of the highway that has eroded to resemble a creature that looks right at home in this rocky desert. The "mouth" of the camel broke off in early 2017, but that hasn't stopped the curious from making the quick stop along Highway 285.

Poeh Museum

78 Cities of Gold Rd.; 505/455-5041;
www.poehcenter.org; 10am-5pm Mon.-Fri.; free

A few miles farther north, the Pojoaque-managed Poeh Museum occupies a striking old-style adobe building just off the highway. It shows (and sells) local artwork, as well as a permanent installation relating the Pojoaque people's path (poeh) through history.

El Parasol

30 Cities of Gold Rd.; 505/455-7185;
6:30am-7:30pm Mon.-Fri., 7am-7pm Sat.,
7am-3pm Sun.; $5-9
Pojoaque's no fuss outpost of the popular local chain **El Parasol** has a long menu of recognizable and dependable New Mexican fare, including chicharrón (fried pork belly) burritos, arroz con pollo, and shredded beef tostados.

★ Rancho Jacona

277 County Rd. 84; 505/455-7948;
www.ranchojacona.com; $175 d
Just west of Pojoaque, a couple of minutes off the road to Los Alamos, Rancho Jacona is a working 35-acre farm dotted with a dozen casitas, each with a kitchen and space for 2-11 people. You'll likely get some fresh eggs for breakfast, and kids can frolic in the pool. There's a two-night minimum.

San Ildefonso

Best known for its black-on-black pottery (first by María Martinez and her husband, Julian, and now from a number of skilled potters), the pueblo of San Ildefonso is off Highway 502, on the way to Los Alamos. Of all the pueblos just north of Santa Fe, it's the most scenic, with even its newer houses done in faux-adobe style, and the main plaza shaded by giant old cottonwoods. You must first register at the **visitors center** (off Hwy. 502; 505/455-3549; 8am-5pm Mon.-Fri.; $10/car), then proceed on foot. There is a small **museum** (8am-4:30pm daily), which is really just an excuse to walk across the village. The only other attractions are pottery shops—which are interesting even if you're not in the market, as it's a chance to peek inside people's homes and chat a bit.

Ceremonial Dances

This is an approximate schedule for dances at pueblos in the Santa Fe area. Pueblo feast days are always on the same date and generally open to all, but seasonal dances (especially Easter and other spring rituals) can vary, and are sometimes closed to visitors. Confirm details and start times—usually afternoon, but sometimes following an evening or midnight Mass—with the **Indian Pueblo Cultural Center** (505/843-7270; www.indianpueblo.org) before setting out.

- **January 1:** Ohkay Owingeh (San Juan): cloud or basket dance; Picurís: various dances

- **January 6:** Picurís: various dances; Nambé: buffalo, deer, and antelope dances

- **January 22:** San Ildefonso: vespers and firelight procession at 6pm

- **January 23:** San Ildefonso: Feast of San Ildefonso, with buffalo and deer dances

- **January 25:** Picurís and Ohkay Owingeh (San Juan) : Feast of San Pablo

- **February 2:** Picurís: various dances for Candlemas (Día de la Candelaria)

- **February, first or second weekend:** Ohkay Owingeh (San Juan): deer dance

- **Easter:** Most pueblos: various dances

- **June 13:** Ohkay Owingeh (San Juan), Santa Clara, and Picurís: Feast of San Antonio

- **June 24:** Ohkay Owingeh (San Juan): Feast of San Juan Bautista

- **July 4:** Nambé: celebration at the waterfall

- **July 25:** San Ildefonso: Feast of Santiago

- **August 9-10:** Picurís: Feast of San Lorenzo

- **August 12:** Santa Clara: Feast of Santa Clara

- **September 8:** San Ildefonso: corn dance

- **October 4:** Nambé: Feast of San Francisco de Asís

- **November 12:** Tesuque: Feast of San Diego

- **December 12:** Pojoaque: Feast of Nuestra Señora de Guadalupe

- **December 24:** Picurís and Ohkay Owingeh (San Juan): torchlight procession at sundown, followed by Los Matachines; Tesuque and Nambé: various dances, beginning after midnight Mass; San Ildefonso: various dances

- **December 25:** San Ildefonso, Ohkay Owingeh (San Juan), Picurís, and Tesuque: various dances

- **December 26:** Ohkay Owingeh (San Juan): turtle dance

- **December 28:** Picurís: children's dances to celebrate Holy Innocents Day

Santa Clara
Puyé Cliff Dwellings

888/320-5008; www.puyecliffdwellings.com; 9am-5pm daily; $25-40

On the land of Santa Clara (Kha P'o, or Shining Water), on Highway 30 south of Española, are the beautiful Puyé Cliff Dwellings, which were occupied until the early 1600s. They're accessible only by guided tour, and a slightly expensive one at that: $25 for a one-hour walk either along the cliffside or the mesa top, or $40 for both. But tour leaders come from the pueblo and connect the ancient ruins with current culture in an intimate and fascinating way.

At the base of the cliffs is a stone building from the Fred Harvey Indian Detour days of the early 1900s, when carloads of intrepid visitors would trundle off the train and out to these exotic sights; it now houses a small museum. The Puyé Cliffs Welcome Center—better recognized as a gas station on Highway 30—marks the turn to the cliffs; you can buy your tickets here (preferred, so they know you're coming) or up the road at the site. **Tours** run on the hour 9am-5pm daily April-September; the rest of the year, tours run 9am-2pm.

Getting There

From downtown Santa Fe, northbound Guadalupe Street turns into U.S. 84/285, which runs north through Tesuque in 5 miles and Pojoaque in 15 miles. Though this stretch of casinos and tax-free cigarette shops isn't particularly scenic, don't be tempted to race through it—the area is a major speed trap.

To reach San Ildefonso, turn off U.S. 84/285 in Pojoaque at the exit for Highway 502 to Los Alamos; the turn for the pueblo is about 6 miles ahead on the right. From San Ildefonso, you can continue to Santa Clara by turning north on Highway 30; the cliff dwellings are 7 miles ahead on the left. The slightly more direct route to Santa Clara is via Española, following signs for Highway 30; the total drive from the edge of Santa Fe is about 23 miles.

LOS ALAMOS

Unlike so many other sights in New Mexico, which are rooted in centuries of history, Los Alamos, home of the atomic bomb, is a product of the modern age. You may spend only a few hours here, visiting the museum and admiring the view from this high plateau, but you'll still sense an atmosphere quite unlike anywhere else in New Mexico. If you can,

visit on a weekday, as more businesses are open; weekends are especially sleepy in this town that draws specialized commuters from around the state—and even beyond.

During World War II, the army requisitioned an elite, rugged boys' school on a remote New Mexico mesa in order to build a top-secret laboratory for development of the nuclear bomb. It was home for a time to J. Robert Oppenheimer, Richard Feynman, Niels Bohr, and other science luminaries. The Manhattan Project and its aftermath, the Cold War arms race, led to the establishment of **Los Alamos National Laboratory** (LANL). Only in 1957 did the former clandestine facility become an actual public community; it's now home to about 18,000 people (if you count the "suburb" of White Rock, just down the hill on Highway 4). The highway up the mountainside is wider than it used to be, but the winding ascent to the mesa of "Lost Almost"—as the first scientists dubbed their officially nonexistent camp—still carries an air of the clandestine. The town can be visually jarring—there is no adobe to be found and the streets have names such as Trinity Drive (named after the first test of a nuclear weapon)—a feeling only enhanced by the dramatic landscape surrounding it.

The townsite is spread over four long mesas that extend like fingers from the mountain behind. Highway 502, also known as the Main Hill Road, arrives on a middle mesa, depositing you on Central Avenue and the main downtown area. The northernmost mesa is mostly residential, while the southernmost mesa is occupied by LANL and Highway 501, which runs back down the mountain and connects with Highway 4.

Los Alamos Historical Museum

1050 Bathtub Row; 505/709-7794;
  www.losalamoshistory.org; 9am-5pm Mon.-Fri.,
10am-4pm Sat.; $5
Though the manufactured feel of Los Alamos would lead you to believe otherwise, the area's

Pueblo Economies in the Gaming Age

North of Santa Fe on U.S. 84/285, Cities of Gold Casino looms beside the road, a sight that would have dazzled any conquistador in search of El Dorado. While it's showing its age, it was the first of the pueblo casinos, and a much-debated project within the community of **Pojoaque** before it opened in the 1990s. Casinos were effectively permitted by the federal Indian Gaming Regulatory Act in 1988 and then legalized in New Mexico in 1994.

The main argument in Pojoaque for getting into the industry was a need for cash and jobs in communities that had virtually no industry. At the time, up to 72 percent of pueblo residents were jobless, and the average income in many communities was less than $10,000 per year—almost inconceivably below national standards. Now, Pojoaque boasts close to zero unemployment as well as attractive apartment housing and a beautifully appointed museum funded by casino profits (including the Buffalo Thunder Resort).

Many other nearby Rio Grande-area pueblos have followed with their own projects, including, most recently, **Tesuque,** whose eponymous casino opened in 2018 to much fanfare. Sleek and modern with a design that complements the nearby Santa Fe Opera, the casino is indicative of many pueblos' willingness to embrace the possibilities the gaming industry affords.

More remote pueblos have taken different strategies, however. Small and somewhat conservative Picurís voted against its own gambling palace; the elders did eventually agree to co-owning the **Hotel Santa Fe,** a venture initiated by a few Anglo entrepreneurs who aimed to capitalize on a unique relationship with a pueblo. Jemez Pueblo attempted to open a casino in southern New Mexico, far from its own land, but its application was denied at the federal level.

Puebloans and Anglos alike complain about the aesthetics of the gaudy, brightly lit casinos, and others worry about the apparent loss of tradition that goes along with courting lowest-common-denominator tourism. But for many pueblo people who, previously, had been considered to be not much more than a scenic backdrop in New Mexico—a mute patch of "local color"—there's no incongruity at all. As George Rivera, the governor of Pojoaque, has put it, "You don't have to be poor to have your culture."

history began long before the construction of LANL. See what the area was like pre-Manhattan Project at the fascinating Los Alamos Historical Museum, set in an old building of the Los Alamos Ranch School, the boys' camp that got the boot when the army moved in. The exhibits cover everything from relics of the early Tewa-speaking people up to juicy details on the social intrigue during the development of "the gadget," as the A-bomb was known. Volunteer docents lead two-hour **walking tours** (11am Mon., Fri., and Sat.; $15) from the museum late May-early October; if you miss this, pick up a brochure for a self-guided walk.

After the completion of ongoing renovation efforts, the nearby modest house Oppenheimer and his family lived in during their time at Los Alamos, also once part of the Los Alamos Ranch School, is expected to open to the public.

Fuller Lodge Art Center
2132 Central Ave.; 505/662-1635; 10am-4pm
Mon.-Sat.; free

In front of the museum is Fuller Lodge Art Center, originally the ranch school's dining room and kitchen. It usually has a community art exhibit downstairs, plus a room upstairs restored to the era when schoolteachers bunked here. The architect John Gaw Meem built the structure in 1928, handpicking more than 700 pine poles to form the walls, and designing the cowboy-silhouette light fixtures in the main hall.

The museum is just west of the main street, Central Avenue—you'll see Fuller Lodge on Central, with the museum set back behind it.

Bradbury Science Museum

*1350 Central Ave.; 505/667-4444; www.lanl.gov/
museum; 10am-5pm Tues.-Sat., 1pm-5pm Sun.-Mon.;
free*

Set up by Los Alamos National Laboratory, the Bradbury Science Museum on the miracles of atomic energy has the feel of an upper-grade science fair, with plenty of buttons to push and gadgets to play with. There's also an air of a convention sales booth—the museum's mission is definitely to promote LANL's work, though a public forum corner gives space to opposing views. Relics of the early nuclear age–Fat Man and Little Boy casings, gadgetry from the Nevada Test Site, and the like—remain the most fascinating items on display.

Recreation

The mountain behind Los Alamos is recovering from the 2011 Las Conchas Fire, but the canyons below Los Alamos were untouched, and are laced by numerous top-notch hiking and mountain biking trails, easily accessible from the town's main roads.

Los Alamos Nature Center

*2600 Canyon Rd.; 505/662-0460; www.peecnature.
org; 10am-4pm Mon. and Wed.-Sun.; free*

Pick up a map and get recommendations from the visitors center or the smartly designed Los Alamos Nature Center, which also is a good place to get to know the plants and animals in the area.

Canyon Rim Trail

Distance: *3 mi round-trip*
Time: *1.5 hours*
Trailhead: *Hwy. 502, just under 2 mi east of town
center*

The dramatic Canyon Rim Trail skirts the edge of Los Alamos Canyon for 1.5 miles; this paved path provides the best vantage point for appreciating the town's setting atop the finger-like mesas.

White Rock Canyon Rim Trail

Distance: *3.6 mi round-trip*
Time: *1.5-2 hours*

Trailhead: *Overlook Park*

There are further spectacular views in White Rock, 15 minutes to the southeast, where the White Rock Rim Trail runs three miles along the cliff edge—you'll have suburban tract homes to your back and a dizzying canyon out in front of you. Even if you don't much feel like a hike, stop by where the walk starts for a view of the Rio Grande; follow signs from Highway 4 at the first stoplight in town.

Red Dot Trail

Distance: *2 mi round-trip*
Time: *1.5 hours*
Trailhead: *Piedra Loop, about 3 mi south of
Overlook Park*

A few miles to the south is the trailhead for Red Dot Trail, a strenuous hike into and out of the gorge. The trail passes a few petroglyphs on its steep descent to the Rio Grande.

Pajarito Mountain

*397 Camp May Rd.; 505/662-5725; www.pajarito.ski;
9am-4pm Fri.-Sun. and holidays*

A bit of a locals' secret, Pajarito Mountain offers good skiing and snowboarding for relatively cheap (from $50 full-day lift ticket), with six lifts giving access to bunny slopes as well as double-black-diamond trails. The area is just a few miles west of Los Alamos, off Highway 501.

On summer weekends, take your mountain bike on the lift (9am-3pm Sat.-Sun.) and explore the **Pajarito Bike Park,** where you'll find several trails of varying difficulty that were built by volunteers.

Food

Los Alamos is not exactly bursting with restaurants, and many are open weekdays only. Plan ahead if you'll be staying overnight.

Morning Glory

*1377 Diamond Dr.; 505/662-4000; 6am-1pm Mon.-Sat.;
$5-12*

For breakfast and lunch, the family-run Morning Glory has tasty breakfast burritos, filling lunch specials, such as chicken-fried steak, and a tempting selection of homemade doughnuts and baked goods.

Blue Window Bistro

1789 Central Ave.; 505/662-6305; 11am-8pm Mon.-Fri.; $8-44

Blue Window Bistro is the fanciest restaurant in Los Alamos, which isn't exactly a tall order. It's a colorful, bustling place; it often feels as if the entire town is crammed inside. Options include huge salads and hot sandwiches for lunch, and creative pasta and steaks in the evening. If you're headed back down the hill for the night, it's not worth staying for dinner, but if you're here overnight, it's your best option.

Bathtub Row Brewing Co-Op

163 Central Park Square; 505/500-8381; 2pm-10pm Mon.-Wed., 2pm-11pm Thurs., noon-11pm Fri.-Sat., noon-10pm Sun.

Tucked away at the end of a small strip mall, Bathtub Row Brewing Co-Op pours pints of its own brews, such as excellent brown and blonde ales, and select offerings from other New Mexico breweries. It's especially lively when the laboratory's day ends.

Farmers Market

2300 Trinity Dr.; 7am-12:30pm Thurs. and 8am-noon Sat. May-Oct.

At the town's small but lively farmers market, you can find a good selection of local produce and homemade foods.

Accommodations

North Road Inn

2127 North Rd.; 505/412-0208; www.northroadinn.com; $98 d

The few hotels in Los Alamos cater primarily to visiting government officials and scientists, though it's a handy place to bunk if you want to get an early start at Bandelier and the Valles Caldera. The chain hotels are functional; the best of the few remaining options is the North Road Inn, a converted apartment complex in a quiet residential area that has large rooms (some are suites with kitchenettes). Those on the upper level are a bit more private. A full breakfast is included.

Information

Tourist Info Center

475 20th St.; 505/662-8105; www.visitlosalamos.org; 9am-5pm Mon.-Fri., 9am-4pm Sat., 10am-3pm Sun.

Stop at the tourist info center, adjacent to Ashley Pond, for maps and advice on hikes. There's another office in **White Rock** (115 Hwy. 4; 505/672-3183; 8am-6pm daily, 10am-2pm daily in winter), en route to Bandelier. The comprehensive events calendar at www.fyilosalamos.com is the best source of the latest happenings.

Getting There

Los Alamos is 36 miles (45 minutes by car) from downtown Santa Fe via U.S. 84/285 north to Highway 502 west. From Española, it's 20 miles (30 minutes) west on Highway 30 to Highway 502. There is an airport (LAM), but the city has no commercial service currently.

★ BANDELIER NATIONAL MONUMENT

15 Entrance Rd.; www.nps.gov/band; $25/car

One of New Mexico's most entrancing ancient sites, Bandelier National Monument comprises 23,000 acres of wilderness, including the remarkable Frijoles Canyon, lined on either side with "cavates"—rooms carved by Ancestral Puebloans that served as their homes—while the remnants of a massive settlement from the 16th century occupy the valley floor. Though signs of human settlement in the canyon date back over 10,000 years, it is these dwellings and the foundations of kivas that were central to Ancestral Puebloan society that the park is most known for today. Several of the cavates are just a short walk from the visitors center—it's possible to climb inside some of them—and there's a network of much longer trails that wend deeper into the canyon, the mesa, and the backcountry.

Bandelier gets so busy in summer that

mid-May–mid-October (9am-3pm) the park is accessible only by shuttle bus from the visitors center in White Rock. The best way to avoid crowds is to arrive early on a weekday, if possible. Another approach is to join a torch-lit, silent **night walk** ($6) into Frijoles Canyon; they're typically on Friday nights, but call the visitors center or check online for the schedule.

In the park, another **visitors center** (505/672-3861; 9am-4:30pm daily) has a museum and the usual array of maps and guides. If you're interested in wildflowers, pick up a Falls Trail guide, as it has good illustrations of what grows in the area. Rangers run free **guided walks** around the main loop a few times a day, or you can pick up the trail guide for $1.

Main Loop Trail and Alcove House Trail

Distance: *1.4 mi round-trip*
Time: *1.5 hours*
Trailhead: *visitors center*

A paved walkway leads out the back of the visitors center into Frijoles Canyon, passing the ruins of the major settlements—or at least the ones that have been thoroughly excavated. You first reach **Tyuonyi** (chew-ON-yee), a circle of buildings that was settled for about 200 years, beginning in the 1300s. Built of bricks cut from tuff (the volcanic rock that makes up most of the area) and adobe plaster, some of the 250 rooms at one time stood several stories tall.

The trail then goes up next to the cliffs, dotted with small caves dug out of the soft stone, and to **Long House,** the remnants of a strip of condo-style buildings tucked into the rock wall. Paintings and carvings decorate the cliff face above. If you're here near sunset, keep an eye on the **bat cave** near the end of the strip, home to thousands of the flying mammals.

Continue another 0.5 mile to the **Alcove House,** accessible by 140 feet of ladders. It's well worth the climb up, if you can handle heights.

Frey Trail

Distance: *1.5 mi one-way; return by shuttle*
Time: *45 minutes*
Trailhead: *Juniper Campground, just off Hwy. 4 northwest of the park access road*

The 1.5-mile Frey Trail used to be the main route to Frijoles Canyon, before the access road was built by the Civilian Conservation Corps in the 1930s. Descending from **Juniper Campground,** it's a nice approach to the area, offering great views over Tyuonyi and a general sense of what it must have been like to "discover" the canyon. The trail has no shade, however, so it's best hiked early in the day. The shuttle bus can drop you at the trailhead, so you can hike down, then ride back to the depot.

Tsankawi

Well before you reach the main entrance to Bandelier, you pass Tsankawi on the east side of Highway 4. (This area is accessible by car year-round.) Unique pottery excavated in this separate section, disconnected from the main park, suggests that it was inhabited by a different people from those who settled in Frijoles Canyon, and some sort of natural border seems to have formed here, despite a shared cliff-dwelling culture: Today the pueblos immediately north of the Bandelier area speak Tewa, while those to the south speak Keresan. A 1.5-mile loop, with ladders to climb along the way, leads past unexcavated ruins, cave houses, and even a few petroglyphs.

Camping

Juniper Campground ($12), just inside the park's northern border, is usually open year-round, with 52 sites. There are no hookups or showers. No reservations are taken, but it's usually not full. The scenery up on the plateau is a bit bleak, due to the 2011 fire, but you will get an early start on the day if you overnight here.

Getting There

Bandelier is 45 miles (one hour) from downtown Santa Fe via U.S. 84/285 north to

Highway 502 and Highway 4 west. From Jemez Springs, it's 41 miles (one hour) via Highway 4 east.

Mid-May–mid-October, access to the park is via free **shuttle bus** only. The service departs from the **White Rock visitors center** (Hwy. 4) every 20 or 30 minutes between 9am and 3pm; before or after that time, you can enter the park by car.

White Rock is a 40-minute drive from Santa Fe via U.S. 84/285 north to Highway 502 and Highway 4 west. From Jemez Springs, it's about an hour's drive via Highway 4 north and east (but you'll have to drive past the Bandelier entrance, and double back in the shuttle bus). The bus also stops at the Frey Trail trailhead en route to the main park.

★ VALLES CALDERA NATIONAL PRESERVE

Highway 4; 575/829-4100; www.nps.gov/vall; $25/car

Spreading out for 89,000 acres to the north of Highway 4, Valles Caldera National Preserve is a series of vast green valleys, rimmed by the edges of a volcano that collapsed into a massive bowl millennia ago. At the center is rounded Redondo Peak (11,254 feet). The surrounding meadows are home to herds of elk; the view down into the caldera from Highway 4 when the elk spread out in front of Redondo Peak can be breathtaking. The land has been carefully managed since it was converted from a ranch in 2000, and it is not heavily visited—it's easy to get out into the wilderness and feel utterly alone under the dome of the sky.

To get oriented, drive in two miles to the **Valle Grande Contact Station** (8am-8pm daily mid-May-Sept., 9am-5pm daily Oct.-mid-May), where you can get a hiking map and the latest trail conditions. A full roster of guided activities is available in winter and summer, including group day hikes, elk sightseeing, and full-moon snowshoeing in winter. There is no camping available in the preserve.

Hiking and Mountain Biking

Hikers have several trails from which to choose. From the contact station, an hour-long trail offers a quick introduction to the preserve. Follow the loop west around the bases of Redondo Peak and neighboring Redonito (10,898 feet) for a relatively flat hike that bisects a few of the preserve's many creeks; short spurs can be tacked on. Further in the preserve, the trails along the slopes of Cerros del Abrigo (10,332 feet) and Cerros Santa Rosa (9,701 feet) are more challenging and heavily forested.

Many of the preserve's hiking trails are also open to mountain bikers, but perhaps the most enjoyable ride can be had by simply following the main dirt road that winds through the preserve to the northwest for approximately 10 miles, crossing through rolling grasslands along the way. As cattle still graze on the land in summer, be prepared to negotiate slow-moving herds.

Winter Sports

More than 25 miles of trails are available for snowshoeing and cross-country skiing; you can also blaze your own trail into the snowy backcountry. The contact station hands out maps for winter activities and is also the staging point for guided outings, including skiing and snowshoeing under the moonlight.

Getting There

Valles Caldera is a scenic, and at times hair-raising, 30-minute drive west from Los Alamos along Highway 501 and Highway 4. From Valles Caldera, continuing west on Highway 4 will bring you to Jemez Springs in 30 minutes; driving east on Highway 4 will take you to Bandelier National Monument in about 20 miles.

If you're carrying on to Santa Fe, it's another hour's drive (about 40 mi). Continue on Highway 4 through the town of White Rock and join Highway 502. This leads to U.S. 285, which then goes south to the capital.

1: Valles Caldera National Preserve **2:** Los Alamos Historical Museum

ESPAÑOLA

Midway between Santa Fe and Taos, Española lacks the glamour or scenery of its neighbors. The town of 10,000 is unquestionably rough around the edges, but don't let that deter you from some of the best New Mexican food in the state. And although it doesn't have much in the way of its own sights (except for the ubiquitous lowriders), it is at a convenient crossroads.

Plaza de Española

Clustered around this public space are the town's museums.

Bond House Museum

706 Bond St.; 505/747-8535; 1pm-3:30pm Mon.-Wed., noon-4pm Thurs.-Fri.; free

The tiny Bond House Museum, built at the turn of the 20th century by a Canadian family that established the Española Mercantile, devotes half its space to artwork and the other small room to various historic artifacts. It's best to call ahead, as hours can vary.

Misión Museum

405 N. Paseo de Onate; 8am-5pm Mon.-Fri.; free

Down the hill, past the replica Alhambra fountain, is the Misión Museum, a replica of the town's original mission church, furnished with traditional craft work from around the valley. It is open sporadically—ask at the Bond House if no one is around.

Chimayó Trading Post

110 Sandia Dr.; 505/753-9414; 9am-4pm Wed.-Mon.

No, you haven't made a wrong turn—you're still in Española. The Chimayó Trading Post, on the west side of the main highway, relocated here in the 1930s, after several decades at its original location in Chimayó. Now it's a listed landmark, as one of the last remaining historic trading posts, and it has everything you'd expect: creaky wood floors, dim lighting, and a jumbled stock of treasures and bric-a-brac that includes Chimayó rugs; pottery from Santa Clara Pueblo; Nepalese silver jewelry; cut-tin candleholders, made locally; skeins of handmade wool yarn; postcards; Pendleton blankets; and even free coffee. After a few lean years when it seemed the inevitable was nigh, it's had a bit of a rebirth and adds Native American crafts regularly.

Santa Cruz de la Cañada Church

Off Highway 76; varied hours; free

Midway through Española, take a right turn at Highway 76 and continue on for just over a mile to reach the village of Santa Cruz, established in 1695. The sizable Santa Cruz de la Cañada Church that's here now (turn left at the traffic light after one mile) dates from 1733, and its altar screen is another colorful work attributed to the Laguna Santero, who also painted the reredos at San Miguel Mission in Santa Fe and the church at Laguna Pueblo. It is dated 1795 but was completely painted over—with the same images—in the mid-19th century, presenting a particular challenge to preservationists, who cleaned and restored the piece in 1995. Each panel presents a different combination of the original artist's work and the fresh paint applied half a century later.

Food

El Parasol

603 Santa Cruz Rd.; 505/753-8852; 7am-8pm Mon.-Wed. and Sun., 7am-9pm Thurs.-Sat.; $5-9

Tucked away underneath a stand of cottonwood trees, takeout stand El Parasol has a no-nonsense Spanglish menu ("pollo with guacamole taco") of cheap and delicious New Mexican classics. It's an ideal pit stop for those taking the high road to Taos; there are a few picnic tables if you want to linger in the shade.

JoAnn's Ranch O Casados

938 N. Riverside Dr.; 505/753-1334; 7am-9pm Mon.-Sat., 7am-4pm Sun.; $6-12

Diner-style JoAnn's Ranch O Casados does all-day breakfast, plus good and inexpensive enchiladas, fajitas, and more. The red chile is rich and mellow, and you can get half orders of many dishes.

Lovin Oven

107 N. Riverside Dr.; 505/753-3493; 6:30am-noon Mon.-Sat.; $10

It might not look like much from the outside, but the family-run Lovin Oven delivers where it counts, with a freshly baked assortment of gooey donuts, fruit-stuffed empanadas, and bizcochitos, among many other delectable baked goods to go. Arrive early for the best selection.

La Cocina

415 S. Santa Clara Bridge Rd.; 505/753-3016; 7am-8pm Mon.-Sat.; $10.50-17

Warm and friendly and nearly always jam-packed during lunch, La Cocina does all the New Mexican classics, including sopaipilla tacos and a combination plate with enchiladas, a tamale, and posole.

Blue Heron Brewing Company

100 Hwy. 503; 505/747-4506; 4pm-7pm Wed.-Sat.

Easily missed, Blue Heron Brewing Company's taproom has an ever rotating selection, but typically include Blue Heron's red ale, IPA, stout, and Scottish ale. It occasionally hosts live music and has frequent game nights.

Accommodations

Española is not an obvious choice for staying overnight, but it has a couple of hotels that are so nice, you might rethink your itinerary. They can be especially handy after a night at the Santa Fe Opera, when all the traffic toward Santa Fe is backed up, but the road north is wide open; you'll also get more bang for your buck staying here than in Santa Fe.

Inn at the Delta

243 Paseo de Oñate; 505/753-9466; www.innatthedelta.biz; $110 s, $140 d

The Inn at the Delta is a beautiful, rambling adobe complex built by a longtime Española family. Each of the positively palatial 10 rooms is decorated with locally made furniture and has a fireplace, a porch, and a jetted tub. Rates include breakfast.

Santa Claran Hotel Casino

460 N. Riverside Dr.; 877/505-4949; www.santaclaran.com; $120 d

A project of the local pueblo, the Santa Claran Hotel Casino also has spacious rooms, tastefully done in subdued grays and browns. Perks include fridges, laundry machines, and satellite TV.

Getting There

Española is about a 35-minute drive from central Santa Fe via U.S. 84/285 north. Leaving Española, take Highway 68 (also called Riverside Drive) north from here to Taos (45 miles), or cross over the Rio Grande and continue on U.S. 84 to Abiquiu (22 miles) or U.S. 285 to Ojo Caliente (25 miles). From an intersection in the middle of Española, Highway 76 leads east to Chimayó (8 miles), then to Truchas and the other high-road towns on the way to Taos. From the old main plaza on the west side of the Rio Grande, Highway 30 is the back road to Los Alamos (20 miles).

OJO CALIENTE

50 Los Banos Dr.; 505/583-2233; http://ojosparesorts.com; 10am-10pm daily; from $45

Twenty-six miles north of Española on U.S. 285, Ojo Caliente is effectively the center of a tiny settlement that built up around the hot springs here. Established in 1916, it's now a somewhat posh resort. The various paved pools ($45 Mon.-Thurs., $65 Fri.-Sun.) have different mineral contents, and there's a mud area with rich local clay, as well as private soaking tubs and a full spa (massage $150/50min). It's a pretty little place, set up against sandstone bluffs; try to go on a weekday, as it gets busy on weekends.

The handsome on-site **Artesian Restaurant** (7:30am-11am, 11:30am-2:30pm and 5pm-9:30pm daily; $15-45), with its creative use of local ingredients, is worth a visit alone. The **hotel** rooms at the resort ($169 d, no shower; $209 d, full bath) are no great value (although rates do include access to the springs); there are **cottages** ($199) and handsome suites ($319) to choose from as well. **Camping** ($40) is also an option; try to choose a shaded site near the river. **The Inn at Ojo** (11 Hwy. 414; 505/583-9131; www.ojocaliente.com; $209 d), just down the road, is a better value; breakfast is included.

Just behind the springs, the one-mile **Posi Trail** leads into public land; centuries-old pottery shards are visible along the route. The longer **Mica Mine** trail wends its way through a scenic landscape of cacti and arroyos, ultimately reaching its eponymous destination after two miles. The resort office has trail maps on these trails and others in the area.

Getting There

Ojo Caliente is 50 miles from downtown Santa Fe, about an hour's drive north on U.S. 84/285, then U.S. 285 east where it splits, north of Española. From Española, allow for 30 minutes' driving time. From Abiquiu, avoid backtracking by going through El Rito; take Highway 554 north to Highway 111 north, coming out on U.S. 285 a few miles north of Ojo Caliente. This route takes about 45 minutes.

From Ojo Caliente, you can continue 41 miles to Taos (about a one-hour drive). Follow U.S. 285 north for 10 miles, then turn right (east) on Highway 567. In nine miles, Highway 567 ends at a T-junction; turn left (north) on Taos County Road and continue about eight miles. You will meet U.S. 64 about one mile west of the Rio Grande Gorge; Taos is to the right (east).

ABIQUIU

Northwest of Española, along U.S. 84, the valley formed by the Rio Chama is one of the most striking landscapes in northern New Mexico. Lush greenery on riverbanks clashes with bright-red mud; roaming sheep and cattle graze by the roadside. The striated hills represent dramatic geological shifts, from purple stone formed in the dinosaur era 200 million years ago to red clay formed by forests, then gypsum from sand dunes, then a layer of lava only eight million years old. Far more recently, Abiquiu became inextricably linked

with the artist Georgia O'Keeffe, who made the place her home for more than 40 years, entranced by the glowing light and dramatic skyline.

Up the hill opposite Bode's is the actual village of Abiquiu, established in 1754 by genízaros (Hispanicized Indians) through a land grant from the Spanish Crown. Georgia O'Keeffe's house forms one side of the old plaza; on the other is the Santo Tomás de Abiquiu Church, built in the 1930s after the community opted for the legal status of village rather than pueblo. Past O'Keeffe's house is the village morada, dramatically set on a hilltop. You're not really welcome to poke around, however—the village maintains a privacy policy similar to those of the pueblos. So, it's best to visit on a guided tour of the house, or come on the village's feast day, for Santa Rosa de Lima, on the weekend closest to August 25.

Bode's

21196 U.S. 84; 505/685-4422; 6:30am-7pm daily; $4.25-10

Although Abiquiu often refers to the whole river valley, the unofficial town center is Bode's, pronounced BO-deez. This long-established general store also has gas, breakfast burritos, pastries, green-chile cheeseburgers, fishing licenses and tackle, camping gear, and local crafts. In winter, it closes earlier on weekends.

Poshuouinge Ruin Trail

About two miles south of Abiquiu proper

On the west side of the road, the 0.5-mile Poshuouinge Ruin Trail leads to an ancestral Tewa site, literally the "village above the muddy river," inhabited only AD 1420-1500—why it was abandoned is unclear. The village contained about 137 rooms, as well as surrounding field grids, though there's not much to see today (thorough excavations took place in 1919, and it has been left to melt away since then). Nonetheless, it's a good place to get out and stretch your legs and take in the view from the hilltop.

Georgia O'Keeffe Home

Welcome center: 21120 U.S. 84; 575/467-2001;
www.okeeffemuseum.org; from $60

The artist's main residence, where she lived 1949-1984, fronts the small plaza in the village center of Abiquiu. The Georgia O'Keeffe Home is open for hour-long guided tours mid-March-November. The price, even for the basic tour, can seem a bit steep, but for fans of modernism of any kind, it's a beautiful place to see. The rambling adobe, parts of which were built in the 18th century, is a great reflection of O'Keeffe's aesthetic, which fused the starkness of modernism with an organic sensuality. If you're on a budget, console yourself with the fact that in many ways the surrounding landscape evokes O'Keeffe's work at least as much as her home does—and stop at Ghost Ranch, for more (and cheaper) info on the painter.

The schedule varies by month, but there are five **tours** (75 min; $60) daily on Tuesday, Thursday, and Friday. June-October, tours are also on Wednesday and Saturday. A "behind-the-scenes" tour (1hr 45min; $85) includes a visit to O'Keeffe's fallout shelter, among other things. Tours depart from the **Georgia O'Keeffe Welcome Center** (575/467-2001; 8am-4pm Tues.-Sat.); you must make reservations in advance.

Dar al Islam and Plaza Blanca

342 County Rd. 0155; 505/685-4515 ext. 21;
https://daralislam.org; 10am-4pm Mon.-Fri.; free

In another chapter of New Mexico's long utopian history, a few American converts established Dar al Islam, an intentional religious community, in 1980. It was meant to be a place in which Muslims—some 30 families to start with—could practice their religion in every aspect of life, from education to food. The group set up a ranch and built the Abiquiu Inn and a few other local businesses, but the village concept eventually foundered. More recently, Dar al Islam has been reinvented as a retreat center that's open to visitors.

Anyone interested in architecture will want to see the adobe mosque by Egyptian architect Hassan Fathy, all organic, sinuous lines; the view from the hilltop across the Chama River valley is a beautiful one, too. The head of the center requests that visitors dress modestly (arms, legs, and cleavage covered) and be quiet, so as not to disturb classes or workshops in session. Stop at the office first (back a bit and to the right of the parking area) to introduce yourself.

The community's land, some 8,500 acres, also includes the towering gypsum formations of **Plaza Blanca** (White Place). The eerie space, bleached as bones, was recorded in a series of Georgia O'Keeffe paintings, and it has also been used for numerous movie shoots. Two main trails lead down from the parking area.

Coming from the south, the community is accessible via Highway 554, which runs east from U.S. 84, just south of Abiquiu (follow signs for El Rito). Immediately after crossing the Chama River, turn left on County Road 0155. Continue 3.2 miles and turn right through a wooden gate made of telephone poles. Coming from the north on U.S. 84, look for County Road 0155, which is unpaved here, just north of Bode's; the wooden gate will be on the left, 2.3 miles on, shortly after the paving starts. Once through the gate, the road forks after less than a mile: To the left is the entrance to Dar al Islam; to the right, Plaza Blanca.

Abiquiu Lake and the Pedernal

An Army Corps of Engineers dam project in the late 1950s-early 1960s created the 4,000-acre Abiquiu Lake, with fingers running into the canyons all around. The view coming in is marred by the power station, but past that the water glimmers at the base of the flat-topped mountain Pedernal ("Flint") Peak, the distinctive silhouette that found its way into so many of O'Keeffe's paintings. ("It's my private mountain," she often said. "God told me if I painted it often enough, I could have it.") The calm waters make this an ideal spot for kayaking, canoeing, and stand-up

paddleboarding, though there are currently no rentals available.

Riana Campground

505/685-4561; www.recreation.gov

The overly paved Riana Campground at the lake is open year-round, but water and electric hookups ($16) are available only from mid-April to mid-October. There's also a small beach suitable for swimming.

TOP EXPERIENCE

★ Ghost Ranch

U.S. 84; 505/685-1000;

www.ghostranch.org; welcome center 9am-4pm daily

Ghost Ranch, a 21,000-acre retreat owned by the Presbyterian Church, is best known because Georgia O'Keeffe owned a small parcel of the land and maintained a studio here. In the science world, it's also known as the place where, in 1947, paleontologists combing the red hills discovered about a thousand skeletons of the dinosaur *Coelophysis* ("hollow form," for its hollow, birdlike bones), the largest group discovered in the world.

The grounds are open to day visitors ($10 day pass) for **hiking.** The best trek, which takes about two hours round-trip, is to **Chimney Rock,** a towering landmark with panoramic views of the entire area. Don't be daunted—the steepest part of the three-mile roundtrip trail is at the start—but do slather on the sunscreen, as there's no shade on this route. **Box Canyon** is an easier, shadier, all-level walk that's about four miles roundtrip. **Kitchen Mesa Trail,** which starts at the same point, is longer (about 4.5 miles roundtrip) and much more difficult, requiring some scrambling to get up the cliffs at the end (though you could hike the easy first two-thirds, then turn around).

Visitors can also see the **Florence Hawley Ellis Museum of Anthropology** and the **Ruth Hall Museum of Paleontology** (both 9am-5pm Mon.-Sat., 1pm-5pm Sun.;

$10), which display the local finds, including remnants of the prehistoric Gallina culture from the ridge above the valley and an eight-ton chunk of *Coelophysis*-filled siltstone in the process of being excavated.

Guided **tours** (various times; $42-80) of the ranch grounds run mid-March-November, on various topics, from local archaeology to movie settings. One walking tour visits O'Keeffe's painting spot in the red Chinle hills behind the ranch. **Horseback rides** (from $95) are another option, visiting various spots key to O'Keeffe's painting life.

Christ in the Desert Monastery

Forest Rd. 151; 575/613-4233; www.christdesert.org; 9am-4pm Mon.-Sat.

Thirteen miles up a winding dirt road, the Benedictine Christ in the Desert Monastery is said to be the remotest monastery in the Western Hemisphere. The drive follows the Chama River through a lush valley, ending at a striking modern church designed in 1972 by the woodworker and architect George Nakashima to blend in with the dramatic cliffs behind. Most of the outbuildings are straw-bale construction, running on solar power, and the monks grow much of their food and brew their own Belgian-style beer, Monks Ale (look for it at Bode's in Abiquiu). A gift shop next to the modern church sells various monastery products. The annual hop harvest, in late August, is a convivial event that draws volunteers from all over. Look for Forest Road 151 off the west side of U.S. 84, north of Ghost Ranch.

For a hike with a view across the valley and the red rocks, **Rim Vista trail** (no. 15) is a good route, climbing up to a mesa in about 2.3 miles one-way. The trailhead is less than 1 mile in on Forest Road 151, off the north side of the road; turn right, then bear right at the fork and park after 0.25 mile. The trail is best in spring and fall, as there is not much shade here.

Echo Amphitheater

U.S. 84; $2/car

The bandshell-shaped rock formation Echo Amphitheater is a natural wonder of acoustics and a great place to let kids run around and yell to their hearts' content. A short, paved trail from the parking area leads up to the Echo Canyon overlook; there are also several pleasant picnic areas tucked in the brush. It's just over three miles north of Ghost Ranch on U.S. 84, a couple hundred feet from the road.

Food and Accommodations

Ghost Ranch

U.S. 84; 505/685-4333; www.ghostranch.org; 2-night minimum; $165

You can stay at Ghost Ranch when it's not full for retreats, in various room options; the older ones are closer to the dining hall, while some of the newer options set on a hill have expansive views. You can also camp (May-Oct.; sites from $25) in a canyon. Rates for rooms (but not campsites) include breakfast, and day visitors can take simple meals (noon-1pm and 5pm-6pm) at the dining hall ($10-14).

Abiquiu Inn

21120 U.S. 84; 505/685-4378; www.abiquiuinn.com; from $199 d

The Abiquiu Inn functions as the area's visitors center. Lodging consists of some pretty casitas ($289) at the back of the property near the river, and a cluster of motel rooms closer to the front (request one facing away from the road). The inn's restaurant, **Café Abiquiu** (7am-9pm daily; $14) serves a nice mix of traditional New Mexican and more creative food, such as a pistachio-crusted salmon, and breakfasts are especially good. When the temperature is warm, the adjacent outdoor seating area, La Terraza, is a wonderful spot for a meal.

Christ in the Desert Monastery

Forest Rd. 151; 801/545-8567; www.christdesert.org; two-night minimum; $90 suggested donation

Christ in the Desert Monastery offers wonderful accommodations in its guesthouse, which includes all meals. Guests can participate in daily life at the monastery, assisting the monks with various tasks.

Rio Chama Campground

At the 11.5-mile mark on Forest Road 151; no fee

The Rio Chama Campground abuts the river and has several shaded sites. If you really want to get away from it all, it's a more serene option than camping at Abiquiu Lake.

Getting There

Abiquiu is about 50 miles (one hour) from downtown Santa Fe; take U.S. 84/285 north for 26 miles to Española. From Española, continue on U.S. 84 north for 23 miles to Abiquiu. From Taos, it's about 70 miles, or 1.5 hours, via El Rito or Ojo Caliente.

LOW ROAD TO TAOS

Following the winding Rio Grande up into the mountains is the highlight of this drive north, mostly along Highway 68. The route begins just beyond Española, passing into a narrowing canyon and finally emerging at the point where the high plains meet the mountains. This dramatic arrival makes it the better route for heading north to Taos; you can then loop back south via the high road.

Embudo

Embudo is really just a cluster of houses at a bend in the river where the Chili Line railroad from Denver, Colorado, used to stop (the old station is across the river).

Classical Gas Museum

1819 Hwy. 68; 505/852-2995; generally 9am-5pm Sat.-Sun.; free

An unexpected treat is the roadside Classical Gas Museum, a front yard filled with old service station accoutrements. If the gate is open, the owner is probably home, and you can peek inside and take a stroll around the grounds

---

1: Christ in the Desert Monastery **2:** Classical Gas Museum **3:** Santuario de Chimayó

to see a beautiful collection of neon signs and restored gas pumps.

Vivác Winery

2075 Hwy. 68; 505/579-4441; 10am-7pm Mon.-Fri., 10am-8pm Sat., noon-7pm Sun. May-Sept., 10am-6pm Mon.-Sat., noon-6pm Sun. Oct.-Apr.; standard tasting $12

If you're into wine, keep an eye out for the various wineries just north of Embudo, starting with Vivác, on the main highway. The acclaimed winery has been producing award-winning wines for over two decades.

Dixon

The pleasant little town of Dixon, known for its dense concentration of artists, organic farmers, and vintners, is home to one of the state's best wineries and a small farmers market.

La Chiripada

Hwy. 75 at CR 1119 #8; 505/579-4437; 11am-4pm daily

At the family-run La Chiripada, on Highway 75 in the center of Dixon, you can sample small-batch wines that have been produced in much the same way for over 40 years.

Dixon Farmers Market

215 Hwy. 75; 3:30pm-6:30pm Wed. early June-early Sept.

The convivial farmers market usually runs in front of the co-op, though be sure to call in advance for the current location. It's not a large operation, but you can count on some of the freshest fruits and vegetables around.

Dixon Studio Tour

First full weekend in Nov.; www.dixonarts.org

If you're in town the first weekend in November, check out the long-running Dixon Studio Tour, which showcases over 25 area galleries and a range of mediums, including woodwork, pottery, jewelry, and glass.

★ Zuly's

234 Hwy. 275; 505/579-4001; 10am-6pm Wed.-Sat.; $8

A good year-round reason to make the turn to Dixon is Zuly's, serving strong coffee and classic New Mexican food with a bit of a hippie flair; hours cut back slightly in winter.

Pilar

Orilla Verde Recreation Area

Hwy. 570; 575/758-8851; www.blm.gov; $3/car

Beginning just south of the village of Pilar, 45 miles north of Santa Fe, and stretching several miles north, Orilla Verde Recreation Area is public land along either side of the Rio Grande, used primarily as a put-in or haul-out for rafting, but you can camp on the riverbanks as well. There are seven campgrounds in Orilla Verde; Petaca and Taos Junction have the best sites ($9/night), while Pilar and Río Bravo have electric hookups.

Running about 1.2 miles one-way along the west edge of the river, the **Vista Verde Trail** is an easy walk with great views and a few petroglyphs to spot in a small arroyo about one-third of the way out. The trailhead is located on the other side of the river, 0.5 mile up the hill from the Taos Junction Bridge off the dirt road Highway 567 (turn left off Hwy. 570 in Pilar, then follow signs into Orilla Verde). Stop first on the main highway at the **Rio Grande Gorge Visitors Center** (Hwy. 68; 575/751-4899; 8:30am-4:30pm daily June-Aug., 10am-3pm daily Sept.-May) for maps and other information.

Pilar Yacht Club

Hwy. 68; 575/758-9072; 8am-6pm daily mid-May-Aug., 9am-2pm daily Apr.-mid-May and Sept.-Oct.

Across the road, Pilar Yacht Club is the hub of local activity, selling tubes for lazy floats, serving New Mexican staples and diner food to hungry river rats, and functioning as an office for a couple of outfitters.

Getting There

The low road is more direct than the high road to Taos, and has fewer potential diversions. Driving the 70 miles from downtown Santa Fe to Taos (on U.S. 84/285 and Hwy. 68), with no stops, takes about 1.5 hours. The only spot for gas along this stretch is at **Michael's Mini Mart** (1410 Hwy. 68; 505/852-4769) in Velarde.

HIGH ROAD TO TAOS

Chimayó, Córdova, Truchas, Las Trampas, Peñasco—these are the tiny villages strung, like beads on a necklace, along the winding highway through the mountains to Taos. This is probably the area of New Mexico where Spanish heritage has been the least diluted— or at any rate relatively untouched by Anglo influence, for there has been a long history of exchange between the Spanish towns and the adjacent pueblos. The local dialect is distinctive, and residents can claim ancestors who settled the towns in the 18th century. The first families learned to survive in the harsh climate with a 90-day growing season, and much of the technology that worked then continues to work now; electricity was still scarce even in the 1970s, and adobe construction is common.

To casual visitors, these communities, closed off by geography, can seem a little insular, but pop in at the shops and galleries that have sprung up in a couple of the towns, and you'll get a warm welcome. During the **High Road Art Tour** (www.highroadnewmexico.com), over two weekends in late September, modern artists and more traditional craftspeople, famed particularly for their woodcarving skills and blanket weaving, open their home studios.

The route starts on Highway 503, heading east off U.S. 84/285 just north of Pojoaque.

Chimayó

From Nambé Pueblo, Highway 503 continues to a T-junction; make a hard left onto Highway 98 to descend into the valley of Chimayó, site of the largest mass pilgrimage in the United States. During Holy Week, the week before Easter, some 50,000 people arrive on foot, often bearing large crosses. At their journey's end is a small church, seemingly existing in a time long since passed, that holds an undeniable pull.

★ Santuario de Chimayó

Hwy. 98; 505/351-4360; www.holychimayo.us; 9am-6pm daily May-Sept., 9am-5pm daily Oct.-Apr.

The pilgrimage tradition began in 1945, as a commemoration of the Bataan Death March, but the Santuario de Chimayó had a reputation as a miraculous spot from its start, in 1814. It began as a small chapel, built at the place where a local farmer, Bernardo Abeyta, is said to have dug up a glowing crucifix; the carved wood figure was placed on the altar. The building later fell into disrepair, but in 1929, the architect John Gaw Meem bought it, restored it, and added its sturdy metal roof; Meem then granted it back to the archdiocese in Santa Fe.

Unlike many of the older churches farther north, which are now seldom open, Chimayó is an active place of prayer, always busy with tourists as well as visitors seeking solace, with many side chapels and a busy gift shop. (Mass is said weekdays at 11am, Sun. at 10:30am and noon year-round.) The approach from the parking area passes chain-link fencing into which visitors have woven twigs to form crosses, each set of sticks representing a prayer. Outdoor pews made of split tree trunks accommodate overflow crowds, and a wheelchair ramp gives easy access to the church.

But the original adobe santuario seems untouched by modernity. The front wall of the dim main chapel is filled with an elaborately painted altar screen from the first half of the 19th century, the work of Molleno (nicknamed "the Chile Painter" because forms, especially robes, in his paintings often resemble red and green chiles). The vibrant colors seem to shimmer in the gloom, forming a sort of stage set for Abeyta's crucifix, Nuestro Señor de las Esquípulas, as the centerpiece. Painted on the screen above the crucifix is the symbol of the Franciscans: a cross over which the arms of Christ and Saint Francis meet.

Most pilgrims make their way directly to the small, low-ceilinged antechamber that holds el pocito, the little hole where the glowing crucifix was allegedly first dug up. From

Walk On, Santo Niño

Santo Niño Chapel

In northern New Mexico, the figure of **Santo Niño de Atocha** is a popular one. This image of Jesus comes from a Spanish legend, when the Christians were battling the Moors in the medieval period. Around 1300, the Muslims took a number of prisoners after a brutal battle in Atocha, near Madrid, and would not allow the captives' families to visit them. After many desperate prayers on the part of Atocha's Christian women, a mysterious child appeared, carrying food and water, to care for the prisoners. The populace guessed that it must be the child Jesus—thus Santo Niño de Atocha became the patron saint of prisoners, and he is depicted carrying a pail for bread and a gourd for water and wearing a large hat emblazoned with a scallop shell, the symbol of pilgrims.

In **Chimayó** alone, Santo Niño de Atocha is installed in the main church and in a separate 1857 chapel just a block away. He is seen now as a broader intercessor not just for those imprisoned, but also for the chronically ill. New Mexicans have developed a unique folk practice, placing baby shoes at the Santo Niño's feet, on the assumption that his own have worn out while he was walking in the night.

this pit they scoop up a small portion of the exposed red earth, to apply to withered limbs and arthritic joints, or to eat in hopes of curing internal ailments. (The parish refreshes the well each year with new dirt, after it has been blessed by the priests.) The adjacent sacristy displays handwritten testimonials, prayers, and abandoned crutches; the figurine of Santo Niño de Atocha is also said to have been dug out of the holy ground here as well. (Santo Niño de Atocha has a dedicated chapel just down the road—the artwork here is modern, bordering on cutesy, but the back room, filled with baby shoes, is poignant.)

Chimayó Museum

Plaza del Cerro; 505/351-0945; 10am-4pm Wed.-Sat. May-Aug.; free

The only other official sight in the village is the tiny Chimayó Museum, set on the old fortified plaza. It functions as a local archive and displays a neat collection of vintage photographs. Look for it behind Ortega's Weaving Shop.

El Potrero Trading Post

17A Santuario Dr.; 505/351-4112;
http://potrerotradingpost.com; 9am-5pm daily

Just to the left of the church, El Potrero Trading Post has been operating in some form for a century and, aside from its collection of santuario souvenirs and local art, is best known for its fresh green and red chile powders and piñon.

★ Rancho de Chimayó

County Rd. 98; 505/351-4444;
www.ranchodechimayo.com; 11:30am-7:30pm Tues.-Fri.,
8:30am-10:30am and 11:30am-7:30pm Sat.-Sun.; $8-21

The family-owned Rancho de Chimayó has earned a James Beard America's Classics award for its great local food, such as sopaipilla relleno (fried bread stuffed with meat, beans, and rice), shrimp pesto green-chile enchiladas, and green-chile stew. Enjoy your meal on a beautiful terrace—or inside the old adobe home by the fireplace in wintertime. The place is also open for breakfast on weekends, and it rents seven rooms (from $79 s, $89 d) in an old farmhouse across the road.

Rancho Manzana

26 Camino de Mision; 505/351-2223;
www.ranchomanzana.com; from $67

Beyond the Rancho de Chimayó's hacienda, the surrounding area holds a few good options for staying overnight. Not far from the church, off County Road 98, Rancho Manzana has a rustic-chic feel, with excellent breakfasts, cozy casitas and much larger lofts. There's a two-night minimum.

Casa Escondida

64 County Rd. 100; 505/351-4805;
www.casaescondida.com; from $169

A couple of miles north of the church, Casa Escondida is a polished country hideaway with nine colorful Southwest-style rooms and a big backyard with lots of birdlife.

Córdova
Sabinita López Ortiz Studio

9 County Rd. 1317; 505/351-4572; variable hours

From Chimayó, turn right (east) on Highway 76 to begin the climb up the Sangre de Cristo Mountains. Near the crest of the hill, about three miles along, a small sign points to Córdova, a village best known for its austere unpainted santos and bultos done by masters such as George López and José Dolores López. Another family member, Sabinita López Ortiz, sells her work and that of five other generations of wood-carvers.

Truchas

Highway 76 winds along to the little village of Truchas (Trout), founded in 1754 and still not much more than a long row of buildings set against the ridgeline. On the corner where the highway makes a hard left north is the village morada, the meeting place of the local Penitente brotherhood.

Nuestra Señora del Rosario de las Truchas Church

37 County Rd. 75; 505/351-4360

Head straight down the smaller road to reach Nuestra Señora del Rosario de las Truchas Church, tucked into a small plaza off to the right of the main street. It's open to visitors only during June-August—if you do have a chance to look inside the dim, thick-walled mission that dates back to the early 19th century, you'll see precious examples of local wood carving. Though many of the more delicate ones have been moved to a museum for preservation, those remaining display an essential New Mexican style—the sort of "primitive" thing that Bishop Lamy of Santa Fe hated. They're preserved today because Truchas residents hid them at home during the late 19th century. Santa Lucia, with her eyeballs in her hand, graces the altar, and a finely wrought crucifix hangs to the right, clad in a skirt because the legs have broken off.

Cordova's Handweaving

32 County Rd. 75; 505/689-1124; variable hours
Mon.-Sat.

Just up the road is Cordova's Handweaving, an unassuming wooden house that echoes with the soft click-clack of a broadloom; this Hispano family turns out subtly striped rugs in flawless traditional style, as it has done for generations. Prices are quite reasonable.

Cardona-Hine Gallery
82 County Rd. 75; 505/689-2253; by appointment only
Truchas has a surprisingly strong—albeit small—gallery scene. A standout is the Cardona-Hine Gallery, which showcases the paintings of the late Alvaro Cardona-Hine and Barbara McCauley.

Las Trampas
San José de Gracia Church
10am-4pm Sat.-Sun. June-Aug.
Farther north on Highway 76, the village of Las Trampas was settled in 1751, and its showpiece, San José de Gracia Church, was built nine years later. It remains one of the finest examples of New Mexican village church architecture. Its thick adobe walls are balanced by vertical bell towers; inside, the clerestory at the front of the church—a typical design—lets light in to shine down on the altar, which was carved and painted in the late 1700s. Other paradigmatic elements include the atrio, or small plaza, between the low adobe boundary wall and the church itself, utilized as a cemetery, and the dark narthex where you enter, confined by the choir loft above, but serving only to emphasize the sense of light and space created in the rest of the church by the clerestory and the small windows near the viga ceiling.

As you leave the town heading north, look to the right—you'll see a centuries-old acequia that has been channeled through a log flume to cross a small arroyo.

Picurís Pueblo
Visitors Center: 575/587-2519; 9am-5pm Mon.-Sat.; suggested donation
One of the smallest pueblos in New Mexico, Picurís is also one of the few Rio Grande pueblos that has not built a casino. Instead, it capitalizes on its beautiful natural setting, a lush valley where bison roam and aspen

leaves rustle. You can picnic here and fish in small but well-stocked Tu-Tah Lake. The **San Lorenzo de Picurís Church** looks old, but it was in fact rebuilt by hand in 1989, following the original 1776 design, a process that took eight years; it underwent a restoration that lasted several years. As at Nambé, local traditions have melded with those of the surrounding villages, and the Hispano-Indian Matachines dances are well attended on Christmas Eve. Start at the **visitors center** to pick up maps and pay a suggested donation. The pueblo is a short detour from the high road proper: At the junction with Highway 75, turn west, then follow signs off the main road for about 0.75 miles.

Peñasco
★ Sugar Nymphs Bistro
15046 Hwy. 75; 575/587-0311; 11am-3pm Wed.-Thurs., 11am-7pm Fri.-Sat., 10am-3pm Sun.; $12
Peñasco is best known to tourists as the home of Sugar Nymphs Bistro, a place with "country atmosphere and city cuisine," where you can get treats such as grilled vegetable tacos, green-chile cheeseburgers, grilled trout, and staggering wedges of triple-layered chocolate cake. In winter, hours are more limited, so call ahead.

Peñasco Theatre
15046 Hwy. 75; 575/587-2726;
www.penascotheatre.org
The adjoining Peñasco Theatre hosts quirky music and theatrical performances as well as a number of youth workshops and classes June-September.

Pecos Wilderness Area
Forest Road 116
This is also the northern gateway to the Pecos Wilderness Area. Follow Highway 73 south out of Peñasco, and then after 3.7 miles turn left on Santa Barbara R Road, which turns into Forest Road 116, eventually ending

1: Truchas **2:** San José de Gracia Church in Las Trampas **3:** El Potrero Trading Post **4:** High Road to Taos

after a further 5.9 miles at Santa Barbara Campground (sites $20), along the Rio Santa Barbara. The north end of the campground is the departure point for the West Fork Santa Barbara Trail to Truchas Peak, a scenic and occasionally arduous 25-mile round-trip hike that passes by No Fish Lake at over 11,500 feet in elevation. Contact the **Española ranger district office** (1710 N. Riverside Dr.; 505/753-7331; 8am-4:30pm Mon.-Fri.) or the one in the town of Pecos (Hwy. 63; 505/757-6121; 8am-4:30pm Mon.-Fri.) for trail conditions before you hike.

Sipapu

Hwy. 518; 800/587-2240; www.sipapu.ski; from $35
Detouring right (east) along Highway 518, you reach Sipapu, an unassuming, inexpensive ski resort—really, just a handful of campsites ($35), suites (from $195), and casitas (from $135), plus an adobe house (from $259), at the base of a 9,255-foot mountain. Cheap lift tickets (from $29 full-day lift ticket) and utter quiet make this a bargain getaway.

Pot Creek Cultural Site

575/587-2255; 9am-4pm Wed.-Sun. late June-early Sept.
Returning to the junction, continue on to Taos

via Highway 518, which soon descends into a valley and passes Pot Creek Cultural Site, a worthwhile diversion for its one-mile loop trail through Ancestral Puebloan ruins from around AD 1200. At its height, it's believed the site was once home to up to 1,000 Ancestral Puebloans.

You arrive in Taos at its southern end—really, in Ranchos de Taos, just north of the San Francisco de Asis Church on Highway 68. Turn left to see the church, or turn right to head up to the town plaza and to Taos Pueblo.

Getting There

From downtown Santa Fe, the high road to Taos is about 90 miles. Follow U.S. 84/285 north for 17 miles to Pojoaque. Turn right (east) on Highway 503, following signs for Nambé Pueblo; turn left where signed, onto County Road 98, to Chimayó, then left again on Highway 76. In about 30 miles, make a hard left onto Highway 518, and in 16 miles, you'll arrive in Ranchos de Taos, just north of the church and about 3 miles south of the main Taos plaza. The drive straight through takes a little more than two hours; leave time to dawdle at churches and galleries, take a hike, or have lunch along the way.

Taos

Adobe buildings cluster around a plaza. Snow-capped mountains beckon. Art galleries, organic bakeries, and yoga studios proliferate. But the town of Taos is anything but a miniature Santa Fe.

It's more isolated, reached by two-lane roads along either the winding mountain-ridge route or the fertile Rio Grande Valley, and it has a less polished, more tied-to-the-earth feel. The glory of the landscape, from looming Taos Mountain to the blue mesas dissolving into the flat western horizon, can be breathtaking. The mysticism surrounding Taos Pueblo is intense, as is the often-wild creativity of the artists who have lived here. No wonder people flock here on pilgrimages: to the hip-deep powder at Taos Ski Valley, to the San Francisco de Asis Church that

Highlights

Look for ★ to find recommended sights, activities, dining, and lodging.

★ **Taos Art Museum at Fechin House:** In the early 1930s, Russian artist Nicolai Fechin designed his home in a fusion of Tartar, Spanish, and American Indian styles. His and other artists' paintings hang inside (page 135).

★ **Mabel Dodge Luhan House:** This idiosyncratic home once hummed with artists drawn to Taos by a freethinking woman from New York City, birthing a thriving counterculture (page 135).

★ **San Francisco de Asis Church:** With its massive adobe buttresses and rich earthy glow, this 350-year-old Franciscan mission is one of the most recognizable in the world, thanks to its frequent depiction in paintings and photographs (page 136).

★ **Taos Pueblo:** The stepped adobe buildings at New Mexico's most remarkable pueblo seem to rise organically from the earth (page 137).

★ **Hiking in Taos Ski Valley:** As the road wends ever higher, trailheads beckon, providing access to mountain vistas and some of the most stunning backcountry in the state—not to mention its highest peak (page 144).

★ **Rafting the Rio Grande Gorge:** As jaw-dropping as this 800-foot-deep channel cut through the rock to the west of Taos looks from above, it can't compare to the thrill of rafting its Class III and Class IV rapids (page 147).

★ **Cumbres & Toltec Scenic Railroad:** Ascending the pass through the Rockies into Colorado on this rumbling old steam train, soot and wind in your hair, you'll feel like you've climbed to the top of the world (page 169).

★ **Live Music in Red River:** Though the alpine setting might seem incongruous, the little village of Red River has a surprisingly strong country and bluegrass scene that plays out in 1950s-era venues that ooze character (page 177).

Georgia O'Keeffe painted, to the ranch where D. H. Lawrence lived. Then they wind up staying. The person pouring your coffee at the café just might have a variation on this story.

Taos has long been associated with artists and writers—and, recently, Hollywood types—but this doesn't translate to wealth and exclusivity. Hispano farmers in Valle Valdez are sustained by acequia-fed farm plots as they have been for centuries. The same goes for residents of old Taos Pueblo, the living World Heritage Site that still uses no electricity or running water. Add to that a strong subculture of ski bums, artists, off-the-grid eco-homesteaders, and spiritual seekers, and you have a community that is more loyal and dedicated to preserving its unique way of life than perhaps any other small town in the western United States.

PLANNING YOUR TIME

Taos's busiest tourist season is **summer,** when a day can be spent gallery-hopping and museum-going, then settling in to watch the afternoon thunderheads gather and churn, followed by the sun setting under lurid red streaks across the broad western mesas. **Wintertime** gets busy with skiers November-April, but as they're all up on the mountain during the day, museums scale back their hours, and residents reclaim the town center, curling up with books at the many coffee shops. **Taos Pueblo closes to visitors** for up to 10 weeks in February and March. By May, the peaks are relatively clear of snow, and you can hike to high meadows filled with wildflowers. **Fall** is dominated by the smell of wood smoke and the beat of drums, as the pueblo and the rest of the town turn out for the Feast of San Geronimo at the end of September.

From Santa Fe, it's possible to visit Taos as a **day trip**—as plenty of people do in the summertime—but you'll get a better sense of the place if you stay overnight. A three- or four-night visit gives you time for an afternoon at Taos Pueblo, a couple of mornings at galleries and museums, a hike or skiing, and a day tour of the Enchanted Circle.

For Chama, you can easily make the drive from Taos and back in a day, though if you plan to ride the train, you'll have to get an early start or book a hotel there. As for the **Enchanted Circle,** the 84-mile loop is typically done as a day trip. By no means attempt to visit Taos *and* do the Enchanted Circle loop in a single day—you'd be terribly rushed, and this is hardly the spirit of Taos.

HISTORY

The first human inhabitants of the area at the base of Taos Mountain were Tiwa-speaking descendants of the Ancestral Puebloans who migrated from the Four Corners area around AD 1000. Taos (how Spaniards heard the Tiwa word for "village") was a thriving village when Spanish explorers, part of Francisco de Coronado's crew, passed through in 1540. By 1615, settlers had arrived. By the mid-18th century, Taos was the hub of a large trade in beaver pelts, which drew French fur trappers, Mexican traders, and local settlers to swap meets.

But in 1879, the railroad arrived in Raton, bumping Taos from its position as a trading hub. Fortunes began to turn nearly two decades later, in 1898, when Bert Geer Phillips and Ernest Blumenschein, two painters on a jaunt from Denver, Colorado, "discovered" Taos after their wagon wheel snapped near town. They established the Taos Society of Artists (TSA) in 1915, making names for themselves as painters of the American West and a name for Taos as a destination for creative types. In the 1960s, creativity took a turn to the communal, with groups such as the New Buffalo commune in Arroyo Hondo—an inspiration for Dennis Hopper's film *Easy Rider*. The culture clash at first was fierce, but in the decades since, hippies (and their richer

Previous: Taos Plaza; Taos Ski Valley village; rafting on the Rio Grande.

Taos

EL SALTO FALLS

To Valle Valdez

HONDO SECO ROAD

Arroyo Seco

LA SANTÍSIMA
TRINIDAD CHURCH

To HIKING IN TAOS
SKI VALLEY

Taos

150

522

To Rio Grande
Gorge (see inset
detail map)

MEDLEY

Taos

TAOS MESA
BREWING

HOTEL LUNA
MYSTICA

TAOS MONTE
BELLO RV PARK

FAR FLUNG
ADVENTURES

64

TAOS REGIONAL AIRPORT

MILLICENT
ROGERS
MUSEUM

FARMHOUSE
CAFÉ

TAOS PUEBLO

TIWA
KITCHEN

SAN GERONIMO
CHURCH

El Prado

Taos

ORLANDO'S

RIFT CYCLES

ELEVATION
COFFEE

GUTIZ

HACIENDA DEL SOL

Blackrock
Springs

CID'S GROCERY

TAOS PIZZA
OUT BACK

TAOS ART MUSEUM AT FECHIN HOUSE

EARTHSHIP
VISITORS
CENTER

Manby Springs

SEE
"DOWNTOWN
TAOS"
MAP

KACHINA LODGE

Taos

Rio Grande

MABEL DODGE LUHAN HOUSE

HACIENDA DE
LOS MARTINEZ

LA LOMA
PLAZA

To Taos

RIO GRANDE
GORGE BRIDGE

64

CUTTHROAT
FLY FISHING

PALACIO DE MARQUESA

CASA GALLINA

TAOS
VALLEY LODGE

INN ON THE RIO

RAFTING THE RIO
GRANDE GORGE

240

BUREAU OF LAND
MANAGEMENT
TAOS FIELD OFFICE

HOTEL DON
FERNANDO

DEVISADERO
TRAIL

Rio Grande
del Norte

TAOS YOUTH &
FAMILY CENTER

585

64

National

TAOS VISITOR CENTER

WILDFLOWER PLAYHOUSE

Monument

ANTONIO'S

SAGEBRUSH
CANTINA/
SAGEBRUSH INN

TAOS CERAMICS CENTER

Taos

Carson

WEST RIM TRAIL

0   1 mi
0   1 km

WILD EARTH LLAMA
ADVENTURES

National Forest

Ranchos
de Taos

JESUS
NAZARENO
CEMETERY

0   1 mi
0   1 km

OLD MARTINA'S HALL

SAN FRANCISCO
DE ASIS CHURCH

RANCHOS
PLAZA GRILL

68

TAOS DRUMS

LOS RIOS RIVER
RUNNERS

518

© MOON.COM

Just as San Francisco de Asis Church has inspired countless painters and photographers, the people of Taos have found their way into novels and short stories.

One of Taos's more revered figures is **Padre Antonio Martinez,** a popular priest in the mid-1800s who clashed with **Bishop Jean-Baptiste Lamy** in Santa Fe. As a result, some Taos residents aren't fond of Willa Cather's *Death Comes for the Archbishop* (New York: Vintage, 1990), even if it is a classic. The 1927 novel is based on the mission of Lamy, with sympathy for his efforts to straighten out "rogue" Mexican priests like Martinez. The padre gets more balanced coverage in *Lamy of Santa Fe* (Middletown, CT: Wesleyan University Press, 2003), a Pulitzer Prize-winning biography by Paul Horgan.

Famous Western novelist Frank Waters, a Taos resident for almost 50 years, fictionalized **Edith Warner,** a woman who ran a small café frequented by Los Alamos scientists while they developed the nuclear bomb. *The Woman at Otowi Crossing* (Athens, OH: Swallow Press, 1987) is his portrait of a woman who seeks isolation in the New Mexico wilderness but is drawn back into the world through the largest event of her time. The novel is fairly true to life, but a biography, *The House at Otowi Bridge: The Story of Edith Warner and Los Alamos* (Albuquerque: University of New Mexico Press, 1973), is stricter with the facts. It's by Peggy Pond Church, who lived at Los Alamos for 20 years before the area was taken over by the government.

Another Taos writer, **John Nichols,** earned acclaim for his 1974 comic novel *The Milagro Beanfield War* (New York: Owl Books, 2000), later made into a film by Robert Redford. The war of the title is an escalating squabble in a tiny village over the acequia, the type of irrigation ditch that's still used in Valle Valdez and other agricultural communities in the area. But if you think it takes comic melodrama and a star such as Redford to make irrigation interesting, look into the beautiful and fascinating *Mayordomo: Chronicle of an Acequia in Northern New Mexico* (Albuquerque: University of New Mexico Press, 1993), **Stanley Crawford**'s memoir about his term as "ditch boss" in the valley where he runs his garlic farm.

relatives, ski bums) have become part of the town's most basic fabric.

ORIENTATION

The area referred to as Taos encompasses a few nearby communities as well. Arriving via the low road, on **Highway 68,** you pass first through **Ranchos de Taos.** From here the road becomes **Paseo del Pueblo Sur,** a wide commercial stretch abutted by chain stores and cheap motels, and continues north for five miles to **Taos Plaza.** The intersection with **Kit Carson Road (U.S. 64)** is the **center of town** proper (Taos Plaza is just west). There's a paid **parking** lot at the light and a free lot a few blocks east on Kit Carson just past Ortiz Lane.

Heading north past Kit Carson, the road becomes Paseo del Pueblo Norte. It curves west after 0.5 mile, and a smaller road continues north about two miles to **Taos Pueblo.**

Paseo del Pueblo Norte carries on through what is technically the separate village of **El Prado,** then to a four-way intersection that will forever be known to locals as "the old blinking light," even though the flashing yellow signal was replaced with a newfangled three-color traffic light in the 1990s. Here U.S. 64 shoots west to the **Rio Grande,** and Highway 522 leads northwest to the outlying village of **Arroyo Hondo,** then to **Questa** and the Enchanted Circle. **Highway 150** goes north to **Arroyo Seco,** and eventually climbs to the **Taos Ski Valley** and the slopes of Kachina Peak.

Heading further northeast and northwest out of Taos leads to two disparate drives, both of which offer stunning scenery. The more well-traveled one is the **Enchanted Circle,** a continuously rewarding 84-mile loop east and north of Taos marked by dramatic mountain landscape, including

Wheeler Peak, the state's highest summit, and the ski resorts of **Red River** and **Angel Fire.** Venturing northwest beyond the Rio Grande Gorge Bridge on Highway 64 leads to vast vistas and a pastoral landscape occasionally interrupted by centuries-old communities such as **Tierra Amarilla** before

leading to the remote **Jicarilla Apache Nation** and the Rockies in the distance. Turning north on Highway 17 25 miles east of the reservation brings you to **Chama,** a charming mountain town which seems to sleep and wake based on the schedule of its steam train.

Sights

DOWNTOWN TAOS
Taos Plaza

Taos Plaza, enclosed by adobe buildings with deep portales, is easy to miss if you just cruise through on the main road—it's just west of the intersection with Kit Carson Road. Once an informal area at the center of a cluster of settlers' homes, the plaza was established around 1615 but destroyed in the Pueblo Revolt of 1680. New homes were built starting in 1710, as defense against Comanche and Jicarilla raiders. Before long a series of fires gutted the block-style buildings, so the structures that edge the plaza all date from around 1930—and unfortunately virtually all are now filled with rather cheesy souvenir shops.

On the plaza's north side, the **Old Taos County Courthouse** contains a series of Works Progress Administration-sponsored murals painted in 1934 and 1935 by Emil Bisttram and a team of other Taos artists. The door is usually open when the farmers market is on, but not reliably so at other times. Still, it's worth a try: Enter on the ground floor through the North Plaza Art Center and go upstairs, toward the back of the building. On the south side, the **Hotel La Fonda de Taos** harbors a small collection of D. H. Lawrence's "erotic" paintings (10am-6pm daily, guided $6, unguided $3, free to guests). The nine paintings are tame by today's standards, but they flesh out (no pun intended) the story of the writer's time in Taos, some of which is described in his book *Mornings in Mexico.*

In the center is a **monument** to New Mexicans killed in the Bataan Death March of World War II. The U.S. flag flies day and night, a tradition carried on after an incident during the Civil War when Kit Carson and a crew of his men nailed the flag to a pole and guarded it to keep Confederate sympathizers from taking it down.

In front of the historic La Fonda hotel, a large bronze **statue of Padre Antonio Martinez** gestures like a visionary. This local hero produced the area's first newspaper, *El Crepúsculo de la Libertad* (The Dawn of Freedom), which later became the *Taos News;* he also established a co-ed school, a seminary, and a law school. Bishop Jean-Baptiste Lamy in Santa Fe criticized his liberal views, especially after Martinez defied Lamy's call for mandatory tithing, and Lamy later excommunicated him. Martinez continued to minister to locals at a chapel in his house until his death in 1867. The statue's enormous hands suggest his vast talent and influence in the town.

Harwood Museum of Art
238 Ledoux St.; 575/758-9826;
www.harwoodmuseum.org; 11am-5pm Wed.-Sun.; $10
The Harwood Museum of Art, set in the sprawling Pueblo Revival-style home of the Harwood patrons, tells the story of Taos's rise as an art colony, beginning with Ernest Blumenschein's fateful wagon accident, which left him and his colleague Bert Phillips stranded in the tiny town in 1898.

Downtown Taos

Modern Taos painters are represented in changing exhibit spaces upstairs and down, and it's interesting to see the same material—the mountain, the pueblo, the river, local residents—depicted in different styles over time. Also upstairs is a small but good assortment of Hispano crafts, including some beautiful 19th-century tinwork and a couple of santos by Patrocinio Barela, the Taos wood-carver who modernized the art in the 1930s. A separate back wing is dedicated to seven ethereal abstractions by painter Agnes Martin; a local teacher offers yoga in the gallery every Thursday morning. The Arthur Bell Auditorium hosts concerts, films, and artist talks.

E. L. Blumenschein Home

222 Ledoux St.; 575/758-0505;
www.taoshistoricmuseums.org; 10am-5pm Mon.-Sat.,
noon-4pm Sun.; $10

Ernest Blumenschein, one of the founding fathers of the Taos Society of Artists, moved into what is now the E. L. Blumenschein Home in 1919 with his wife, Mary Shepherd Greene Blumenschein, also an accomplished artist. The house's decoration largely reflects her taste, from the sturdy wood furnishings in the dining room to the light-filled studio and the cozy wood-paneled library.

The original rooms of the house feature rotating exhibits, while other rooms, including the "Green Room," are hung with works by their contemporaries, including a beautiful monotype of Taos Mountain by Oscar E. Berninghaus. The main bedroom, entered through a steep arch, is decorated with Mary's lush illustrations for *The Arabian Nights*. Throughout, you can admire the variety of ceiling styles, from rough-hewn split cedar (rajas) to tidy golden aspen boughs (latillas).

Admission to the E. L. Blumenschein Home is also good for entrance to Hacienda de los Martinez.

Taos Walking Tour

Governor Bent House and Museum

The major sights around Taos Plaza are listed in the order of a potential walking tour. Stroll quickly to get oriented or take your time and visit the museums along the way. Either way, you'll pass a few other historical spots as well.

Starting on **Taos Plaza,** walk out the southwest corner to Ledoux Street and the museums (such as the **Harwood Museum of Art**). Make a short jog left (southwest) down Lower Ranchitos Road to **La Loma Plaza.** Return to Ranchitos, and then turn left into Padre Martinez Lane, where the influential pastor lived until his death in 1867. At the end of the street, turn right and walk to Camino de la Placita, then turn left.

After a couple of blocks, turn right (east) on Bent Street, passing **Governor Bent House and Museum,** home of the first U.S. governor, Charles Bent. At Paseo del Pueblo Norte, turn left and walk to **Taos Art Museum at Fechin House,** at least to admire the structure. Backtrack and enter **Kit Carson Park** to find the **cemetery** where many Taos notables are buried. Cut out the back of the park, past the baseball diamonds to Morada Lane—at the end is the **Mabel Dodge Luhan House.**

Take Morada Lane back to Kit Carson Road, passing the **Couse-Sharp Historic Site** and the **Kit Carson Home and Museum.** Turn right (west) to get back to Paseo del Pueblo. Another right turn gets you to a well-deserved drink at the **Taos Inn.**

Governor Bent House and Museum

117 Bent St.; 505/758-2376; 9am-5pm daily May-Sept., 10am-4pm Oct.-Apr.; $3

This dusty little backroom exhibit space is odd and not well cared for, but worth a quick visit if it happens to be open (the posted hours aren't always maintained). The Governor Bent House and Museum is the former residence of Charles Bent, who, following the onset of the Mexican-American War, was appointed the first governor of the territory of New Mexico in 1846, based on his extensive experience as a Western trader (he and his brother had built Bent's Fort, an important trading center in southern Colorado). But Bent died in 1847, at the hands of an angry mob dissatisfied by the new U.S. government.

Amid the slightly creepy clutter, which includes a malevolent-looking ceremonial buffalo head and photos of Penitente rituals from an old *Harper's* magazine, is the very hole in the very wall that Bent's family quickly dug to escape while Bent tried to reason with the murderous crowd. The back room only gets stranger, with weird taxidermy (including an eight-legged lamb), sinister early 1900s doctor's instruments, and lots of old guns. The place may feel like an antiques store where nothing's for sale, but it's a unique overview of the period nonetheless.

Kit Carson Park and Cemetery

211 Paseo del Pueblo Norte, north of the Taos Inn

A shady sprawl of gravestones in a corner of Kit Carson Park, the cemetery was established in 1847 to bury the dead from the Taos Rebellion, a melee incited by wealthy Spanish landowners and Catholic priests anxious about their loss of influence under the Americans. Mobs killed New Mexico's first U.S. governor, the veteran merchant Charles Bent, as well as scores of other Anglo landowners in the area. The cemetery earned its current name when the bodies of Carson and his wife were moved here in 1869, according to his will.

Many of Taos's oldest families, particularly the merchants of the late 1800s, are buried here. Mabel Dodge Luhan had been a close friend of the trader Ralph Meyers, and they often joked about being buried together. When Mabel died in 1962, a few years after Ralph, writer Frank Waters recalled their wishes and suggested that Meyers's grave be scooted over to make room for Mabel. She was the last person to be buried in the cemetery, in 1962, and her grave is squeezed into the far southwest corner. Other local luminaries at rest here include Padre Antonio Martinez, who stood up to Catholic bishop Lamy, and an Englishman named Arthur Manby, whose grave actually stands outside of the cemetery proper, due to his lifetime of shady business deals, land

grabs, and outright swindles perpetrated in town. Manby was found beheaded in his mansion in 1929, and the unsympathetic populace was happy to attribute the death to natural causes.

The park itself is a popular picnic and barbecue spot in summer, when it also holds concerts by local and national acts.

Couse-Sharp Historic Site

146 Kit Carson Rd.; 575/751-0369; www.couse-sharp.org; 9am-5pm Mon.-Sat., May-Oct.; donation

Tours of the Couse-Sharp Historic Site are by appointment (2 hrs, Mon.-Sat.) and during open houses (3pm-5pm, first Sat. of the month June-Oct.), but it is well worth arranging to see the interior of painter Eanger Irving Couse's home and studio. Couse, a friend of E. L. Blumenschein's, came to Taos in 1902 with his wife, Virginia, and spent the summers here, working as a figurative painter, until he died in 1936.

Not only has the Couse home and garden been meticulously kept up, as has adjacent property owned by friend and fellow painter Joseph Henry Sharp, but the tours (typically 1.5 hours) are led by Couse's granddaughter and her husband, who have a wealth of stories to share. And not only artists will be intrigued; Couse's son, a mechanical engineer who developed mobile repair vehicles, built a vast machine shop here.

Kit Carson Home and Museum

113 Kit Carson Rd.; 575/758-4945; http://kitcarsonhouse.org; 11am-4pm Mon.-Sat., noon-4pm Sun.; $10

Old photographs, memorabilia, and assorted trinkets from the frontier era conjure the spirit of the legendary scout at the Kit Carson Home and Museum, where he lived with his third wife, Josefa Jaramillo, from 1843 until they both died in 1868.

The definitive mountain man, Carson was of the most acclaimed of the many solitary scouts, trackers, and trappers who explored the West. He was an intrepid adventurer who, after a childhood on the barely settled edge

of Missouri, joined a wagon train headed down the Santa Fe Trail; he arrived in Taos in 1826. His talent for tracking, hunting, and translating from Spanish and various Indian languages soon put him in high demand. Whether he was scouting for John C. Frémont as the explorer mapped the trails west to Los Angeles or serving as an officer in the Civil War or, less heroically, forcing the Navajos on the Long Walk to Fort Sumner, he called Taos home.

Taos Inn

125 Paseo del Pueblo Norte; 575/758-2233; www.taosinn.com

Distinguished by its large glowing thunderbird sign, the Taos Inn was as central to previous generations of Taoseños's lives as it is now. Granted, today it's the hotel bar that everyone goes to, but starting in the 1890s, it was the home of T. P. Martin, Taos's first and only county doctor, who had a reputation for accepting chickens or venison from his poorer patients in lieu of cash. His home looked out on a small plaza and a well—which has since been covered over and made into the hotel lobby.

CENTRAL TAOS
La Loma Plaza

To see what Taos Plaza looked like before the spread of souvenir-shops, stroll down Lower Ranchitos Road and turn on Valdez Road to reach La Loma Plaza. The center of a fortified settlement created by 63 Spanish families in 1796, the ring of adobe homes around a central open space is dusty and little changed through the centuries. Exit the plaza by continuing uphill and bearing right—this takes you past La Loma's tiny old chapel and onto paved San Antonio Street, which leads downhill and back to Lower Ranchitos.

1: Mabel Dodge Luhan House **2:** Kit Carson Park and Cemetery **3:** Taos Plaza

★ Taos Art Museum at Fechin House

227 Paseo del Pueblo Norte; 575/758-2690; www.taosartmuseum.org; 10am-5pm Tues.-Sun. May-Oct., 10am-4pm Nov.-Apr.; $10

This sunny space, the former home of artist and wood-carver Nicolai Fechin, is a showcase not only for a great collection of paintings, but also for Fechin's lovely woodwork. When the Russian native moved to Taos in 1927, hoping to cure his tuberculosis, he purchased seven acres of land, including the small, two-story Taos Art Museum at Fechin House. He proceeded to hand-carve the lintels, staircases, bedsteads, and more, in a combination of Russian Tartar and local styles. His blending of traditions is flawless and natural—a small altar, also in the dining room, is set with Orthodox icons but could just as easily hold local santos.

The permanent collection rotates through three times a year, so the exhibits vary depending on the season. One thing you can count on is that all will be eclectic: Victor Higgins's 1936 *Indian Nude* recalls Paul Gauguin, while Dorothy Brett's *Rainbow and Indians* from 1942 is more enamored of the powerful landscape. One room is dedicated to Fechin's own portrait work, characterized by broad, dynamic brushstrokes and a canny eye for distinctive facial features. After all the work Fechin did on the house, he stayed in Taos only six years, when his wife divorced him. He moved on to Los Angeles with his daughter, Eya (her sunny study, on the ground floor, contains the child-scale furniture that her father made for her). After her father died in 1955, Eya, by then practicing psychodrama and dance therapy, returned to live in the studio (the back building that also houses the gift shop) and helped establish the main house as a museum.

★ Mabel Dodge Luhan House

240 Morada Ln.; 575/751-9686; http://mabeldodgeluhan.com; 9am-7pm daily; free

While it mainly operates as a hotel and retreat, the Mabel Dodge Luhan House is also open to curious visitors. Knock at the main building first; the caretaker will give you a history brochure for a self-guided tour around the public areas of the house.

Mabel Dodge, a well-off, freethinking woman who had fostered art salons in New York City and Florence, Italy, decamped to Taos in 1916, following her third husband. Eventually she got married again, to Taos Pueblo member Tony Luhan, and her name became inextricably linked with Taos's 20th-century history, thanks to all the budding artists and writers she encouraged to visit. Novelist D. H. Lawrence dubbed Taos "Mabeltown," and figures as grand and varied as actress Greta Garbo, writer Willa Cather, photographer Ansel Adams, artist Georgia O'Keeffe, poet Robinson Jeffers, and psychiatrist Carl Jung made the long trek to her home.

Bordering the Taos reservation, the house was built to Luhan's specifications starting in 1918. Unsurprisingly, given her artistic taste, she exercised a firm hand in its design. Alongside a small original structure—a low row of adobe rooms that were already a century old at that point—she added a three-story main building, topped with a huge sunroom open on three sides. This, and the similarly glass-enclosed bathroom on the 2nd floor, scandalized her neighbors, the pueblo residents.

One of them, however, didn't seem to mind: Tony Luhan, the foreman of the construction project, became her next husband. But Mabel's custom love nest brought out some latent prudery even in D. H. Lawrence, who objected to the curtainless bathroom windows; to soothe his sensibilities, if not Mabel's, he painted colorful swirls directly on the glass.

WEST OF TAOS
Hacienda de los Martinez

708 Hacienda Rd., off Lower Ranchitos Rd.; 575/758-1000; www.taoshistoricmuseums.org; 10am-5pm Mon.-Sat., noon-5pm Sun. Apr.-Oct., 10am-4pm Mon. and Thurs.-Sat., noon-4pm Sun. Nov.-Mar.; $10

The word hacienda conjures a sprawling complex and fields, but the reality in 19th-century Taos was quite different, as seen at the carefully restored 1804 Hacienda de los Martinez, one of the last remaining homes of its kind in the Southwest. Its builder and owner, Don Antonio Severino Martinez, was a prominent merchant who hosted the Taos trade fairs at the hacienda and eventually became the mayor of Taos in the 1820s. His oldest son was Padre Antonio Martinez, the valley leader who clashed with the French bishop Jean-Baptiste Lamy.

Despite the family's high social standing, life was fairly rugged, cramped, and dangerous. The 21 simple rooms arranged around two courtyards allowed room for sleeping, cooking, and protection against raids. Some of the spaces have been furnished to reflect their original use; others are dedicated to exhibits, such as an interesting display on enslavement in the area, and a wood carving of Doña Sebastiana, Lady Death, with her glittering mica eyes, in the collection of Penitente paraphernalia. During the spring and summer, local craftspeople are on hand to demonstrate weaving, blacksmithing, and the like in the house's workshops; in the fall, the trade fair is reenacted over a weekend.

Admission to Hacienda de los Martinez also is good for entrance to the **E. L. Blumenschein Home.**

RANCHOS DE TAOS
★ San Francisco de Asis Church

East side of U.S. 68 in Ranchos de Taos; 575/758-2754; 9am-4pm daily, Mass 8am, 9:30am, and 11:30am Sun.; donation

Just as photographs of the Great Pyramid of Cheops seldom show the sprawl of modern Cairo crowding up to its base, San Francisco de Asis Church as depicted in, say, Georgia O'Keeffe's paintings and Ansel Adams's photographs, is a shadow-draped fortress isolated on a hilltop. In fact, the iconic church, completed in the early 19th century as a Franciscan mission, is at the center of a plaza, ringed with buildings.

It's easy to see what has fascinated so many

Dennis Hopper in Taos

In 1968, a Taos Pueblo elder told Dennis Hopper, "The mountain is smiling on you!" No wonder the *Easy Rider* actor and real-life renegade claimed the town as what he called his "heart home." His early years here were wild: He's notorious for having ridden his motorcycle across the roof of the Mabel Dodge Luhan House, which he bought in 1969. Over the decades, he mellowed just a bit, and Taos locals came to think of him as one of their own. In 2009, as part of a 40th-anniversary celebration of the Summer of Love, the Harwood Museum mounted an exhibit of his photography and paintings, along with works by some of his compatriots from that era.

Hopper died not long after, in 2010. His funeral was held at the San Francisco de Asis Church, and attended by fellow *Easy Rider* actors Peter Fonda and Jack Nicholson. Following Pueblo tradition, Hopper was buried in a pine box under a dirt mound, in the nearby **Jesus Nazareno Cemetery.** Fans can pay their respects there. To find it, take Highway 518 south; about 0.25 mile along, turn left (east) on Espinoza Road. The cemetery is a short way from here, off the left side of the road. From the main gate, Hopper's grave is near the back, on the right-hand side.

artists: the clean lines, the shadows created by the hulking buttresses, the adobe bathed in the sun's glow. The church is living architecture, as much a part of the earth as something raised above it. As with every traditional adobe structure, it must be refinished every year with a mix of clay, sand, and straw; it is then coated with a fine layer of water and sand, and buffed with sheepskin. This process, known as the enjarre, happens over two weeks in early June, during which the church is open only at lunchtime and on Sunday.

Inside, the whitewashed walls are covered with the stations of the cross; two Spanish Colonial reredos decorate the altars. In the **parish hall** (10am-3pm Mon.-Fri.; $3) is the 1896 painting *The Shadow of the Cross,* an eight-foot-high canvas in which the figure of Christ can be seen to luminesce—allegedly miraculously.

TOP EXPERIENCE

★ TAOS PUEBLO

120 Veterans Hwy.; 575/758-1028; www.taospueblo. com; 9am-5pm Mon. and Thurs.-Sun., closed for 10 weeks Feb.-Mar.; $25

Even if you've been in New Mexico for a while and think you're inured to adobe, Taos Pueblo is an amazing sight. Two clusters of multistory mud-brick buildings make up the core of this village, which claims, along with Acoma Pueblo, to be the oldest continually inhabited community in the United States. The current buildings, annually repaired and recoated with mud, are from the 1200s, though it's possible that all their constituent parts have been fully replaced several times since then.

About 150 people (out of the 1,900 or so total Taos reservation residents) live here year-round. These people, along with the town's designation as a United Nations Educational, Scientific, and Cultural Organization (UNESCO) World Heritage Site, have kept the place remarkably as it was in the pre-Columbian era, save for the use of adobe bricks (as opposed to clay and stone), which were introduced by the Spanish, as the main structural material. The apartment-like homes, stacked upon each other and reached by wooden ladders, have no electricity or running water, though some use propane gas for heat and light.

You are free to explore, but be mindful not to intrude on private space: Enter only buildings that are clearly marked as shops, and stay clear of the ceremonial kiva areas on the east side of each complex. These round structures form the ritual heart of the pueblo, a secret space within an already private culture.

You're welcome to wander around and enter any of the craft shops and galleries that

1

2

3

are open—a good opportunity to see inside the earthen structures and to buy some of the distinctive Taos pottery, which is only lightly decorated but glimmers with mica from the clay of this area. These pots are also renowned for cooking tender beans.

Don't miss the ceremonial dances performed here, about eight times a year.

You can also purchase arts and crafts sold by Taos Pueblo artisans in the **Taos visitor center** (1201 Paseo del Pueblo Sur) in town.

San Geronimo Church

The path from the Taos Pueblo admission gate leads directly to the central plaza, a broad expanse between Red Willow Creek (source of the community's drinking water, flowing from sacred Blue Lake high in the mountains) and San Geronimo Church. The church, built in 1850, is perhaps the newest structure in the village, a replacement for the first mission the Spanish built, in 1619, using forced Indian labor. The Virgin Mary presides over the room roofed with heavy wood beams; her clothes change with every season, a nod to her dual role as the Earth Mother. (Taking photos is strictly forbidden inside the church at all times and, as at all pueblos, at dances as well.)

The older church, to the north behind the houses, is now a cemetery—fitting, given its tragic destruction. It was first torn down during the Pueblo Revolt of 1680; the Spanish rebuilt it about 20 years later. In 1847, it was again attacked, this time by U.S. troops sent in to quell the rebellion against the new government, in retaliation for the murder of Governor Charles Bent. The counterattack brutally outweighed what had sparked it. More than 100 pueblo residents, including women and children, had taken refuge inside the church when the soldiers bombarded and set fire to it, killing everyone inside and gutting the building. Since then, the bell tower has been restored, but the graves have simply intermingled with the ruined walls and piles of dissolved adobe mud. All of the crosses—from old carved wood to newly finished stone—face the sacred Taos Mountain.

EL PRADO AND WEST ON U.S. 64
Millicent Rogers Museum

1504 Millicent Rogers Rd., El Prado; 575/758-2462; www.millicentrogers.org; 10am-5pm daily Apr.-Oct., 10am-5pm Mon.-Tues. and Thurs.-Sun. Nov.-Mar.; $15

A dashing, thrice-married New York City socialite and designer, Millicent Rogers visited Taos in 1947 after breaking things off with actor Clark Gable. After moving to Taos, she brought Southwestern fashion to national attention, as she modeled Navajo-style velvet broomstick skirts, concha belts, and pounds of silver-and-turquoise jewelry for photo spreads in *Vogue* and *Harper's Bazaar*. Though she died just six years after she arrived in Taos, at the age of 51, she managed to accumulate a fantastic amount of local art. El Prado's Millicent Rogers Museum was established by her son, Paul Peralta-Ramos, and is set in the warren of adobe rooms that make up her former home.

Her belongings form the core collection, with flawless pieces of pottery, rugs, baskets, and jewelry—both local works and her own designs. Peralta-Ramos also contributed his own collection, including beautiful pieces of Navajo rugs and Hispano devotional art. An entire gallery is devoted to the work of San Ildefonso potter Maria Martinez. Aside from the works' individual beauty, they make an excellent broad introduction to the crafts of the area, from ancient times to modern. But it's not all rooted in local culture: Rogers's goofy illustrations of a fairy tale for her children fill the last room. The gift shop here is particularly thorough and includes beautiful vintage jewelry and circa-1900 rugs.

Rio Grande Gorge

12 miles northwest of Taos Plaza

Heading west on U.S. 64 from its intersection with Highway 150 and Highway 522, you pass the Taos airstrip on the left; then,

1: San Francisco de Asis Church **2:** Rio Grande Gorge **3:** San Geronimo Church at Taos Pueblo after a few more miles, the ground simply drops away into the Rio Grande Gorge (also called the Taos Gorge). Plunging at its most vertigo-inducing point 800 feet down into malevolent-looking basalt as the river courses through it, the gorge presents one of the most awe-inspiring vistas in the state. It's not just millions of years of rushing water that have carved out the canyon—seismic activity also caused a rift in the earth's surface. The crack extends north to just beyond the Colorado state line and south almost to Española.

The elegant, unnervingly delicate-looking **Rio Grande Gorge Bridge** that spans it was built in 1965 to supplement entrepreneur John Dunn's rickety old toll crossing eight miles north. Critics mocked the newer structure as "the bridge to nowhere" because the highway on the western bank had yet to be built, but the American Institute of Steel Construction granted it the Most Beautiful Steel Bridge award in 1966. At 650 feet above the river, the cantilever truss was a stunning engineering feat; it is still the seventh-highest bridge in the United States. On either side of the bridge is the stretch of white water called the Taos Box, two words that inspire wild tales in any seasoned river-runner. This series of Class III and IV (and occasionally class V, if the water is high) rapids is the pinnacle of rafting in New Mexico.

A pedestrian path along the bridge brings the depths below you into extremely sharp relief; viewing the gorge from here at sunset with the mountains looming in the backdrop can make for a stunning end to the day. On the west side of the gorge is a rest area, and the start of the **West Rim Trail,** running south from the parking lot and yielding great views of the bridge to the north.

Greater World Earthship Development

Earthship visitors center: 2 Earthship Way; 575/613-4409; www.earthship.com; 9am-4pm daily; $8 self-guided tours

If you brave the slender gorge bridge and continue a mile or so west on U.S. 64, you soon see some whimsically curved and creatively stuccoed houses along the right side of the road. These are Earthships: modular, low-priced homes that function entirely on collected rainwater and wind and solar power. Although they look like fanciful hobbit homes or Mars colony pods, Earthships are made of rather common stuff: The walls, built into hillsides for efficient heating and cooling, are stacks of used tires packed with rammed

the Rio Grande Gorge Bridge

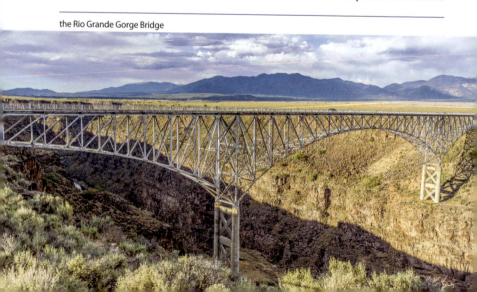

earth, while bottles stacked with cement and crushed aluminum cans form front walls and colorful peepholes.

Greater World is the largest of three local all-Earthship subdivisions and headquarters of the architecture office that developed the design. The **Earthship visitors center** is the most unconventional model home and sales office you'll ever visit. You can take the self-guided tour of a basic Earthship and watch a video about the building process and the rationale behind the design. If you're hooked, you can, of course, get details on buying a lot in the development or purchasing the plans to build your own place elsewhere. Or try before you buy: You can stay the night in an Earthship here, starting at $165. Look for the green building on the right, 1.5 miles past the bridge.

HIGHWAY 150
Arroyo Seco
When Taos's downtown core becomes too overrun for your liking, it's a good time to make for the village of Arroyo Seco, reached by driving past El Prado on U.S. 64 and heading north on Highway 150. This cluster of buildings at a bend in the road to the ski valley feels very much of another era. Sure, there's art up here, too, but this diminutive community, though only a half-hour drive (8.5 miles) from the Taos Plaza, maintains an even more laidback and funky attitude than Taos—if such a thing is possible. It has been a retreat for decades: Frank Waters, celebrated author of *The Man Who Killed the Deer* and *The Woman at Otowi Crossing,* lived here off and on from 1947 until his death in 1995.

"Downtown" Arroyo Seco, all one block of it, has grown up around the bend in the road and **La Santísima Trinidad Church** (480 NM-150), set back from Highway 150 on the left. The church, built in 1834, has adobe walls that are alarmingly eroded in patches, but it sports a cheery red-metal roof; the spare traditional interior is decorated with bultos (an image of a saint carved in wood) and retablos

(altarpieces), but the doors are often locked. Secular pursuits in this area are more sure-fire draws: a fine bar and general store, for instance, and El Salto Falls, up the mountain a bit.

The Rim Road
As Highway 150 continues north, the road to the ski valley eventually makes a hard right just over a mile past Arroyo Seco, and the aptly named Rim Road heads to the left for a little under three miles, along the canyon's southern edge. It gives a great view of **Valle Valdez** below, where tidy farm plots are set along Rio Hondo and the traditional acequia irrigation that has been used here for more than four centuries. In typical modern real-estate distribution, the not-so-well-off native Taoseños value their fertile soil, while wealthy arrivistes (actress Julia Roberts, most famously) have claimed the swoon-inducing views on the rim road, which was developed only in the later part of the 20th century. On the north side of the valley, the ritzy Turley Mill development is built on the site of a still that produced the powerful bootleg hooch known as "Taos lightning" from the 1700s to 1847. (Also glossed over in the development: The still was burned and its owner and customers killed during the uprising against Governor Bent.) The area was once home to former defense secretary Donald Rumsfeld and is dotted with million-dollar casitas.

Taos Ski Valley
Highway 150 winds relentlessly up through Hondo Canyon, the steep mountain slopes crowded with tall, dense pines that in winter disappear into a wreath of clouds. The paved road ends at the ever-expanding village of Taos Ski Valley, 10 miles northeast of Arroyo Seco; from there it's another two miles along a rough dirt road to the Wheeler Peak and Williams Lake trailhead. When you get out of the car at the village and take in the vertiginous view up to Kachina Peak (elevation

12,481 feet and often white-capped even in July), you'll see why it inspires legions of reverential skiers every winter, when an average of 305 inches of snow falls on the mountain—almost 10 times the amount they get down in town.

For decades, it was only skiers here. Snowboarders were banned, allegedly because the slopes were too steep—more than half the trails are rated expert level, and many of them are left ungroomed. The mountain was opened to all in 2008, and the ski valley's ambition has grown with each passing year.

In the summer, the village is the site of a burgeoning mountain social scene with live music, and Hondo Canyon's many trails make for good hiking or picnicking. The road is dotted on either side with picnic areas and campgrounds—Cuchilla del Medio is a particularly nice area for a picnic. The small **visitors center** (575/776-1413; www.taosskivalley. com; 9am-2pm daily) in the ski area parking lot stocks trail descriptions and maps.

Recreation

The wild setting presses in all around Taos, and the mountains frame every town view. Downhill skiing is the main draw in the winter, but snowshoeing and Nordic skiing are also wildly popular. In summer, peak-baggers will want to strike out for Wheeler, the state's highest, and mountain bikers should seek out—but not underestimate—the adrenaline rush that is descending the nearby dedicated trails in the ski valley. Not quite as intense, but no less dramatic, is the ride along the Rio Grande Gorge. In the waters below, kayakers and rafters challenge the churning rapids of the legendary Taos Box (late May and early June, with winter runoff, are the most intense season for this).

Sudden thunderstorms are common in summer, as are flash floods and even freak blizzards. Well into May, snow can blanket higher passes, so wherever you go, always carry more warm clothing than you think you'll need. Carry plenty of water with you—your adventures are taking place at over 7,000 feet, after all—and don't skimp on the sunscreen, even when it's below freezing.

Information
Carson National Forest Supervisor's Office

208 Cruz Alta Rd.; 575/758-6200; 8am-4pm Mon.-Fri.
Stop in at the Carson National Forest Supervisor's Office for booklets on recommended trails and maps.

Bureau of Land Management Taos Field Office

1024 Paseo del Pueblo Sur; 575/758-8851;
8am-4:30pm Mon.-Fri.
The Bureau of Land Management Taos Field Office can help with rafting or camping trip prep, with plenty of maps and brochures.

Taos Youth and Family Center

407 Paseo del Cañon; 575/758-4160;
8:30am-6pm daily
The Taos Youth and Family Center has a big indoor pool, as well as an ice-skating rink and skate park. Hours are limited in fall and winter.

HIKING

With Taos Mountain and Wheeler Peak in the backyard, you can ramble along winding rivers or haul up 2,000 feet in less than four miles. Be prepared for a cold snap or storm at any time, and don't plan on anything before May—it takes that long for the snow to

1: Greater World Earthship Development **2:** Arroyo Seco thaw. You can still hit white stuff in the alpine meadows well into summer.

Outfitters
Wild Earth Llama Adventures
800/758-5262; www.llamaadventures.com
If you'd like to lighten your load and enjoy unique animal companionship to boot, contact Wild Earth Llama Adventures, which runs day hikes with lunch ($175), as well as multiday treks (from $825). What follows are just a few of the many trails worth seeking out.

Mudd N Flood
103 Bent St.; 575/751-9100; www.muddnflood.com; 10am-6pm daily
In Taos, Mudd N Flood is a great spot to fill any last-minute gear needs before hitting the trails.

Devisadero Trail
Distance: *6 mi round-trip*
Time: *3-4 hours*
Trailhead: *3 mi east of Taos on the north side of U.S. 64; park across the road*
Leading to ever-expansive views over Taos, the Devisadero Trail (also known as **Loop Trail 108**) is a popular hike close to town that goes up the eponymous mountain. Located in the Carson National Forest, the moderately difficult loop trail presents a steady climb up from either approach. There are numerous lookouts along the way, and it's usually possible to see the Rio Grande Gorge to the northwest. Plan on about 3-4 hours for the round-trip.

West Rim Trail
Distance: *9 mi one-way*
Time: *3-4 hours one-way*
Trailhead: *rest area adjacent to Rio Grande Gorge Bridge, 20 minutes northwest of center of Taos*
The West Rim Trail offers dramatic views as it hugs the rim of the gorge. The trail is fairly flat and easy to negotiate, with good opportunities to see bighorn sheep along the sides of the gorge. Spurs near the halfway point can be tacked on and bring you down closer to the river. If your time is limited, consider an hour-long out-and-back walk, which will get you away from the crowds near the bridge and provide a reasonable taste of the trail's entire length.

El Salto Falls
Some theorize that the mysterious "Taos Hum"—the faint, low drone that many in the area claim to hear—emanates from the caves at El Salto Falls (575/776-2371; generally dawn until dusk; $5), a scenic spot on a patch of private land in Arroyo Seco. That mystery aside, the series of waterfalls (the tallest drops 200 feet) is an iconic Taos natural landmark, and an easy hike or a challenging one, depending on just how much you'd like to see. Save this hike for dry weather, unless you have a four-wheel drive—the road is rough when muddy or snowy.

In Arroyo Seco, take El Salto Road east (go straight where Highway 150 makes a hard right); after about a mile is a sign on the left asking visitors to pay. Leave cash in the honor box on the porch of the green house just off the road, and fill out a waiver and a permit to place on your dashboard. Continue driving another 0.7 mile and bear left; from here, it's 0.9 mile up to a green gate and small parking area. Walk in, following the road as it curves left, then bearing right. This leads in just a few minutes to the lowest, largest cave and the first waterfall—though most of the year, it is often just a trickle. Intrepid hikers can climb up to the right of the cave, to ever-smaller falls and notches in the cliff face. In total, it's less than a mile roundtrip.

★ Taos Ski Valley
Highway 150 winds through Hondo Canyon, the paved road ending at the village of Taos Ski Valley. The **visitors center** (575/776-7852; www.taosskivalley.com) in the ski area parking lot off Thunderbird Road stocks trail descriptions and maps.

1: Taos Ski Valley in winter **2:** Cottam's Ski Shop **3:** Devisadero Trail **4:** Williams Lake

Just before the parking lot for the ski area, **Gavilan Trail** (no. 60) begins at the north side of the road. It's plenty steep but leads to a high mountain meadow. The route is five miles round-trip (budget about three hours), or you can connect with other trails once you're up on the rim.

The relatively easy and popular **Williams Lake Trail** (no. 62) starts near the end of Twining Road, a narrow dirt road that leads out of the top of the ski valley parking lot. The out-and-back hike is four miles round-trip; budget about three hours. After just under two miles of a gradual climb, the **Wheeler Peak Summit Trail** (no. 67), which scales New Mexico's highest mountain, branches off to the left. Hiking the additional two miles or so up to Wheeler Peak from here requires no technical skill, but it's a fairly relentless ascent and should not be undertaken lightly; it'll add an additional two hours round-trip to your hike. Or continue on the Williams Lake Trail for the short final stretch to reach an overlook, which takes in the aquamarine waters of Williams Lake (11,040 feet). After negotiating a rocky stretch, the trail to the lakeshore is straightforward. For either hike, plan on an early morning start to avoid afternoon thunderstorms (and to time your return with a well-earned pint at the Bavarian Lodge). In summer, on the night of the full moon, there's a free guided **moonlight hike** to Williams Lake, starting at 7:30pm; check the schedule at www.taosskivalley.com.

If all that sounds too strenuous, in summer you can take the **chairlift** (9am-4pm Thurs.-Mon. June-Aug.; $20) up to the top of the mountain, then wander down any of several wide, well-marked trails, all with stunning views.

BIKING
Outfitters
Rift Cycles
1029 Paseo del Pueblo Norte; 575/694-2096;
11am-5pm Tues.-Thurs., 10am-6pm Fri.-Sat.
In El Prado, Rift Cycles rents full suspension mountain bicycles for $120 per day and provides a full range of services. If you're bringing your bicycle with you, consider having it shipped here. The shop will reassemble it and have it waiting when you arrive.

Cottam's Ski & Outdoors
207-A Paseo del Pueblo Sur; 575/758-2822;
7:30am-7pm Mon.-Fri., 7:30am-8pm Sat.-Sun.; $85/day
Though better known as Taos' go-to ski shop, Cottam's Ski & Outdoors boasts a large selection of bike rentals, including full-suspension bikes and e-bikes, and sells a wide range of bike gear, too.

Mountain Biking
Taos has several great trails for mountain biking. A popular ride close to town is **West Rim Trail** along the Rio Grande Gorge, either from the gorge bridge up to John Dunn Bridge, about 15 miles round-trip, or from the gorge bridge south to the Taos Junction Bridge near Pilar, about 18 miles out and back. Either way, you'll have great views and fairly level but rugged terrain.

For some serious downhill action, **Taos Ski Valley** offers mountain biking in summer and early fall; the **Northside** (daily, late June-Oct.) trail network contains about 18 miles of exhilarating trails mostly suited for intermediate to advanced riders. The **Alpine Wildflower Loop** (10.3 miles) offers the best introduction and some of the most dramatic scenery in the area. The 3.6-mile **Berminator** route, which sets off from the top of the Taos Ski Valley, is a wildly bouncy and heart-pounding descent from 12,500 feet. Fill out the required permit at the trailhead before starting your ride.

Road Biking
For road touring, the pleasant 25-mile loop from **Taos through Arroyo Hondo and Arroyo Seco,** with no steep grades, is a good way to get adjusted to the altitude. Head north up Paseo del Pueblo Norte, straight through the intersection at Highway 150, then, in Arroyo Hondo, turn right onto County Road B-143. Cross Highway 230, and you arrive in

Arroyo Seco, behind The Snowmansion. Turn right on Highway 150 to loop back to Taos.

For a longer road challenge, take on the 84-mile **Enchanted Circle**—even better if you do so with more than 1,000 fellow riders. Usually held in August or September, the **Enchanted Circle Century Tour** (575/754-3104; www.redriver.org), the four-decade-old ride kicks off in Red River and is marked by grueling climbs and hairpin descents.

WATER SPORTS

★ Rafting the Rio Grande Gorge

The **Taos Box,** the 16-mile stretch of the Rio Grande between the John Dunn Bridge and Pilar, provides the most exhilarating rafting in New Mexico, with Class III and Class IV rapids with ominous names like Boat Reamer and Screaming Left-Hand Turn. The river mellows out south of the Taos Box, then leads into a shorter Class III section called the **Racecourse**—the most popular run, usually done as a half-day trip. Beyond this, in the Orilla Verde Recreation Area around Pilar, the water is wide and flat, a place for a relaxing float with kids; you can flop in an inner tube if you really want to chill. North of the John Dunn Bridge and accessed only by hiking 1.25 miles down the La Junta trail in the Wild Rivers Recreation Area, is another highly rated run called **La Junta.** It's usually done as a half-day outing and offers some of the best opportunities to see bighorn sheep.

The best month to be on the river is late May-late June, when the water is high from mountain runoff; if the snowmelt is particularly extensive, that period typically extends by a few weeks.

Los Rios River Runners

575/776-8854; www.losriosriverrunners.com
The experienced Los Rios River Runners lead a number of rafting trips to the most popular sections of the Rio Grande and Rio Chama as half-day outings ($65), day trips (from $105), and overnight trips (from $348). They also have offer rafting trips paired with climbing, biking, and horseback riding.

Far Flung Adventures

575/758-2628; www.farflung.com
As well as half-day rafting ($59) and stand-up paddleboarding ($70) outings on the Rio Grande, Far Flung Adventures can also offer

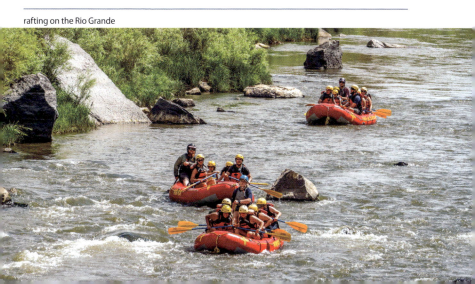

rafting on the Rio Grande

river trips that add rock climbing ($150) and horseback riding ($165) to their outings. Multi-day trips are also an option, including one to a little-visited spot on the Upper Pecos River (from $325).

New Mexico River Adventures

800/983-7756; www.newmexicoriveradventures.com
New Mexico River Adventures offers stand-up paddleboarding half-day ($90) and multi-day trips (from $525) on the tamer sections of the Rio Grande and the Rio Chama. As these outings can be tailored based on skill level, they are suited for those new to the sport as well as those with more experience. All gear is included.

ROCK CLIMBING

From popular rock-climbing spots such as the basalt **Dead Cholla Wall** in the Rio Grande Gorge to the more traditional routes 35 minutes west of Taos at **Tres Piedras,** the area around Taos is a climber's dream. One of the most impressive pitches is at **Questa Dome,** 29 miles north of Taos on Highway 378, where the flawless granite on the Questa Direct route is graded 5.10 and 5.11. And climbers are not limited to the summer, as winter sees some terrific ice climbs at higher elevations.

For climbing lessons for all skill levels and guided climbs (from $230 for a half day), contact **Mountain Skills** (575/776-2222; www.climbtaos.com) in Arroyo Seco.

Taos Mountain Outfitters

*113 N. Plaza; 575/758-9292; www.
taosmountainoutfitters.com; 9am-6pm Mon.-Wed.,
9am-8pm Thurs.-Fri., 9am-8pm Sat., 10am-6pm Sun.*
Taos Mountain Outfitters can provide maps, ropes, and more details.

SKIING, SNOWBOARDING & SNOWSHOEING
Taos Ski Valley

*866/968-7386; www.skitaos.com; $155 full-day lift
ticket*
Taos Ski Valley is a mecca for downhill skiing and snowboarding, with an enticing mix of demanding and accessible runs coupled with spectacular mountain scenery and first-class facilities. The resort is open late November-first weekend in April, with over 110 trails served by 15 lifts, and snowmaking capacity on all beginner and intermediate areas in dry spells. Having opened a lift to just shy of the 12,481-foot Kachina Peak—making it some of the highest lift-served terrain in North America—much of the focus is currently on improving and expanding the beginner area. Devotees of hike-to terrain still have areas dedicated to them, including a 35-acre tree-skiing area. The highly regarded **Ernie Blake Snowsports School** (866/968-7386) is one of the best places to learn the basics or polish your skills. Group (from $75) and private lessons (full day $175) are available; rates are cheaper in the afternoon for the latter.

Enchanted Forest

*575/754-6112; www.enchantedforestxc.com;
$24 full-day pass*
For cross-country skiing and snowshoeing, Enchanted Forest, between Elizabethtown and Red River on the Enchanted Circle loop, offers 20 miles of groomed trails.

Carson National Forest

www.fs.usda.gov/carson
There are several easy cross-country skiing and snowshoeing access points in the Carson National Forest. Two of the best options are Capulin Trail 494 in Capulin Canyon five miles east of Taos on Forest Road 10 just off U.S. 64. The 5-mile loop trail follows an old logging road through a pretty forest and sees less use than you would expect.

In Hondo Canyon on Highway 150, four miles before the ski valley, Manzanita Canyon Trail 58 is a more taxing 4.2-mile trail along a canyon bottom before climbing over 3,000 feet in elevation.

Outfitters
Cottam's Ski & Outdoors

*207-A Paseo del Pueblo Sur; 575/758-2822;
7:30am-7pm Mon.-Fri., 7:30am-8pm Sat.-Sun.*

The family-run Cottam's Ski & Outdoors has the area's biggest stock of rental skis, snowboards, and snowshoes. The shop also sells everything else you'll need to get out and enjoy the snow; there's another location at the ski valley (101 Sutton Pl.; 575/776-8719) and one at the Angel Fire ski resort (575/377-3700).

HOT SPRINGS

Two spots along the Rio Grande have natural pools of warm water, by-products of the seismic upsets that formed the gorge. They're free and popular with locals, and clothing is optional. Don't crowd in if several people are already in the spring, and never leave trash behind.

Blackrock Springs

The easier location to reach is Blackrock Springs, accessible by a 0.25-mile hike. From the intersection with U.S. 64, head north on Highway 522 about six miles to where the road dips; immediately after the bridge, turn left on County Road B-005, which runs along the north side of the small Rio Hondo and past the New Buffalo commune. The road crosses the water, then climbs a hill and descends again, toward the Rio Grande. Cross the old John Dunn Bridge to reach the west side, then turn left and park at the first switchback. Hike down the rocks and downstream to the two pools.

Manby Springs

Also called Stagecoach Springs, Manby Springs are at the edge of the river where the stage road used to meet a bridge and cross to the west side of the gorge. The hike down is on the old road, now quite rocky, and takes about 20 minutes. (In the late afternoon, keep an eye out for bighorn sheep near the trail.) To find the parking area, take U.S. 64 four miles west, just past the airport, and turn right on Tune Drive; follow this to the end, approximately another four miles. The old road is off the southwest side of the parking area.

FISHING AND HUNTING
Fishing

Taos's mountain streams and lakes teem with fish. The feisty cutthroat trout is indigenous to Valle Vidal, north of Questa, or you can hook plenty of browns in the wild waters of the Rio Grande. Eagle Nest Lake and Cabresto Lake (northeast of Questa) are both stocked every year.

Cutthroat Fly Fishing

575/776-5703; www.cutthroatflyfishing.com
If you'd like a guide to show you where to cast, Cutthroat Fly Fishing can bring you to the best spots around Taos and farther afield (half-day trips from $225).

The Solitary Angler

866/502-1700; www.thesolitaryangler.com
The Solitary Angler is another knowledgeable operator (half-day trips from $325) who specializes in spots throughout much of northern New Mexico not likely to filled by others.

Taos Fly Shop

338 Paseo del Pueblo Sur; 575/751-1312;
https://taosflyshop.com
Stop at the tidy Taos Fly Shop for tackle and info on flows and other conditions. They also offer guided trips (half-day from $325), including one for three days into the Rio Grande Box in the fall (from $2,500).

Hunting

Elk are the primary target in hunters' rifle scopes, but you can also bag mule deer, bear, and antelope.

New Mexico Department of Game and Fish

505/476-8000; www.wildlife.state.nm.us
Reach out to the New Mexico Department of Game and Fish for details on seasons, permits, and licenses.

Entertainment

Taos is a small town: no glitzy dance clubs, no bars where you're expected to dress up. Nighttime fun is concentrated in places where, even after just a couple of visits, you'll get to know the regulars. The various town-wide celebrations—including music and dancing on the plaza on summer Thursdays—draw a good cross section of the population.

NIGHTLIFE
Bars and Clubs
Adobe Bar

125 Paseo del Pueblo Norte; 575/758-1977; 4pm-9pm Thurs.-Mon.

Starting around 4pm, the Adobe Bar, in the lobby of the Taos Inn (look for the neon thunderbird sign), is where you'll run into everyone you've seen over the course of the day, sipping a Cowboy Buddha ($13)—Herradura silver tequila, Cointreau, and lime—or some other expertly made specialty margarita. Mellow jazz or acoustic guitar sets the mood from 7pm. To give hotel residents a break, the bar closes at 9pm.

The Lounge by Rolling Still

110 Paseo del Pueblo Norte; 575/613-0326; 4pm-9:30pm Tues.-Thurs., 4pm-10:30pm Fri., 3pm-10:30pm Sat.

Occupying an old adobe, The Lounge is a relaxed, understated spot with outside seating and a strong selection of cocktails, many of which feature the Rolling Still distillery's vodkas. Options include a red or green chile vodka with lime and ginger beer as well as more traditional margaritas and whiskey drinks.

The Alley Cantina

121 Teresina Ln.; 575/758-2121; 11:30am-midnight Mon. and Thurs.-Sun., kitchen open until 9pm; cover $5-10

For many locals, the default late-night spot is The Alley Cantina. This warren of interconnected rooms (one of which is supposedly the oldest in Taos … but don't they all say that?) can be potentially baffling after a few drinks. There's shuffleboard for entertainment if you're not into the ensemble onstage, whose name usually ends in "Blues Band."

Wine and Cocktail Lounges
The Treehouse Bar

123 Bent St.; 575/758-1009; 4:30pm-9pm daily; $10

The Treehouse Bar, located on the upper floor of Lambert's and softly lit, is Taos's most sophisticated late-night option, with a full bar and no shortage of creative cocktails. It also has a happy hour.

Parcht

103 E. Plaza; 575/758-1994; 3pm-8:30pm Thurs.-Sat.

On the plaza, the wine shop Parcht pops the cork on a dozen bottles a night, offering glasses and tastings along with perfectly paired small plates, such as pear slices with bleu cheese and honey. It's popular with both the après-work and après-ski sets.

Live Music
Taos Mesa Brewing

20 ABC Mesa Rd.; 575/758-1900; www.taosmesabrewing.com; noon-10pm daily May-Sept.; cover from $5, food from $10

If your style is cramped by old adobes, check out Taos Mesa Brewing, on U.S. 64 opposite the airport, where there's plenty of room to groove. The metal Mothership looms like a far-flung Burning Man theme camp, and the entertainment roster is suitably eclectic, with everyone from grizzled blues masters to major global artists performing outside. The crowd is all of Taos's younger hippies, plus hops aficionados of all stripes. The menu features tacos and a couple of filling house-made veggie burgers, and naturally showcases their own brews, including several IPAs and a potent Scottish ale.

The brewery's in town **tap room** (201 Paseo del Pueblo Sur; 575/758-1900; 11am-9pm Mon.-Tues. and Thurs.-Sun.), which also hosts bands and fuels the crowd with pizza, is a good option in offseason.

Old Martina's Hall

4140 Hwy. 68; 575/758-3003;
www.oldmartinashall.com

Check the schedule at Old Martina's Hall for special events in this recently renovated old adobe theater. It may not get as wild as back in the days when Dennis Hopper owned the joint, but the wooden dance floor is a treat.

Sagebrush Cantina

1508 Paseo del Pueblo Sur; 575/758-2254;
www.sagebrushinn.com; 4pm-close daily

The Sagebrush Cantina, inside the Sagebrush Inn, hosts live music nightly in a historic and handsome space with wood paneling, leather seats, and wall art featuring Taos luminaries. There's a good selection of drinks to choose from while you take in the show.

THE ARTS

Taos Center for the Arts

133 Paseo del Pueblo Norte; 575/758-2052;
www.tcataos.org

Given the high concentration of artists of all stripes, it's no surprise that Taos's theater scene is so rich for such a small town. Check at the Taos Center for the Arts to find out what shows may be on; the group also organizes chamber music performances and film screenings at the adjacent **Taos Community Auditorium** (145 Paseo del Pueblo Norte; 575/758-4677).

SMU in Taos

6580 Hwy. 518; 575/758-8322; www.smu.edu/taos

SMU in Taos organizes a summer lecture series at its Fort Burgwin campus about seven miles east of Ranchos de Taos. The Tuesday night gatherings (from 7pm; free), late May-mid-August, bring noted historians, anthropologists, authors, and others with an interest in the Southwest.

The Storyteller

110 Old Talpa Canyon Rd.; 575/751-4245;
www.storyteller7.com

The Storyteller shows first-run films on seven screens, with an occasional arty option.

Wildflower Playhouse

1339 Paseo del Pueblo Sur;
https://wildflowerplayhouse.org

An 80-seat community theater just north of Rancho de Taos, the Wildflower Playhouse hosts plays, film screenings, and local and regional musical acts.

FESTIVALS AND EVENTS

Taos Shortz Film Fest

www.taosshortz.com; Mar.

The end of winter sees the town hosting the Sundance of short film gatherings, the Taos Shortz Film Fest, which screens 150 films from around the globe over one weekend in March.

Monolith on the Mesa

Taos Mesa Brewing;
www.monoliththemesa.com; mid-May

Late spring marks the unofficial start of Taos's festival season. The nascent Monolith on the Mesa, held on three stages, sees some of the best regional psych and space rockers—and a few national ones, too—descending on Taos; of course, there's plenty of locally crafted beer to be had as well.

Taos Opera Institute

Various locations; www.taosoi.org; June

Throughout June, the Taos Opera Institute hosts a series of mostly free weekend concerts across town and in the ski valley performed by students from across the country studying at the institute. The variety of venues—ranging from private homes to ones framed by the Sangre de Cristos—and the enthusiasm of the

Ceremonial Dances at Taos Pueblo

In addition to the Feast of San Geronimo, ceremonial dances are open to visitors. This is only an approximate schedule—dates can vary from year to year, as can the particular dances. Contact the **pueblo** (505/758-1028; www.taospueblo.com) for times, or check the listings in the Tempo section of *The Taos News* for that week.

Every night May-October, there are demonstration dances at the **Kachina Lodge** (413 Paseo del Pueblo Norte)—a little touristy, but nice if your trip doesn't coincide with a dance at the pueblo itself.

- **January 1:** Turtle dance
- **January 6:** Deer or buffalo dance
- **Easter:** Various dances
- **May 3:** Feast of Santa Cruz, corn dance
- **June 13:** Feast of San Antonio, various dances
- **June 24:** Feast of San Juan, corn dance
- **July 25-26:** Feast of Santiago and Santa Ana, corn dances and footraces
- **September 29-30:** Feast of San Geronimo
- **December 24:** Sundown procession and bonfire
- **December 25:** Various dances

artists can make these shows feel like a special treat.

Taos Pueblo Powwow

West of the center of Taos Pueblo and northeast of El Prado at the end of Ben Romero Rd.; second week of July; from $15

The Taos Pueblo Powwow is a major get-together of Pueblo Indians and tribal members from around the country. Try to be there for the Grand Entry, the massive opening procession.

Fiestas de Taos

www.fiestasdetaos.com; third weekend of July

The town turns out for the Fiestas de Taos, a three-day celebration of Santiago de Compostela and Santa Ana. Highlights include a parade, food and crafts booths in Kit Carson Park, and the crowning of the Fiestas Queen.

Taos Fall Arts Festival

Various galleries; www.taosfallarts.com; Sept. and Oct.

Taos galleries put out their finest at the Taos Fall Arts Festival, a 10-day-long exhibition that shows the works of more than 150 Taos County artists.

Feast of San Geronimo

Taos Pueblo; www.taospueblo.org; Sept. 29-30

Taos's biggest annual festivity (for which many local businesses close) is the Feast of San Geronimo, the patron saint assigned to Taos Pueblo by the Spanish when they built their first mission there in 1619. The holiday starts the evening of September 29 with vespers in the pueblo church and continues the next day with footraces and a pole-climbing ritual. Hacienda de los Martinez usually reenacts a 19th-century Taos trade fair, with mountain men, music, and artisans' demonstrations.

Taos Wool Festival
Revolt Gallery; www.taoswoolfestival.org; first weekend of Oct.

The Taos Wool Festival has drawn textile artists as well as breeders since 1983. Admire the traditional Churro sheep or an Angora goat and then pick up a fleece or scarf made from its wool.

Tree-Lighting Ceremony
Town plaza; first weekend of Dec.

In winter, the glow of luminarias and torchlight on snow produces a magical effect. On the first weekend in December, the tree-lighting ceremony on the plaza draws the whole town, and the rest of the season sees numerous celebrations, such as the reenactments of the Virgin's search for shelter, called **Las Posadas,** which take place at Our Lady of Guadalupe Church west of the plaza on the third weekend in December. At the pueblo, vespers is sung at San Geronimo Church on Christmas Eve, typically followed by a children's dance. On Christmas Day, the pueblo hosts either a deer dance or the Spanish Matachines dance.

Shopping

ARTS AND CRAFTS
Magpie
218 Paseo del Pueblo Norte; 781/248-0166; 11am-5pm Tues.-Sat.

Magpie promises "wonderful things for your nest." The owner, a Taos native returned from living on the East Coast, has selected a colorful array of handcrafted furniture, pottery, handmade jewelry, and more, nearly all produced by Taos residents.

Taos Drums
3956 Hwy. 68; 800/424-3786;
9am-5pm Mon.-Fri., 10am-5pm Sat.,
11am-5pm Sun.

Taos Drums is a giant shop and factory dedicated to making Taos Pueblo-style percussion instruments, from thin hand drums to great booming ones, out of hollow logs. Trying out the wares is encouraged. The shop is located on the west side of the highway five miles south of the plaza.

Taos Ceramics Center
114 Este Es Rd.; 575/758-2580; noon-5pm Wed.,
10am-5pm Thurs.-Sat., noon-4pm Sun.

Taos Ceramics Center is a homegrown affair. Local artists turn the ceramics at the on-site studio; classes are available, too (series from $325). There's also a gallery that showcases pieces by local and regional artists.

GIFT AND HOME
Seconds Eco Store
120 Bent St.; 575/751-4500; 10am-6pm daily May-Oct.,
10am-5pm daily Nov.-Apr.

Tap into Taos's environmental ethic at Seconds Eco Store, with nifty upcycled and green goods, such as earrings made of skis and circuit boards turned into key chains.

CFT Décor and Gifts
303 Paseo del Pueblo Norte; 575/613-3486; 11am-3pm
Thurs., 10:30am-4:30pm Fri.-Sat., 11am-3pm Sun.

CFT Décor and Gifts is packed with a wide-ranging selection of colorful home goods and tchotchkes, from lamps and candles to brightly painted cabinets and tables.

Arroyo Seco Mercantile
488 Hwy. 150; 575/776-8806; 10am-5:30pm Mon.-Sat.,
11am-5pm Sun.

Up Highway 150, Arroyo Seco Mercantile is the town's former general store, now a highly evolved junk shop that has maintained the beautiful old wood-and-glass display cases. Its stock ranges from the practical (books on passive-solar engineering and raising llamas) to the beautiful, like antique wool blankets.

BOOKS
Op.cit.
124-A Bent St., No. 6 Dunn House; 575/751-1999;
10am-5pm daily
Op.cit. stocks new and used books, local titles, and maps, and hosts author readings.

TOYS
Twirl
225 Camino de la Placita; 575/751-1402; www.twirltaos.
org; 10am-6pm Tues.-Sat., noon-5pm Sun.

Food

Taos is also home to an exceptionally magical toy store, the nonprofit Twirl. Tucked in a series of low-ceilinged adobe rooms, it's crammed with everything from science experiments to wooden trains to fairy costumes. Even the kiva fireplace gets a fantastical 1,001 Nights treatment, and it has the best playground in town out back—it even includes a handcrafted hobbit house.

Taos has no shortage of restaurants that can deliver memorable meals—even in the ski valley. At one of the New Mexican places, try some posole—it's more common here than in Albuquerque or Santa Fe, often substituted for rice as a side dish alongside pinto beans. Also—especially given the hiking and skiing opportunities nearby—don't overlook the breakfast burrito. This unfussy combo of scrambled eggs, green chile, hash browns, and bacon or sausage in a flour tortilla commonly wrapped in foil makes for the perfect meal on the go.

Most restaurants close relatively early, and many smaller places don't take plastic—so load up on cash and get seated by 8pm. You'll need reservations for the more upscale restaurants on the weekends, but the whole scene is relatively casual.

DOWNTOWN TAOS
Mexican
La Cueva
135 Paseo del Pueblo Sur; 575/758-7001;
10am-8pm Mon.-Fri., 10am-5pm Sun.; $7-14
Tiny La Cueva looks like a New Mexican restaurant at first glance, as it has all the usual green-chile-smothered dishes. But its owners are from south of the border and round out the menu with fantastically fresh and homemade-tasting dishes such as chicken mole enchiladas and a heaping steak and relleno, as well as exceptionally savory beans. Breakfasts are especially inexpensive. Beer and wine are also served.

Fine Dining
Byzantium
112 Camino de la Placita; 575/751-0805;
noon-4pm Mon.-Tues. and Sat.-Sun.; $19-39
Sitting down for lunch at Byzantium feels not unlike stumbling upon the environs of a secret gastronomic society, with its dim lighting and low vigas-beam ceilings. The menu is lean and changes often, with a focus on rice bowls and sandwiches. It's a small space; reservations are recommended.

Lambert's
123 Bent St.; 575/758-1009; 5pm-9pm daily; $23-38
Set inside a cozy adobe house, Lambert's is a Taos favorite, long a popular choice for celebrations and special occasions. Its menu is a bit staid, but everything is executed perfectly. The filet mignon in a peppercorn demi glace is fantastic; less obvious, but equally gratifying, is the zucchini pasta with arugula pesto and oyster mushrooms. Brunch is also served on Sundays in summer and worth it for the shrimp and cheddar grits alone. A full liquor license means good classic cocktails, which you can also enjoy upstairs at **The Treehouse Lounge.**

Cafés

World Cup

102 Paseo del Pueblo Norte; 575/737-5299;
7am-6pm daily; $3

The location of World Cup on the corner of the plaza makes it a popular pit stop for both tourists and locals—the latter typically of the drumming variety, lounging on the stoop. Espressos and matcha drinks are the specialties, along with tasty baked goods.

CENTRAL TAOS

Mexican

★ Antonio's

1379 Paseo del Pueblo Sur; 575/758-2599; 11am-8pm
Mon.-Fri. and Sun., 11am-5pm Sat.; $10-22

Antonio's is a goldmine of authentic and unfussy Mexican cuisine and New Mexican heavy hitters. Though a number of the dishes will be familiar—chicken tacos, beef burritos and the like—their execution elevates them well above you might have come to expect. Standouts include a crispy cheese relleno and veggie tamale, a chicken mango enchilada, and the pork carnitas street taco.

Fresh and Local

★ The Love Apple

803 Paseo del Pueblo Norte; 575/751-0050;
5pm-close Wed.-Sun.; $9-18

The Love Apple wears its local, organic credentials on its sleeve, and the food delivers in simple but powerful flavor combinations for less than you'd expect. The menu is seasonal, with dishes such as a grilled trout topped with chipotle créme, and beef wagyu tenderloin with mesquite red chile gratin. There's an extensive wine list, too. Set inside a thick-walled adobe chapel dating back to the early 19th century, the place oozes atmosphere, with candles glimmering softly against whitewashed walls. It's one place in town where reservations should be considered essential, and in an old-school move, it accepts cash only.

Burgers

★ The Burger Stand

401 Paseo del Pueblo Norte; 575/758-5522;
11am-11pm daily; $9

The Burger Stand is an outpost of a Kansas restaurant—but it fits right in in Taos, in large part because it makes not one but three killer veggie burgers. We recommend the lentil one topped with feta cheese, pickled green beans, and toasted almonds. The beef and lamb burgers are great, too, and decked out in similarly creative ways. The same can be said for the fries, which come in a whopping seven varieties; try a basket tossed in white truffle oil. It doesn't hurt that the restaurant's set inside the lively **Taos Ale House,** where there's a strong beer selection.

Italian

Taos Pizza Out Back

712 Paseo del Pueblo Norte; 575/758-3112;
11am-9pm daily; $8-23

Taos Pizza Out Back serves up the best pie in town, using mostly local and organic ingredients. Sure, you can design your own pizza, but there's little need to with specialty options such as marinated chicken, peppers, onions, and garlic with a honey chipotle chile sauce and smoked mozzarella or basil pesto, green chile, smoked mozzarella, feta, roasted garlic, and fresh tomatoes.

Breakfast and Lunch

Michael's Kitchen

304-C Paseo del Pueblo Norte; 575/758-4178;
7am-2pm Wed.-Sun.; $8

A down-home, wood-paneled family restaurant, Michael's Kitchen is filled with chatter, the clatter of dishes, and the sense that your fellow patrons have been here many times before. It's famous for New Mexican breakfast items like huevos rancheros and blue-corn pancakes with pine nuts, served all day, but there's quite a bit more on the extensive menu. "Health Food," for instance, is a double order of chile-cheese fries and there are blintzes, deli sandwiches, and a handful of steak dishes, too.

TAOS
FOOD

The front room is devoted to gooey doughnuts, Frisbee-sized cinnamon rolls, and pie.

★ Gutiz

812-B Paseo del Pueblo Norte; 575/758-1226;
http://gutiztaos.com; 8am-2pm Wed.-Sun.; $8-19

The menu at Gutiz, occupying a welcoming and unassuming adobe, borrows from France and Spain and adds a dash of green chile. Start your day with a chocolate croissant or an impressive tower of scrambled eggs and spinach. Lunch sees traditional croques monsieurs, grilled chicken with hummus sandwiches, and paella that doesn't skimp on the scallops, shrimp, clams, and mussels.

Markets
Cid's Grocery

623 Paseo del Pueblo Norte; 575/758-1148;
8am-8pm Mon.-Sat.

If you're planning a picnic or a meal in, stop at Cid's Grocery for great takeout food, as well as freshly baked bread and a whole range of organic and local goodies, from New Mexican wines to fresh elk steaks. **Cid's Mountain Market** (200 Thunderbird Rd., Unit 102; 575/776-2303; 7:30am-6pm daily) is the newer, smaller location in the ski valley village.

Taos Farmers Market

105 Albright St.; www.taosfarmersmarket.org;
8am-12:30pm Sat.

The excellent Taos Farmers Market takes place at the Taos County Courthouse parking lot mid-May-late October. As well as fresh produce and meats, vendors sell prepared food and locally made products such as lavender, honey, jams, and spices.

EL PRADO
Elevation Coffee

1110 Paseo del Pueblo Norte; 575/758-3068;
6:30am-2pm daily; $3

Elevation Coffee boasts the best coffee in town without a whiff of snobbery—in fact, its knowledgeable baristas are some of the friendliest around. The fancifully designed mochas are as tasty as they look, while the pour-overs are consistently on the mark. Grab a seat with your drink and admire the art; there's a small patio, too. This spot is cash only.

★ Orlando's

1114 Don Juan Valdez Ln.; 575/751-1450;
10:30am-3pm and 5pm-9pm daily; $7-14

A small, festively painted place on the north side of town, the family-run Orlando's is invariably the first restaurant named when the question of the best chile comes up. It enlivens all of the New Mexican classics, such as tamales, tostados, and chiles rellenos, most of which are satisfying and freshly made. A standout is the green-chile chicken enchiladas, and the pozole is quite good, too—perfectly firm, earthy, and flecked with oregano. The restaurant is always busy, but a fire pit outdoors makes the wait more pleasant on cold nights.

Farmhouse Café

1405 Paseo del Pueblo Norte; 575/758-5683;
www.farmhousetaos.com; 9am-3pm daily; $7-17

Set in bucolic gardens with a view of Taos Mountain, Farmhouse Café is a beautiful spot to revive over a hearty salad, veggie shepherd's pie, or a bison burger. There are several gluten-free options, too, including a shepherd's pie and a chocolate-peanut-butter crispy-rice bar. Service can be a little spotty, but the meals are worth the wait.

RANCHOS DE TAOS
Ranchos Plaza Grill

6 St. Francis Plaza; 575/758-5788; 8am-2pm Wed.-Sun.; $11

Just off the plaza near the church, Ranchos Plaza Grill is a casual breakfast and lunch spot, known for its red-chile caribe, made from crushed, rather than ground, chiles. New Mexican dishes fill the menu, and the sopaipillas are gargantuan.

TAOS
FOOD

1: Op.cit. bookstore **2:** Orlando's iconic sign **3:** Elevation Coffee **4:** The Love Apple

Old Martina's Hall

4140 Hwy. 68; 575/758-3003;
www.oldmartinashall.com; 11am-2pm and 5pm-9pm
Wed.-Sat., 11am-2pm Sun.; $12-15

Across the road from the turn to St Francis de Asis, Old Martina's Hall, a once-derelict adobe theater with a soaring ceiling that has been lovingly redone, is a wonderfully welcoming place with a menu of sophisticated regional standbys, such as grilled pork tenderloin carnitas, as well as a few surprises. There is green chile, but it's dialed down and accentuates rather than overtakes. It's more casual for lunch ($10 for sandwiches).

TAOS PUEBLO
Tiwa Kitchen

328 Veterans Hwy.; 575/751-1020; 11am-4pm Fri.-Mon.;
$9-17

On the road to the center of Taos Pueblo, Tiwa Kitchen is a friendly, family-run place that specializes in Pueblo food, much of which is laced with chile. The hearty lunch options include stuffed blue corn fry bread and a red chile beef and vegetable stew. For dessert there are homemade baked goods to choose from, including a decadent chocolate squash cake.

HIGHWAY 150
Abe's Cantina y Cocina

489 Hwy. 150; 575/776-8643; 7am-3pm daily; $4

A creaky, old, all-purpose general store/diner/saloon, Abe's Cantina y Cocina has earned fans from all over for serving a breakfast burrito that is both cheap and immensely satisfying. There's a full menu of tacos and green-chile cheeseburgers—pair them with the satisfying chili cheese fries—an impressive beer list featuring several top-notch regional ales, and a nice shaded back patio. Don't miss the sweet, flaky empanadas next to the cash register in the store.

Taos Cow

485 Hwy. 150; 575/776-5640; 7:30am-5:30pm daily;
$3-9.50

For coffee and ice cream head next door to Taos Cow, a chilled-out coffee bar par excellence, with writers scribbling in one corner and flute players jamming in another. But it's the ice cream that has made the

the Bavarian Lodge

Taos Cow name (you'll see it distributed all around town, and elsewhere in New Mexico and Colorado). The most popular flavors are tailored to local tastes: Café Olé blends cinnamon and Mexican chocolate chunks in its coffee ice cream, while Cherry Ristra is cherry with piñon nuts and dark chocolate. There are plenty of breakfast options, too, including a bagel sandwich with lox, cream cheese, and capers.

★ Medley
100 Hwy. 150; 575/776-8787; 4pm-9pm Tues.-Sat.; $17-38

The husband-and-wife chef team at the restaurant, bar, and wine shop Medley have cooked all over the world. Their menu mixes eclectic global flavors (chili, curry, aioli, saffron) with New American staples such as roasted red peppers and squash. The food is great, if not flawless—even the bread plate is worthy of a lengthy post-dinner recap—and the atmosphere is casual.

TAOS SKI VALLEY
Rhoda's Restaurant
116 Sutton Pl.; 575/776-2291; 11am-5pm Mon.-Sat.; $12

In the village center, welcoming Rhoda's Restaurant is a decent casual option. The menu has lunch staples such as fish tacos, burgers, and a nice selection of salads. The patio has great views, which are best enjoyed with a glass of the house margarita.

★ Bavarian Lodge
100 Kachina Rd.; 575/776-8020; 11:30am-9pm daily in ski season; $15

More adventurous drivers should head for Bavarian Lodge, way up Twining Road near the southeast edge of the ski area and Kachina Lift 4. You'll need four-wheel drive in winter; in summer, the expanded front deck is a lovely place to have a stein of ale (served by actual German speakers) in the pines, though note that it's typically open only around the weekend (11:30am-close Thurs.-Sun.). The menu is hearty Wiener schnitzel and spaetzle; the bread pudding with pretzel pieces is as dense as it sounds—and delicious, too.

Accommodations

Taos hotels can be overpriced, especially at the lower end, where there are few reliable bargains. But because Taos is awash in centuries-old houses, bed-and-breakfasts have thrived. For those skeptical of B&Bs, don't despair: The majority have private bathrooms, separate entrances, and not too much country-cute decor. Certainly, just as in Santa Fe, the Southwestern gewgaws can be applied with a heavy hand, but wood-burning fireplaces, well-stocked libraries, hot tubs, and big gardens make up for that.

For better deals, consider staying outside of Taos proper. Arroyo Seco is about a half-hour drive from the plaza, and rates here and in Ranchos de Taos can be a little lower. In the summer, the lodges in the ski valley cut prices by almost half—a great deal if you want to spend time hiking and don't mind driving into town on occasion.

DOWNTOWN TAOS
$150-200
Hotel La Fonda de Taos
108 S. Plaza; 575/758-2211; www.lafondataos.com; $179 d

Of the two landmark hotels in town, Hotel La Fonda de Taos has a few more modern perks, such as gas fireplaces in some rooms and mostly reliable Wi-Fi. As can be expected of an older hotel, rooms tend to be on the small side, and you're certainly paying a premium for its history. Its location can't be beat if you're looking for something central—plus, it can feel quite grand opening your balcony doors over the plaza (though you may also be subjected to predawn street-cleaning noise).

Historic Taos Inn

125 Paseo del Pueblo Norte; 575/758-2233;
www.taosinn.com; $195 d

The Historic Taos Inn, established in 1936 in the former home of the town doctor, like La Fonda, has long been intertwined with the town's past and present, though it is cozier and slightly overpriced. Rooms in the main building have more character and are cheaper (from $170 in high season); in the courtyard section or other outbuildings, you may get a kiva fireplace. All 44 rooms offer free Wi-Fi and access to the on-site fitness center and yoga studio.

CENTRAL TAOS
Under $100
Taos Valley Lodge

615 Paseo del Pueblo Norte; 575/737-0447;
www.taosvalleylodge.com; from $89 d

The Taos Valley Lodge is a solid budget-friendly option, with over 100 nicely appointed rooms and atypical extras for this price bracket, such as an indoor pool, free continental breakfast, and outdoor grills. Be sure to stop by the cheerful onsite **Espresso Bar** (575/751-1131; 7am-7pm Mon.-Sat., 7am-3pm Sun.) to get your coffee fix.

$100-150
Sagebrush Inn

1508 Paseo del Pueblo Sur; 575/758-2254;
www.sagebrushinn.com; $118

On the southern edge of town, the Sagebrush Inn has expanded significantly beyond its roots as a family-run hotel serving travelers heading west decades ago. Today, it's a sprawling compound that has largely been successful in preserving its history, with the newest rooms offering more comfort than the original ones, including some that open to a pretty courtyard. Rooms vary in size

and amenities; some have kiva fireplaces and there's even a loft with touches inspired by Georgia O'Keeffe.

Taos Lodging

109 Brooks St.; 575/751-1771;
www.taoslodging.com; $130 studio

Not a hotel at all, but a clutch of well-maintained one- and two-bedroom private casitas, Taos Lodging is in a quiet, convenient block about a 10-minute walk north from the plaza. Here, eight cottages (from $130), arranged around a central courtyard, have assorted floor plans, but all have porches, full kitchens, living rooms, and fireplaces as well as access to a shared outdoor hot tub. The smallest, a 350-square-foot studio, sleeps two comfortably; the largest sleep up to six. The same group manages two additional properties nearby, for those who want a larger condo.

Mabel Dodge Luhan House

240 Morada Ln.; 575/751-9686;
www.mabeldodgeluhan.com; $135 d

In addition to being a tourist attraction, the Mabel Dodge Luhan House also functions as a homey bed-and-breakfast. Even the least expensive rooms, in a 1970s outbuilding, feel authentically historic and cozy, with wood floors and antique furniture. In the main house, Mabel's original bedroom ($255) is the grandest (you can even sleep in her bed). The pick of the 21 rooms, though—if you don't mind waking at the crack of dawn—is the upstairs solarium ($175), which is gloriously sunny, with gorgeous views of the mountain. Either way, you'll feel a little like you're bunking in a museum (which means those who want modern amenities like air-conditioning should look elsewhere). Breakfast is a cut above standard B&B fare.

Hotel Don Fernando

1005 Paseo del Pueblo Sur; 575/751-4444;
www.hoteldonfernando.com; $137 d

Of the various motels on the south side, none

is excellent—and most are not memorable in a good way, for that matter—but Hotel Don Fernando is a cut above. The hotel has more than 120 rooms spread throughout six buildings. Rooms are generally bright and cheerful, though not all have benefitted equally from a 2018 renovation. There's a medium-sized pool and fitness center.

$150-200
El Pueblo Lodge
412 Paseo del Pueblo Norte; 575/758-8700;
www.elpueblolodge.com; $159 d

Walking distance from the plaza, El Pueblo Lodge is a budget operation with nice perks such as a full breakfast and free use of barbecue grills. The cheerful rooms vary from a snug nook in the oldest adobe section to new, slick motel rooms complete with gas fireplaces. Those in the 1960s motel strip are a good combo of atmosphere and amenities. The grounds are pleasant and shaded, with a hot tub and a heated pool in the summertime.

★ Inn on the Rio
910 E. Kit Carson Rd.; 575/758-7199;
www.innontherio.com; $159 d

Inn on the Rio might be more accurately called Motel on the Creek. But what a motel: Each of the 12 thick-walled rooms has been decorated with rich colors and retro Western details. The vintage wall heaters, still cranking from the old motor-court days, keep the rooms as toasty as a fireplace would. A hot tub and summer-only pool between the two wings, plus luxe sheets and locally made bath gels, are nice upgrades. Pair this with longtime resident owners, a great morning meal, and very reasonable rates, and you have all the benefits of a bed-and-breakfast without the feeling that you have to tiptoe in late at night.

Hacienda del Sol
109 Mabel Dodge Ln.; 575/758-0287;
www.taoshaciendadelsol.com; from $199 d

Everything at Hacienda del Sol is built in relation to Taos Mountain. With this view, even the smallest of the 11 rooms in the adobe complex feel expansive. The style is cozy without being too oppressively Southwestern. Once owned by Mabel Dodge Luhan, the house was where she often put up guests; perks like plush robes and kiva fireplaces make it feel homey; some rooms have skylights.

Dreamcatcher
416 La Lomita Rd.; 575/758-0613;
www.dreambb.com; from $199 d

The seven rooms at the central Dreamcatcher look out on to a pretty courtyard with hammocks. Three of the rooms are attached to the main house, while the four others are split between two cute casitas. All are thoughtfully designed and appointed and evoke the region; think warm earth tones, wood furniture, and Native American rugs and artwork; some have kivas as well.

$200-250
Casa Gallina
613 Callejon; 575/758-2306;
www.casagallina.net; from $250 d

Decorated with an artist's eye, the five bright and colorful guest cottages at Casa Gallina showcase beautiful handicrafts from Taos and around the globe. All are well appointed and cared for, and the kitchens can be stocked with occasional goodies from the garden and eggs from resident hens (they're also pressed into service for the fresh and delicious breakfasts). There's a two-night minimum stay.

Over $250
Palacio de Marquesa
405 Cordoba Rd.; 575/758-4777;
www.marquesataos.com; $349 d

Palacio de Marquesa is an exquisite eight-room inn, also run by Heritage Hotels and Resorts. The rooms have an air of what might be called pueblo minimalism: dark viga ceilings, with white walls, white leather chairs, and marble baths. What could come off as too austere is warmed up with pops of color, skylights, and kiva fireplaces. Rooms are

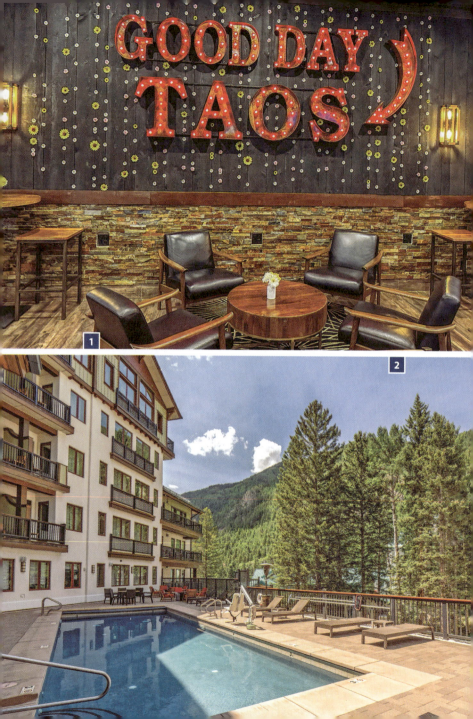

dedicated to Taos women of influence, such as Mabel Dodge Luhan and Agnes Martin. Spa services and the option of a made-to-order breakfast delivered to your room add to the cocoon-like feel.

El Monte Sagrado

317 Kit Carson Rd.; 575/758-3502; www.elmontesagrado.com; $359 d

A somewhat storied and star-crossed luxury hotel, El Monte Sagrado is owned by the excellent New Mexico company Heritage Hotels and Resorts, which enlivened the overall look and restored some of its eco-friendly infrastructure. The hotel has eclectic style in the Global Suites ($599 and up), but entry-level Taos Mountain rooms, while a little generic with their white linens and dark wood, are reasonably priced and have balconies. The grounds are immaculate, and there's a lovely spa.

RANCHOS DE TAOS
$100-150
★ **Adobe & Pines Inn**

4107 Hwy. 68; 575/751-0947; www.adobepines.com; $140 d

At the south edge of Ranchos de Taos, Adobe & Pines Inn is built around an 1830s hacienda, shaded by old trees and overlooking a lush garden. Of the eight rooms, six are quite large (from $240), with especially lavish bathrooms. But even the two smallest rooms ($140) have fireplaces—and everyone gets the exceptionally good breakfasts, with fresh eggs from the on-site chickens and veggies from the garden.

HIGHWAY 150
Under $100
The Snowmansion

Hwy. 150, Arroyo Seco; 575/776-8298; www.snowmansion.com; dorm beds $55, private rooms from $109

The best bargain option in the area is The Snowmansion. Conveniently set midway to the Taos Ski Valley in bustling "downtown" Arroyo Seco, this cheerful place offers comfy private rooms and bunks in basic dorm rooms ($55). Its roots as a hostel are evident, and a laidback charm pervades throughout.

TAOS SKI VALLEY
Over $250
★ **The Blake**

116 Sutton Pl.; 575/776-8298; www.skitaos.com; $300 d

The Blake is a clear signal of the Taos Ski Valley positioning itself squarely among the top ski resorts in the West. A model of sustainability and replete with thoughtful touches and features, the property at once pays homage to the ski valley's European roots and proudly displays the area's Native American and Southwestern influences. The 80 rooms vary in size from two queen beds or a king to lavish 1,400-square-foot suites. All are handsomely designed and include access to a hot tub, pool, spa services, and breakfast at the on-site 192 at The Blake restaurant. Hitting the slopes from here couldn't be any easier—there's a ski lift outside the doors and a full equipment shop on-site.

NORTH AND WEST OF TAOS
$150-200
Taos Goji Eco Lodge

Old State Rd. 3; 575/776-3971; www.taosgoji.com; $160 d

Nestle into a snug sheepherder's cabin at Taos Goji Eco Lodge, in the village of San Cristobal, 11 miles north of Taos. Blessedly devoid of Internet access and TVs, the 10 cozy and comfortable cabins, each over a century old, have wood stoves and kitchens, and the surrounding 40-acre farm is lively with sheep, goats, and chickens. If you'd like to get even closer to nature, there are also a couple of tipis ($119) equipped with queen beds and basic furnishings.

1: Espresso Bar at the Taos Valley Lodge **2:** The Blake

Earthship

U.S. 64; 575/751-0462; www.earthship.com; from $165 d

For an only-in-Taos experience, stay the night in an Earthship. Five of the curvy, off-the-grid homes are available, with room for up to six people in the largest one. Evoking a stay in a hobbit house with banana trees (in the south-facing greenhouse areas), you're out in the larger, all-Earthship subdivision, with great views of the mountain. And, yes, you'll have running water, a refrigerator, and all the other comforts. It's a bit of a drive from town (west of the Rio Grande), but it's well worth it. It's now also possible to stay in the Earthship that started it all ($140 d), a short drive east of the Taos Plaza.

Camping
Hotel Luna Mystica

25 ABC Mesa Rd.; 575/977-2424; www.hotellunamystica.com; hostel bunks $30, trailers from $120, campsites $10

Hotel Luna Mystica, conveniently located across the road from the Taos Mesa Brewing, offers cheerful accommodation in an assortment of vintage trailers from the 1950s and '60s—there's even one done up as a hostel. All are smartly appointed and comfortable, and the morning coffees from their decks can't be beat. There are also several dozen primitive campsites equipped with hammocks for some of the best stargazing around.

Taos Monte Bello RV Park

24819 U.S. 64; 575/751-0774; www.taosmontebellorvpark.com; from $43

Just over a 10-minute drive northwest of Taos Plaza, Taos Monte Bello RV Park has a variety of tidy RV sites with full hook-ups. The friendly host is a good source of area information, and there's an on-site laundromat, a walking path, and Wi-Fi throughout.

Information and Services

TOURIST INFORMATION
Taos Visitor Center

1201 Paseo del Pueblo Sur; 575/732-8267; www.taos.org; 9am-5pm daily

A few miles south of the plaza, the Taos Visitor Center is helpful, as long as you don't show up right before closing time. Stop here for flyers and maps galore, free coffee, and the thorough weekly news and events bulletin (also posted online), which includes gallery listings, concerts, festivals, and more. Artists from the Taos Pueblo Collective sell their works here.

SERVICES
Banks

US Bank (120 W. Plaza; 575/737-3540; 9am-5pm Mon.-Fri.), just off the southwest corner of the plaza, is the most convenient bank and ATM while on foot. The drive-through service at **Centinel Bank of Taos** (512 Paseo del Pueblo Sur; 575/758-6700; 9am-5pm Mon.-Fri.) is easily accessible from the main drag.

Post Offices

The Taos post office (710 Paseo del Pueblo Sur; 575/751-1801; 9am-1pm and 2pm-4:30pm Mon.-Fri.) is on the south side; there's another on the north side (318 Paseo del Pueblo Norte; 575/758-2081; 8:30am-5pm Mon.-Fri.).

Getting There and Around

CAR

From Santa Fe, the drive to Taos takes about 1.5 hours (70 miles) along the direct "low road" through the river valley (via Española, U.S. 84/285 to Hwy. 68). If taking the more circuitous "high road" (via Chimayó and Truchas, mostly on Hwy. 76), plan on at least two hours for the 80-mile drive.

From Albuquerque, add at least an hour's travel time for the 60-mile drive up I-25 (the most direct route) to Santa Fe.

Once in Taos, you will need a car to get to outlying sights but will also have to negotiate the frequent traffic jams on Paseo del Pueblo. There are paid parking lots close to the plaza, and a free one less than 0.25 mile down Kit Carson Road. Of the rental car options, **Enterprise** (1350 Paseo del Pueblo Sur; 575/758-5333; www.enterprise.com; 9am-3pm Mon.-Fri.) is the most convenient, a block south of the visitors center.

BUS AND SHUTTLE

For pickup at the Albuquerque airport, the **Taos Rides** (575/613-3256; www.taosrides. com; $125 one-way from town, $145 one-way from the ski valley) shuttle service is the best option. Allow at least 2.5 hours for travel time; advance reservations are required.

The **North Central Regional Transit District** (NCRTD; 866/206-0754; www. ncrtd.org) serves the Taos area. Its long-running **Taos Express** (Route #305; $10 round-trip) makes the trip between Taos and Santa Fe once in the morning and once in the afternoon. The one-way trip takes 1 hour and 50 minutes. In Taos, it stops at Our Lady of Guadalupe parking lot, one block west of the plaza; southbound, it also picks up passengers at the Sagebrush Inn (1508 Paseo del Pueblo Sur). In Santa Fe, the bus stops near the Rail Runner main depot (Montezuma at Guadalupe) and at the South Capitol station (Sunday). The schedule syncs with the Rail Runner's arrival in Santa Fe (and it can carry bicycles), making it a potentially seamless three-hour trip all the way from Albuquerque.

The NCRTD also runs the commuter weekday **Taos** (Route #300; free) that runs four times a day and will take you as far as Española, stopping in Dixon and Pilar along the way. Pick it up at the **Taos County Administration Building** (105 Albright St.). Within Taos, the NCRTD's **Chile Line bus** (Route #340) runs north-south from the Ranchos de Taos post office to the Taos Pueblo, approximately every 40 minutes 7:30am-5:30pm Monday-Friday. In town, it's free. Mid-December-April, the **TSV Green** (Route #341; free) runs to Taos Ski Valley, with five buses daily making stops at select hotels and motels en route to the mountain; not all buses stop at all hotels.

AIR
Taos Regional Airport
800-435-9579; www.jsx.com/taosair
For a select few gateways—Austin and Dallas in Texas and San Diego and Burbank in California—it's possible to fly in summer and winter into the Taos Regional Airport (TSM), 15 minutes northwest of the plaza on Hwy. 64, on Taos Air. From there a free Taos Air shuttle is available to the ski valley, while the NCRTD provides a free shuttle to several destinations throughout Taos.

For most everyone else, Santa Fe's airport is the next best option—though it's nearly a two-hour drive away. While flights into Albuquerque's airport are cheaper and offer a greater selection, the drive from Albuquerque takes about two hours and 45 minutes.

Outside Taos

The Road to Chama

U.S. 64 leads west out of Taos into an undulating landscape of thick patches of forest and open grassy plains interrupted sparingly by resolute ranching communities, most of which have long since passed their heyday. After winding through mountains, a dramatic descent brings you into the lush Chama Valley and the likeable town of Chama, a few miles from the border with Colorado.

TRES PIEDRAS

Named for nearby jutting granite rocks, the tiny community of Tres Piedras is a big draw for rock climbers who come here to test themselves on several difficult routes.

Chili Line Depot Café

38429 U.S. 285; 575/758-1701; 8am-7pm Mon.-Fri. and Sun., 8am-9pm Sat.; $7

This settlement about 30 miles west of Taos is not much more than a handful of houses scattered around the crossroads of U.S. 64 and U.S. 285 and the welcoming Chili Line Depot Café, just north of the intersection. With friendly staff, hearty burritos, green-chile cheeseburgers, and apple pies, it's well worth the detour. Call ahead to check hours; the restaurant may close early if business is slow. It also has a few cozy guest rooms (from $70) and a cabin ($110).

TIERRA AMARILLA AND LOS OJOS

U.S. 64 climbs up and over the Brazos Mountains—the view from the pass takes in the sheer limestone of 3,000-foot-high cliffs to the north. Descending into the golden valley along the Rio Chama, you soon reach the junction with U.S. 84 and the village of Tierra Amarilla, off the east side of the highway. Most of the buildings have long been vacant and the limited places it had in recent years to grab a bite to eat or a cup of coffee have now closed.

Just a few miles north of Tierra Amarilla and west of the highway, Los Ojos is a two-block-long main street of adobe and Victorian wood-frame buildings, most connected in some way with the now defunct Ganados del Valle, a cooperative established in 1983 to preserve the economy in the region, which, for hundreds of years, had been based on raising sheep and selling their products. But young people could no longer earn a living from this, and many of the most traditional weaving and spinning techniques had already been lost. The cooperative was gradually able to provide employment for dozens of artists, administrators, and sheepherders, and in 1990, one of its founders, Maria Varela, who got her start as a Chicana activist in the Student Nonviolent Coordinating Committee in the 1960s, earned a MacArthur "genius grant" for her efforts.

EL VADO LAKE AND HERON LAKE STATE PARKS

El Vado Lake State Park

575/588-7247; www.emnrd.nm.gov; $5/car day use

The two reservoirs west of Tierra Amarilla are nearly linked and are prime spots for trout and kokanee salmon fishing. El Vado Lake State Park is smaller but busier, as motorboats are permitted here, and it's a popular recreation spot, with large **campgrounds** (sites $10) at its south end (accessible via Hwy. 112, 17 miles southwest of Tierra Amarilla; the turnoff to the park is about 2 miles north of the village). A 5.5-mile one-way hiking trail leads from Shale Point, north of all the campgrounds, up along the Rio Chama, across a bridge, up past Heron Dam, and into the south end of Heron Lake State Park.

Heron Lake State Park

575/588-7470; www.emnrd.nm.gov; $5/car day use

Much more sedate, Heron Lake State Park is also accessible via U.S. 64/84 and Highway 95. Boats can only operate at no-wake speeds, which also makes it ideal for kayakers. During the week, free ranger-led hikes are available on request—ideally, call ahead to the visitors center to let the staff know you're coming. Scores of attractive **campsites** (from $8) line the park's southern and eastern shores.

Three miles north of Heron Lake and about 14 miles west of the U.S. 64/84 turnoff, sprawling **Stone House Lodge** (1409 Hwy. 95; 575/201-3232; www.stonehouselodge.com) has

a range of places to spend the night, including recently renovated barebones cabins (from $150), campsites ($35), and RV sites ($35).

Rafting

The stretch of the Chama River from El Vado Dam to Abiquiu Lake is one of the state's more scenic rafting runs and can be done as a leisurely multiday trip.

Kokopelli Rafting Adventures

1164 Parkway Dr., Unit A; 505/983-3734; www.kokopelliraft.com; 7-8 hours $124

Kokopelli Rafting Adventures in Santa Fe provides full day outings on the Chama River, and while there are rapids to contend with, they are decidedly on the mild side.

Los Rios River Runners

4003 Hwy. 68; 575/776-8854; www.losriosriverrunners. com; day trip $125, overnight $375, 3-day trip $530

Los Rios River Runners in Rancho de Taos runs day-trips and multiday trips through remote canyons of the Chama River.

CHAMA

A picturesque high-mountain town, Chama is the last population center of any size until you're well inside Colorado. With just 1,000 residents, the place has always been centered on the railroad that begins here and threads its way northeast between the mountains and over the state line to Antonito. Even if the steam train isn't your thing, you can drive north on Highway 17 for the views, though note that when the train isn't running, neither is much of the town; check for winter closures.

Chama is bordered on both sides by land belonging to the Jicarilla Apache. The tribe operates an elite hunting ranch south of town, The Lodge at Chama, that's a favorite politico getaway. But the natural attractions here are accessible to all—with the Rio Chama running right through town, you could theoretically walk out the front door of your (affordable) rental cabin, snag a trout, and cook it for dinner. On a day visit, the star of the show is the great steam train. If you stay a little longer, you'll have a chance to appreciate the remarkable vistas—particularly in the fall, when the mountains are blanketed with a thick patchwork of color.

★ Cumbres & Toltec Scenic Railroad

500 S. Terrace Ave.; 888/286-2737; www.cumbrestoltec.com; June-Oct. and Dec.; 6-hour excursion to Osier and back adults $115, children $60

The biggest attraction in Chama is the historic steam-driven Cumbres & Toltec Scenic Railroad, which has been running 64 miles from Chama up through a pass in the Rockies to Antonito, Colorado, since 1880. It is now jointly owned by the two neighboring states and maintained as a sort of museum.

You can travel the route in several ways, depending on how long of an outing you want. The standard outing is from Chama to the midpoint, the ghost town of Osier, just over the state border—you hop off there, have lunch, stroll around, and get back on the train for the ride back down the pass. Hard-core rail fans can go the whole way to Antonito—stopping in Osier for lunch—and return to Chama by bus, which takes eight hours ($135 adults, $80 children); this way, you'll get to see the dramatic Toltec Gorge, just north of Osier.

Trains run most frequently early June-August and less often September-mid-October for autumn leaf season; there are limited runs in late December around the holidays on occasion as well. Reservations are advised, and you can choose from three classes of service (windows open in tourist class, which is fun, but soot from the steam engine can make things a little gritty). The hot lunch included in the ticket price is pretty generous, with turkey and all the standard vegetables, plus pie to finish.

You can also prowl around the depot and rail yards. Pick up a flyer at the station that identifies all the structures, as well as distinguishes between drop-bottom gondolas, flangers, and other specialized train cars.

Tierra Wools

2450 Hwy. 64.; 575/756-1650; www.handweavers.com; 9:30am-5pm Mon.-Sat., 11am-4pm Sun.

Formerly in Tierra Amarilla and once a Ganados project, Tierra Wools has become a pilgrimage site for anyone engaged in fiber arts. The shop showcases the work of local weavers—rugs, pillows, ruanas—as well as brilliantly dyed skeins of handwoven wool yarn from the hardy, four-horned Churro sheep, a breed the conquistadors introduced

Take a ride back in time aboard the Cumbres & Toltec Scenic Railroad.

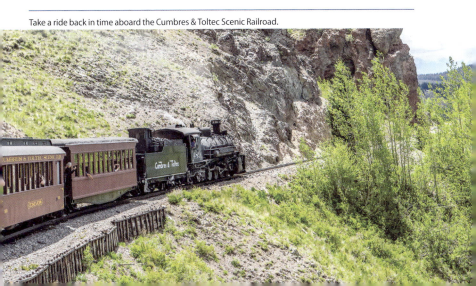

King Tiger and the Mercedes

The pastoral village of **Tierra Amarilla** gives little indication that it was once a battleground in the Chicano rights movement and the local Hispano fight for land-grant restitution. The Tierra Amarilla merced (land grant) was established in the 19th century, and when Nuevo México became a U.S. territory in 1848, the Treaty of Guadalupe Hidalgo specified it would be preserved. But cattle ranchers and the national forest system gradually appropriated it, so that, by the 1960s, many families in largely Hispano Rio Arriba County found themselves landless and subsisting on less than $1,500 per year.

BATTLE AT THE COURTHOUSE

Around this time, Reies López Tijerina, a charismatic activist in the growing Chicano movement, took up the land-grant cause. In 1967, he and more than 150 local men stormed the Tierra Amarilla courthouse, calling themselves the Political Confederation of Free City States and bearing a banner proclaiming "Give Us Our Land Back." Their plan was to make a citizen's arrest of the district attorney (DA). But the DA was nowhere around, the activists wound up taking everyone in the courthouse hostage, and 300 National Guard troops were called in. The incident made headlines across the country, and Tijerina was an overnight legend. The press dubbed him King Tiger, and he was praised in the ballad "El Corrido de Rio Arriba," penned within weeks by the band Los Reyes de Albuquerque.

Trials the next year were equally gripping: Tijerina wept on the witness stand, a lawman present at the raid turned up murdered, and even New Mexico's governor gave heartfelt testimony. Tijerina came away with a minimal sentence for second-degree kidnapping. He went on to lead the Chicano faction as part of Martin Luther King Jr.'s Poor People's Campaign.

CHANGE COMES SLOWLY

In Tierra Amarilla, meanwhile, the battle lines became hopelessly tangled. With seed money from a generous donor, the Sierra Club announced in 1970 that it would donate a new "land grant" to the area, but it failed to materialize—perhaps because environmentalists soon were battling the local sheepherders over the effects of grazing. In 1995, a local shepherd successfully sued the Sierra Club for the never-applied donation, and the economic situation in the valley has somewhat improved.

to New Mexico. If you're interested in the process, you can join a four-day workshop ($725) or try your hand at a two-day hand spinning immersive class ($400).

Recreation
Edward Sargent Wildlife Area
575/476-8000; www.wildlife.state.nm.us

Elk are prevalent throughout the mountains around Chama, and in the fall, the elk's distinctive mating call, or bugle, can be heard. North of town, accessed at the end of Pine Street, the Edward Sargent Wildlife Area has a viewing spot just inside the borders of the reserve, overlooking a big basin where the animals often graze; the best times to spot them

are at dawn and dusk. You can also hike into the center of the 20,000 acres, along the Rio Chama (for excellent fishing)—ask at the Chama visitors center for more information and other area hiking spots. If you want to hike or explore further, you'll need a Gaining Access into Nature (GAIN) permit, which you can pick up at Lowe's Market in Chama (2451 S. U.S. 84; 575/756-2545; 7am-8pm daily; $20).

Food
Box Car Café
425 Terrace Ave.; 575/756-2706; 10am-9pm Tues.-Sat. Apr.-Nov.; $8

Across the street from the train yard, Box Car Café serves hearty breakfast burritos (smothered in piquant chile) and juicy burgers for lunch. The menu is fairly limited, but the food is good and priced well.

Fina's Diner

2298 Hwy. 17; 575/756-9195; 6am-2pm daily; $7-14

Fina's Diner serves dependable New Mexican dishes and homemade baked goods. It's a friendly spot often filled with regulars, and for good reason; the prices are reasonable and there's no shortage of comforting meals to choose from, such as a stack of hot cakes for breakfast and chopped sirloin and a bowl of chile with sopaipillas for lunch.

Elk Horn Café

2663 S. U.S. 64; 575/756-2229; 7:30am-2:30pm Mon. and Thurs.-Sun.

Choose from a full selection of New Mexican breakfast and lunch staples at the Elk Horn Café, where the portions are generous and the red chile does not disappoint.

Accommodations and Camping

Chama has several decent places to stay.

Vista del Rio Lodge

2595 U.S. 64; 575/756-2138; www.vistadelriolodge.com; from $85 d

Vista del Rio Lodge is one of the nicest in town. The spacious 19 rooms are furnished in a contemporary Southwest style and have modern bathrooms.

The Chama Hotel

501 S. Terrace Ave.; 575/756-2416; www.thehotel.org; from $98 d

Some of the least expensive beds can be found at The Chama Hotel, a 1930s building with small, clean rooms that are a pleasant throwback.

★ Chama Station Inn

423 Terrace Ave.; 575/756-2315; www.chamastationinn.com; May-mid-Oct.; from $115 d

The pretty Chama Station Inn is just across from the train depot. Most of the nine rooms have wood floors, and all are decorated sparingly with country touches; the extra $10 for a deluxe room is well worth it, as it gets you a kiva fireplace, a graceful high ceiling, and a little more space.

Chama River Bend Lodge

2625 U.S. 64; 575/756-2264; www.chamariverbendlodge.com; rooms from $99 d, cabins from $139

The south side of town is largely devoted to rustic riverside cottage operations. Chama River Bend Lodge offers clean, basic rooms in a motel-like strip as well as cabins closer to the water.

Rio Chama RV Park

U.S. 64; 575/756-2303; May to mid-Oct.; tent sites $25, RV sites from $36

Campers will do well at the Rio Chama RV Park, on the north edge of town, where tent sites and RV sites with hookups are nestled amid tall trees, and the river flows right by.

Information and Services

Chama's **visitors center** (2372 Hwy. 17; 575/756-2306; 10am-3pm Tues.-Sat.) is located at the junction of U.S. 64/84 and Highway 17, on the southern edge of town. In addition to maps and other info (for the whole state), it also provides free Internet access and coffee.

JICARILLA APACHE NATION

The village of **Dulce** is the main town of the 750,000-acre Jicarilla Apache Nation (575/759-3242), which stretches north to the state line and south almost to the town of Cuba. The area is not the ancestral homeland of this band of Apache—originally, they had lived around the Platte and Arkansas Rivers in what is now central Colorado. But they were pushed south by white settlers in the 19th century, eventually scattering to live with other tribes as far south and east as Tucumcari. The current reservation wasn't designated until 1887, when the band's numbers had dwindled to just 330 and the group had split into two factions. Although the land was hard-won, it proved fortunate when oil and gas were discovered on it in the 1930s. Profit from these resources, as well as a casino in Dulce and the luxurious Lodge at Chama, has made this a relatively prosperous reservation.

The tribe now numbers about 3,000 members, with 2,500 or so based in Dulce, 25 miles west of Chama on U.S. 64. The village is set in a high, grassy valley that feels hidden away from the rest of the world, with bison, cattle, and sheep grazing beneath the snowcapped Rockies.

Sights
Jicarilla Cultural Affairs
13533 U.S. 64; 575/759-1343; 8am-5pm Mon.-Fri.; free
The Jicarilla Cultural Affairs has a small museum that describes the role of buffalo, medicinal herbs, and other aspects of the Jicarilla Apache Nation's heritage.

Jicarilla Apache Cultural Arts and Heritage Center
U.S. 64; 575/759-4380; 8am-5pm Mon.-Fri.; free

In a trailer south of the tribal headquarters, the Jicarilla Apache Cultural Arts and Heritage Center is more of a shop, where you can also see people making the intricate baskets for which the tribe is known.

Recreation
Most visitors come here to hunt mule deer and elk on the reservation lands, or to fish in one of the many lakes; contact **Jicarilla Game and Fish** (575/759-3255; www.jicarillahunt.com) for rules and permits. **Stone Lake** ($5, or free with fishing and hunting licenses), 18 miles south of Dulce, has pretty campsites around its three miles of shoreline.

Festivals and Events
On the third week in July, the Little Beaver Roundup is a well-attended and long running powwow and rodeo in Dulce that's open to visitors, and photography is permitted. Similar events, plus traditional footraces, mark **Go-Jii-Ya,** the tribe's feast day on September 15; it takes place at Stone Lake.

The Enchanted Circle

The Enchanted Circle, the loop formed by U.S. 64, Highway 38, and Highway 522, is named for its breathtaking views of the Sangre de Cristo Mountains, including Wheeler Peak. The area is a cultural shift from Taos, much of it settled by Anglo ranchers and prospectors in the late 1800s and currently populated by transplanted flatlander Texans enamored of the massive peaks. The main towns on the route—Angel Fire and Red River—are ski resorts and, increasingly, mountain biking hotbeds. As the scenery is really the thing, you can drive the 84-mile route in a short day, with time out for a hike around Red River or a detour along the Wild Rivers scenic byway. If you like country music, you might want to plan to be in Red River for the evening.

Driving counterclockwise around the loop, as described below, gives you the arresting

descent into the Taos Valley from Questa—not to be missed, if you can manage it. Avoid driving the circle on a Sunday and early in the week, as significantly more attractions and businesses are closed.

To start, head east out of Taos on Kit Carson Road, which turns into U.S. 64, winding along next to the Taos River and past numerous campgrounds and hiking trails. At Palo Flechado Pass, the road descends into the high Moreno Valley, a gorgeous expanse of green in early spring and a vast tundra in winter.

ANGEL FIRE
Angel Fire Resort
800/633-7463; www.angelfireresort.com;
$104 full-day lift ticket
After about 20 miles, a right turn up Highway

The Enchanted Circle

434 leads to this tiny ski village, a cluster of timber condos at the base of a 10,600-foot mountain. In comparison with Taos Ski Valley, Angel Fire Resort looks like a molehill, with a vertical drop of 2,077 feet. But it's friendly to families, has two freestyle terrain parks, and is the only place in the state for night skiing. For those with no snow skills at all, the 1,000-foot-long tubing hill provides an adrenaline rush.

In summer, the resort transforms itself with a full slate of activities on offer, though mountain biking is the clear highlight. Rightly acclaimed by regional riders, the **Angel Fire Bike Park** ($68/day) is larger than the one at Taos Ski Valley and has more varied runs, including a handful that are suitable for beginners. There are enough trails here to easily occupy several weekends. Near the resort, the storied **South Boundary Trail** (no. 164) runs from a trailhead off Forest Road 76 south of Angel Fire. The route to Taos is about four vertical-seeming miles over the pass, then another 16 or so back to El Nogal trailhead on U.S. 64, a couple of miles east of Taos.

The cool alpine waters of the resort's

Monte Verde Lake are particularly appealing at the height of summer. Try your hand at stand-up paddleboarding and kayaking (each $40/hour) and fishing ($40 permit; $50/boat), or enjoy the elaborate zipline course (Mon. and Fri.-Sun. late May-late Oct; $125). Off the slopes, **Roadrunner Tours** (27500 Hwy. 64; 575/377-6416; www.nancyburch.com) offers a variety of trail rides on horseback into the mountains (from $55).

Festivals and Events
Balloons Over Angel Fire
Angel Fire Airport; www.angelfirenm.gov; mid-June
While not at the level of Albuquerque's Balloon Fiesta, there's no doubt Balloons Over Angel Fire is growing in stature with each passing year. Held over a weekend in the middle of June, the event sees dozens of colorful and imaginatively designed hot-air balloons take to the skies around dawn from the Angel Fire Airport. With the unobstructed Sangre de Cristos as a backdrop, the mass ascension is quite a spectacle.

Food
★ Mikuna Grill
48 N. Angle Fire Rd.; 575/377-7009; 4pm-9pm Tues.-Sun.; $5-16
Taste Peruvian specialties at the Mikuna Grill. Lunch dishes include a hearty quinoa soup filled with ribeye chunks. For dinner, seafood lovers will want to zero in on the tasty ceviche appetizer—featuring red snapper, shrimp, and sweet potato—and the flavorful arroz con mariscos, a tantalizing plate of calamari, mussels, and shrimp with seasoned rice.

The Bakery & Café
3420 Mountain View Blvd.; 575/377-3992; 7:30am-2:30pm Mon.-Fri., 7am-2pm Sat.-Sun.; $7-11
Before hitting the slopes, stop in at The Bakery & Café for generously sized and tasty burritos, burgers, and chicken-fried steak and eggs.

Angel Fired Pizza
3375 Mountain View Blvd.; 575/377-2274; 4pm-8pm Tues.-Thurs., noon-8pm Fri.-Sun.; $7-20

If you're craving a slice, Angel Fired Pizza is the place to go. As well as several thin-crust whole wheat pizza specialties, it serves a green-chile carbonara and an unwieldy, but supremely tasty, meatball sub.

Information
The Angel Fire CVB maintains a **visitors center** (3365 Hwy. 434; 575/377-6555; www.angelfirenm.gov; 9am-5pm daily) just south of the T-intersection with Angel Fire Road. The **Angel Fire Chamber of Commerce** (3407 Hwy. 434; 575/377-6353; www.angelfirechamber.org; 9am-5pm Mon.-Fri.) has its own office where the lobby is open 24 hours, so you can pick up brochures and maps anytime.

VIETNAM VETERANS MEMORIAL STATE PARK
34 Country Club Rd.; 575/377-2293; www.vietnamveteransmemorial.org; 8am-5:30pm daily; chapel open 24 hours
Back on U.S. 64, a little more than a mile past the turn for Angel Fire, a swooping white structure rises on the hill to your left. This is the Vietnam Veterans Memorial, built by Victor "Doc" Westphall as a remembrance of his son David, who was killed in the war. When Westphall commissioned Santa Fe architect Ted Luna to design the graceful white chapel in 1968, it was the first such memorial dedicated to the casualties of Vietnam. An adjacent visitors center was built later and now holds a small but moving museum about the conflict and its aftermath. In the garden are a Huey helicopter and the graves of Victor Westphall and his wife, Jeanne.

EAGLE NEST
At the junction of U.S. 64 and Highway 38, Eagle Nest is a small strip of wooden buildings, all that's left of what was a jumping gambling town in the 1920s and 1930s, when bars hosted roulette and blackjack, and enterprising businesspeople would roll slot machines out onto the boardwalks to entice travelers en route to Raton and the train. The pretty

lake here now is the main focus of fun, but there's also good hiking just east in Cimarron Canyon State Park.

Eagle Nest Lake State Park

42 Marina Way; 575/377-1594; www.emnrd.nm.gov; 8am-4:30pm daily; $5/car day use

East of U.S. 64 and just south of town, Eagle Nest Lake was created in 1918 with the construction of a privately financed dam on the Cimarron River. Today it's a pretty state park, stocked with trout, and a popular recreation spot year-round—the Fourth of July fireworks display and winter ice fishing are legendary. For the marina and **visitors center,** look for the turn off U.S. 64 marked by a large RV park sign. Stop here for an exhibit on the dam, as well as camping ($10). The lake is also accessible via three day-use areas, two of which are to the south of the visitors center, while the third is on the lake's northeast shore.

Eagle Nest Visitor Center & Gateway Museum

U.S. 64; 575/721-0704; generally 10am-4pm Fri.-Sun., mid-May-mid-Oct.; donation

The Eagle Nest Visitor Center & Gateway Museum, at the eastern edge of Eagle Nest, gives an overview of the good old days and often hosts events, such as a mountain-man rendezvous. This is also the spot to pick up local and regional information, though the hours are spotty.

Food and Accommodations

Kaw-Lija's

200-236 E. Therma St.; 575/377-3424; 8am-8pm Mon.-Sat.; $8

You'll find filling favorites at Kaw-Lija's, such as chicken fried steak, cowboy chili, and a baked potato loaded with half a dozen ingredients. Perhaps the best treats are the sliders; there are two types to choose from—cheeseburger and BBQ pulled pork—and neither disappoints.

Cowboy's Corner

50 Hwy. 38; 575/377-9525; 11am-2pm Mon.-Fri.; $8

During the week, the rustic Cowboy's Corner is a great spot for lunch and the views are tough to beat. There are sandwiches and wraps, but it's the burgers—think juicy and oversized patties with buns heated just right—that get the most acclaim. Be sure to call ahead, as the hours can be sporadic.

Eagle Nest Lake

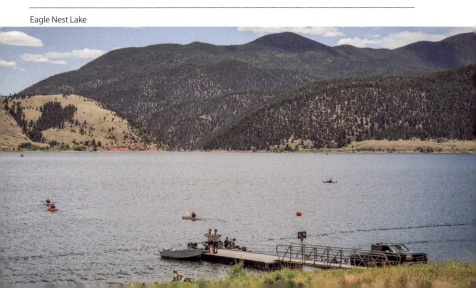

Laguna Vista Lodge

51 Therma Dr.; 575/377-6522;
www.lagunavistalodge.com; from $149
Laguna Vista Lodge has pleasant motel rooms connected by a screened porch, as well as cabins and apartments with a view of the lake.

Angel Nest RV Retreat

28418 U.S. 64; 575/377-0533; www.angelnestrvretreat.
com; RV sites $42, cabins $69, tent sites $18
Just west of Eagle Nest Lake State Park, Angel Nest RV Retreat has more than 60 pleasant and roomy RV sites with full hook-ups, as well as seven cabins and tent sites. There's not much in the way of shade, but the views of the lake make up for it.

ELIZABETHTOWN

Blink and you'll miss it: A small sign on the right side of the road 4.8 miles past Eagle Nest points to a left turn to the former gold rush site of Elizabethtown, the first incorporated village in New Mexico. When gold was discovered in 1866, it grew to more than 7,000 people, and then faded to nothing after a dredge-mining project failed in 1903. It's now a barely discernible ghost town, with the meager stone ruins of the Mutz Hotel, the former center of social activity. The only signs of life are, ironically, in the **cemetery,** which is still used by residents of Colfax County and contains graves dating as far back as 1880.

RED RIVER

The ski village of Red River is a cluster of tidy rows of wooden buildings, all done up in Old West facades, complete with boardwalks and swinging saloon doors. Like Elizabethtown, this was once a community of wild prospectors, but when mining went bust, the town salvaged itself by renting out abandoned houses to vacationers escaping the summer heat. Just when air-conditioning started to become widespread in the 1950s, the ski area opened, saving the town from a major slump. Red River still thrives, with a year-round population of only about 500.

The town hosts several outsized **events** throughout the year, including a rowdy Memorial Day Motorcycle Rally, a large Fourth of July parade, the Enchanted Circle Century Tour in September, a lively three-day Oktoberfest in early October, and a Mardi Gras street party; contact the **Red River Chamber of Commerce** (575/754-2366; www. redriverchamber.org) for more details.

Skiing
Red River Ski & Summer Area

575/754-2223; www.redriverskiarea.com;
$106 full-day lift ticket
Compared with Taos Ski Valley, Red River Ski & Summer Area may be a bunny hill, but it's nothing if not convenient: The trails run into town, so the two chairlifts are walking distance from anywhere in town.

Enchanted Forest

575/754-6112; www.enchantedforestxc.com;
9am-4:30pm daily; $20 full-day pass
Cross-country skiers should follow Highway 38 east of town, to the Enchanted Forest cross-country ski area, which has more than 20 miles of groomed trails through the trees and up the mountainside. Cross-country skis are available for rent, as are snowshoes (both from $16). And, for a special overnight experience, you can trek to a **yurt** (from $75, depending on season), nicely appointed with a woodstove and clean bedding. They're available year-round, and snowmobile delivery of your gear is an option in winter ($50).

Hiking

The town abuts the back side of Wheeler Peak, so the ascents here are much more gradual, while still yielding dramatic views. Stop in at the **visitors center** (101 W. River St.; 575/754-3030; www.redriver.org; 8am-5pm daily), in the town hall, for area maps and trail guides.

In summer, you can ride the **Platinum Chairlift** ($22) to the ski area, where you can hike around the summit, grab a bite to eat on the deck of The Tip restaurant, and negotiate the steep trail back into town; it's also popular with experienced mountain bikers. The 360-degree views from the top are worth the trip up alone.

Red River Nature Trail

Distance: *2 mi round-trip*
Time: *45 minutes*
Trailhead: *101 River St.*

The easy Red River Nature Trail can be accessed behind the conference center just past the covered bridge. It includes interpretive signs identifying plants and geological formations.

Pioneer Creek Trail

Distance: *3.4 mi round-trip*
Time: *1.5 hours*
Trailhead: *Arrowhead Lodge, off Pioneer St.*

The more demanding and scenic Pioneer Creek Trail (FR 485) follows an old mining road through the forest before ending at just over 10,000 feet; there are a few signs of long-closed silver and copper mines along the way.

Columbine Trail

Distance: *10 mi round-trip*
Time: *4-5 hours*
Trailhead: *Columbine Campground, 8 mi west of town/4 mi east of Questa*

West of town, Highway 38 leads past a number of trailheads that make for a good amble. Columbine Trail (no. 71), on the left, is the one to choose if your time is limited. The trail starts out easy, crossing Deer Creek, but soon climbs switchbacks that lead through a large aspen grove, then above the tree line to the ridge. As an incentive, wild berry bushes flourish alongside the trail in late summer. The right side of the road, however, is a little less scenic because a molybdenum mine has stripped a good chunk of the mountain.

Bobcat Pass

1670 Hwy. 38; 575/754-2769; www.bobcatpass.com; 8am-5pm daily mid-May-late Aug. and Dec.-Mar.; horseback rides $55, snowmobile tours $75

Bobcat Pass offers horseback rides by day and hosts "cowboy evenings," which include a home-style steak dinner along with a night of singing and picking and a bit of poetry. In winter, they provide two-hour snowmobile tours on a private ranch, including a highly recommended one at sunset.

★ Live Music

Red River has a lively country music scene, heavily influenced by the Texans and Oklahomans who have long come here for vacation. "Outlaw country" singer and songwriter Michael Martin Murphey, whose song "The Land of Enchantment" is the official state ballad, has been an enduring presence in the music scene here, and he performs regularly July-first week of September at **Rockin' 3M Chuckwagon Amphitheater** (178 Bitter Creek Rd.; 575/754-6280; 5pm-close daily).

Motherlode Saloon

406 E. Main St.; 575/754-6280; 6pm-2am daily

The barn-like Texas Reds holds two live music venues, one of which is the adjacent Motherlode Saloon, where local rock and country acts take the stage and make it the most rollicking place in town on weekends.

Lost Love Saloon

400 E. Main St.; 575/754-2922; 4:30pm-9pm daily

The cozy Lost Love Saloon features more sedate country and western crooners throughout the week. It's a great spot to settle in shoulder to shoulder and get lost for a bit, listening to forlorn tales.

Food

The largest selection of lunch options on the Enchanted Circle is in Red River, but there are few standouts.

Dairy Bar

417 E. Main St.; 575/754-9969; 11am-10pm daily summer, 11am-7pm Thurs.-Mon. in winter; $5

For a quick in-and-out meal, the throwback Dairy Bar offers burgers, chile, quesadillas, and, naturally, soft-serve ice cream—its floats are an ideal summer treat.

Farther Afield: Cimarron

Cimarron Canyon State Park

From Eagle Nest, continuing east on U.S. 64 takes you through **Cimarron Canyon State Park** (575/377-6271; www.emnrd.nm.gov; $5/car), known for excellent trout fishing in the Cimarron River, the dramatic granite palisades that form the canyon walls, and a few scenic hikes. Of the three campgrounds (sites from $10) along the riverbanks, Maverick and Ponderosa are closest to the trails.

Twelve miles east of the canyon, you reach the town of Cimarron, where the **St. James Hotel** (Hwy. 21; 575/376-2664; www.exstjames.com; $95 d shared bathroom, $130 private bathroom) is one of the state's most historic hotels, notorious for gunfights in the years of the Colfax County War and still rich with atmosphere.

Lambert's in the St. James Hotel (7am-9pm daily; $6-28) serves standard fare—burgers, steaks, and burritos—though there's no doubt it suits the dark paneling and evident fondness for taxidermy. The bar here is open 11am-midnight, or "whenever the bartender gets tired of looking at people."

The Tip

Red River Ski and Summer Area; 575/754-2223; $7

Though the food—burgers, brats, and hot dogs—isn't exactly remarkable, the summit views from the deck of The Tip warrant a stop alone.

Sundance

401 High St.; 575/754-2971; 5pm-9pm daily; $13

For Tex-Mex, including gut-busting stuffed sopaipillas, Sundance is equally reliable—it's on the street uphill and parallel to the main drag.

Texas Reds

400 E. Main St.; 575/754-2922; 4:30pm-9pm Mon.-Thurs., 11:30am-9pm Fri.-Sun.; $15

Business turnover can be high here, but at least Texas Reds is consistent; it packs 'em in with Texas-sized steaks and elk burgers in a wood-paneled Western-look room; the floors are scattered with peanut shells.

Der Market

307 W. Main St.; 575/754-2974; 7am-8pm daily

The best place in town to stock up for a picnic and hike is the central Der Market. Its deli casts a particularly wide net: breakfast burritos, catfish strips, and egg rolls are just a few of the items you can choose from.

Accommodations

Red River is an ideal base for exploring the Enchanted Circle's hiking and skiing options; there are plenty of choices, and most are pleasant and reasonably priced, if somewhat dated.

Three Bears Lodge

301 E. Main St.; 575/754-2272; from $94

Three Bears Lodge, at the village's center, is one of the better lodging options. It's a quaint, well cared for place with rustic cabins of various sizes.

Alpine Lodge

417 W. Main St.; 575/754-2952; $109 d, two-night minimum

Spread along the river, the Bavarian-themed Alpine Lodge is the best deal in the village. Accommodations range from nicely appointed rooms with balconies in the hotel to spacious log cabins that can fit up to twelve. The property has its own private park, and you can even cast a line in the river out back.

Information
Visitors Center

101 W. River St.; 575/754-1708; 8am-5pm daily

The chamber of commerce staffs a very well-stocked visitors center inside the town hall, off the north side of the main drag.

QUESTA

Arriving in Questa, at the junction of Highway 38 and Highway 522, it's hard not to get a sense you're back in Spanish New Mexico. The town, which now has a population of about 1,700, was established in 1842 and is still primarily a Hispano farming village, though a few Anglo newcomers have set up art spaces here. The **Questa Art Tour** (http://questacreative.org) takes place in the middle of August and features pieces by local artists, often in their homes.

The heart of town is the 1841 **San Antonio Church** (16 St. Anthonys Rd.), which was restored in 2016 by volunteers over about eight years of night-and-weekend work.

Recreation
Yoga Sala

2331 Hwy. 522; 575/224-202; gallery 11am-5pm Fri.-Sun.

Questa is home to one of the best yoga studios in northern New Mexico: Yoga Sala. The sunny space hosts a full schedule of healing modality classes, including yoga, meditation, and tai chi.

Food
The Wildcat's Den

2457 Hwy. 522; 575/586-1119; 11am-6pm Mon.-Fri., 11am-4pm Sat.; $7

Of the few places to grab a bite to eat, The Wildcat's Den is the best bet; its burgers—juicy and unwieldy—are rightly revered by locals.

My Tia's Café

107 Hwy. 378; 575/586-2203; 11am-6pm Wed.-Sun.; $7

For a meal more in line with Questa's roots, head about four miles north to the village of Cerro and My Tia's Café, which does New Mexican home cooking, including chiles rellenos and taco salads.

Information
Visitors Center

1 Hwy. 38; 575/586-2278; https://visitquesta.com; 10am-3pm daily June-Aug.

The small visitors center has maps, souvenirs, and helpful staff with information on the nearby Wild Rivers Recreation Area.

Wild Rivers Recreation Area

The **Río Grande del Norte National Monument** (575/758-8851; www.blm.gov/visit/rgdnnm) protects the river from the Colorado state line to Pilar, south of Taos. Perhaps the wildest section of the land is found north of Questa, in the Wild Rivers Recreation Area, where the Red River meets the Rio Grande. Red-tailed hawks circle over gnarled, centuries-old piñon and juniper

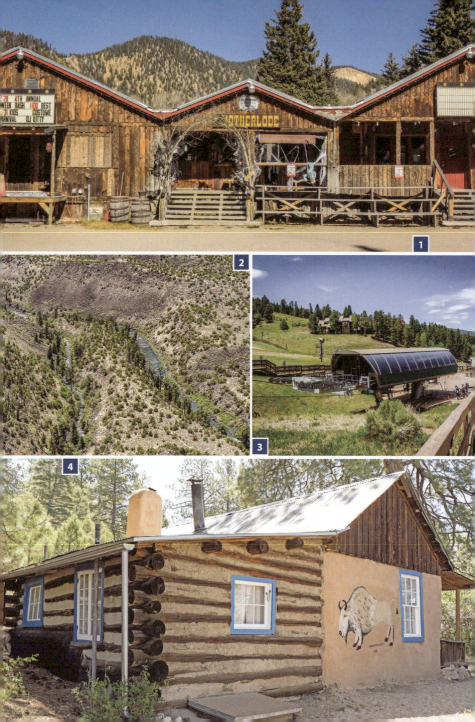

trees, and river otters thrive here, after their reintroduction in 2008. White-water **rafting** is popular in the Class III rapids of the Red River Confluence run; contact an outfitter in Taos.

The access road to the recreation area is three miles north on Highway 522 from the main Questa intersection, then west on Highway 378, which leads through Cerro and to the area's **visitors center** (575/586-1150; 10am-3pm daily June-Aug.; $3/car day use).

Hiking

Steep hiking trails lead down into the gorge and along the river, so you can make a full loop, starting down from **La Junta Point,** named for where the two rivers come together over 800 feet below. Once at the bottom, take **Little Arsenic Trail** back up (about 4.5 miles total), or **Big Arsenic Trail** for a longer hike (6 miles). If you'd prefer not to descend (and, necessarily, ascend) the canyon, follow the more level 1.7-mile **Pescado Trail** along the Red River rim and gently down to the Red River Fish Hatchery.

Camping

Five developed campgrounds (but no RV hookups; $7/car) on the rim can be reached by car, or you can hike in to campsites by the river ($5). There's a scenic picnic area near the gorge's rim.

D. H. LAWRENCE RANCH

506 D. H. Lawrence Ranch Rd.; 575/776-2245; 9:30am-3:30pm Tues.-Thurs.

After Questa, the view opens up as you descend into Taos Valley, with mesas stretching far to the west. Five miles east on the rutted San Cristobal Road is the 160-acre D. H. Lawrence Ranch, also known as the Kiowa Ranch, where English writer and provocateur D. H. Lawrence lived in 1924 and 1925 with his wife, Frieda, and the painter Dorothy Brett. A docent is on-site to answer questions. It's a serene spot, with not much to see beyond a shrine to the writer and a few small buildings, but the lonely drive up a back road into the fragrant pine forests has its own appeal. (Don't bother driving up on a closed day—the property is fully fenced and locked.)

The 160-acre spread was a gift from Mabel Dodge Luhan—generous, but nonetheless it offered a bare-bones existence, as you can see in the cabins the artists occupied. Lawrence soon returned to Europe, but Frieda stayed on. Years after the writer died of tuberculosis in France in 1930, Frieda exhumed and cremated his body and brought the ashes to New Mexico. This plan sparked anger among Lawrence's friends, including Mabel, who characterized Frieda's planned site for the ashes as "that outhouse of a shrine." Tales abound about how the ashes never made the trip. Some of the earliest visitors to pay their respects at the ranch include playwright Tennessee Williams and artist Georgia O'Keeffe, whose painting *The Lawrence Tree* was inspired by the view from the base of a gnarled pine in front of the Lawrences' cabin.

The turn for D. H. Lawrence Ranch Road is about 10 miles north of Taos off Highway 522. Once on the road, proceed slowly 4.7 miles to the ranch.

1: Motherlode Saloon **2:** view from La Junta Point
3: a ski lift taking riders to Angel Fire Bike Park
4: cabin at the D. H. Lawrence Ranch

Albuquerque

As a tourist destination, Albuquerque has long labored in the shadow of the arts meccas to the north, but times are changing—and rightly so. The Duke City is fun, down-to-earth, and affordable.

If Santa Fe is the "City Different" (a moniker Albuquerqueans, or Burqueños, razz for its pretentiousness), then New Mexico's largest city, with a population of 900,000 in the greater metro area, is proudly the "City Indifferent," unconcerned with fads and fanciful facades.

The city does have its pockets of historic charm—they're just not visible from the arteries of I-40 and I-25, which intersect in the center in a graceful tangle of turquoise-trimmed bridges. Albuquerque was founded three centuries ago, its cumbersome name that of a Spanish

Highlights

Look for ★ to find recommended sights, activities, dining, and lodging.

★ **ABQ Trolley Co.:** Take the best city tour in the state, aboard an open-sided, faux-adobe tram, with lively, knowledgeable owners sharing Albuquerque lore (page 188).

★ **KiMo Theatre:** A fantasia of Southwestern decorative styles and downtown's showpiece, this former cinema and now more varied arts space is one of the few examples of Pueblo Deco style (page 196).

★ **Sandia Peak Tramway:** Zip up the world's longest single-cable tram to the crest of the mountain that looms over the east side of Albuquerque for vertigo-inducing views across the whole metro area (page 202).

★ **Petroglyph National Monument:** Basalt boulders throughout the city's West Mesa are covered with several thousand fine rock carvings etched centuries ago by the ancestors of the local Pueblo people (page 202).

★ **Ballooning:** In the country's hot-air balloon capital, enjoy a dawn flight—or at least witness hundreds of brightly colored balloons take part in the wildly popular Balloon Fiesta (page 205).

★ **Acoma Pueblo:** This windswept village atop a mesa west of Albuquerque is one of the oldest communities in the United States. Visit for the views as well as for the delicate black-on-white pottery made only here (page 232).

★ **Bosque del Apache National Wildlife Refuge:** Nothing quite prepares you for the sight of thousands of sandhill cranes suddenly taking flight against the backdrop of a burnt orange sky at one of North America's premier birding destinations (page 237).

★ **Tinkertown Museum:** An enthralling collection of one man's lifetime of whittling projects, this folk-art exhibit delights kids and adults alike (page 240).

★ **Kasha-Katuwe Tent Rocks National Monument:** Break up the otherwise unremarkable freeway drive to Santa Fe with a hike in this eerie canyon landscape marked by dozens of bleached-white conical formations (page 249).

Albuquerque

ALBUQUERQUE

To Coronado
Historic Site

313

528

Rio Grande

Sandia

Corrales

CASA SAN
YSIDRO

448

25

OLD SAN
YSIDRO CHURCH

PEREA'S TIJUANA
BAR & RESTAURANT

MARBLE
TAPROOM

VILLAGE
PIZZA

MCMAHON BLVD.

UNSER BLVD.

TRACTOR
BREWING

CORRALES ROAD
SCENIC BYWAY

ROY AVE.

SANDIA
CASINO

FLYING
STAR CAFÉ

PIEDRAS
MARCADAS
CANYON

ADOBE
THEATER

ANDERSON ABRUZZO
ALBUQUERQUE
INTERNATIONAL
BALLOON MUSEUM

RAINBOW
RYDERS

ALAMEDA BLVD.

PASEO DEL NORTE BLVD.

423

GRUET
WINERY

Petroglyph
National
Monument

COORS BLVD.

Rio Grande

Los
Ranchos

2ND ST.

SAN ANTONIO DR.

BOCA NEGRA
CANYON

VERNON'S
SPEAKEASY

OSUNA RD.

NATIVO LODGE

PETROGLYPH
NATIONAL
MONUMENT

LA CUMBRE
TAPROOM

LOS POBLANOS
FARM SHOP

4TH ST.

ACADEMY RD.

RINCONADA
CANYON

LOS POBLANOS
HISTORIC INN

MONTAÑO RD.

25

SAN MATEO BLVD.

RIO GRANDE
NATURE CENTER
STATE PARK

BOOKWORKS

GRIEGOS RD.

MONTGOMERY BLVD.

Rio Grande
Nature Center
State Park

BETTY'S BATH
& DAY SPA

LA MONTAÑITA
CO-OP

CANTEEN
BREWHOUSE

VORTEX
THEATRE

CANDELARIA RD.

LITTLE
BEAR
COFFEE

INDIAN PUEBLO
CULTURAL CENTER

MARY &
TITO'S CAFÉ

LA CUMBRE
BREWING

BALLOONING

LOUISIANA BLVD.

FORK & FIG

40

BOW &
ARROW

ABQ
UPTOWN

UNSER BLVD.

COORS BLVD.

40

SEE
"OLD TOWN
ALBUQUERQUE"
MAP

TRACTOR
BREWING

SEE
"DOWNTOWN
ALBUQUERQUE"
MAP

GREEN
JEANS
FARMERY

SEE
"THE UNIVERSITY
AND NOB HILL"
MAP

ABQ BIOPARK
AQUARIUM &
BOTANICAL
GARDENS

KIMO
THEATRE

LOMAS BLVD.

SANDIA
PEAK INN

ABQ
TROLLEY CO.

Albuquerque

CENTRAL AVE.

FLEA
MARKET

WYOMING BLVD.

CENTRAL AVE.

DOG HOUSE

RIO
GRANDE
POOL

ABQ BIOPARK ZOO

ISOTOPES
PARK

CODA
BAKERY

BRIDGE BLVD.

TORTUGA
GALLERY

THE PIT

ISLETA BLVD.

ARENAL RD.

NATIONAL HISPANIC
CULTURAL CENTER

GIBSON BLVD.

ROY E. DISNEY CENTER
FOR PERFORMING ARTS

Rio Grande

To
Twisters
(Los Pollos Hermanos)

25

ALBUQUERQUE
INTERNATIONAL
SUNPORT

© MOON.COM

RIO BRAVO BLVD.

South
Valley

0   1 mi
0   1 km

CAPULIN SPRINGS
SNOW PLAY SITE

LA LUZ TRAIL

10K TRAIL

SANDIA PEAK
SKI AREA

SANDIA
CREST

CREST TRAIL

SANDIA PEAK TRAMWAY

TRAMWAY RD

Juan Tabo Arroyo

La Cueva Arroyo

536

PASEO DEL NORTE BLVD

BOESE BROTHERS

Sandia
Park

TINKERTOWN
MUSEUM

Cibola

National

Forest

Pino Arroyo
Open Space

Pino Arroyo

ELENA GALLEGOS
PICNIC AREA

SIMMS PARK RD

Bear Canyon Arroyo

Bear Canyon Arroyo
Open Space

Embudito

Arroyo

Gutierrez
Canyon-Milne
Open Space

EUBANK BLVD

ANNAPURNA'S

MARBLE
TAPROOM

O'NIELL'S

TRAIL 365

TRAMWAY BLVD

Sandia Foothills

14

Sandia
Foothills
Open Space

MENAUL BLVD

A1A CAR WASH

JUAN TABO BLVD

Embudu Arroyo

BURGER
BOY

Cedar Crest

Ojito de San
Antonio
Open Space

EMBUDITO
CANYON TRAIL

Embudo
Canyon

333

CANTEEN
TAPROOM

Carlito Springs
Open Space

Tijeras

CENTRAL AVE

333

40

TIJERAS PUEBLO
ARCHAEOLOGICAL SITE

NATIONAL MUSEUM
OF NUCLEAR
SCIENCE & HISTORY

Sandia
Foothills
Open Space

Tres Pistolas
Open Space

East Tijeras
Arroyo
Open Space

Cibola

National

Forest

TUNNEL
CANYON TRAIL

Sabino Canyon
Open Space

Otero Canyon

nobleman (hence its nickname, the Duke City). But its character is the product of later eras: the post-1880 downtown district; the University of New Mexico campus, built in the early 20th century by John Gaw Meem, the architect who defined Pueblo Revival style; and Route 66, the highway that joined Albuquerque to Chicago, Illinois, and Los Angeles, California, in 1926.

Spread out on either side of the Rio Grande, from volcanic mesas on the west to the foothills of the Sandia Mountains along the east, Albuquerque has accessible hiking and biking trails that run through diverse landscapes. In the morning, you can stroll under centuries-old cottonwood trees near the wide, muddy river; in the afternoon, you can hike along the edge of a windswept mountain range with views across the vast empty land beyond the city grid. And at the end of the day, you'll see Albuquerque's most remarkable feature, the dramatic light show on the Sandia Mountains—Spanish for "watermelon," for the bright pink hue they turn at sundown.

The city is also an excellent base for exploring the many interesting pueblos and natural attractions nearby. In the Manzano Mountains southeast of town, for instance, lie a series of pueblos remnants, last inhabited during the early years of the Conquest. The road that links them also winds past a canyon known for its fall colors and a historic hotel in a distinctly New Mexican style.

Albuquerque is also just an hour's drive to Santa Fe, with easy day trips or scenic drives through the mountains in between. The most direct is I-25, which cuts through dramatic rolling hills; take a short detour to Kasha-Katuwe Tent Rocks National Monument, where pointed white rocks tower above a narrow canyon. Beginning east of Albuquerque, the historic Turquoise Trail winds along the back side of the Sandias, then through the former mining town of Madrid, resettled as an arts colony, with galleries occupying the cabins built against the black, coal-rich hills. The most roundabout route north is along the Jemez Mountain Trail, a scenic byway northwest of Albuquerque through the brick-red rocks surrounding Jemez Pueblo, then past natural hot springs.

PLANNING YOUR TIME

Precisely because it's not so full of must-see historic attractions, Albuquerque fares best as the primary focus of a trip, so you have time to enjoy the natural setting, the food, and the people. It makes financial sense, too: Your money will go further here than it will farther north, especially when it comes to hotels, which offer great value and don't dramatically hike rates for **summer** high season, as is standard in Taos and Santa Fe. Ideally, you would spend a leisurely **three days** here, soaking up a little Route 66 neon, enjoying the downtown entertainment, hiking in the Sandias, taking scenic drives, and bicycling along the Rio Grande.

But if you're also planning to visit other parts of the state, it is difficult to recommend more than a **couple of days** in Albuquerque—preferably on the way out, as the city's modern, get-real attitude is best appreciated after you've been in the adobe dreamland of Santa Fe for a bit. Spend a day cruising the neighborhoods along Central Avenue, and for a last dose of open sky, take the tramway up to Sandia Crest and hike along the Crest Trail. At the end of your trip, the altitude will likely be more manageable.

In the city proper, the weather for most of the year is enjoyable. **Winters** are mild in the low basin around the river, though the Sandias often get heavy snow. **Fire season** is generally from April through June, though it can last longer if the monsoon rains start late in July. Note that a **summer** day here can be 5-10°F hotter than farther north, though, as elsewhere in the state the heat of July and

August is usually broken by heavy afternoon rainstorms. And because Albuquerque is seldom at the top of tourists' lists, there's never a time when it's unpleasantly mobbed.

HISTORY

Albuquerque was established in 1706 as a small farming outpost on the banks of the Rio Grande, where Pueblo Indians had been cultivating crops since 1100, and named after a Spanish duke. Decades later, the Villa de San Felipe de Alburquerque (the first "r" was lost over the years) flourished as a waypoint on the Camino Real trade route.

The city began to transform in 1880, when the railroad arrived, two miles from the main plaza—this sparked the growth of "New Town" (now the downtown business district) and drew tuberculosis patients, who saw the city's crisp air as beneficial. By 1912, these patients made up nearly a quarter of the state's population.

More modernization and growth came from Route 66, which was laid down Central Avenue in the 1930s, and the establishment of Sandia National Labs in 1949, in response to the escalating Cold War. Tourism boomed (and neon signs buzzed on), and new streets were carved into the northeast foothills for lab workers' tract homes. In the 1940s, the population exploded from 35,000 to 100,000; by 1959, 207,000 people lived in Albuquerque.

Growth has been steady ever since, and recent development has been spurred by a growing film industry and other technical innovations. Subdivisions have spread across the West Mesa, and small outlying communities have become suburbs—though portions along the river retain a village feel that's not too far from the city's roots as a farming community three centuries back.

ORIENTATION

Albuquerque's greater metro area covers more than 100 square miles, but visitors will likely see only a handful of neighborhoods, all linked by Central Avenue (historic Route 66),

the main east-west thoroughfare across town. The Albuquerque Rapid Transit (ART; www. cabq.gov) offers bus options along Central Avenue.

A few blocks from the Rio Grande, which runs north-south through the city, the **Old Town** makes for an ideal introduction to the city. The best museums are clustered here, and the area exudes history without feeling overly manufactured. East from Old Town lies **downtown,** with most of the city's bars and clubs, along with the bus and train depots. Immediately to the east, the aptly named East Downtown (more commonly known as EDo) neighborhood, bordered by Martin Luther King Jr. Avenue to the north and Coal Avenue to the south, holds historic homes and some of the city's better restaurants. Central Avenue continues under I-25 and past the **University of New Mexico** campus, followed by the lively **Nob Hill** district, which occupies about 10 blocks of Central. Taking Louisiana Boulevard NE north from here will bring you through the largely nondescript shopping district known as **Uptown.** After this, the rest of Albuquerque blurs into the broad area known as the **Northeast Heights;** the main attractions up this way are hiking trails in the foothills and the Sandia Peak Tramway. The other notable parts of town—technically, separate villages—are **Los Ranchos de Albuquerque** and **Corrales.** These are two districts in the **North Valley**—the stretch of the river north of Central—that contain a few of the city's better lodging options; from Old Town, head north on Rio Grande Boulevard to reach Los Ranchos, then jog west over the river and north again to Corrales.

To keep your bearings, remember that the mountains run along the east side of the city. Street addresses are followed by the city quadrant (NE, NW, SE, SW); the axes are Central and 1st Street. When locals talk about "the Big I," they mean the relatively central point where I-40 and I-25 intersect.

Sights

Most sightseeing destinations are along or near Central Avenue (historic Route 66), with the remaining sights scattered elsewhere in the greater metro area.

OLD TOWN

Until the railroad arrived in 1880, this wasn't just the old town—it was the *only* town. The labyrinthine old adobes have been repurposed as souvenir emporiums and galleries; the city's major museums are nearby on Mountain Road. Despite the chile-pepper magnets and cheap cowboy hats, the residential areas surrounding the shady plaza retain a strong Hispano flavor, and the historic Old Town buildings have a certain endearing scruffiness—they're lived-in, not polished.

★ ABQ Trolley Co.

800 Rio Grande Blvd. NW; 505/240-8000; www.tourabq.com

To cruise the major attractions in town and get oriented, put yourself in the hands of the excellent locally owned and operated ABQ Trolley Co.—even if you're not normally the bus-tour type. The difference here is, first of all, in the bus itself: in summer, a goofy faux-adobe open-sided trolley-bus; in winter, a stealthy black van. But much more important are the enthusiastic owners, who give the tours themselves. Their love of the city is clear as they wave at pedestrians and tell stories about onetime Albuquerque resident and Microsoft founder Bill Gates.

All tours depart from the Hotel Albuquerque at Old Town. The 120-minute **tour** (10am and noon daily; $30) runs through downtown and some off-the-beaten-track old neighborhoods, passing many TV and movie locations. Buy tickets online to guarantee a spot; the tickets also get you discounts around town, so it's good to do this early in your visit.

ABQ BioPark

505/768-2000; www.cabq.gov/biopark; 9am-5pm daily; $10-16

The earnest ABQ BioPark is made up of several components, linked by parkland along the river. On the riverbank just west of Old Town are an **aquarium** and **botanical gardens**

ABQ Trolley Co.

Old Town Albuquerque

ZEARING AVE

PAXTON'S ▼

SAWMILL MARKET ▼

BELLAMAH AVE

HOTEL CHACO

HOTEL ALBUQUERQUE

RIO GRANDE BLVD

20TH ST

18TH ST

0   200 yds

0   200 m

MOUNTAIN RD

Old Town Founder & Gateway Park

VISITORS CENTER ℹ️

ROUTES

CHARLEVOIX ST

THE CANDY LADY

MUSEUM OF NATURAL HISTORY & SCIENCE ★

MOUNTAIN RD

CASA FLAMENCA ■

CAPILLA DE NUESTRA SEÑORA DE GUADALUPE

ALBUQUERQUE MUSEUM OF ART & HISTORY

¡EXPLORA! ★

BLUE PORTAL GALLERY

CHURCH ST

SLATE STREET CAFÉ ★

ROMERO ST

SAN FELIPE DE NERI CHURCH

19TH ST

Tiguex Park

POST OFFICE ■

BREAKING BAD RV TOUR ★

NORTH PLAZA ST

BREAKING BAD STORE ABQ ■

SOUTH PLAZA ST

⭐ ABQ TROLLEY CO.

OLD TOWN RD

OLD TOWN PIZZA PARLOR ▼

TREASURE HOUSE ★

RIO GRANDE BLVD

AMERICAN INTERNATIONAL RATTLESNAKE MUSEUM

SAN FELIPE ST

SAN PASQUAL AVE

19TH ST

MARBLE AVE

CENTRAL AVE

BOTTGER MANSION ■

CENTRAL GRILL ▼

LOMAS BLVD

SAN PASQUALE AVE

DURAN CENTRAL PHARMACY ▼

CENTRAL AVE

VINAIGRETTE ▼

To ABQ BioPark Aquarium & Botanical Gardens ↓

ALBUQUERQUE LITTLE THEATRE ■

CHACOMA PL

© MOON.COM

(2601 Central Ave. NW). The aquarium is small but well stocked, with a giant shark tank and displays on underwater life from the Gulf of Mexico and up the Rio Grande. The well-conceived adjoining gardens include a desert hothouse, a butterfly habitat, a Japanese garden, a garden railroad, and a surprisingly compelling "BUGarium" full of insects in close approximations of their natural habitats. The gardens also include the 10-acre Rio Grande Heritage Farm, a re-creation of a 1930s operation with heirloom apple orchards and rare types of livestock, such as Percheron horses and Churro sheep, in an idyllic setting near the river. The whole facility is very kid friendly, but in the desert rose garden, there's a pleasant **mini café** where you can enjoy a glass of wine, too.

A few blocks away is the **zoo** (903 10th St. SW), which you can reach from the aquarium via a miniature train. While not exactly groundbreaking, in recent years the zoo has received a series of updates, which included several enclosures receiving upgrades and the introduction of a sleek so-called Penguin Chill. Throughout the zoo there's plenty of space for kids to run around; aside from the new penguin exhibit, the window into the gorilla nursery is probably the most fascinating. Tickets for each section (zoo or aquarium/gardens) are $10, and a combo ticket for entry to all three, which includes the mini-train ride when available, is $16. Ticket booths close 30 minutes before the attractions' closing times.

The land between the zoo and aquarium, on the east bank of the river, south of Central, is **Tingley Beach** (1800 Tingley Dr. SW; sunrise-sunset; free), 18 acres of paths and three ponds for fishing; you can also relax at the small **café** (late May-early Sept.).

Albuquerque Museum of Art and History

2000 Mountain Rd. NW; 505/243-7255; www.cabq.gov/museum; 9am-5pm Tues.-Sun.; $6
The Albuquerque Museum of Art and History has a permanent collection ranging

from a few choice Taos Society of Artists members to contemporary work by the likes of Nick Abdalla, whose sensual imagery makes Georgia O'Keeffe's flower paintings look positively literal. The history wing covers four centuries, with emphasis on Spanish military trappings, Mexican cowboys, and Albuquerque's early railroad years. Free guided tours run daily around the sculpture garden, or you can join the informative **Old Town walking tour** (11am Tues.-Sun. mid-Mar.-mid-Dec.). The museum has free admission Saturday after 2pm, Sunday 9am-1pm, and the third Thursday night of the month, when it's open until 8:30pm.

American International Rattlesnake Museum

202 San Felipe St. NW; 505/242-6569; www.rattlesnakes.com; 11:30am-5:30pm Tues.-Sat., 1pm-5pm Sun. June-Aug., 11:30am-5:30pm Tues.-Sat. Sept.-May; $8.95
You'd never guess that a small storefront just off the plaza houses the largest collection of live rattlesnakes in the world. An outsized gift shop tempts at the entrance to the American International Rattlesnake Museum; press past the snake swag to view the live critters in the back. You'll also see some fuzzy tarantulas and Gila monsters; the enthusiastic staff are usually showing off some animals outside to help educate the phobic.

Capilla de Nuestra Señora de Guadalupe

404 San Felipe St. NW; noon-5pm Thurs.-Sat.
One of the nifty secrets of Old Town, the tiny adobe Capilla de Nuestra Señora de Guadalupe is tucked off a small side alley. It's dedicated to the first saint of Mexico; her image dominates the wall facing the entrance. The dimly lit room, furnished only with heavy carved seats against the walls, is still in regular use (although, unfortunately, a fire put an end to lit votive candles, and the image of the Virgin was repainted in a more modern style). Despite the building's diminutive size, it follows the scheme of many traditional New

Breaking Bad

The Candy Lady tempts *Breaking Bad* viewers with bags of blue treats.

Walter White and Jesse Pinkman may be gone from television, but their legacy lives on in Albuquerque. The AMC show about a high school chemistry teacher turned meth cook, *Breaking Bad* was originally written for a California setting, but production moved to Albuquerque following tax incentives. It was a happy accident, and unlike other productions shot here anonymously, *Breaking Bad* was explicitly down with the 505.

Dedicated fans can book a tour in the **Breaking Bad RV** (1919 Old Town Rd. NW, Suite 11; 505/205-7292; www.breakingbadrvtours.com; 3 hours; $95), which is a strong facsimile of the one from the show (on the outside, natch) as it takes you to no less than twenty sites from both *Breaking Bad* and the *Better Call Saul* series, the latter of which has equally strong ties to the Duke City. The bike rental company **Routes** (2113 Charlevoix St. NW; 505/933-5667; www.routesrentals.com; $95) offers three-hour "Biking Bad" tours on request.

A few other sights around town include:

- The **Dog House** hot dog stand, with its exceptionally fine neon sign, is at 1216 Central Avenue Southwest, near Old Town.

- **The Grove** (600 Central Ave. SE), where Lydia loved her stevia too well, is a popular café downtown.

- **Los Pollos Hermanos** is actually Twisters, at 4257 Isleta Boulevard Southwest, but the PH logo is painted on the wall outside.

- Walt and Skyler's **A1A Car Wash** is at Menaul and Eubank (9516 Snow Heights Circle NE, for your GPS).

As for souvenirs of your Albuquerque visit, **Great Face & Body** (123 Broadway SE; 505/430-5053) sells "Bathing Bad" blue bath salts. **The Candy Lady** (424 San Felipe St. NW; 505/243-6239), which cooked the prop "meth" for a few episodes, sells its blue hard candy in zip-top plastic bags. For everything from a Los Pollos Hermanos apron to a Walter White blue hazmat figure, look no further than the imaginatively stocked **Breaking Bad Store ABQ** (2047 S. Plaza St. NW; 505/242-6944) in Old Town.

Mexican churches, with a clerestory that allows sunlight to shine down on the altar.

¡Explora!

1701 Mountain Rd. NW; 505/224-8300; www.explora. us; 10am-5pm daily; adults $10, children $6

A 50,000-square-foot complex adjacent to the natural history museum, ¡Explora! is dedicated to thrilling—and educating—with science. Its colorful geodesic-dome top reflects the enthusiastic and engaging tone within; inside, more than 250 interactive exhibits demonstrate the scientific principles behind everything from high-wire balancing to gravity. Since this is the desert, a whole section is dedicated to water, where kids can build a dam using Lego pieces.

Museum of Natural History and Science

1801 Mountain Rd. NW; 505/841-2800; www.nmnaturalhistory.org; 9am-5pm Mon. and Wed.-Sun.; museum adults $8, children $5, planetarium or theater $7

The Museum of Natural History and Science is a large exhibit space containing three core attractions: a planetarium and observatory, a wide-format theater screening the latest vertigo-inducing nature documentaries, and an exhibit of Earth's geological history. Discounted admission is available if you buy tickets to more than one attraction.

The museum section devotes plenty of space to the crowd-pleasers: dinosaurs. New Mexico has been particularly rich soil for paleontologists, and several species that once lived in the area now known as the Bisti Badlands are on display, such as *Coelophysis* and *Pentaceratops*. Highlighting much smaller animals from today, the Naturalist Center exhibit shares insight into the flora and fauna throughout the state.

San Felipe de Neri Church

2005 N. Plaza St. NW; 10am-4pm daily

Established in 1706 along with the city itself, San Felipe de Neri Church was originally built on what would become the west side of the plaza—but it dissolved in a puddle of mud after a rainy season in 1792. The replacement structure, on the north side, has fared much better, perhaps because its walls, made of adobe-like terrones (sun-dried bricks cut out of sod) are more than five feet thick. As they have for two centuries, local parishioners attend Mass here, which is conducted three times a day, once in Spanish.

Like many religious structures in the area, this church received a late-19th-century makeover from Eurocentric bishop Jean-Baptiste Lamy of Santa Fe. Under his direction, the place got its wooden folk Gothic spires, as well as new Jesuit priests from Naples, who added such non-Spanish details as the gabled entrance and the widow's walk. The small yet grand interior has brick floors, a baroque gilt altar, and an elaborate pressed-tin ceiling with Moorish geometric patterns. A tiny **museum** (505/243-4628; usually 10am-4:30pm daily; free), accessible through the gift shop, contains some historic church furnishings.

DOWNTOWN

Albuquerque's downtown district, along Central Avenue between the train tracks and Marquette Avenue, was once known as bustling New Town, crowded with mule-drawn streetcars, bargain hunters, and wheeler-dealers from the East Coast. At Central Avenue and 4th Street, two versions of Route 66 intersect. When the original highway was commissioned in 1926, the road from Chicago to the West Coast ran along 4th Street; after 1937, the route was smoothed so that it ran east-west along Central. The route brought more business, but spread it through the city: In the 1950s and 1960s, shopping plazas farther east in Nob Hill and the Northeast Heights drew business away from downtown. By the 1970s, the neighborhood was a wasteland of government office buildings. Thanks

1: Museum of Natural History and Science 2: Capilla de Nuestra Señora de Guadalupe 3: Albuquerque Museum of Art and History 4: San Felipe de Neri Church

Downtown Albuquerque

JUNO BREWERY

KINLEY AVE

SUMMER AVE

12TH ST
11TH ST

GOLDEN
CROWN
PANADERIA

MOUNTAIN RD

Wells
Park

6TH ST
5TH ST
4TH ST
3RD ST
2ND ST
1ST ST

HARWOOD
ART CENTER

7TH ST

GRANITE AVE

FORRESTER AVE

CHATTER SUNDAY

MARBLE AVE

MARBLE BREWERY

LOMAS BLVD

McClellan
Park

KEELER AVE
8TH ST

CELL THEATRE

MARQUETTE AVE

TIJERAS AVE

DOCTOR MARTIN LUTHER KING JUNIOR AVE

KENT AVE

CAFÉ LUSH

CENTRAL AVE

TIJERAS AVE

Washington
Middle
School Park

Robinson
Park

COPPER AVE

TELEPHONE
MUSEUM

MÁS TAPAS Y VINO/
HOTEL ANDALUZ

505
CENTRAL

LAUNCHPAD

ANODYNE

HOLOCAUST AND
INTOLERANCE
MUSEUM

516 ARTS

BOESE
BROTHERS

KIMO THEATRE

CENTRAL AVE

GOLD AVE

8TH ST
7TH ST

CECILIA'S
CAFÉ

POST
OFFICE

OCCIDENTAL
LIFE BUILDING

SUNSHINE
THEATER

SILVER AVE

6TH ST
5TH ST
4TH ST
3RD ST

BOX
PERFORMANCE
SPACE

Alvarado
Transportation
Center

GREAT FACE
& BODY

EXHIBIT/208

2ND ST
1ST ST

LEAD AVE

BROADWAY BLVD

TURQUOISE
MUSEUM

COAL AVE

© MOON.COM

to an aggressive urban-renewal scheme, downtown has regained some of its old vigor, and Central is now a thoroughfare best known for its bars.

By day there aren't many attractions to detain you, but you can join a walking tour with **Albuquerque Tourism & Sightseeing Factory** (219 Central Ave. NW; 505/200-2642; www.tourabq.com), the friendly, informed crew that also runs the city trolley tours. Walks are currently limited to the Albucreepy (2.5 hours; $30), a nighttime ghost tour with three stops at Old Town bars along the way.

★ KiMo Theatre

423 Central Ave. NW; 505/768-3522;
www.cabq.gov/kimo

Albuquerque's most distinctive building is the KiMo Theatre. In 1927, local businessman and Italian immigrant Carlo Bachechi hired Carl Boller, an architect specializing in movie palaces, to design this marvelously ornate building. Boller was inspired by the local adobe and native culture to create a unique style dubbed Pueblo Deco—a flamboyant treatment of Southwestern motifs, in the same vein as Moorish- and Chinese-look cinemas of the same era. The tripartite

stucco facade is encrusted with ceramic tiles and Native American iconography (including a traditional Navajo symbol that had not yet been appropriated by WWII Germany's Nazi Party when the KiMo was built).

To get the full effect, catch one of the concerts, plays, or special film screenings the KiMo hosts throughout the year, or else take a **self-guided tour** during the theater's Meet the KiMo event (check the website for current dates, free) of the interior to see the cow-skull sconces and murals of pueblo life; enter through the business office, just west of the ticket booth.

Occidental Life Building

Gold Ave. at 3rd St.

The one-story Occidental Life Building is another of Albuquerque's gems, built in 1917 by H. C. Trost, whose work defines downtown El Paso, Texas. With its ornate facade of white ceramic tile, it looks a bit like the Doge's Palace in Venice rendered in marshmallow fluff. After a 1933 fire, the reconstructing architects added even more frills, such as the crenellations along the top. The entire building is surfaced in white terra-cotta; the tiles were made in a factory in Denver, Colorado, that sprayed the ceramic glaze onto concrete

KiMo Theatre

blocks, each individually molded and numbered, and the blocks were then assembled in Albuquerque according to an overall plan. (The building is owned by local-boy-made-good Jared Tarbell, a cofounder of Etsy, the online craft site. Tarbell's high-tech toy- and art-manufacturing company and event space, Levitated, is located nearby, on Silver Avenue at 7th Street.)

Museums
Holocaust and Intolerance Museum
616 Central Ave. SW; 505/247-0606; http://nmholocaustmuseum.org; noon-3:30pm Wed.-Sat.; $6
Production value is basic at the storefront Holocaust and Intolerance Museum, but the message is compelling. Displays cover not just World War II, but also the Armenian genocide, actions against Native Americans, and a new permanent exhibit on African Americans and enslavement.

Telephone Museum
110 4th St. NW; 505/841-2937; 10am-1:30pm Mon., Wed., and Fri.; $2
Nearby, the surprisingly detailed three-story Telephone Museum is worth a visit—if you happen to get there during its limited open time.

Turquoise Museum
400 2nd St. SW; 505/247-8650; http://turquoisemuseum.com; tours 11am and 1pm Mon.-Sat.; $20
Occupying the opulent eyeful that is Zachary Castle, the Turquoise Museum now occupies a setting much better suited to its collection. Exhibits present the geology and history of turquoise, along with legendary trader J. C. Zachary's beautiful specimens from all over the world. But most folks can't help but think how this relates to all the jewelry they plan to buy. So come here to learn the distinction between "natural" and "real" turquoise and arm yourself for the shopping ahead. The castle itself, built by one of Albuquerque's most successful businesswomen, is worth a visit.

THE UNIVERSITY AND NOB HILL
When it was established in 1889, what's now the state's largest university was only a tiny outpost on the far side of the railroad tracks. Surrounding the campus, which sprawls for blocks, is the typical student-friendly scrum of cheap-pizza places and dilapidated bungalow rentals. To the east along Central is Nob Hill, a thriving neighborhood developed around a shopping plaza in the late 1940s and still showing that decade's distinctive style in marquees and shop facades.

The University of New Mexico
Between Central Ave. and University Blvd.; 505/277-5020; www.unm.edu
Approximately 25,000 students are enrolled at the University of New Mexico (UNM) campus. The school's oldest buildings were designed in a distinct pueblo-inspired style, commissioned in the early 1900s by college president William George Tight. Trustees later fired Tight in part for his non-Ivy League aesthetics, but the style was in motion. Pueblo Revival pioneer John Gaw Meem carried on the vision through the 1940s, and even with contemporary structures now set among the original halls—of these **Mesa Vista Hall** and **Zimmerman Library** stand out—it's still a remarkably harmonious vision, uniting the pastoral sanctuary feel of the great East Coast campuses with a minimalist interpretation of native New Mexican forms.

Visitors can park in a complex just inside the UNM campus across from Cornell Street. The info center, where you can pick up a detailed map, is in the southwest corner of the structure.

University Art Museum
203 Cornell Dr. NE; 505/277-4001; http://artmuseum.unm.edu; noon-5pm Wed.-Thurs., noon-6pm Fri.-Sat.; $5 donation
Just across the way, the University Art Museum displays treasures from the permanent fine art collection of more than 30,000 pieces from all over the globe.

The University and Nob Hill

Maxwell Museum of Anthropology

Off University Blvd., north of M. L. K. Jr. Blvd.;
505/277-4405; http://maxwellmuseum.unm.edu;
10am-4pm Tues.-Sat.; free

Rest up at the bucolic duck pond, then head for the Maxwell Museum of Anthropology, a Meem building designed as the student union. The museum has a strong overview of Southwestern Indian culture, numerous Native American artifacts from university-sponsored digs all over the state, and a surprisingly extensive collection of objects depicting cultures from around the world.

Nob Hill

At Girard Street, a neon-trimmed gate marks the start of the Nob Hill district, which extends east along Central Avenue about 10 blocks to Washington Boulevard. The area began to grow after 1937, when Route 66 was rejiggered to run along Central. The Nob Hill shopping plaza, at Central and Carlisle, signaled the neighborhood's success when it opened as the glitziest shopping district in town a decade later. The area went through a slump from the 1960s through the mid-1980s, but it's now lined with brightly painted facades and neon signs, making it a lively district where the quirk factor is high—whether you want designer underwear or an antique Mexican mask, you'll find it here.

Bart Prince House

3501 Monte Vista Blvd. NE

Head off of Central on Monte Vista and keep an eye out for the Bart Prince House, known affectionately as The Spaceship. The home and studio of one of the city's most celebrated contemporary architects, it's the residential counterpart to the eccentric businesses that flourish in this area.

NORTH VALLEY

The stretch of the river north of Central is one of Albuquerque's prettier areas, shaded with cottonwoods and dotted with patches of farmland. The scenic route through North Valley is Rio Grande Boulevard; the commercial strip is 4th Street.

Indian Pueblo Cultural Center

2401 12th St. NW; 505/843-7270;
www.indianpueblo.org; 9am-4pm Tues.-Sun.; $12
Just north of I-40 from Old Town, the Indian Pueblo Cultural Center is a must-visit before heading to any of the nearby Indian communities. The horseshoe-shaped building (modeled after the Pueblo Bonito ruins in

Chaco Canyon in northwestern New Mexico) houses a large museum that traces the history of the first settlers along the Rio Grande. It is illustrated with some beautiful artifacts and showcases distinctive craftwork from each pueblo.

The central plaza hosts **dance performances** (11am and 2pm Sat.-Sun. Apr. and Sept.-Oct., 2pm Fri., 11am and 2pm Sat.-Sun. May-Aug., noon Sat.-Sun. Nov.-Mar.), one of the only places to see them outside of the pueblos themselves. The extensively stocked gift shop is a very good place to buy pottery and jewelry; you can also have a lunch of stew and fry bread at the Indian Pueblo Kitchen. Don't miss the south wing, which contains a gallery for contemporary art. At the information desk, check on ceremony schedules and get directions to the various pueblos.

The Rebirth of Route 66

Route 66 is one of the biggest repositories of U.S. nostalgia, a little neon ribbon of cool symbolizing the country's economic growth in the 20th century. But the "mother road," on which so many Dust Bowl refugees made their way west and so many beatniks got into their grooves, officially no longer exists; the highway was decommissioned in 1985. You can still follow the brown historic-marker signs from Chicago to Los Angeles, however, including along **Central Avenue.**

the De Anza

The businesses that thrived in the early highway era—especially the numerous 1940s motor courts—fell on hard times long ago. As part of Albuquerque's aggressive urban-renewal program, city planners demolished a number of motels, leaving dead neon signs standing like tombstones amid the rubble. But the city had a change of heart with the 1939 **De Anza** (4305 Central Ave NE), on the east edge of Nob Hill, and bought it in 2003 to protect, among other things, beautiful interior murals by American Indian painters. In the meantime, Burqueños developed fresh affection for their neon-lit heritage. So, when the owner of the **El Vado Motel,** near Old Town, threatened his vintage property with the wrecking ball, the city bought that, too. Construction began apace and El Vado has been reborn as a motor-themed boutique hotel complete with a taproom and restaurants. The De Anza underwent a somewhat similar rebirth and has been remodeled into luxury apartments, with some set aside for extended stays.

The city's ongoing interest in preserving its Route 66 heritage just might yield similar rebirths in the future. In the meantime, check out a 4.5-mile self-guided tour of the fabled highway at www.visitalbuquerque.org.

Rio Grande Nature Center State Park

2901 Candelaria St. NW; 505/344-7240; www.emnrd.nm.gov; 8am-5pm daily; $5/car

Explore a secluded wetland landscape at the Rio Grande Nature Center State Park. The sleek, concrete **visitors center** (10am-5pm daily) houses an exhibit on water conservation and river ecology, while just beyond is a comfortable glassed-in "living room," where you can watch birds on the pond from the comfort of a lounge chair, with the outdoor sounds piped in through speakers.

Outside, several **paved trails** run across irrigation channels and along the river, shaded by towering cottonwoods. In the spring and fall, the area draws all manner of migrating birdlife. Borrow binoculars from the staff if you want to scout on your own, or join one of the frequent **nature walks** (including full-moon tours) that take place year-round.

Los Ranchos and Corrales Road Scenic Byway

For a pretty drive (or bike ride) through historic villages that have been all but consumed by greater Albuquerque, head north from Old Town on Rio Grande Boulevard; you first reach Los Ranchos, then cross the river at Alameda to Corrales Road (Hwy. 448) and continue north up the west bank. This

Corrales Road Scenic Byway still holds pockets of pastoral calm, a practical melding of old agricultural heritage with modern suburban trappings.

Old San Ysidro Church

966 Old Church Rd.; 505/897-1513; 1pm-4pm Sat.-Sun. June-Oct.

The only real sights are in central Corrales, two blocks west of Hwy. 448. The folk Gothic Old San Ysidro Church stands where the center of the village was in 1868, when its bulging adobe piers were first constructed. Every spring, the church gets a fresh coat of mud from the community. The church hosts several concerts and arts shows throughout the year; check with the Corrales Historical Society (www.corraleshistory.org) for upcoming events.

Casa San Ysidro

973 Old Church Rd.; 505/898-3915;
www.cabq.gov/museum; guided tours $6

Across the road, Casa San Ysidro was the home of obsessive collectors Alan and Shirley Minge. While they lived in the place, 1952-1997, they heated with firewood and squirreled away New Mexican antiques and craftwork. It is a lovingly preserved monument to a distinct way of life. The Albuquerque Museum gives **tours** (10:30am, noon, and 1:30pm Tues.-Sat. June-Aug.) of the interior with its beautiful brickwork and wood carving; tours are less frequent September-November and February-May (9:30am and 1:30pm Tues.-Fri., 10:30am, noon, and 1:30pm Sat.). You can just show up, but it's a good idea to call to confirm the times.

ALBUQUERQUE METRO AREA

Beyond Central Avenue, Albuquerque is largely a haze of nondescript houses and shopping centers built during the 1960s and later—decades one local journalist dubbed the city's Asphalt Period. A few sights are well worth seeking out, however.

National Hispanic Cultural Center

1701 4th St. SW; 505/246-2261; www.nhccnm.org

Just south of downtown (but not quite walking distance), the modern National Hispanic Cultural Center lauds the cultural contributions of Spanish speakers the world over. It has had a positive influence in the down-at-the-heels district of Barelas (even the McDonald's across the street mimics its architecture), but numerous houses—occupied by Hispanic people, no less—were demolished for its construction. One woman refused the buyout, and her two small houses still sit in the parking lot, a kind of exhibit of their own.

The central attraction is the **museum** (10am-4pm Tues.-Sun.; $6), which shows work ranging from the traditional bultos and retablos by New Mexican craftspeople to contemporary painting, photography, and even furniture by artists from Chile, Cuba, Argentina, and more. If you can, visit on Saturday or Sunday, when the **torreón** (tower) is open (noon-5pm) to show Frederico Vigil's amazing fresco *Mundos de Mestizaje,* a decadelong project depicting the many strands—Arab, Celtic, African—that have contributed to Hispanic culture today.

Adjacent to the museum is the largest Hispanic genealogy library in existence, as well as the giant **Roy E. Disney Center for Performing Arts.**

National Museum of Nuclear Science & History

601 Eubank Blvd. SE; 505/245-2137;
www.nuclearmuseum.org; 9am-5pm daily; $15

The spiffy National Museum of Nuclear Science & History covers everything you wanted to know about the nuclear era, from the development of the weapon on through current energy issues. Exhibits cover the ghastly elements of the atomic bomb, but also wonky tech details (check out the display of decoders set in suitcases for emergency deployment) and pop-culture artifacts, such as "duck and cover" films from the Cold War. Don't miss the beautiful posters by Swiss

American artist Erik Nitsche. The adjoined nine-acre Heritage Park offers close-up views of a vast collection of missiles and jet rocket launchers, and even a replica of the tower from Trinity Site.

★ Sandia Peak Tramway

30 Tramway Rd.; 505/856-7325; www.sandiapeak.com; 9am-9pm daily June-Aug., 9am-8pm Wed.-Mon. and 5pm-8pm Tues. Sept.-May; $3 parking, $33 round-trip, $22 one-way

The longest tramway of its type in the world, the Sandia Peak Tramway whisks passengers 2.7 miles and 4,000 feet up, along a continuous line of Swiss-made cables. The ride from Albuquerque's northeast foothills to Sandia Crest, the highest point in the Sandia Mountains, takes about 15 minutes; the views of the cityscape and beyond along the way can be breathtaking. You can also take in views from inside **Ten 3** (30 Tramway Rd. NE; 505/764-8363; 11am-8pm Thurs.-Sun.; from $15), a restaurant at the top of Sandia Crest that opened in 2019; it serves steaks and the like in the evening and less expensive meals during the day.

The tramway is also a convenient means to get to the ski area in winter, and in summer and fall you can hike along the ridgeline via the Crest Trail (no. 130) to the Sandia Crest House gift shop. The tramway runs frequently year-round, but check the website for periodic maintenance closures in fall and spring.

At the base of the tram, there's a small, free museum about skiing in New Mexico, and even from this point, the view across the city is very good.

★ Petroglyph National Monument

Visitors center: Unser Blvd. at Western Tr.; 505/899-0205; www.nps.gov/petr; 8:30am-4:30pm daily

Albuquerque's west side is marked by the black boulders of Petroglyph National Monument, some of which are the canvas for 20,000 carved lizards, birds, and assorted other beasts. Most of the images, which were created by chipping away the dark "varnish"

of the volcanic rock to reach the paler stone beneath, are 400-700 years old, while others may date back three millennia. A few later examples of rock art include Maltese crosses made by Spanish settlers and initials left by explorers (not to mention a few by idle teenagers in more recent years).

Stop in first at the **visitors center** for park maps, flyers on flora and fauna, and general orientation. From here, you will have to drive to the major trails that crisscross the monument's 7,500 acres: **Boca Negra Canyon,** a short, paved loop and the only fee area ($1/car on weekdays, $2 on weekends); **Piedras Marcadas Canyon,** a 1.5-mile unpaved loop; and **Rinconada Canyon,** an out-and-back hike (2.2 miles round-trip) that can be tedious going in some spots because the ground is sandy. The clearest, most impressive images can be found here, in the canyon at the end of the trail. Everywhere in the park area, keep an eye out for millipedes, which thrive in this environment; dead, their curled-up shells resemble the spirals carved on the rocks—coincidence?

For the best overview (literally) of this area's geology, head for the back (west) side of the parkland, the **Volcanoes Day Use Area** (9am-5pm daily), where three cinder cones mark Albuquerque's western horizon. Access is via Atrisco Vista Boulevard (exit 149) off I-40; turn right (east) 4.3 miles north of the highway at a dirt road to the parking area.

From this vantage point, you can look down on the lava "fingers" that stretch east to form the crumbled edges of the escarpment where the petroglyphs are found. The fingers were formed when molten rock flowed between sandstone bluffs, which later crumbled away. The volcanoes were last reported emitting steam in 1881, though a group of practical jokers set smoky fires in them in the 1950s, briefly convincing city dwellers of an impending eruption. But the peaks are not entirely dead: Patches of green plants flourish

1: Sandia Peak Tramway **2:** Petroglyph National Monument

Albuquerque's Hot-Air History

How did it come to be that one of the most iconic sights in Albuquerque is the pairing of Darth Vader and Yoda, each several stories tall, floating in front of the Sandias? Albuquerque, it turns out, enjoys the world's most perfect weather for navigating hot-air balloons. A phenomenon called the Albuquerque Box, created by the steep mountains adjacent to the low river bottom, enables pilots to move at different speeds at different altitudes, and even to backtrack, if necessary. Combine that with more than 300 days of sunshine per year, and it's no wonder that now more than 600 balloons convene each October to show off their colors and compete in precision flying contests.

a balloon preparing for liftoff at Balloon Fiesta

The city's air currents were discovered to be friendly to balloons for the first time in 1882. That was when an adventurous bartender piloted a hydrogen-filled craft into the sky as part of the New Town's Fourth of July celebrations, much to the delight of the assembled crowd, which had waited almost two days for *The City of Albuquerque*, as the balloon was dubbed, to fill. "Professor" Park Tassell, the showman pilot, went aloft alone and landed successfully; the only mishap was that a ballast sandbag was emptied on a spectator's head.

Ninety years passed, and in 1972, Albuquerque again drew attention to this venerable pursuit. This was the year the first balloon fiesta was held, with 13 aircraft participating. The gathering, a rudimentary race, was organized as a publicity stunt for a local radio station's 50th-anniversary celebration. The spectacle drew 20,000 people, most of whom had never even seen a hot-air balloon before—but within a few short years, the event was internationally renowned, and the **Balloon Fiesta** has been a hugely popular annual event ever since.

around the steam vents that stud the hillocks, particularly visible on the middle of the three volcanoes.

Anderson Abruzzo Albuquerque International Balloon Museum

9201 Balloon Museum Dr. NE; 505/768-6020; www.balloonmuseum.com; 9am-5pm Tues.-Sun.; $6

Boosters of Albuquerque's hot-air balloon scene—which has been flourishing since the first rally in 1972—include locals Ben Abruzzo, Larry Newman, and Maxie Anderson, who in 1978 made the first Atlantic crossing by balloon in the *Double Eagle II* helium craft. Abruzzo and Anderson also crossed the Pacific and set a long-distance record (5,678 miles) in the *Double Eagle V*.

These pioneers are honored at the so-called **BaMu,** in Balloon Fiesta Park just off Alameda Boulevard. The displays are a great mix of historical background, interactive physics lessons, and inspiring footage of record-setting balloon ventures. As long as you don't dwell too long on the zeppelin exhibit, complete with china and tableware from the *Hindenburg,* you may come away sufficiently inspired by the grace of balloons to seek out a ride in one yourself.

Coronado Historic Site

485 Kuaua Rd., Bernalillo; 505/867-5351; 10am-4pm Wed.-Mon.; $5

Though named for Spanish explorer Francisco Vásquez de Coronado, who camped on this lush riverside spot during his 1540 search for gold, the Coronado Historic Site is actually a Native American relic, the partially restored pueblo of Kuaua (Tiwa for "evergreen"), inhabited between 1300 and the early 1600s. The centerpiece is one of the partially sunken kivas, or ceremonial chambers, inside which murals of life-size human figures and animals were discovered in the 1930s. The images were carefully salvaged, then reproduced in the kiva by Velino Herrera (Ma Pe Wi), a member of a key group of early American Indian figurative painters who also painted murals in the U.S. Department of the Interior in Washington DC.

With Herrera's reproductions in place, this is the only opportunity to witness the usually protected, sacred space of a kiva close to how it originally appeared. And once you've seen the complete images, it's easier to pick out the representations on the original frescoes mounted in the visitors center—some of the oldest examples of Indigenous art on display anywhere in the United States.

Join a tour of the kiva, if possible—the guides add a lot to the story. On occasional weekends, there are traditional craft and music demonstrations as well. And even if none of that is going on, this is a beautiful

spot for a picnic. Facing the river and the mountains, with the city hidden from view behind a dense screen of cottonwoods, you get a sense of the lush, calm life along the Rio Grande in the centuries before the Spanish arrived. To reach the monument, exit I-25 in Bernalillo and head west on Highway 550; Kuaua Road is on your right, before the Santa Ana Star casino.

Gruet Winery

8400 Pan American Fwy. NE; 505/821-0055; www.gruetwinery.com; 11am-7pm Sun.-Wed., 11am-9pm Thurs.-Sat.; wine tasting $16

Spanish missionaries planted the first vineyards in North America in New Mexico in the 17th century, and the industry persisted until a series of floods finally wiped out the vines by the 1920s. So New Mexico's current wine scene, while strong, is still somewhat young. One of the state's best wineries, Gruet began producing its excellent sparkling wines (the Gruet family hails from Champagne, France) only in 1987; look out especially for its nonvintage sparkling rosé, which is delicious and affordable. A wine-tasting visit includes four pours; **tours** are offered at 2pm.

Recreation

From the river basin up to mountain peaks, Albuquerque has plenty to keep you active in the outdoors for days on end. Late summer (after rains have started and fire danger is past) and fall are the best times to head to the higher elevations on the Sandia Mountains. Once the cooler weather sets in, the scrub-covered foothills and the bare, rocky West Mesa are more hospitable. The valley along the Rio Grande, running through the center of the city, is remarkably pleasant year-round: mild in winter and cool and shady in summer. As everywhere in the desert, always pack extra layers of clothing and plenty of water before you set out, and don't go charging up Sandia

Crest (10,678 feet above sea level) your first day off the plane.

★ BALLOONING

For most people, the Balloon Fiesta is a spectator event, but the truth is you can go up, up, and away yourself just about any day of the year, thanks to the ideal conditions nearly always present around Albuquerque. A trip is admittedly an investment (and you have to wake up well before dawn for sunrise trips), but there's no other ride quite like it and the views can forever change how you see the city.

Rainbow Ryders

505/823-1111; www.rainbowryders.com; from $179 pp

One of the longest established operations is Rainbow Ryders. Typically, you're up in the balloon for about an hour, depending on wind conditions, and a champagne toast awaits when you're back on solid ground.

HIKING
Rio Grande Nature Center State Park

2901 Candelaria St. NW; 505/344-7240; www.rgnc.org; 8am-5pm daily; $3/car

Between the West Mesa and the East Mountains, there are plenty of day hikes to choose from. The least strenuous is the bosque (the wooded area along the Rio Grande), where level paths lead through groves of cottonwoods, willows, and olive trees. The Rio Grande Nature Center State Park is the best starting point for any walk around the area. The park has a combination of hiking paths and interpretive trails, all of which are less than a mile long and mostly flat.

Sandia Foothills

The city's greatest concentration of trails can be found to the east of the city, in the Sandia foothills, where hikes are ideal in winter but a little hot in summer. They're best accessed at the **Elena Gallegos Picnic Area** (7am-9pm daily Apr.-Oct., 7am-7pm daily Nov.-Mar.; $1 on weekdays, $2 on weekends), east of Tramway Boulevard and north of Academy, at the end of Simms Park Road. Various trails lead into the foothills from the picnic area.

Embudito Canyon Trail

Distance: *12 mi round-trip*
Time: *7-8 hours*
Trailhead: *Off Glenwood Hills Dr., south of Elena Gallegos Picnic Area*

The challenging and scenic Embudito Canyon Trail (no. 192) travels through the namesake canyon gradually up to 9,768-foot South Sandia Peak. Most of the hike is in the shade, though the majority of the exposed portions are during the final stretch to the peak. For this reason, it's advisable to head out early in summer.

La Luz Trail

Distance: *7.5 mi up, take tram down*
Time: *3-4 hours*
Trailhead: *Far north end of Tramway Blvd., before the road turns west; parking $3 per car*

The foothills are also the starting point for the popular but tough La Luz Trail (no. 137), which offers a dramatic ascent to Sandia Crest. The trail has a 12 percent grade at certain points, and passes through four climate zones (pack lots of layers) as you climb 3,200 vertical feet. Near the top, you can take a spur that leads north to the Sandia Crest observation point or continue on the main trail south to the ski area and the Sandia Peak Tramway, which you can take back down the mountain. Ideally, you'd have someone pick you up at the bottom, because the 2.5-mile trail from the tram back to the trailhead has no shade. (You might be tempted to take the tram up and hike down the La Luz Trail, but the steep descent can be deadly to toes and knees.)

Crest Trail

Distance: *3.2 mi round-trip*
Time: *2 hours*
Trailhead: *Sandia Peak Tramway terminus or Sandia Crest House gift shop*

A 1.6-mile (one-way) section of the Crest Trail (no. 130) takes you on a hike along the Sandia Crest ridgeline, between the Sandia Peak Tramway terminus and the Sandia Crest House gift shop to the east. Views along the way are fantastic. The trail is fairly level and can be hiked in either direction. Budget about two hours round-trip. Arriving by tramway to the western trailhead is the easiest approach, but you can also drive up the east face of the mountain via scenic Highway 536, aka the Sandia Crest Road, to arrive at the trailhead adjacent to the Sandia Crest House gift shop.

Birding on the Crest

gray-crowned rosy finch

In the dead of winter, **Sandia Crest** does not seem hospitable to life in any form, much less flocks of delicate-looking birds the size of your fist, fluffing around cheerfully in the frigid air. But that's precisely what you'll see if you visit right after a big snowfall. These are rosy finches, a contrary, cold-loving variety (sometimes called "refrigerator birds") that migrate from as far north as the Arctic tundra to the higher elevations of New Mexico, which must seem relatively tropical by comparison.

What's special about Sandia is that it draws all three species of **rosy finch,** which in turn draws dedicated birders looking to add the finches to their life lists, and it's one of the few places to see them that's close to a city and accessible by car. So, if you see the finches—they're midsize brown or black birds with pink bellies, rumps, and wings—you'll probably also spy some human finch fans. But they might not have time to talk, as it's not unheard-of for the most obsessive birders—those on their "big year," out to spot as many species as possible in precisely 365 days—to fly in to Albuquerque, drive to the crest, eyeball the finches, and drive right back to the airport again.

BIKING

Albuquerque maintains a great network of paved trails in the city, and the mountains and foothills have challenging dirt tracks.

Outfitters

Routes

2113 Charlevoix St. NW; 505/933-5667; www.routesrentals.com; 9am-5pm daily; $25/4 hours, $40/day

The most visitor-friendly bike store in town is Routes, which rents city cruisers, mountain bikes, and more at its handy location in Old Town; pickup and drop-off from hotels is free. It also runs fun daylong **bike tours** along the Rio Grande (from $85), and rents snowshoes ($25/day) in the winter.

Mountain Biking

Mountain bikers can explore the 30 miles of wooded trails at **Sandia Peak Ski Area.** Bikes aren't allowed on the tram, though, so if you have your own ride, you can drive up via Highway 536 on the east side of the mountain.

Also on the east side of the mountains, a whole network of trails leads off Highway 337 (south of I-25), through **Otero Canyon** and other routes through the juniper-studded Manzanos. Or stay in the city and ride the popular 16-mile long **Trail 365,** which covers a nice mix of terrain without being too difficult; access it via the Elena Gallegos Open Space Park. The trail is part of the **Sandia Foothills Trails,** a vast network of dirt tracks all along the edge of the Northeast Heights. Locals built a small but fun BMX terrain park at **Embudo Canyon;** park at the end of Indian School Road.

Road Biking
Paseo del Bosque
Recreational cyclists should look no farther than the river, where the Paseo del Bosque, a 16-mile-long, completely flat biking and jogging path, runs through the Rio Grande Valley State Park. The northern starting point is at **Alameda/Rio Grande Open Space** (7am-9pm daily Apr.-Oct., 7am-7pm daily Nov.-Mar.) on Alameda Boulevard. You can also reach the trail through the **Rio Grande Nature Center State Park** (www.rgnc.org; 8am-5pm daily; $3/car), at the end of Candelaria, and at several other major intersections along the way. For details on this and other bike trails in Albuquerque, download a map from the city's bike info page (www.cabq.gov/bike) or pick up a free copy at bike shops around town.

Corrales Road Scenic Byway
Corrales, in the far North Valley, and the gentle 6.7-mile long Corrales Road Scenic Byway that you can take Alameda Boulevard NW to reach the village, both make for a relaxing afternoon ride. The speed limit on Corrales' main street is low, and you can dip into smaller side streets and bike along the acequias.

Sandia Crest
A popular and more challenging tour is up to Sandia Crest via Highway 536, also known as Sandia Crest Road, on the east side—you can park and ride from any point, but cyclists typically start somewhere along Highway 14 north of I-40, then ride up Highway 536, which winds 13.5 miles along increasingly steep switchbacks to the crest. The **New Mexico Touring Society** (www.nmts.org) lists descriptions of other routes and organizes group rides.

SWIMMING
Rio Grande Pool
1410 Iron Ave. SW; 505/848-1397; www.cabq.gov; noon-5pm and 5:30pm-7:30pm Mon.-Fri., 1pm-5pm Sat.-Sun. late May-mid-Aug.; $3
Beat the heat at the Rio Grande Pool, Albuquerque's nicest public place to take a dip; the outdoor 25-meter pool is shaded by giant cottonwoods.

WINTER SPORTS
For trail conditions, call or visit the **Sandia ranger station** (505/281-3304) on Highway 337 in Tijeras.

Sandia Peak Ski Area
505/242-9052; www.sandiapeak.com; mid-Dec.-mid-Mar.; $60 full-day lift ticket
Though Sandia Peak Ski Area opens in mid-December, it often takes until about February for a good base to build up. The 10 main trails, serviced by four lifts, are not dramatic, but they are good and long. The area is open daily in the holiday season, then Wednesday-Sunday for the rest of the winter.

Capulin Springs Snow Play Site
Hwy. 536; 9:30am-3:30pm Fri.-Sun. in winter; $3/car
Groomed cross-country skiing trails start from Capulin Springs Snow Play Site, where there are also big hills for tubing and sledding. Look for the parking lot nine miles up Highway 536 on the way to Sandia Crest.

10K Trail
Hwy. 536; $3/car
Nine minutes farther up on the mountain on Highway 536 is the trailhead for the 10K Trail,

usually groomed for cross country skiers, as is a service road heading south to the upper tramway terminal; the latter is wide and relatively level—good for beginners.

SPAS

Betty's Bath & Day Spa

1835 Candelaria Rd. NW; 505/341-3456;
www.bettysbath.com

Betty's Bath & Day Spa is the place to get pampered, whether with a massage ($125/60 minutes) and a facial (from $85) or with an extended dip in a hot tub (from $30/30 minutes).

Love's Healing Touch

1218 Broadway NE; 505/289-0495;
www.loveshealingtouch.com

Closer to downtown, Love's Healing Touch has similar facilities, including a solar-heated communal tub; the sauna is done in Finnish cedar. The reasonable rates ($35/two hours) include the use of robes and sandals, and massages ($100/60 minutes) are available, too.

SPECTATOR SPORTS

Albuquerque Isotopes

1601 Avenida Cesar Chavez NE; 505/924-2255;
www.milb.com

Minor-league baseball thrives in Albuquerque, apparently all because of some clever name: The so-so Dukes petered out a while back, but a fresh franchise, under the name of the Albuquerque Isotopes, draws crowds. It's hard to judge whether the appeal is the cool **Isotopes Park,** the whoopee-cushion theme nights, or just the name, drawn from an episode of *The Simpsons*. Regardless, a summer night under the ballpark lights is undeniably pleasant; it helps that you can usually get good seats for around $15.

The Pit

Avenida Cesar Chavez at University Blvd.;
505/925-5626; www.golobos.com

Burqueños also go crazy for UNM Lobos **basketball,** packing the raucous University Arena, aka The Pit—one of the largest college venues in the country. Tickets start at $20, but the seats with the best vantage points and comfort start at $40.

New Mexico United

Isotopes Park, 1601 Avenida Cesar Chavez NE;
505/209-7529; www.newmexicoutd.com

Albuquerque's newest sports team is New Mexico United, which played its inaugural season in 2019 in the United Soccer League's second division. Matches are played at Isotopes Park from spring until fall, with most tickets ranging $16-42. As the state's only professional soccer team, the club has quickly gathered an enthusiastic following, though efforts to secure city financing for a dedicated stadium have stalled.

Entertainment

NIGHTLIFE

Albuquerque's drinking dens can host a remarkable cross section of subcultures, and even the most chic-appearing places could see a Sandia National Laboratories physicist and a veteran Earth Firster propping up the bar next to well-groomed professionals.

That said, the city's main bar and club scene, in a few square blocks of downtown, can feel a bit generic, with free-flowing beer specials for non-choosy students. It ends in a rowdy scene after closing time on weekends, when crowds spill out onto several blocks of Central that are closed to car traffic. So, although this area does have a few good bars, you'll find more interesting entertainment elsewhere.

Downtown
Hotel Andaluz

125 2nd St. NW; 505/242-9090; lobby bar 11am-10pm
Sun.-Thurs., 11am-11pm Fri.-Sat., rooftop bar 4pm-11pm
Sun.-Thurs., 4pm-1am Fri.-Sat.

The Hotel Andaluz lobby touts itself as "Albuquerque's living room"—hotelier Conrad Hilton's original vision for the place—and it's a comfy spot to sip cocktails and nibble tapas, especially if you reserve one of the six private booths ("Casbahs") on the weekend. **Ibiza,** its rooftop bar, is a sleek and cozy spot to watch the sunset over drinks.

Apothecary Lounge

806 Central Ave. SE; 505/242-0040; 4pm-10pm Sun.-Thurs., 3pm-11:30pm Fri.-Sat.

A great spot to watch the Sandia Mountains turn pink at sunset, the Apothecary Lounge is the rooftop bar at the Parq Central hotel in East Downtown. Fitting with the historic atmosphere of the hotel, the bar specializes in vintage cocktails.

Anodyne

409 Central Ave. NW; 505/244-1820; 4pm-midnight Sun.-Thurs., 4pm-1am Fri.-Sat.

One of the best all-purpose casual bars downtown, Anodyne is a long, wood-floored room filled with pool tables and thrift-store sofas. Choose from more than a hundred beers, and get some quarters to plug in to the good collection of pinball machines. Happy hour is 4pm-8pm Monday-Thursday, and until 9pm on Friday.

Sister

409 Central Ave. NW; 505/242-4900; www.sisterthebar.com; 4pm-11pm Mon.-Thurs., 11am-1am Fri.-Sat., 11am-11pm Sun.

Downstairs in the same building as Anodyne, the more cavernous Sister has tacos, live bands, and more pinball.

The University and Nob Hill
Gecko's

3500 Central Ave. SE; 505/262-1848; 11am-11pm Sun.-Thurs., 11am-midnight Fri.-Sat.

In the Nob Hill shopping plaza, Gecko's is a good place for finger food (anything from taquitos to buttermilk onion rings) and a drink in the sidewalk seats.

O'Niell's

4310 Central Ave. SE; 505/255-6782; 11am-10pm daily

Sporting its own breezy patio, the venerable O'Niell's is a great Irish pub that draws a varied crowd, whether for the quiz nights or weekend folk bands; the kitchen is open until 11pm. There's a second location in the Northeast Heights with the same hours (3301 Juan Tabo Blvd. NE; 505/293-1122).

THE ARTS

It's no stretch to say Albuquerque has the liveliest theater scene in the Southwest, with dozens of troupes in action.

Vortex Theatre

2900 Carlisle Blvd. NE; 505/247-8600; www.vortexabq.org

One of the city's standbys, the black box Vortex Theatre has been running since 1976. After a couple of lean years due to COVID, the theater is back to a regular full slate of plays.

Albuquerque Little Theatre

224 San Pasquale St. SW; 505/242-4750; www.albuquerquelittletheatre.org

The more standard repertory Albuquerque Little Theatre was founded in 1930 and hosts performances in an intimate 500-seat Works Progress Administration-era building

Adobe Theater

9813 4th St. NW; 505/898-9222; www.adobetheater.org

Up in the North Valley, the Adobe Theater has been running in some form since 1957. Its full calendar features performances based on the works of nationally known playwrights as well as collaborative pieces by local artists.

Cell Theatre

700 1st St. NW; 505/766-9412; www.fusionnm.org

The 70-seat Cell Theatre is home to the long-running FUSION, a theater company of professional union actors. It often runs recent Broadway dramas and is part of the FUSION Forum, a campus for the theater company

Albuquerque Beer Culture

Burque's beer scene is a lively one, with taprooms regularly putting on some of the city's best events and enticing with new drafts and food pairings. Nob Hill is a center for the city's beer culture, and below are some of the best spots in the neighborhood as well as Albuquerque at large. For more, see the **New Mexico Brewers Guild** (www.nmbeer.org). The *Albuquerque Journal* also has a dedicated Brews News beat. For car-free sampling, check out **Duke City Pedaler,** a so-called party bike that fits over a dozen passengers and makes a few stops at Old Town and Sawmill area bars and tasting rooms (www.tourabq.com; $30).

- **Il Vicino** (3403 Central Ave. NE; 505/266-7855; 11am-9pm Sun.-Thurs., 11am-10pm Fri.-Sat.): This Nob Hill pizza parlor, the original of the three locations now in Albuquerque, has been brewing its own beer since 1994. It has a large brewing facility at the **Canteen Brewhouse** (2381 Aztec Rd. NE; noon-9pm Sun.-Wed., noon-10pm Thurs.-Sat.). There's also the **Canteen Taproom** (417 Tramway Blvd. NE; 505/200-2344; noon-9pm Sun.-Wed., noon-10pm Thurs.-Sat.), serving the same brews with close-up views of the Sandias.

- ★ **Bow & Arrow** (600 McKnight Ave. NW; 505/247-9800; 3pm-9pm Mon.-Wed., 3pm-10pm Thurs., noon-11pm Fri.-Sat., noon-9pm Sun.): This bright, spacious Native-American-owned beer hall has an impressive variety of Southwest-themed offerings, including a blue corn lager, hazy IPA, and a farmhouse red ale.

- **Paxton's** (1909 Bellamah Ave. NW; http://sawmillmarket.com; 11am-9pm Sun.-Thurs., 11am-10pm Fri.-Sat.): An airy taproom in the Sawmill Market food hall, Paxton's serves a number of regional ales from the likes of Tractor, La Cumbre, and Marble, as well as a strong mix of stouts and IPAs. The outdoor seating area is usually packed in summer.

- **Boese Brothers** (601 Gold Ave. SW; 505/382-7060; 5pm-11pm Tues.-Wed., 5pm-1am Thurs.-Sat.): This downtown brewery is big and lively, usually with six house brews on tap and a menu of sandwiches. A second location is in Northeast Heights (7849 N. Tramway Blvd., Ste. C; 505/821-0752; 3pm-10pm Tues.-Fri., noon-10pm Sat., noon-9pm Sun.).

- **Marble Brewery** (111 Marble Ave. NW; 505/243-2739; 11am-midnight Mon.-Sat., 11am-10:30pm Sun.): The brewery is located pleasantly out of the downtown fray, with a dog-friendly outdoor area featuring eclectic bands. In Northeast Heights there's the **Marble Taproom** (9904 Montgomery Blvd. NE; 505/323-4030; 11am-10pm Mon.-Wed., 11am-midnight Thurs.-Sat., 11am-10:30pm Sun.), and another is on the west side (5740 Night Whisper Rd. NW; 505/508-4368; 11am-10pm Mon.-Wed., 11am-midnight Thurs.-Sat., 11am-10:30pm Sun.).

- ★ **Juno Brewery** (1501 1st St. NW; 505/219-3938; 4pm-11pm Mon., 4pm-10pm Tues.-Wed., 4pm-midnight Thurs.-Fri., 2pm-midnight Sat., 2pm-10pm Sun.): Funky and friendly, much like its previous incarnation as Dialogue Brewing, this brewery fosters a strong community feel and showcases works by local artists. There are DJs and live acts some nights, too. Beers on tap include lagers, IPAs, and a smooth stout.

- **Tractor Brewing:** This popular brewing company has three locations near central Albuquerque. Its brewery is in the industrial area north of downtown (1800 4th St. NW; 505/243-6752; 3pm-10pm Mon., 2pm-11pm Tues. and Fri., 2pm-10pm Wed.-Thurs., 1pm-11pm Sat., 1pm-10pm Sun.), an airy bar is in Nob Hill (118 Tulane St. SE; 505/433-5654; noon-midnight Sun.-Thurs., noon-2am Fri.-Sat.), and there's an outpost on the west side (5720 McMahon Blvd. NW; 505/361-1834; 1pm-10pm Sun.-Thurs., 1pm-midnight Fri., 1pm-11pm Sat.). The brewery and bar feature live music regularly, while the west side outpost occasionally has food trucks parked outside.

- **La Cumbre Brewing** (3313 Girard Blvd. NE; 505/872-0225; noon-10pm Sun.-Mon., noon-11pm Tues.-Thurs., noon-midnight Fri.-Sat.): La Cumbre's brewery is in a fairly isolated industrial area, with only the occasional food truck for sustenance, but locals love this beer. Its newer **La Cumbre Taproom** is farther out on the west side (5600 Coors Blvd. NW, Ste. C1; 505/916-0787; noon-10pm Sun.-Mon., noon-11pm Tues.-Thurs., noon-midnight Fri.-Sat.).

that also includes the spacious indoor venue **@708** and the adjacent outdoor space **The Meadow.**

Box Performance Space

114 Gold Ave. SW; 505/404-1578; www.theboxabq.com
The neighboring Box Performance Space hosts various improv groups and satirical comedians, and it conducts workshops.

Blackout Theatre

505/672-8648; www.blackouttheatre.com
Blackout Theatre doesn't have its own space, but it mounts interesting shows in interesting places: improv Dickens, for instance, or an interactive alien invasion commemorating the UFO incident at Roswell. Other groups of note include the **Duke City Repertory Theatre** (505/797-7081; www.dukecityrep.com) and **Mother Road Theatre Company** (505/243-0596; www.motherroad.org).

LIVE MUSIC
KiMo Theatre

423 Central Ave. NW; 505/768-3522;
www.cabq.gov/kimo
Albuquerque's arts scene graces a number of excellent stages. The most beautiful is the city-owned KiMo Theatre, often hosting locally written plays and dance, as well as the occasional musical performance and film screening.

Roy E. Disney Center for Performing Arts

1701 4th St. SW; 505/724-4771; www.nhccnm.org
Bigger classical and folkloric acts perform at the Roy E. Disney Center for Performing Arts at the National Hispanic Cultural Center, a modernized Mesoamerican pyramid that contains three venues, the largest of which is a 691-seat proscenium theater. This is the place to catch a performance by visiting or local flamenco artists; with the National Institute of Flamenco headquartered in Albuquerque, there's often someone performing.

Popejoy Hall

UNM campus; 505/925-5858; http://popejoypresents.com
UNM's Popejoy Hall hosts the New Mexico Symphony Orchestra (which also plays at the Rio Grande Zoo in the summer) as well as a selection of marquee touring Broadway musicals and dance performances.

Chatter Sunday

912 3rd St. NW; 505/234-4611; www.chatterabq.org;
10:30am Sun.
A more intimate classical event is Chatter Sunday. Originally known as Church of Beethoven, this chamber-music show aims to offer all the community and quiet of church, with none of the religious overtones. The "service" lasts about an hour, with two musical performances, interspersed with a poem and a few minutes of silent contemplation. It's all fueled by free espresso.

Casa Flamenca

401 Rio Grande Blvd. NW; 505/247-0622;
www.casaflamenca.org
Flamenco enthusiasts should check the schedule at Casa Flamenca in Old Town. The dance school in an old adobe house hosts a monthly tablao, in which local teachers and visiting experts perform.

Isleta Amphitheater

5601 University Blvd. SE; www.isletaamphitheater.net
For rock and rap concerts, the biggest venue in town is Isleta Amphitheater, with space for some 15,000 people.

Sandia Casino

I-25 at Tramway; 505/796-97500; www.sandiacasino.com
The next step down is one of the Albuquerque-area casinos, the ritziest of which is Sandia Casino, which has a 4,000-seat outdoor amphitheater.

Sunshine Theater

120 Central Ave. SW; 505/764-0249;
http://sunshinetheaterlive.com
Sunshine Theater is a converted movie

house with excellent sightlines. The schedule features a wide mix of shows with a more alternative bent, including frequent national acts.

Launchpad

618 Central Ave. SW; 505/764-8887;
www.launchpadrocks.com

To catch touring indie rockers or the local crew about to hit it big, head to the lively Launchpad. Arrive early as shows are often packed and space is a premium; there are a few arcade games, too.

FESTIVALS AND EVENTS

Gathering of Nations Powwow

Tingley Coliseum and Expo New Mexico, both at 300 San Pedro Dr. NE; 505/836-2810;
www.gatheringofnations.com; Apr.

The colorful Gathering of Nations Powwow is the largest tribal get-together in the United States, with more than 3,000 dancers and singers in full regalia from over 500 tribes coming together. Miss Indian World earns her crown by showing off traditional talents such as spearfishing and storytelling.

Albuquerque Summerfest

Various outdoor venues in Nob Hill, Northeast Heights, and the North Valley; www.cabq.gov; one Sat. per month June-Aug.; free

Held in three different parts of Albuquerque, the city-run Summerfest features free concerts, local crafts, food trucks, and plenty of beer from local breweries.

New Mexico State Fair

Expo New Mexico, 300 San Pedro Dr. NE;
www.exponm.com; Sept.; $15

Just after Labor Day, the state's agricultural roots get their due at the New Mexico State Fair: two weeks of fried foods, prizewinning livestock, midway rides, and really excellent rodeos, which often end with shows by country music legends.

¡Globalquerque!

National Hispanic Cultural Center, 1701 Fourth St. NW;
www.globalquerque.org; mid-Sept.; from $50

The eclectic and never dull two-day world-music fest ¡Globalquerque! draws top-notch pop and traditional performers from around the world as well as plenty of international arts and crafts and cuisine.

Sunshine Theater

Ceremonial Dances

This is an approximate schedule for dances at Albuquerque-area pueblos. Pueblo feast days are always on the same date and generally open to all, but seasonal dances (especially Easter and other spring rituals) can vary, and are sometimes closed to visitors. Confirm details and start times with the **Indian Pueblo Cultural Center** (2401 12th St. NW; 505/843-7270; www.indianpueblo.org) before setting out.

- **January 1:** Jemez: Los Matachines; Kewa (Santo Domingo): corn dance
- **January 6:** Most pueblos: various dances to honor new tribal officials
- **Easter:** Most pueblos: various dances
- **May 1:** San Felipe: Feast of San Felipe
- **Memorial Day weekend:** Jemez: craft show and powwow
- **June 13:** Sandia: Feast of San Antonio
- **June 29:** Santa Ana and Kewa (Santo Domingo): Feast of San Pedro
- **July 14:** Cochiti: Feast of San Bonaventura
- **July 26:** Santa Ana: Feast of Santa Ana
- **August 2:** Jemez: Feast of Santa Persingula
- **August 4:** Kewa (Santo Domingo): Feast of Santo Domingo
- **August 10:** Jemez: Pueblo Independence Day and Fair
- **August 15:** Zia: Feast of the Assumption of Our Blessed Mother
- **August 28:** Isleta: Feast of San Agustín (ends September 4)
- **Labor Day:** Kewa (Santo Domingo): craft market
- **November 12:** Jemez: Feast of San Diego
- **December 12:** Jemez: Los Matachines
- **December 25:** Santa Ana, Kewa (Santo Domingo), and Zia: various dances
- **December 26-28:** Kewa (Santo Domingo): corn dance; also dances at most other pueblos

ALBUQUERQUE ENTERTAINMENT

Albuquerque International Balloon Fiesta

Balloon Fiesta Park, 4401 Alameda Blvd. NE; 505/821-1000; www.balloonfiesta.com; Oct.; $15

The city's biggest annual event is the Albuquerque International Balloon Fiesta, nine days dedicated to New Mexico's official state aircraft, with more than 700 hot-air balloons of all colors, shapes, and sizes gathering at a dedicated park on the north side of town, west of I-25. During the fiesta, the city is packed with "airheads," who claim this is the best gathering of its kind in the world. If you go, don't miss an early morning mass ascension, when the balloons glow against the dark sky, then lift silently into the air in a great wave. Parking can be a nightmare—take the park-and-ride bus ($25, including admission), or ride a bike (valet parking available!).

Marigold Parade

South Valley; 505/363-1326; www.muertosymarigolds.org; early Nov.

Don't miss the Marigold Parade, celebrating

The Albuquerque Art Scene

When it comes to art, the Duke City may not have the buzz or the wealth that's concentrated farther north in Santa Fe, but it does have DIY energy, refreshing diversity, and a long history, thanks to the highly respected fine arts program at the University of New Mexico. On the first Friday of every month, the citywide **Artscrawl** (www.artscrawlabq.org; 5pm-8pm) keeps galleries and shops open late in Nob Hill, Old Town, and downtown. The rest of the time, check out these arts spaces and galleries:

- **Exhibit/208** (208 Broadway Blvd. SE; www.exhibit208.com; 10am-4pm Thurs.-Sat.): Work by full-time artists, some well-known in the state. Openings are usually the second Friday evening of the month.

- **516 Arts** (516 Central Ave. SW; 505/242-1445; www.516arts.org; noon-5pm Tues.-Sat.): Polished downtown space with numerous international artists.

- **Harwood Art Center** (1114 7th St.; 505/242-6367; www.harwoodartcenter.org; 10am-3pm Wed.-Thurs.): Classes, exhibits, and special events, all with a strong community connection.

- **Mariposa Gallery** (3500 Central Ave. SE; 505/268-6828; http://mariposa-gallery.com; 11am-6pm Mon.-Sat., noon-5pm Sun.): In Nob Hill, long established (since 1974) and eclectic, with jewelry, fiber art, and other crafts.

- **Matrix Fine Art** (3812 Central Ave. SE; 505/917-8054; www.matrixfineartabq.com; 1pm-5pm Thurs.-Sun.): In east Nob Hill, showing only New Mexico artists, usually figurative.

- **Tamarind Institute** (2500 Central Ave. SE; 505/277-3901; tamarind.unm.edu; 1pm-4pm Thurs.-Fri.): Long-established and nationally renowned lithography center; gallery on the second floor shows expert prints.

- **Tortuga Gallery** (901 Edith Blvd. SE; 505/506-0820; www.tortugagallery.org; hours vary): Music, poetry, and more, with a super-grassroots vibe.

the Mexican Day of the Dead and general South Valley pride. The parade is a procession of skeletons, cars bedecked in flowers, and a little civil rights activism.

Winter Holiday Season

Multiple locations; Dec.

During the holiday season, the city is trimmed with luminarias (paper-bag lanterns), especially in Old Town and the Country Club neighborhood just to the south. The Albuquerque Botanic Garden (www.cabq.gov/culturalservices/biopark/garden) is decked out with holiday lights and model trains for much of December, and ABQ Ride, the city bus service, offers the **Luminaria Tour** (45 minutes; $1.50) around the prettiest neighborhoods on Christmas Eve.

Shopping

You can pick up traditional American Indian jewelry and pottery for very reasonable prices in **Old Town** and the surrounding area, while **Nob Hill** is the commercial center of Albuquerque's counterculture, with body-piercing studios adjacent to comic book shops next to herbal apothecaries.

OLD TOWN
Blue Portal Gallery

2107 Church St. NW; 505/243-6005;
11am-4pm Tues.-Sat. 1pm-4pm Sun.

The galleries and gift shops around the plaza can blur together after just a little bit of browsing, but the Blue Portal Gallery is a nice change, with well-priced and often very refined arts and crafts, from quilts to woodwork, by Albuquerque's senior citizens. And the **street vendors** set up on the east side of the plaza are all artisans selling their own work, at fair prices.

Duran Central Pharmacy

1815 Central Ave. NW; 505/247-4141;
9am-6pm Mon.-Fri., 9am-4pm Sat.-Sun.

For a huge selection of interesting New Mexico gifts and books, as well as local herbal treatments, visit Duran Central Pharmacy, just outside Old Town.

Treasure House

2012 S. Plaza St.; 505/242-7204;
11:30am-5pm Sun.-Tues., 11am-5:30pm Thurs.-Sat.

On the plaza, Treasure House has a nice collection of New Mexican and Southwestern-themed books and gifts. Most of the titles are from independent publishers, and there are several cookbooks to choose from as well.

THE UNIVERSITY AND NOB HILL
Nob Hill Music

3904-B Central Ave. SE; 505/266-4200;
noon-6pm Thurs.-Sun.

Among the various quirky boutiques in this area, of particular note is Nob Hill Music, hands down the city's best record store and in a new location a few blocks east of its old spot. Flipping through vinyl albums here is very satisfying and can quickly transport you to a bygone era that is enjoying something of a resurgence.

University of New Mexico Bookstore

2301 Central Ave. NE; 505/277-5451; 9am-5pm
Mon.-Fri.

The University of New Mexico Bookstore maintains a good stock of travel titles and maps, along with state history tomes and the like. In summer, it closes an hour earlier on weekdays.

NORTH VALLEY
Bookworks

4022 Rio Grande Blvd. NW; 505/344-8139;
www.bkwrks.com; 9am-6pm daily

Bookworks has a large stock of New Mexico-related work as well as plenty of other titles, all recommended with the personal care of the staff.

Indian Pueblo Store

2401 12th St. NW; 505/843-7270;
www.indianpueblo.org; 9am-4pm Tues.-Sun.

For excellent crafts, head to Indian Pueblo Store, the shop at the Indian Pueblo Cultural Center. Not only are prices reasonable, but the staff is happy to explain the work that goes into various pieces.

Los Poblanos Farm Shop

4803 Rio Grande Blvd. NW; 505/938-2192;
9am-6pm daily

Los Poblanos Farm Shop sells soaps, bath salts, and lotions scented with the organic lavender grown in the adjacent field. It also stocks an excellently curated selection of garden gear, books, kitchen supplies, and locally made snacks.

ALBUQUERQUE METRO AREA
Rail Yards Market

777 1st St. SW; www.railyardsmarket.org;
10am-2pm Sun. May-Oct.

Set in the old Santa Fe workshops south of downtown, Rail Yards Market is a festive gathering of arts and crafts, produce, snacks, and live music. It's a good place to shop for offbeat souvenirs—and it's a great chance to see inside the majestic old buildings where locomotives for the Santa Fe line were built from the ground up.

Flea Market

300 San Pedro Dr. NE; 505/319-2849; $2, $7 parking

Every Saturday and Sunday, Albuquerque's flea market takes place at the Expo New Mexico fairgrounds (enter at Gate 1, on Central just west of Louisiana). It's an interesting outlet where you can pick up anything from new cowboy boots to loose nuggets of turquoise; socks and beef jerky are also well represented. Stop off at one of the myriad food stands for a snack—refreshing aguas frescas (fruit juices, in flavors such as watermelon and tamarind) and Indian fry bread are the most popular. In theory it starts at 7am, but most vendors get rolling around 9am and go until a little after 3pm.

ABQ Uptown

2200 Louisiana Blvd. NE; 505/899-6918

If you're looking for central one-stop mall shopping, your best bet is ABQ Uptown, where stores like the North Face, Lush, Anthropologie, and Apple are chock-a-block at the intersection of Louisiana Boulevard NE and Indian School Road NE.

Food

Albuquerque has a few dress-up establishments, but the real spirit of the city's cuisine is in its lower-rent spots where dedicated owners follow their individual visions. The more traditional New Mexican places tend to be open only for breakfast and lunch, so plan accordingly.

OLD TOWN

Aside from the few recommended here, the restaurants in the blocks immediately adjacent to the Old Town plaza are expensive and only so-so; better to walk another block or two for real New Mexican flavor, or drive a short way west on Central.

New Mexican

★ Duran Central Pharmacy

1815 Central Ave. NW; 505/247-4141;
9am-4pm Sun.-Tues., 9am-7pm Wed.-Sat.; $8.75-15

Look behind the magazine rack at Duran Central Pharmacy, and you'll find an

Sawmill Market

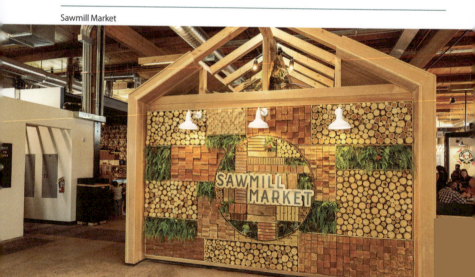

old-fashioned lunch counter. Regulars pack this place at lunch for all the New Mexican staples: huevos rancheros, green-chile stew, and big blue corn enchilada plates.

Fresh and Local
Sawmill Market

1909 Bellamah Ave. NW; 505/563-4470; 8am-9pm Sun.-Thurs., 8am-10pm Fri.-Sat.; prices vary by vendor

Occupying a former lumberyard building, Sawmill Market, with its collection of top-notch food merchants, filled a void in Old Town when it opened in 2020. Each site within the food hall offers something different, but they all share a common focus on local ingredients. Highlights include **Plata Coffee,** which can expertly address your caffeine fix; **Dr. Field Goods,** a farm-to-table spot with a focus on fresh meats; **Notorious P.O.K.E,** which features colorful poke bowls, including an excellent one with salmon and another with Hatch green chile shrimp; and **Neko Neko,** a Japanese-inspired soft ice cream shop. Stalls are added regularly, and the space also contains a few artisan shops.

★ Vinaigrette

1828 Central Ave. SW; 505/842-5507; 11am-9pm Mon.-Sat.; $9-18

Founded in Santa Fe, Vinaigrette is an excellent "salad bistro" with more substantial plates than you might imagine—its apple-cheddar chop with arugula is especially satisfying, and it has sandwiches including a Reuben and tuna melt. It's a welcome spot of healthy eating around Old Town.

Italian
Old Town Pizza Parlor

108 Rio Grande Blvd. NW; 505/999-1949; 11am-7pm Sun.-Thurs., 11am-8pm Fri.-Sat.; $9-15

It's not necessarily a destination from elsewhere in the city, but Old Town Pizza Parlor is an unpretentious, kid-friendly place to eat in Old Town, with generously topped pizzas, ultra-creamy pastas, dense calzones, and cheesy garlic fingers. The back patio is a welcomed bonus.

Cafés
Slate Street Café

2000 Mountain Rd. NW; 505/243-2210; 9am-2pm Tues.-Sun.; $8-14

Inside the Albuquerque Museum, Slate Street Café is great for coffee and cupcakes, as well as more substantial breakfast and lunch entrées, such as a seared salmon club with applewood bacon. Its larger, original location is at 515 Slate Ave. NW (505/243-2210).

Diners
Central Grill

2056 Central Ave. SW; 505/554-1424; 7am-2pm daily; $3.50-12

Built on the bones of an old fast-food joint, Central Grill still makes quick food, but with a fresher, more homemade feel and free Wi-fi. Like a good diner should, it serves breakfast all day, including real maple syrup and strong coffee. Its daily special plate is usually a solid deal, with a main like a grilled tortilla burger plus sides and a drink for around $10.

DOWNTOWN

While there's no shortage of bars and coffee shops in this area, there's not exactly a huge selection of places when it comes to finding a sit-down meal.

Food Halls
505 Central

Corner of Central Ave. SW and 5th St. NW; www.505central.com; 11am-9pm Sun.-Wed., 11am-10pm Thurs.-Sat.; prices vary by vendor

The opening of 505 Central in 2020 went some ways toward enlivening not just the downtown's food scene but also the area in general. The split-level industrial warehouse is home to about 10 vendors that offer everything from Detroit-style pizza at **Thicc Pizza Co.** (505/450-2487), spicy fried chicken sandwiches at **Kukri Chicken** (505/582-8891), New Mexican beer and spirits at **Moᵒnwalk**

(505-505/8777), and hot coffee and donuts at **Humble Coffee** (505/609-7099).

New Mexican
★ Cecilia's Café

230 6th St. SW; 505/243-7070;

7am-1:30pm Mon.-Fri.; $8-12

Even though it's in the middle of Albuquerque's main business district, Cecilia's Café feels more like a living room than a restaurant. Maybe it's the woodstove in the corner—as well as the personal attention from Cecilia and her daughters—and the food is clearly made with care. The rich, dark-red chile really shines, elevating dishes such as a chorizo burrito, chicken enchiladas, and a sopaipilla burger.

Fresh and Local
★ The Grove

600 Central Ave. SE; 505/248-9800;

8am-2pm Tues.-Sun.; $9-16

Past the railroad tracks in EDo, The Grove draws devoted diners with its dedication to local and organic ingredients, big front windows facing Central, and a screened-in patio. The chalkboard menu features creative salads (mixed greens, roasted golden beets, asparagus, and almonds is one combo) as well as sandwiches and cupcakes. Hearty breakfast dishes, such as pancakes with crème fraiche and poached eggs, are served all day.

Farmers Markets

There are a number of farmers markets throughout the city; one of the largest is downtown at Robinson Park on Central Avenue at 8th Street (8am-noon Sat. Apr.-Sept.). For other markets around the city, visit www.farmersmarketsnm.org.

Spanish
Más Tapas y Vino

125 2nd St. NW; 505/923-9080;

7am-9pm daily; $10-26 tapas, $18-48

Chef James Campbell Caruso made his name in Santa Fe as a maestro of Spanish cuisine. His Albuquerque outpost, Más Tapas y Vino,

in the Hotel Andaluz, shows off many of his best dishes, but it's not quite as chummy as his other restaurants. If you're not also visiting Santa Fe and want a creative bite of Iberian goodness, including grilled octopus and vegetarian paella, though, consider this a possible special-occasion meal. It also has happy hour 4pm-6pm daily.

Italian
★ Farina Pizzeria

510 Central Ave. SE; 505/243-0130;

11am-9pm Mon.-Fri., 4pm-9pm Sat.; $13-26

A popular hangout for urban pioneers in the EDo neighborhood, Farina Pizzeria has exposed brick walls and a casual vibe. The pies come out of the wood-fired oven suitably crisp-chewy and topped with seasonal veggies. Make sure you get a cup of the Gorgonzola-crème fraîche-chive dip for your crusts—it's the upscale version of the ranch dressing that's more commonly offered. Sunday-Tuesday there are pint-and-pizza combo specials as well.

Cafés
Café Lush

700 Tijeras Ave. NW; 505/508-0164;

7am-1:30pm Mon.-Fri., 8am-1pm Sat.; $7-9

There's a lot to like on Café Lush's wide-ranging breakfast and lunch menus, including a sweet kale salad with butternut squash, bacon grilled pears and pistachios, breakfast pizza with a scallion-potato crust, a sauteed curried tofu wrap, and a house-made green chile turkey burger. The diner evokes Route 66 with its aluminum counter and tables, while dishes feature local and organic ingredients; even the croissants somehow feel healthy.

Golden Crown Panaderia

1103 Mountain Rd. NW; 505/243-2424;

7am-8pm Wed.-Sat., 10am-8pm Sun.; $4-16

A 10-minute walk from Old Town, Golden Crown Panaderia is a real neighborhood hangout that's so much more than a bakery. Famous for its green-chile bread and bizcochitos (the anise-laced state cookie), it also does pizza with blue-corn or green-chile crust, to take away or to eat at the picnic tables out back. Wash it down with a coffee milkshake.

THE UNIVERSITY AND NOB HILL

Thanks to the large student population, this area has several great and varied spots to grab a cheap bite; Nob Hill has some upscale options, too.

New Mexican
★ The Frontier

2400 Central Ave. SE; 505/266-0550;
5am-midnight; $3-13

You haven't been to Albuquerque unless you've been to The Frontier, across from UNM. Everyone in the city passes through its doors at some point; pick a seat in one of the five Western-themed rooms and watch the characters file into the place. You'll want some food, of course: a green-chile-smothered breakfast burrito filled with crispy hash browns, or a juicy hamburger, or one of the signature cinnamon rolls—a deadly amalgam of flour, sugar, and some addictive drug that compels you to eat them despite all common sense.

El Patio

142 Harvard Dr. SE; 505/268-4245;
11am-8pm daily; $9-20

Near the university, El Patio is the kind of old-reliable place that ex-locals get misty-eyed about after they've moved away. The green-chile-and-chicken enchiladas are high on many citywide-favorites lists and the Sunrise Burger—a hamburger with egg and bacon—makes a great case for kicking off your day with a large meat patty. It doesn't hurt that the setting, in an old bungalow with a shady outdoor space, feels like an extension of someone's home kitchen. The menu is more vegetarian-friendly than most New Mexican joints, including burrito and enchilada options. There's also a location just east of the Rio Grande (3851 Rio Grande NW; 505/433-4499; 11am-8pm Tues.-Sun.).

Latin American
Guava Tree Café

118 Richmond Dr. SE; 505/990-2599;
11am-4pm Tues.-Sat.; $7.95-15

Guava Tree Café is a cheerful place serving succulent Cubano sandwiches, as well as pan-Central-American treats such as arepas and coconut flan, plus tropical fruit juices. There are a few vegetarian options too, including a sandwich stuffed with roasted vegetables, provolone cheese, avocado, and topped with chimichurri sauce. Their second location near Balloon Fiesta Park (6110 Alameda Blvd. NE; 505/319-5813; 11am-8pm Sun.-Wed., 11am-9pm Thurs.-Sat.) has longer hours.

French
Frenchish

3509 Central Ave. NE; 505/433-5911;
4:30pm-8:30pm Wed.-Sat.; $12-38

Sleek and modern Frenchish has quickly built a reputation for serving French-inspired meals that look as good as they taste, and personal touches on dishes such as a sautéed trout with capers and a braised pheasant pasta. The menu's not extensive and all the better for its focus.

Vegetarian
Annapurna's

2201 Silver Ave. SE; 505/262-2424;
8am-8pm Mon.-Sat., 10am-8pm Sun.; $6.25-13.50

Venerable Annapurna's, for some, remains the city's de facto vegetarian option. There are two branches (the other location is to the northeast at 5200 Eubank Blvd. NE), both serving an extensive menu of meat-free dishes, such as the Yogi Bowl—veggies with rice or quinoa, a dosa crepe, and yogurt or chutney sauce. A bit dark and replete with earth tones, the decor hasn't seemingly changed in years, which is part of its appeal.

Mata G

116 Amherst Dr. SE; 505/266-6374;
10am-6pm Mon.-Sat.; $7-14.50

Mata G specializes in homemade and ready-to-eat vegetarian sandwiches, salads, and

soups. There are plenty of tasty options to choose from—try the spicy tempeh wrap, which is stuffed with black pepper tempeh, Vegenaise sauce, lettuce, and tomato. There's also a hot bar with a focus on a different international cuisine daily.

Cafés
★ Humble Coffee
4200 Lomas Blvd. NE; 505/289-9909; 7am-6pm daily
Great single-source coffee, attentive baristas, and a smartly designed space give the Nob Hill institution Humble Coffee plenty of reasons to boast—the selection of fresh pastries and savory breakfast burritos only adds to its considerable appeal. There's also an outpost in the 505 Central food hall.

La Montañita Co-Op
3500 Central Ave. SE; 505/265-4631; 7am-9pm daily; $6-12
Pick up goods for a picnic at La Montañita Co-Op, where fresh breakfast burritos, sandwiches, and salads are all the rage; look as well in the dairy section for samples of locally made cheese. There's a second location in the North Valley (2400 Rio Grande Blvd. NW; 505/242-8800).

Tia B's La Waffleria
3710 Campus Blvd. NE; 505/492-2007; 8am-2pm daily; $8-16
Waffles sweet or savory are the thing at Tia B's La Waffleria, set in a funky old house with front and back patios. Of course, you can get a blue-corn waffle with eggs and scorching chile or layer your waffle with smoked salmon or ham and cheese. The adventurous can build their own, too.

Flying Star Café
3416 Central Ave. SE; 505/255-6633; 7am-9pm Sun.-Wed., 7am-10pm Thurs.-Sat.; $8-18
Step in to Flying Star Café, and you'll likely be mesmerized by the pastry case, packed

with triple-ginger cookies, lemon-blueberry cheesecake, and fat éclairs. But try to look up to appreciate the all-encompassing menu: Asian noodles, hot and cold sandwiches, mac-and-cheese, and enchiladas sit alongside salads, Buddha bowls, and shrimp tacos. The food isn't always quite as great as it looks, but with speedy service and locations all over town, including two locations in North Valley (Los Ranchos: 4026 Rio Grande Blvd. NW, 505/344-6714; Corrales: 10700 Corrales Rd., 505/938-4717), it's a handy place to zip in or to lounge around (Wi-Fi is free).

NORTH VALLEY
New Mexican
★ Mary & Tito's Café
2711 4th St. NW; 505/344-6266; 11am-3pm Mon.-Thurs., 11am-5pm Fri.-Sat.; $6-9.45
Mary & Tito's Café is *the* place to go for carne adovada, the dish of tender pork braised in red chile, which is irresistible in what the café calls a Mexican turnover (a stuffed sopaipilla). The meat is flavorful enough to stand alone, but the fruity, bright red-chile sauce, flecked with seeds, is so good you'll want to put it on everything. This place is such a local icon, seemingly untouched since the 1980s (note the dusty-rose vinyl seats), it won a James Beard America's Classics award. Sadly, both Mary and Tito have passed on now, but it is holding strong, however, and the prices can't be beat.

Perea's Tijuana Bar and Restaurant
4590 Corrales Rd.; 505/898-2442; 10am-2pm Wed.-Sat.; $5-11
Out in Corrales, dependable Perea's Tijuana Bar and Restaurant has limited hours, but if you know you'll be out this way, try to fit it in. Everything in this cozy adobe is home-cooked, from Frito pie to carne adovada, and the underrated green-chile cheeseburger oozes flavor.

Indian Pueblo Kitchen
2401 12th St. NW; 505/724-3510; 9am-4pm Tues.-Sun.; $8-23
For New Mexican food with a strong

American Indian influence, hit the Indian Pueblo Kitchen, at the Indian Pueblo Cultural Center. The menu has standard burgers and fries, but it also has specialties such as a hearty pueblo stew with bison, cabbage, and oven bread. Breakfast is also good, with the atole—blue corn porridge, piñon, quinoa, amaranth, currants, sunflower seeds, berries, and toasted bread—among the standouts.

Fresh and Local
★ Campo
4803 Rio Grande Blvd. NW; 505/344-9297; 8:30am-1pm and 5pm-9pm daily; $16-60

The restaurant at Los Poblanos Historic Inn, Campo occupies a restored dairy building, and the site is a perfect extension of a menu steeped in a farm-to-table ethos. Local ingredients are featured heavily in menus that change seasonally; expect flawless takes on traditional New Mexican dishes and New American cuisine, too. For brunch, that means meals such as hominy grits with grilled sausage and quail eggs, while dinner might feature dishes such as a seared duck breast with pickled mulberry sauce. The adjoining bar is open daily from 4pm-9pm.

Italian
★ Village Pizza
4266 Corrales Rd.; 505/898-0045; 11am-8:30pm Sun.-Thurs., 11am-9pm Fri.-Sat.; $12.50-32.50

Family-owned Village Pizza in Corrales has long served some of the best pizza in and around Albuquerque, which is why it's often packed, particularly in the summer when the shaded outside dining area in the back is positively humming. Choose from a variety of crusts, toppings, and house combos—ultimately, the secret is the sauce, which locals rightly swear by.

Steakhouse
Vernon's Speakeasy
6855 4th St. NW; 505/341-0831; 4pm-10pm Wed.-Sun.; $28-$74

Vernon's Speakeasy, in Los Ranchos, is nothing if not earnest about crafting an experience quite unlike any other. As the name suggests, it's one that leans heavily on a Prohibition theme, with texted passwords to gain entry, staff playing the role of gangsters, and upright bass players thumping away in a dimly lit corner. It's not all show, however—the service is first rate and the food is impeccable, with prices to match. Choose from steak and seafood classics for mains and a long list of tempting appetizers, such as seared scallops and steamed mussels.

ALBUQUERQUE METRO AREA
Great places to eat are scattered all over the city, often in unlikely looking strip malls. These places are worth making a trip for or will provide a pick-me-up when you're far afield.

Mexican
El Modelo
1715 2nd St. SW; 505/242-1843; 7am-7pm daily; $2.15-8.60

Cruise down by the rail yards south of downtown to find El Modelo, a local go-to for a hangover-curing chicharrón burrito, chile-smothered spareribs, or tamales for the whole family—you can order a single tamale or a whole platter of food. Because it's really a front for a tortilla factory, the flour tortillas are also particularly tender. If the weather's nice, grab a seat at a picnic table outside and watch the freight trains go by.

Barelas Coffee House
1502 4th St. SW; 505/843-7577; 7:30am-3pm Mon.-Fri., 7:30am-2:30pm Sat.; $4-9

Just two blocks from the National Hispanic Cultural Center, popular Barelas Coffee House is potentially confusing to the first-timer: The attraction is not coffee, but chile—especially the red, which infuses hearty, New Mexican standards such as posole, chicharrones, and menudo. The restaurant occupies several storefronts, and even then, there's often a line out the door at lunchtime. But it's worth the wait—this is timeless food.

Fresh and Local
★ Fork & Fig
6904 Menaul Blvd. NE; 505/881-5293; 11am-8pm Tues.-Thurs., 11am-9pm Fri.-Sat.; $13-21

Firmly ensconced as one of the city's best and most inventive restaurants, Fork & Fig was founded by Josh Kennon, a Le Cordon Bleu-trained chef from Deming, a few hours south of the city. His background and New Mexican heritage are reflected in unpretentious and irresistible sandwiches, burgers, and wraps such as a sammy with turkey, poached pear, and fig jam, or the wrap stuffed with grilled salmon, greens, and aioli. The atmosphere is industrial and modern, yet casual; reserve ahead if possible, as the space is compact and the word has long been out.

Green Jeans Farmery
3600 Cutler Ave. NE; www.greenjeansfarmery.com; hours vary by store

For one-stop noshing, head to Green Jeans Farmery, a kind of outdoor food court and general hangout spot built from shipping containers. Pick from tacos at **Fusion Tacos,** juicy burgers at **Rustic,** Neapolitan pizza at **Amore,** ice cream at **Nitro Fog Creamery,** and a pint at **Santa Fe Brewing,** among other options. It draws a nice cross section of the city's denizens.

Steak
Monte Carlo Steakhouse
3916 Central Ave. SW; 505/836-9886; 11am-10pm Tues.-Sat.; $9-29

With a brown, windowless cinderblock facade and a package-liquor store in the front, Monte Carlo Steakhouse doesn't do itself any favors as far as winning over new customers. That said, it's a wondrous time machine, lined with vintage Naugahyde booths and serving good, hearty food, with scant care for calorie counts or arterial impact. The prime-rib special Thursday-Saturday, a softball-size green-chile cheeseburger, and marinated pork kebab all come with delicious hand-cut fries. Greek ownership means you get a tangy feta dressing on your salad and baklava for dessert. And even though there's a full bar, you're still welcome to buy wine from the package store up front and have it with your dinner, for a nominal markup.

Asian
Talin Market World Food Fare
88 Louisiana Blvd. SE; 505/268-0206; 9am-6pm daily

Can't decide what kind of food you're craving? Cruise the aisles of Talin Market World Food Fare, a megamarket near the fairgrounds that's stocked with items from Bombay to the United Kingdom. Its Asian stock is the largest, though, and you can get a variety of hot Laotian, Korean, and Filipino lunch items from the small cafeteria section in one corner and sweets such as pumpkin custard from the bakery. There's also a bubble-tea joint next door, and the parking lot draws a few food trucks.

Coda Bakery
230-C Louisiana Blvd. SE; 505/232-0085; 9am-5:30pm Mon.-Sat., 10:30am-5pm Sun.; $5.25-8.50

Just across the parking lot from Talin is the excellent Vietnamese café Coda Bakery, which specializes in banh mi sandwiches (try the pork meatball) and serves chewy-sweet coconut waffles and Vietnamese iced coffee.

Cafés
★ Bike in Coffee
949 Montoya St. NW; 505/764-9116; 8am-2pm Wed.-Sun. Mar.-Oct.; $3-10

Its location at the historic Old Town Farm, framed by towering cottonwoods and a floral garden, is a large part of the appeal of Bike in Coffee. As the name suggests, it caters to cyclists (though there's parking if you come by car), who stop by to fuel up for (or recover from) rides—the Paseo del Bosque is a few blocks west—with coffee, breakfast burritos, and baked goods.

Little Bear Coffee
2632 Pennsylvania St. NE; 505/300-4685; 7am-6pm daily

In Northeast Heights, Little Bear Coffee features multi-roast pour-overs and methodically prepared drinks. The modern interior is simple and unfussy with open seating. In the warmer months, the covered patio is a great place to linger for an hour or two. If you like doughnuts, you're in luck; you can pair your drink with Bristol Doughnut Company's finest—perhaps the most revered doughnuts in the city. Little Bear also has a location with a strong industrial feel in Nob Hill that recently underwent expansion (3123 Central Ave. NE; 505/917-8290; 7am-9pm daily).

Accommodations

Albuquerque isn't quite a tourist mecca, which means you can find some good-value hotels; you'll pay less here than you would in Santa Fe for similar amenities, for example—but not as much as was once the case. The only time you'll need to book in advance is early October, during Balloon Fiesta (when prices are usually higher).

OLD TOWN
$150-250
★ Bottger Mansion

110 San Felipe St. NW; 505/243-3639;
www.bottger.com; $160 d

The stately and very reasonably priced Bottger Mansion is smack in the middle of Old Town, making this an excellent central choice. The seven themed rooms are nicely appointed; most are also fairly spacious and include a queen- or king-size bed. Breakfasts are generous, and the owners are quick to provide insight into area attractions.

Over $250
Hotel Albuquerque

800 Rio Grande Blvd. NW; 505/843-6300;
www.hotelabq.com; $279 d

Wrought-iron chandeliers, viga beams, and earthen tones lend Hotel Albuquerque a traditional Southwestern aesthetic in its public areas, while guest rooms exude a more contemporary feel and have surprisingly competitive rates given the central location in Old Town. There's a full range of amenities, including restaurants, lounges, and an outdoor pool open year-round.

Hotel Chaco

2000 Bellamah Ave; 855/997-8208;
www.hotelchaco.com; $349 d

One of the city's newer hotels and on the edge of Old Town, Hotel Chaco stands out in terms of its size, scope, and the execution of its heavy Southwestern influences, with muted colors and earth tones, vigas, latillas, and works by Native American artists featured in public spaces and guest rooms. A rooftop restaurant and lounge, pool, and sleek and well-appointed fitness center round out the high-end touches; a daily all-inclusive resort fee is added for use of many of the amenities.

DOWNTOWN
$150-250
Parq Central

806 Central Ave. SE; 505/242-0040;
www.hotelparqcentral.com; $158 d

Set in the original AT&SF railroad hospital and sporting a storied past is the stylish Parq Central. Rooms are a bit small but feel light and airy thanks to big windows and gray and white furnishings, with retro chrome fixtures and honeycomb tiles in the bath. The hospital vibe is largely eradicated, though whimsical vitrines in the halls conjure old-time medical treatments, and the rooftop bar sports a gurney. Perks include free parking, a decent continental breakfast, and an airport shuttle.

★ Hotel Andaluz

125 2nd St. NW; 505/242-9090;
www.hotelandaluz.com; $206 d

A beautiful relic of early 20th-century travel, Hotel Andaluz was first opened in 1939 by

New Mexico-raised hotelier Conrad Hilton. It received a massive overhaul in 2009, keeping all the old wood and murals but updating the core to be fully environmentally friendly, from solar hot-water heaters to a composting program. The neutral-palette rooms are soothing and well designed, with a little Moorish flair in the curvy door outlines. The place is worth a visit for the lobby alone; check out the exhibits from local museums on the second-floor mezzanine.

NORTH VALLEY
Over $250
★ Los Poblanos Historic Inn

4803 Rio Grande Blvd. NW; 505/344-9297; www.lospoblanos.com; $355 d

At Albuquerque's nicest place to stay, you don't actually feel like you're anywhere near the city. Los Poblanos Historic Inn sits on 25 acres, the largest remaining plot of land in the city, and the rooms are tucked into various corners of a sprawling ranch built in the 1930s by John Gaw Meem and beautifully maintained and preserved. Even the huge, old kitchen ranges are still in place, as are murals by Taos artist Gustave Baumann and frescoes by Peter Hurd. In the main house, the

guest rooms are set around a central patio and retain their old wood floors and heavy viga ceilings. Newer, larger rooms have been added and fit in flawlessly—deluxe rooms have a very light Southwest touch, while the farm suites have a whitewashed rustic aesthetic, accented by prints and fabrics by modernist designer Alexander Girard, of the folk-art museum in Santa Fe. There's also a saltwater pool and a gym, as well as extensive gardens. The included breakfast is exceptional, as is dinner at Campo, the on-site restaurant.

ALBUQUERQUE METRO AREA
$100-150
★ Sandia Peak Inn

4614 Central Ave. SW; 505/831-5036; $118 d

A family-run motel on the west side, just over the river from Old Town, Sandia Peak Inn is named not for its proximity to the mountain, but its view of it. It's certainly the best value in this category, offering large, spotless rooms, all with bathtubs, fridges, microwaves, and huge TVs. Continental breakfast is included in the rate, and the proprietors are positively sunny. There's a small indoor pool and free Wi-Fi throughout.

Los Poblanos Historic Inn

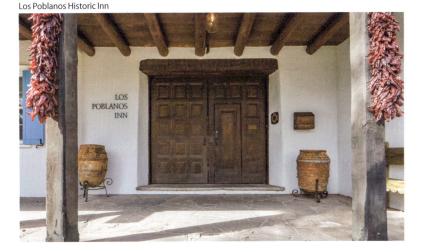

$150-250
★ El Vado Motel

2500 Central Ave SW; 505/361-1667;
http://elvadoabq.com; $159 d

Lovingly restored, El Vado Motel captures the Route 66 charm of the original incarnation with several touches that elevate it well beyond a standard roadside motel. Centered around a large courtyard and pool, the surprisingly spacious rooms and open spaces are brightly decorated, with viga ceilings and several cheerful nods to its history throughout. Its Plaza, an event space in the motel's courtyard, hosts local musicians and art markets in summer. There's a taproom onsite as well as a handful of small eateries and a coffee shop.

Nativo Lodge

6000 Pan American Fwy. NE; 505/798-4300;
www.nativolodge.com; $199 d

On the north side of town, Nativo Lodge is convenient for the Balloon Fiesta, an early start to Santa Fe, or a cheap off-airport rental-car pickup, as a Hertz office is within walking distance. The price is great for this level of comfort and style, with several rooms designed by local American Indian artists. Request a room in the back so you're not overlooking I-25.

Hyatt Regency Tamaya

1300 Tuyuna Tr., Santa Ana Pueblo; 505/867-1234;
www.hyattregencytamaya.com; $239 d

North of the city, on Santa Ana Pueblo land, Hyatt Regency Tamaya is a pretty resort. Rooms aren't always maintained as well as they could be, but even the standard ones are quite large, with either terraces or balconies. Three outdoor heated swimming pools and a full spa offer relaxation; more active guests can play golf or tennis, take an archery class, or attend an evening storytelling program with a pueblo member.

Information and Services

TOURIST INFORMATION

The **City of Albuquerque** website (www.cabq.gov) is very well organized, with all the essentials about city-run attractions and services.

Visit Albuquerque

800/284-2282; www.visitalbuquerque.org

Visit Albuquerque offers the most detailed information on the city, with an office in Old Town (522 Romero St.; 10am-5pm Mon.-Sat., 10am-4pm Sun.) and a desk at the airport near the baggage claim (9:30am-8pm Sun.-Fri., 9:30am-4:30pm Sat.).

SERVICES
Banks

Banks are plentiful, and grocery stores and pharmacies increasingly have ATMs inside. Downtown, look for **New Mexico Bank &** **Trust** (320 Gold Ave. SW; 505/830-8100; 9am-4pm Mon.-Fri.). In Nob Hill, **Wells Fargo** (3022 Central Ave. SE; 505/255-4372; 9am-5pm Mon.-Fri.) is on Central at Dartmouth. Both have 24-hour ATMs.

Post Offices

Most convenient for visitors are the **Old Town Plaza Station** (303 Romero St. NW; 505/242-5927; 11am-4pm Mon.-Fri., noon-3pm Sat.), **Downtown Station** (201 5th St. SW; 505/346-1256; 9am-4:30pm Mon.-Fri.), and an office near **UNM** (115 Cornell Dr. SE; 505/346-0923; 9am-3:30pm Mon.-Fri.).

Internet

The city's free **wireless hotspots** are listed at www.cabq.gov/wifi; many businesses around town also provide service.

Getting There and Around

AIR
Albuquerque International Sunport
(ABQ, 2200 Sunport Blvd.; 505/244-7700; www.abqsunport.com) is a pleasant single-terminal airport served by all major U.S. airlines. It's on the south side of the city, just east of I-25, about four miles from downtown. It has free wireless Internet access. Near baggage claim is an info desk maintained by the convention and visitors bureau.

Transit from the airport includes **bus Route 50** ($1), which runs to the Alvarado Transportation Center downtown (Central and 1st St.) every half hour 7am-8pm, and on Saturday every hour and 10 minutes 9:45am-6:50pm; there is no Sunday service. The ride takes about 25 minutes.

Less frequent, but free, the **Airport Connection shuttle** (aka city bus **Route 250**) runs weekdays only (9:10am, 4:01pm, 5:09pm, and 6:10pm) to the downtown Alvarado Transportation Center. The schedule is timed to meet the Rail Runner train to Santa Fe, departing about 30 minutes later. Another free weekday bus (Route 222) runs to the Bernalillo Rail Runner stop, though this is less convenient for visitors. Verify online at www.riometro.org, as the train schedule can change.

TRAIN
Amtrak (320 1st St. SW; 800/872-7245; www.amtrak.com) runs the Southwest Chief through Albuquerque. It arrives daily in the afternoon from Chicago and Los Angeles. The depot shares space with the Greyhound terminal, downtown on 1st Street, south of Central Avenue and the Alvarado Transportation Center.

The **Rail Runner** (866/795-7245; www.riometro.org) connects downtown Santa Fe with Albuquerque and continues as far south as Belén. The main stop in Albuquerque is downtown, at the Alvarado Transportation Center, at Central and 1st Street. If the not-so-frequent schedule fits yours, it's fantastic service to or from Santa Fe, but within Albuquerque, the system doesn't go anywhere visitors typically go. If you ride, keep your ticket—you get a free transfer from the train to any city bus.

BUS
Greyhound (800/231-2222; www.greyhound.com) runs buses from all major points east, west, north, and south, though departures are not frequent. The **bus station** (320 1st St. SW; 505/243-4435) is downtown, just south of Central Avenue. Cheaper *and* nicer are the bus services that cater to Mexicans traveling across the Southwest and into Mexico, though they offer service only to Las Cruces and Denver; **El Paso-Los Angeles Limousine Express** (2901 Pan American Fwy. NE; 505/247-8036; www.eplalimo.com) is the biggest operator, running since 1966.

With the city bus system, **ABQ Ride** (505/243-7433; www.cabq.gov/transit), it's possible to reach all the major sights along Central Avenue, but you can't get to the Sandia Peak Tramway or anywhere in the East Mountains. The most tourist-friendly bus line is Route 66 (of course), along Central Avenue, linking Old Town, downtown, and Nob Hill; service runs until a bit past 1am on summer weekends. The Route 766 bus follows the same route but stops at only the most popular stops. The fare for all buses, regardless of trip length, is $1 (coins or bills; no change given); passes are available for one ($2), two ($4), and three ($6) days and can be purchased on the bus. The D-Ride bus is a free loop-route bus around downtown that runs weekdays 6:30am-5:30pm. Note that the city may be testing a no-fare pilot program, which may apply to ABQ Ride fares; see their website to learn more.

CAR

From Santa Fe, Albuquerque is 60 miles (one hour) south on I-25; from Las Cruces, it is 225 miles (a little more than three hours) north on I-25. From Denver, the drive takes about 6.5 hours (445 miles); Phoenix is about the same distance west on I-40.

All the major car-rental companies are in a single complex adjacent to the airport, connected by shuttle bus. **Hertz** and **Enterprise** offer service at the Amtrak depot (really, just a refund for the cab ride to the airport offices). Hertz's two other city locations are usually less expensive because you bypass the airport service fee; if you're renting for more than a week, the savings can offset the cab fare. The prominent ride-sharing companies **Uber** (www.uber.com) and **Lyft** (www.lyft.com) both operate in Albuquerque.

BIKE

Albuquerque's bike-route system (www.cabq.gov/bike) is reasonably well developed, the terrain is flat, and the sun is usually shining. Rent bikes from Routes (2113 Charlevoix St. NW; 505/933-5667; www.routesrentals.com; 9am-5pm daily; $25/4 hours, $40/day).

Outside Albuquerque

Albuquerque is encircled by some of the state's top attractions, many of which are less than an hour away. Southeast of the city, a winding mountain road brings you to the ruined Salinas Pueblo Missions, intriguing remnants of early Conquest history. To the east off I-40 is the start of one of three routes to Santa Fe, the Turquoise Trail, which leads through proudly independent communities still exhibiting vestiges of New Mexico's mining past. An equally scenic route north is the much more circuitous Jemez Mountain Trail, which passes a dramatic landscape marked by red rocks and hot springs. The most direct route north, on I-25, brings you to the windswept Kasha-Katuwe Tent Rocks National Monument and its otherworldly formations.

WEST TO ACOMA

I-40 climbs the West Mesa out of Albuquerque and heads dead straight across a plateau lined with flat mesas—archetypal Southwest scenery. Perched on top of one of these mesas is the ancient **Acoma Pueblo,** an unforgettable village that has endured for nearly a thousand years.

Laguna Pueblo

505/552-6654; www.lagunapueblo-nsn.gov
About 18 miles west of Albuquerque, I-40 crosses the border onto the 45 square miles of Laguna Pueblo, on which 7,000 Keresan-speaking Ka-waikah (Lake People) live in six villages. From the highway, the only impression you get of Laguna is its Dancing Eagle Casino, but if you have time, get off at exit 114 to visit the **San José Mission Church** (505/552-9330). Established in 1699 when the Laguna people requested a priest (unlike any other pueblo), it stands out for its stark white stucco coating, but this is a relatively recent addition, following a 19th-century renovation. It was mudded and whitewashed every year until the 1950s, when the boom in uranium mining in the area left no time for this maintenance; it's now sealed with stucco.

Inside, between a packed-earth floor and a finely wrought wood ceiling, the late-18th-century altar screen dominates the room. It's the work of the so-called Laguna Santero, an unidentified painter who made the innovation of placing icons inside a crowded field of decorative borders and carved and painted columns, creating a work of explosively colorful folk art that was copied elsewhere in the region in subsequent decades.

The doors, and the small on-site gift shop, are usually open 9am-3pm daily (and after a 7am Mass).

Outside Albuquerque

THE JEMEZ
MOUNTAIN TRAIL
502
84
Los Alamos
550
Spence Hot
Springs
McCauley
Warm Springs
Bandelier
National
Monument
Santa Fe
National
Forest
Tesuque
285
Jemez
Santa Fe
National
Forest
Santa Fe
Jemez
Springs
GILMAN
TUNNELS
4
599
KASHA-KATUWE TENT ROCKS
NATIONAL MONUMENT
Jemez
Cochiti
Lake
Zia
Jemez
Pueblo
Santo
Domingo
Cochiti
16
"OLD MAIN"
STATE
PENITENTIARY
Cibola
National
Forest
Santa
Ana
Zia
SANTO DOMINGO
TRADING POST
Kewa
Rio Puerco
Laguna
550
Santa
Ana
Jemez
Canyon
Reservoir
San
Felipe
25
Galisteo
Reservoir
Madrid
Cerrillos
THE
TURQUOISE
TRAIL
Laguna
Laguna
PUEBLO
RESTAURANT
14
SAN FRANCISCO
DE ASIS CHURCH
CORONADO
HISTORIC SITE
Rio
Rancho
Bernalillo
SPRING
LOOP TRAIL
Golden
41
SAN JOSÉ
MISSION CHURCH
PETROGLYPH
NATIONAL
MONUMENT
Sandia
SANDIA PEAK
TRAMWAY
344
Navajo
Nation
Albuquerque
VOLCANOES
DAY USE AREA
TINKERTOWN
MUSEUM
472
SKY CITY
CASINO & HOTEL
Laguna
Pueblo
ABQ TROLLEY CO.
BALLOONING
SEE
"ALBUQUERQUE"
MAP
Edgewood
40
ACOMA PUEBLO
South
Valley
KIMO THEATRE
Moriarty
CHURCH OF
SAN ESTEBAN
DEL REY
Laguna
TWISTERS
(LOS POLLOS
HERMANOS)
45
ISLETA
AMPHITHEATER
Acoma
Isleta
Isleta
6
Los
Lunas
337
Peralta
Laguna
25
Fourth of
July Canyon
Estancia
Acoma
47
55
41
Belen
Rio Communities
Cibola
National
Forest
Navajo
Nation
304
47
Quarai
Mountainair
Abó
60
55
Cibola
National
Forest
Rio Salado
60
Sevilleta
National
Wildlife
Refuge
RANCHO
BONITO
Gran Quivira
Salinas Pueblo
Missions National
Monument
60
Cibola
National
Forest
107
QUEBRADAS
BACKCOUNTRY
BYWAY
Socorro
Rio Grande
25
Cibola
National
Forest
San Antonio
1
BOSQUE
BIRDWATCHERS
RV PARK
380
BOSQUE DEL APACHE NATIONAL WILDLIFE REFUGE

0   15 mi
0   15 km

© MOON.COM

Each of the six villages of Laguna celebrates its own feast day, and then the whole pueblo turns out at the church September 19 for the Feast of San José, one of the bigger pueblo events in the Albuquerque area.

Food

★ Laguna Burger

Old Rte. 66; 505/552-7762; 7am-3pm daily; $5

One of New Mexico's most acclaimed green-chile cheeseburgers is served at Laguna Burger, at the 66 Pit Stop gas station at exit 114. The ragged patties are made of fresh, never frozen beef, the buns are toasted on the griddle, and the fries are hand-cut, with skins on. Still, the cheery staff's T-shirts wonder, "Is it the beef, or is it the love?" There's also a branch of Laguna Burger at exit 140, at the 66 Pit Stop north of the highway (505/352-7848; 6am-7pm daily) and one in Albuquerque near the Indian Pueblo Cultural Center (2400 12th St. NW; 505/352-8282; 11am-8pm Sun.-Thurs., 11am-9pm Fri.-Sat.).

TOP EXPERIENCE

★ ACOMA PUEBLO

On the road to Acoma, you may feel as though you've crossed through a pass into a Southwestern Shangri-La, for none of this great basin is visible from the highway. Down in the valley, the route runs directly toward a flat-topped rock that juts up like a tooth.

Atop the rock is the original Acoma Pueblo, the village aptly known as **Sky City.** The community covers about 70 acres and is built largely of pale, sun-bleached adobe, as it has been since at least AD 1150. Only a hundred or so people live on the mesa top year-round, given the hardships of no running water or electricity. But many families maintain homes here, and the place is thronged on September 2, when the pueblo members gather for the **Feast of San Esteban.** The rest of the 2,800 Acoma (People of the White Rock, in their native Keresan) live on the valley floor, which is used primarily as ranchland.

Visiting Sky City

All visitors must stop at the **Sky City Cultural Center and Haak'u Museum** (Indian Rte. 23; 800/747-0181; www.acomaskycity.org; 8am-5pm daily Mar.-Oct., 9am-5pm Fri.-Sun. Nov.-Feb.) on the main road, which houses a café and shop stocked with local crafts, along with beautiful rotating exhibits on Acoma art and tradition. From here, you must join a **guided tour** (first tour 9:30am

Acoma Pueblo

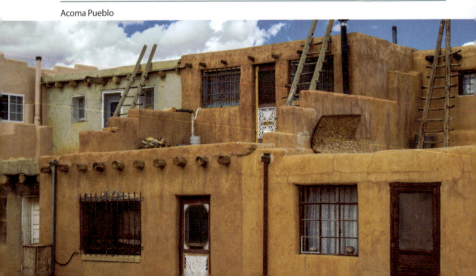

and last tour 3:30pm mid-Mar.-Oct., first tour 9:30am and last tour 2:30pm Nov.-early Mar.; $25), which transports groups by bus to the village. The road to the top is the one concession to modernity; previously, all goods had to be hauled up the near-vertical cliff faces. The tour lasts about 1.5 hours, after which visitors may return by bus or climb down one of the old trails, using hand- and footholds dug into the rock centuries ago. Definitely call ahead to check that the tours are running and verify times, as the pueblo closes to visitors periodically.

Arriving at the mesa top, with winds gusting through gaps in the cluster of adobe homes and views stretching out vast distances below, can be a moving experience, particularly as you learn how the village was built. The centerpiece is the **Church of San Esteban del Rey,** one of the most iconic of the Spanish missions in New Mexico. Built between 1629 and 1640, the graceful, simple structure has been inspiring New Mexican architects ever since. Its interior is, like many New Mexican pueblo churches, spare and simple, the white walls painted with rainbows and corn. As much as it represents the pinnacle of Hispano-Indian architecture in the 17th century, the church is also a symbol of the brutality of Spanish colonialism, as it rose in the typical way: forced labor. The men of Acoma felled and carried the tree trunks for the ceiling beams from the forest on Mount Taylor, more than 25 miles across the valley, and up the cliff face to the village.

Acoma is well known for its pottery, easily distinguished by the fine black lines that sweep around the curves of often creamy-white vessels. On the best works, the lines are so fine and densely painted, they shimmer almost like a moiré. The clay particular to this area can be worked so thin that the finest pots will hum or ring when tapped. Throughout the tour, there are several opportunities to buy pieces. This can feel slightly pressured, but in many cases, you have the privilege of buying work directly from the artisan who created it.

Food and Accommodations

Yaak'a Café

505/552-7878; hours vary; $8

The cultural center contains the Yaak'a Café, which serves earthy local dishes like stuffed acorn squash, pueblo tacos, red chile beef posole, and burgers served on fry bread.

Sky City Casino & Hotel

888/759-2489; www.skycity.com; $79 d

Acoma Pueblo operates the small-scale Sky City Casino & Hotel, also at exit 102. Its rooms are perfectly clean, functional, and reasonably priced, and there's an exercise room and a little pool.

Getting There

Take exit 102 off I-40 (about 55 miles west of downtown Albuquerque), and follow signs south to Sky City—this drive, along Indian Service Route 38, is the best signposted and offers the most dramatic views of the valley around Acoma. Allow about 1.5 hours for the drive out, and an additional 2 hours for the tour. Leaving Acoma, to avoid backtracking, you can take Indian Service Route 23, from behind the cultural center, northeast back to I-40.

SALINAS PUEBLO MISSIONS NATIONAL MONUMENT

The Salinas Pueblo Missions are a trio of pueblo remains (**Quarai, Gran Quivira,** and **Abó**) southeast of Albuquerque, on the plains on the far side of the Manzano Mountains. The eerily affecting foundations and frames of the mission churches, built by the pueblo residents under pressure from Franciscan brothers in the early years of the Conquest, stand starkly amid the other remnants of nearby buildings. The drive here also passes one of the area's most beautiful fall hiking spots, a few very old Hispano villages, and the little town of Mountainair.

Allow the better part of a day for a leisurely drive. The whole loop route, starting and ending in Albuquerque, is about 200 miles, and

Ceremonial Dances at Acoma and Laguna Pueblos

Feast days typically involve carnivals and markets in addition to dances. Dates can vary from year to year. Confirm details and start times—usually afternoon, but sometimes following an evening or midnight Mass—with the **Indian Pueblo Cultural Center** (505/843-7270; www.indianpueblo.org) before setting out.

- **February, first or second weekend:** Acoma (Sky City): governor's feast, various dances
- **March 19:** Laguna (Old Laguna): Feast of San José
- **Easter:** Various dances
- **May 7:** Acoma: Feast of Santa María
- **July 26:** Laguna (Seama): Feast of Santa Ana
- **August 10:** Acoma (Acomita): Feast of San Lorenzo
- **August 15:** Laguna (Mesita): Feast of the Assumption
- **September 2:** Acoma (Sky City): Feast of San Esteban
- **September 8:** Laguna (Encinal): Feast of the Nativity of the Blessed Virgin Mary
- **September 19:** Laguna (Old Laguna): Feast of San José
- **September 25:** Laguna (Paguate): Feast of Saint Elizabeth
- **October 17:** Laguna (Paraje): Feast of Saint Margaret Mary
- **Thanksgiving:** Acoma (Sky City): craft show
- **December 24:** Acoma (Sky City): luminaria display; Laguna (Old Laguna): dances after evening Mass
- **December 25-28:** Acoma (Sky City) and Laguna (Old Laguna): Christmas dances

straight driving time is about four hours. From Albuquerque, take I-40 east to exit 179, to the village of Tijeras and then turn south on Highway 337.

Tijeras

Established in the 1850s, Tijeras (*scissors*, for the way two canyons meet here) is a quiet spot at a crossroads with some excellent hiking close at hand. Stop by the **Sandia ranger station** (11776 Hwy. 337; 505/281-3304) for maps and tips on the area's hikes. A short interpretive trail behind the station leads to the **Tijeras Pueblo Archaeological Site,** which dates back to the 14th century. The ruins have been covered over for their protection, but signs help illuminate what the pueblo was like in its prime.

Roots Farm Café
11784 Hwy. 337; 505/900-4118; 8am-3pm Wed.-Sun.; $6
Kick your tour off right with a stop for breakfast at Roots Farm Café, in a cheerful cabin run by a couple who also own a farm up the road. In high season, their produce shapes a menu that often changes daily. The coffee is exceptionally good.

Hiking
Tunnel Canyon
Distance: *2.4 mi one-way*
Time: *1.5-2 hours each way*

Trailhead: *On the right side of the road heading out of Tijeras, about 2.5 miles south of I-40*

Of the several hikes available off Highway 337 south out of Tijeras, the Tunnel Canyon trail provides one of the best and least taxing introductions to the Manzano Mountains. After rising gently from the canyon floor, the trail leads to a series of exposed ridges with expansive mountain views. Yucca and colorful paintbrush and penstemon dot the trail. The trail connects with the West Ridge and Birdhouse Ridge trails, making a longer outing possible.

Fourth of July Canyon

After you pass through the Spanish land grant of Chililí, Highway 337 runs into Highway 55—make a right and head to Tajique, then turn onto Forest Road 55 to reach Fourth of July Canyon. The area in the foothills of the Manzanos, seven miles down the dirt road, is well worth a detour in late September and early October, when the red maples and oak trees turn every shade of pink, crimson, and orange imaginable. (Surprisingly, the place got its name not for this fireworks-like show of colors, but for the date an Anglo explorer happened across it in 1906.) The canyon is also pretty in late summer, when the rains bring wildflowers. You can explore along the short **Spring Loop Trail** or **Crimson Maple Trail,** or really get into the woods on **Fourth of July Trail** (no. 173), which wanders into the canyon 1.8 miles and connects with **Albuquerque Trail** (no. 78) to form a 4.4-mile loop.

Camping

Technically, Forest Road 55 continues on to rejoin Highway 55 farther south, but after the Fourth of July campground, the road is not always maintained and can be very rough going. It's wiser to backtrack rather than carry on, especially if you're in a rental car. Sites at the campground ($7) are fairly close to each other, but the scenic setting and ample shade more than make up for it. The sites can accommodate tents and smaller RVs.

Quarai

505/847-2290; www.nps.gov/sapu; 9am-6pm daily; free

The first Salinas Pueblo Missions ruins you reach are those at Quarai, a pueblo inhabited in the 14th-17th centuries. Like the other two Salinas pueblos, Quarai was a hardscrabble place with no natural source of water and very little food, though it did act as a trading outpost for salt, brought from small salt lakes (salinas) farther east. When the Franciscans arrived, they put more than the usual strain on this community. The 400 or so Tiwa speakers nonetheless were pressed to build a grand sandstone-and-adobe mission, the most impressive of the ones at these pueblos.

The priests also found themselves at odds with the Spanish governors, who helped protect them but undermined their conversion work by encouraging ceremonial dances. At the same time, raids by Apaches increased because any crop surplus no longer went to them in trade, but to the Spanish. *And* there were terrible famines 1663-1670. No wonder, then, the place was abandoned even before the Pueblo Revolt of 1680. Only the mission has been excavated; the surrounding hillocks are all pueblo structures.

Mountainair
B Street Market

204 W Broadway St.; 505/847-2223; 8am-6:30pm Mon.-Sat., 10am-3pm Sun.

Highway 55 meets U.S. 60 in the village of Mountainair, once known as the Pinto Bean Capital of the World. It's less booming now, but you can still pick up a pound of local beans and a good selection of supplies at the B Street Market grocery store.

Salinas Pueblo Missions Visitors Center

505/847-2585; www.nps.gov/sapu; 8am-5pm daily

You'll find the Salinas Pueblo Missions Visitors Center on U.S. 60, west of the intersection—though it offers not much more information than what's available at the small but detailed museums at each site.

Acoma vs. Oñate: Grudge Match

The early history of the conquistadors at Acoma was one of brutal back-and-forth attacks, each escalating in violence after the initial Spanish incursion. In a 1599 attack following many previous skirmishes, Don Juan de Oñate, the first governor of Spain's newest province, killed 800 people, leaving only 80 men alive in the hilltop village.

But Oñate was not content. He then brought his enemies into a makeshift court and tried them for the murder of 11 Spaniard soldiers. The sentence for the inevitable guilty verdict was that every male in Acoma over the age of 25 would have one foot cut off; everyone between the ages of 12 and 25 was pressed into slavery; and the children were sent to convents in Mexico.

Oñate was eventually recalled from his post and chastised for his actions. But in 1640, as if to add insult to injury, the Spanish friars presented the Church of San Esteban del Rey—built by enslaved Acoma people over more than a decade—to the maimed pueblo population as "restitution" for Oñate's cruelties. As a further gift of salvation, the friars publicly purged and hanged the village's spiritual leaders in the churchyard.

Variations on this treatment happened up and down the Rio Grande, eventually inspiring the Pueblo Revolt of 1680. But Oñate's particular brand of viciousness is probably the most remembered. Shortly after a monument to the conquistador was erected north of Española in 1998, the right foot of the bronze statue turned up missing—someone had snuck in at night and sawed it clean off. An anonymous letter to newspapers stated that the act was "on behalf of our brothers and sisters at Acoma Pueblo." Rumor adds that the prankster vandals also left behind at the statue two miniature feet made of clay, attached to a shield inscribed with the words "The Agony of Defeat."

Mountainair Ranger Station

505/847-2990; 8am-noon and 12:30pm-4:30pm Mon.-Fri.

The Mountainair ranger station is here as well; coming from the north, follow signs west off Highway 55 before you reach the U.S. 60 intersection.

Shaffer Hotel

103 Main St.; 505/847-2888; $79 d

Mountainair is also home to the weird architectural treasure that is the Shaffer Hotel, a 1923 Pueblo Deco confection with a folk-art twist, built by one Clem "Pop" Shaffer, who had a way with cast concrete—look for his name in the wall enclosing the little garden. (Similar stonework of his can also be spotted in the garden at Los Poblanos in Albuquerque.)

The hotel's **dining room** (10am-6pm Mon.-Tues. and Fri.-Sun.) reopened in 2019 after being shuttered for several years. It's worth at least a peek to admire the ceiling, Shaffer's masterpiece of carved and painted

turtles, snakes, and other critters. The dining room's menu ($8) is limited—burgers, steak, and pizza are among the mainstays—though there are regular specials as well as indoor and outdoor seating. The historic rooms have been renovated with a light touch, in character with the rest of the hotel.

Alpine Alley

210 N. Summit Ave.; 505/847-2478; 8am-3pm Tues.-Sat., 8am-1pm Sun.; $8

Bustling Alpine Alley, just north of the main intersection on Highway 55, features freshly baked treats, tasty soups, and creative sandwiches. Many of the items were inspired by the regular crew that settles in at the café for long periods.

Gran Quivira

505/847-2770; www.nps.gov/sapu; 9am-5pm daily; free

South from Mountainair 26 miles lies Gran Quivira—a bit of a drive, and you'll have to backtrack. On the way, about one mile south of town, you'll pass another Pop Shaffer creation, **Rancho Bonito,** his actual home. As it's private property, you can't go poking around, but from the road you can see a bit of the little log cabin painted in black, red, white, and blue. (If you happen to be in Mountainair in May for its art tour, the house is open then.)

Where Highway 55 makes a sharp turn east, Gran Quivira looks different from the other two Salinas pueblos because it is built of gray San Andres limestone slab and finished with plaster that was painted with symbols. It's the largest of the three, and once was home to an estimated population of 1,500-2,000. The array of feathers and pottery styles found here indicate the community was devoted to trade. Like the people of Abó, the residents spoke Tompiro, and the Spanish dubbed them Los Rayados, for the striped decorations they wore on their faces. They appear to have outwardly accepted the Franciscan mission after the first sermon was preached here in 1627. But they took their own religion literally underground, building hidden kivas underneath the residential structures even as they toiled on two successive missions ordered by the Catholics. Nonetheless, the place was deserted by 1671, after more than one third of the population had starved to death.

Abó

505/847-2400; www.nps.gov/sapu; 9am-5pm daily; free

From Gran Quivira, drive back the way you came and turn west on U.S. 60 in Mountainair to reach Abó, nine miles on. This was the first pueblo the Franciscans visited, in 1622; the mission here, constructed over more than 60 years, shows details such as old wood stairs leading to the choir loft. (The Franciscans were so dedicated to re-creating the Catholic church experience here in the desert that they brought in portable pipe organs and trained their converts to sing.)

Abó is also notable for the placement of its kiva, right in the center of the convento (the compound adjoining the mission) and apparently dating from the same period. This suggests that the local populace came to some

agreement with the priests, though no archaeologist or historian has been able to find proof of this. The excellent condition of all of these ruins is due in part to the efforts of the family that owned the land from the mid-19th century. One member, Federico Sisneros, is buried near the mission, at his request.

From Abó, continue west through the mountain pass, then down into the long, flat Rio Grande Valley on U.S. 60. It runs straight into I-25 at Bernardo, but if you're heading back to Albuquerque, you can take Highway 47 northwest to Belén, about 25 miles closer to the city.

★ BOSQUE DEL APACHE NATIONAL WILDLIFE REFUGE

Bosque del Apache National Wildlife Refuge ($5/car), 57,000 acres of wetlands along the river, is the site of a winter sojourn for some 15,000 giant sandhill cranes and hundreds of other migratory species. It's one of the country's top birding destinations as a result, but you don't need an ability to differentiate a great blue heron from a little blue heron to appreciate the spectacle of thousands of birds rising in unison at sunrise.

Access to the bosque is via Highway 1, south from U.S. 380, where the small town of **San Antonio,** just a blip on the map and a 10-minute drive from the reserve, provides a couple of lunch spots for hungry birders. Five miles inside the north border of the reserve, you pass the **visitors center** (1000 Hwy. 1; 575/835-1828; www.fws.gov; 8am-4pm daily), where you can pick up maps and find out which birds have been spotted that day.

A bit farther south on Highway 1, a 12-mile paved car loop passes through all the marshlands and the grain fields; at certain points along the drive, you can get out and hike set trails, such as a quarter-mile boardwalk across a lagoon or a trail to the river. Some areas are open to mountain bikers. The **loop drive** through the wetlands opens when birdlife is at its best, one hour before sunrise; cars need to be out by an hour after dark. The so-called Flight Deck adjacent to the bosque's main pool is the place to be at dawn; arrive at least 30 minutes before sunrise to ensure an unobstructed view of massive flocks of snow geese taking flight. With all its marshland, the bosque could just as well be called a mosquito sanctuary—slather on plenty of repellent before you start your drive.

The biggest event of the year is the arrival of the sandhill cranes—they were the inspiration for the refuge, as their population had dwindled to fewer than 20 in 1941. But now more than 15,000 of these graceful birds with six-foot wingspans winter over in the bosque. They're celebrated annually at the four- to five-day **Festival of the Cranes** (http://friendsofbosquedelapache.org) in late November or early December, when birders gather to witness the mass morning liftoffs and evening fly-ins.

Just north of San Antonio, **Socorro** also has a few good places where you can refuel post-birdwatching.

Food
Owl Bar & Café
77 U.S. 380; 575/835-9946; 8am-8pm Mon.-Sat.; $6-14
San Antonio, the nearest town just eight miles north, is best known for its green-chile cheeseburgers, especially at the legendary Owl Bar & Café. And the Owl gets extra points for historic details: It kept atomic-bomb engineers such as Robert Oppenheimer supplied with cheeseburgers and booze while they worked at Trinity Site, about 20 miles away. And the Owl's wooden bar is salvaged from the world's first Hilton hotel, started here in San Antonio by the father of modern hospitality, magnate Conrad Hilton.

Buckhorn Burgers
68 U.S. 380; 575/835-4423; 11am-8pm Mon.-Fri., 11am-3pm Sat.; $5-9
Seemingly untouched by time, Buckhorn Burgers is a good spot for a spicy Frito pie, though it's not easy to come here and pass on the vast selection of burgers, including its award-winning namesake offering topped with green chile, chopped onion, and pickles.

El Camino
707 N. California St.; 575/835-1180; 11:30am-7:30pm Mon.-Tues., 6am-9:30pm Wed.-Sun.; $6-9
Vintage Americana fans should head for Socorro and El Camino, a diner that's plucked straight from the early faux-wood-paneling

Bosque del Apache National Wildlife Refuge

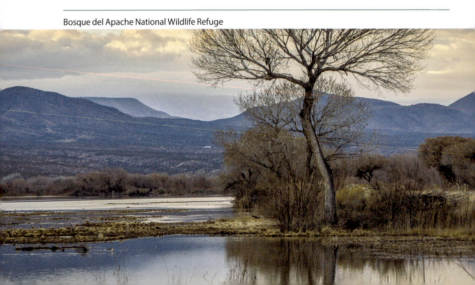

era. Its chicken-fried steak and eggs is a good bet at any time of the day.

San Antonio Crane
17 Pino St.; 575/835-2208; 8:30am-4pm Tues.-Sat.; $3.50-12
If, for some reason, you're not in the mood for a burger, follow the signs for San Antonio Crane, one block south off U.S. 380, for home-made New Mexican food (including especially good tamales) served in a tiny dining room. In the winter, during birding season, it opens for breakfast, too.

Capitol Bar & Brewery
575/835-1193; 3pm-11pm Mon., 11:30am-midnight Tues.-Sat., 3pm-10pm Sun.
Wet your whistle at the Capitol Bar, on the plaza in Socorro; it doesn't seem to have changed much in more than 125 years of doing business—this is one of those creaky-wood-floor saloons that you thought existed only on movie sets. But with friendly bartenders, a great selection of beers on tap, pool tables, and live bands, it also has what every modern bar-goer needs.

Accommodations and Camping
Casa Blanca B&B
13 Montoya St.; 575/835-3027; from $125 d
In San Antonio, the pleasant Casa Blanca B&B has three cozy rooms and a full breakfast is included. You can also use the kitchen, and there's a pretty patio that's perfect for relaxing as you review your photos from the reserve.

Dos Casitas en Socorro
317 Eaton Ave.; 575/835-2858; https://doscasitasensocorro.com; open Sept.-mid-May; $140 d
A few blocks west of I-25 in Socorro, Dos Casitas en Socorro's two stand-alone cottages are done in bright colors, with gas fireplaces. It's open only in birding season.

Bosque Birdwatchers RV Park
1481 Hwy. 1; 575/835-1366; www.birdwatchersrv.com; from $35
For RV road-trippers, Bosque Birdwatchers RV Park is just 100 yards north of the reserve on Highway 1. It's basic, with few amenities, but it's clean and you stand a good chance of spotting a number of birds from your site.

Getting There
From Albuquerque, Bosque del Apache is a straight shot south on I-25, a little less than 100 miles and about a 1.5-hour drive. (To continue to the wildlife refuge from Abó, head west on U.S. 60 to the interstate, and head south.)

Quebradas Backcountry Byway
The Quebradas Backcountry Byway is a 24-mile dirt road, which runs in a jagged arc down to U.S. 380, just south of Socorro. Requiring 2-3 hours, the route makes a particularly scenic—albeit very slow—way to or from the Bosque del Apache. It cuts through arroyos and rounded hills striped with rainbow hues, while the scrub desert teems with hawks, mule deer, and foxes. Don't attempt the drive if it has rained recently—the route is named for the deep "breaks," or drainage channels it crosses, and the mud in the bottoms can be impossible to pass. Look out for sandy patches at all times, as well as the occasional hardy mountain biker.

Heading south, leave I-25 at Escondida (exit 152), then go north for 1.3 miles on the east-side frontage road; turn east at Escondida Lake and continue for 0.8 mile, crossing the river, to Pueblito, where you turn right at a T-intersection. After about a mile, you see a sign for the byway beginning on your left (west); the road ends on U.S. 380 about 10 miles east of San Antonio and the road to the bosque. Coming north, the start is easier to find: From the intersection of the bosque road (Highway 1) in San Antonio, in front of the Owl Café, head east on U.S. 380 for just over

240

10 miles; then turn north on County Road A-129, the beginning of the byway.

THE TURQUOISE TRAIL

This scenic back route to Santa Fe, along the east side of the Sandias and up across high plateaus, revisits New Mexico's mining history as it passes through a series of former ghost towns. From Albuquerque, it's about 70 miles and can be driven straight through in 1.5 hours.

Take I-40 east from Albuquerque to exit 175. For hiking maps of the area, bear right to go into the village of Tijeras and the **Sandia ranger station** (11776 Hwy. 337; 505/281-3304). Go left to continue directly to the junction with Highway 14, the beginning of the Turquoise Trail.

East Mountains

The four-lane road heads north through alternating communities of old Spanish land grants and modern subdivisions collectively referred to as the East Mountains. Despite a few strip malls, the area still has a distinct identity from the city.

Cedar Crest

One hub of mountain culture is the **Burger Boy** (12023 Hwy. 14; 505/281-3949; 9am-4pm Wed.-Sun.; $8) in the community of Cedar Crest. Its green-chile cheeseburger can hold its own against the state's best, plus the restaurant offers a range of breakfast and lunch specials. Don't miss the paintings, inside and out, of founding owner Green Chili Bill, by Ross Ward.

Sandia Park

In Sandia Park, several miles north, is a large triangle intersection—to the left is Highway 536 (also known as **Sandia Crest Road,** or the **Sandia Crest Scenic Byway**), which heads up to Sandia Crest. The road offers a beautiful, winding 13-mile-drive through the steadily thinning trees of the Cibola National Forest to the exposed top of the mountain, more than 10,000 feet above sea level and

more than 5,500 feet above the center of Albuquerque. You'll find spectacular views at the top, as well as the **Sandia Crest House** (701 Sandia Crest Rd.; 505/243-0605) gift shop and a trailhead for the 1.6-mile **Crest Trail.** Note that there is a $3 fee to park anywhere in the national forest.

★ Tinkertown Museum

121 Sandia Crest Rd.; 505/281-5233; www.tinkertown. com; 10am-4pm Mon. and Fri.-Sun. Apr.-Oct.; $6

Just 1.5 miles up Sandia Crest Road is Tinkertown Museum, a temple to the ambitious use of downtime. Artist **Ross Ward,** a certified circus-model builder and sign painter who learned his trade making banners for carnivals, was also a master whittler and creative engineer who built, over 40 years, thousands of miniature figures and dioramas out of wood, clay, and found objects. Some of the scenes are even animated with tiny pulleys and levers: A man with a cleaver chases chickens in a circle; circus performers soar; the blacksmith's bellows huff and puff.

Much of the building is Ward's creation as well—undulating walls made of bottles and studded with odd collectibles, for instance. The museum, ever bulging at its seams, even took over a neighbor's 35-foot wooden boat. Ward died in 2002; his family keeps up the museum, and even though it's no longer growing as it used to, it remains a remarkable piece of pure folk art.

Golden

Back on Highway 14, continue north through rolling hills and ever-broader skies. After 15 miles, you reach the all-but-gone town of Golden, site of the first gold strike west of the Mississippi, in 1825. All that's left now is a handful of homes, the attractive adobe **San Francisco de Asis church** (Hwy. 14; 505/471-1562), and **Henderson Store** (1710 Hwy. 14; 10am-3:30pm Wed.-Sat.), open since 1918. It's largely given over to Indian jewelry

---

1: Tinkertown Museum **2:** the former ghost town of Madrid **3:** Mine Shaft Tavern **4:** Black Bird Saloon

and pottery, and antique trinkets line the upper shelves. The house across the road, bedecked with thousands of colored bottles, is worth a quick look.

Madrid

Thirteen miles beyond Golden, and about midway along the drive to Santa Fe, Madrid (pronounced MAD-rid) is a ghost town back from the dead. Built by the Albuquerque & Cerrillos Coal Co. in 1906, it once was home to 4,000 people, but by the end of World War II, when natural gas became the norm, it was deserted. By the late 1970s, a few of the sway-backed wood houses were squatted by hippies willing to live where indoor plumbing was barely available.

Over the decades, Madrid was slowly reborn. Portable toilets are still more common than flush models, but the arts scene has flourished along with a strong off-grid mindset, and a real sense of community pervades the main street, which is lined with galleries and pretty painted bungalows. In 2006, the village was the setting for the John Travolta film *Wild Hogs,* and the set-piece café built for the production (now a souvenir shop) has become a minor pilgrimage site for bikers. While you're in the area, tune in to local radio station KMRD, 96.9 FM.

Old Coal Town Museum

2846 Hwy. 14; 505/473-0743;
www.themineshafttavern.com; hours vary Sat.-Sun.; $5
The best place in Madrid to learn more about its history is the Old Coal Town Museum, which can be unfortunate, given its nebulous opening hours and the less-than-attentive care taken with its collection. When it's open, you can wander among sinister-looking machine parts and old locomotives.

★ The Hollar

2849 Hwy. 14; 505/471-4821; 11am-5pm Thurs.-Sun.;
$6.75-18.25
The Hollar serves excellent Southern standards such as shrimp po'boys and fried okra, plus several New Mexican dishes, and there's

even a dedicated menu for dogs. The green tomatoes and goat cheese are both local, and the outside patio makes for a great place to linger in summer.

Mine Shaft Tavern

2846 Hwy. 14; 505/473-0743;
www.themineshafttavern.com; 11:30am-8pm
Sun.-Thurs., 11:30am-9pm Fri.-Sat.; $8-17
The Mine Shaft Tavern is a vibrant remnant of Madrid's company-town days, where you can belly up to a 40-foot-long pine-pole bar. Above it are murals by local artist Ross Ward, who built the Tinkertown Museum in Sandia Park. "It is better to drink than to work," reads the Latin inscription interwoven among the mural panels, and certainly everyone in the bar, from long-distance bikers to gallery-hoppers, is living by those encouraging words. It serves solidly satisfying "New Mexico roadhouse cuisine," though that belies its award-winning Mad Chile Burger. It is, as the name suggests, not for those with delicate palates.

Java Junction

2855 Hwy. 14; 505/438-2772;
www.java-junction.com; 7am-close daily
For morning coffee, pastries, and local gossip, hit Java Junction, which has mostly shaded patio seating. It also rents a comfy **suite** ($129 d, with breakfast) on its 2nd floor that includes a stocked kitchen and coffee below.

Cerrillos

Though the source of turquoise that has been traced to Chaco Canyon, Spain, and Chichén Itzá in Mexico's Yucatán Peninsula, Cerrillos hasn't been gallery-fied the way Madrid, its neighbor down the road, has—even if many residents are wealthy escapees from Santa Fe.

Casa Grande

17 Waldo St.; 505/438-3008; 10am-4pm daily; $4
Representing old-time Cerrillos is the combo petting zoo-trading post Casa Grande, with some llamas and goats, plus turquoise nuggets and taxidermied jackalopes.

Cerrillos Station

15-B First St.; 505/474-9326; 10am-5:30pm Mon.-Sat., 11am-5pm Sun.

New-look Cerrillos is a few doors down at Cerrillos Station, a rather swank shop and gallery, with an adjacent dance studio space that occasionally offers spa services, such as massages.

Cerrillos Hills State Park

Co. Rd. 59; www.emnrd.nm.gov; 6am-9pm daily; $5/car

For some of the smoothest horseback rides around, head north on County Road 59 to Cerrillos Hills State Park and visit the long-running **Broken Saddle Riding Co.** (505/424-7774; www.brokensaddle.com; $90 for two hours) on the edge of the state park, which has more than 1,000 acres of rolling hills and narrow canyons that are also ideal for hiking and mountain biking.

★ Black Bird Saloon

29 Main St.; 505/438-1821; 11am-7:45pm Thurs.-Sat., 10am-3pm Sun.; $9-15

Friendly and oozing a rustic Wild West vibe, the saloon offers plenty of local brews to wash down creative breakfast and lunch dishes such as scrambled eggs with venison and blueberry sausage and grilled bread.

Mary's

15-A First St.; erratic hours

Opposite the Black Bird Saloon is the barest ghost of a dive bar, Mary's, filled with cats and serving primarily as a liquor store.

North to Santa Fe

After ascending from the canyons around Cerrillos onto a high plateau (look out for pronghorn), you're on the home stretch to Santa Fe.

If you're heading into central Santa Fe, take the on-ramp to I-25 north (signs point to Las Vegas) to the Old Pecos Trail exit, and follow signs as it eventually merges with the Old Santa Fe Trail and ends at the plaza. This is faster and prettier than continuing straight in on Highway 14, which turns into Cerrillos Road, a particularly slow and non-scenic route to the plaza. Along the way, grab a bite and visit the historic penitentiary.

San Marcos Café

3877 Hwy. 14; 505/471-9298; 8am-2pm Mon.-Fri.; $10

The San Marcos Café shares space with a working feed store where chickens and the occasional peacock roam the yard. Hearty meals are served in a country-style dining room (complete with potbellied stove); breakfast customarily starts with fresh cinnamon buns and from there can include homemade chicken sausage and a variety of egg dishes.

Beer Creek Brewing Company

3810 Hwy. 14; 505/471-9271; 11:30am-9pm Tues.-Sun.; $12-28

A rustic, solitary oasis on Hwy. 14, Beer Creek Brewery has an interior that oozes character, but it's the huge, semicircular patio and a welcoming, relaxed air that makes the place feel truly special. Expert craft beer and tasty specialty pizzas fill a menu that pairs perfectly with a summer afternoon outside.

"Old Main" State Penitentiary

4337 Hwy. 14; www.cd.nm.gov; tours 8am-2pm; tours from $30

Five miles farther is the "Old Main" State Penitentiary, site of a vicious riot in 1980 that is still counted as one of the worst in U.S. history. The state corrections department offers surprisingly detailed and thought-provoking tours of the old facility.

THE JEMEZ MOUNTAIN TRAIL

Beginning just northwest of Albuquerque, the Jemez (HAY-mez) Mountain Trail is a beautiful drive that takes you through the Jemez Pueblo, Santa Fe National Forest, and village of Jemez Springs, before continuing on to the Valles Caldera National Preserve as you near Santa Fe (page 109). It's the least direct way of getting to Santa Fe from Albuquerque—it covers about 140 miles, and you wind up near Los Alamos and must backtrack a bit south to

reach the city. But anyone in search of natural beauty will want to set aside a full day for the trip, or plan an overnight in **Jemez Springs,** especially in the fall, when the aspen leaves are gold against the red rocks.

The drive begins on U.S. 550, northwest out of the satellite town of Bernalillo, just west of I-25. (Stop here for gas, if necessary—stations are few on this route.) At the village of San Ysidro, bear right onto Highway 4, which forms the major part of the route north.

Jemez Pueblo

This community of some 1,800 tribal members was settled in the late 13th century, and Highway 4 runs through the middle of the 89,000 acres it still maintains. Before the Spanish arrived, the Hemish (literally, "the people," and which the Spanish spelled Jemez) had established more than 10 large villages in the area. Jemez Pueblo is quite conservative and closed to outsiders except for holidays. Because Jemez absorbed members of Pecos Pueblo in 1838, it celebrates two feast days, San Diego (November 12) and San Persingula (August 2), as well as Pueblo Independence Day (August 10), commemorating the Pueblo Revolt of 1680. It's also the only remaining pueblo where residents speak the Towa language, the rarest of the related New Mexico languages (Tewa and Tiwa are the other two).

The pueblo operates the **Walatowa Visitor Center** (575/494-1965; www.jemezpueblo.com; 8am-5pm daily Apr.-Dec., 9am-4pm daily), about five miles north of San Ysidro. You might miss it if you're gawking off the east side of the road at the vivid red sandstone cliffs at the mouth of the **San Diego Canyon;** from April-October, another, tastier distraction is the Indian fry bread and enchiladas sold by roadside vendors. The center has exhibits about the local geology and the people of Jemez, and doubles as a ranger station, dispensing maps and advice on outdoor recreation farther up the road. You can take

a 1.5-mile guided hike ($6) up into the red rocks; it's a good idea to call ahead and arrange a time.

Gilman Tunnels

Blasted in the 1920s for a spur of a logging railroad, the two narrow Gilman Tunnels over scenic Highway 485 make a good excuse to drive up this narrow road and through a dramatic canyon. Look for the turn left (west) off Highway 4, a couple of miles after the Walatowa Visitor Center, after mile marker 9; the tunnels are about five miles along. After the tunnels, the road turns to dirt and heads into the national forest. (Sturdy vehicles can make a big clockwise loop from here via Forest Service Road 376, rejoining Highway 4 north of Jemez Springs, about a 1.5-hour drive.)

Jemez Springs

A funky old resort village where hippies and Jemez Pueblo residents meet, Jemez Springs is a collection of little clapboard buildings tucked in the narrow valley along the road. As the most convenient place to indulge in the area's springs, which have inspired tales of miraculous healing since the 1870s, the town makes for a nice afternoon pause or an overnight getaway.

Jemez Hot Springs

Hwy. 4; 575/829-9175; www.jemezhotsprings.com; 10am-6pm Sun.-Mon. and Wed.-Thurs., 11am-7pm Fri.-Sat.; $25/1 hour, $50/2 hours

Jemez Hot Springs has a spring-fed pool enclosed in an attractively landscaped flagstone area right near the Jemez River; occupancy is capped at 10 and reservations are not accepted. Arrive early in summer, as it can fill up.

Jemez Springs Bath House

Hwy. 4; 575/829-3303; www.jemezspringsbathhouse. com; 10am-4pm Fri.-Mon.; $25/50 minutes

The Jemez Springs Bath House, in one of the original historic buildings, is operated by the village. (The source is in a gazebo next door—check out the mineral buildup!) Here, the springs have been diverted into eight concrete

1: breakfast samosa at Highway 4 Café & Bakery
2: Beer Creek Brewery

soaking tubs—a bit austere, but with a cool historic vibe. Reservations are required; massages ($85/60 minutes) and other spa treatments are available.

Bodhi Manda Zen Center

Hwy. 4; 575/829-3854; www.bmzc.org; 9am-4pm Wed.-Sun.; $10 donation

The most natural springs (expect some algae) are on the riverside at the Bodhi Manda Zen Center; payment is cash only and on the honor system.

Jemez Ranger District Office

51 Woodsy Ln.; 575/829-3535; 8am-4:30pm Mon.-Fri.

If you're planning to explore the wilderness and missed the Walatowa Visitor Center at Jemez Pueblo, you can stop at the Jemez Ranger District office for info; it's on the north edge of town just off Highway 4.

★ Highway 4 Café & Bakery

17502 Hwy. 4; 575/829-4655; 8am-4pm Thurs.-Sun.; $6-11

Highway 4 Café & Bakery has a great selection of pastries and hearty homemade lunches—there's plenty of coffee, too.

Los Ojos Restaurant & Saloon

17596 Hwy. 4; 575/829-3547; 11am-10pm daily; $11-18

For dinner, the only place open all the time is Los Ojos Restaurant & Saloon, where horseshoes double as window grills, tree trunks act as bar stools, and the atmosphere hasn't changed in decades. Burgers and the steak burrito are the way to go. The kitchen shuts around 9pm, and bar closing time can come earlier if business is slow, so call ahead in the evenings.

Bodhi Manda Zen Center

Hwy. 4; 575/829-3854; www.bmzc.org; rooms available Dec.-Mar. $90 s, $175 d

The Bodhi Manda Zen Center has its own hot pools, rents bare-bones rooms, and offers vegetarian meals to guests.

Laughing Lizard Inn

17526 Hwy. 4; 575/829-4377; www.thelaughinglizard.com; $95 d, $160 suite

Another bargain place to stay, with a few more amenities, is the Laughing Lizard Inn, next door to Highway 4 Café & Bakery; its four simple but pretty rooms, plus one suite, open onto a long porch.

Jemez Mountain Inn

17555 Hwy. 4; 575/829-3926; $85 d

Just across the street, Jemez Mountain Inn is slightly plusher, and its rooms a bit quieter, as they're back from the road. Hot springs are within easy walking distance.

Jemez Historic Site

18160 Hwy. 4; 575/829-3530; 10am-4pm Wed.-Sun.; $7

Just north of Jemez Springs, you pass the Jemez Historic Site, a set of ruins where ancestors of the present Jemez people settled more than 700 years ago and apparently lived until 1694 or so, when Diego de Vargas returned after the Pueblo Revolt. The old pueblo, named Giusewa, has almost entirely dissolved; as at the Salinas Pueblo Missions south of Albuquerque, the attraction is the Franciscan convent and church. Built starting around 1620, it has been partially reconstructed, enough to show how the architecture—a floor that sloped up to the altar, a unique octagonal bell tower—created maximum awe in the local populace. If you pay the admission, you can also visit **Coronado State Monument,** on the north edge of Albuquerque, on the same or next day. If you're in the area in early to mid-December, check for the date of the **Light Among the Ruins,** during which hundreds of farolitos are lit at the site and traditional Native American dances take place in front of a bonfire.

A couple of curves in the highway past the monument, you reach the rocks of **Soda Dam** off the right side of the road. The pale,

1: Light Among the Ruins at the Jemez Historic Site **2:** Gilman Tunnels **3:** the Jemez Mountains **4:** hiking Kasha-Katuwe Tent Rocks National Monument

bulbous mineral accretions that have developed around this spring resemble nothing so much as the top of a root beer float, with a waterfall crashing through the middle. You can't really get in the water here, but it's a good photo op.

Hot Springs
McCauley Warm Springs

Outside Jemez Springs, you pass two other opportunities to soak in hot water. Five miles north, where the red rocks of the canyon have given way to steely-gray stone and Battleship Rock looms above the road, is the start of the East Fork Trail (no. 137)—there's a dedicated parking lot just north of the picnic area. From here, the hike up the trail to McCauley Warm Springs is a bit more than two miles, mostly uphill; follow the trail until it meets a small stream flowing down from your left (north), then walk up the creek about 0.25 mile to the spring, which has been diverted so it flows into a series of pools, only 85°F at most points. (You can also reach the springs from the other direction along East Fork Trail, parking at Jemez Falls, farther north on Highway 4; from here, the hike is downhill—but of course a slog back up.)

Spence Hot Springs

More accessible are Spence Hot Springs, about two miles north of Battleship Rock, between mile markers 24 and 25. Look for a loop parking area on the east side of the road (if it's full, there is another lot a short way north along the highway). The 0.5-mile trail down to the river is wide and well tended, but then it's a bit more strenuous heading up the steep hillside to two sets of 100°F pools with milky-blue mineral water.

Hiking
East Fork Trail

Several trails run through the Jemez, but damage from the 2011 Las Conchas Fire has made some less scenic. Portions of East Fork

Trail (no. 137) are still quite nice, however. The route runs between Battleship Rock (on the southwest end) and Las Conchas (on the northeast), crossing Highway 4 at a convenient midpoint. If you head south from the highway parking area (about 3 miles after a hairpin turn southeast), you reach Jemez Falls after 1 mile, then gradually descend to Battleship Rock in about 6 miles, passing McCauley Springs on the way. Heading north from the highway is fine, too, following a stream through a pine forest, though near the end of 4.5 miles, you approach the burned area.

THE INTERSTATE TO SANTA FE

The most direct route north from Albuquerque to Santa Fe is along I-25, a one-hour drive without stops. The road, which passes through the broad valley between the Sandia and Jemez mountain ranges, is not as scenic as the more meandering routes, but it does cross wide swaths of the undeveloped pueblo lands of Sandia, San Felipe, and Kewa (formerly Santo Domingo).

Kewa (Santo Domingo)

505/465-2214; www.santodomingotribe.org
The pueblo of Kewa is a short drive from exit 259, via Highway 22. Formerly known as Santo Domingo, this Keresan-speaking community of 2,500 people has been here since the 1200s. If you're going to Kasha-Katuwe Tent Rocks anyway, you'll pass a freshly repainted old-time curio stand, the **Santo Domingo Trading Post** (by the Rail Runner station stop). Then it's worth a short detour west on Indian Service Route 88, to the center of the pueblo, to see the whitewashed village church, its facade adorned with two large horses. Set against the red earth here, it's a vivid image—but remember, no photography is allowed on pueblo land.

To continue to Kasha-Katuwe Tent Rocks, backtrack to Highway 22; the Indian service route to Cochiti does not go through.

★ Kasha-Katuwe Tent Rocks National Monument

Forest Rd. 266; 505/331-6259; www.blm.gov/visit/kktr; 7am-7pm daily mid-Mar.-Oct., 8am-5pm daily Nov.-mid-Mar.; $5/car

A bit west of I-25, Kasha-Katuwe Tent Rocks National Monument is one of the region's most striking natural phenomena. The wind-whittled clusters of volcanic pumice and tuff resemble enormous tepees, some up to 90 feet tall.

To reach the area, continue past Kewa Pueblo and head northwest toward Cochiti Pueblo on Highway 22. After about 15 miles, turn south in front of Cochiti Dam. In less than two miles, in the middle of the pueblo, turn right on Indian Service Route 92. From the monument parking area, you have the choice of two short trails: An easy, relatively flat loop runs up to the base of the rocks, passing a small cave, while a longer option runs 1.5 miles into a narrow canyon where the rock towers loom up dramatically on either side. The latter trail is level at first, but the last stretch is steep and requires a little clambering. Even if you just want to take a quick peek and don't intend to hike, don't come too late in the day: The gates (close to the junction with Highway 22) are locked one hour before official closing time.

To get back to the freeway without backtracking, continue northeast on Highway 22, which makes a sharp turn at the base of Cochiti Dam (turn left, or north, and you'll reach **Cochiti Lake,** a popular summer destination for boaters). Follow Highway 22 back southeast, then take Highway 16 to rejoin the interstate at exit 264.

Food

★ Pueblo Restaurant

26 Hagen Rd.; 505/867-4706; 7am-7pm Mon.-Sat.; $7-17

At exit 252, hop off for a meal at the Pueblo Restaurant, adjacent to the Black Mesa Casino, inside the San Felipe Travel Center, and past a short hall of dinging slot machines. Its broad diner menu offers spaghetti and meatballs as well as New Mexican favorites and breakfast all day. The pueblo dishes, such as posole with extra-thick tortillas, are excellent. Dig in alongside pueblo residents, day-trippers, and long-haul truckers.

Background

The Landscape

Santa Fe, Taos, and Albuquerque are located in New Mexico's high desert, an arid landscape west of the Sangre de Cristo and the Sandia Mountains that's generally at least a mile above sea level—and often much higher than that. Though the adjectives commonly used to describe the land—stark, unforgiving, rugged—are all true, they fall short of capturing its essence. Marked by jagged mountains, endless and impossibly blue skies, and flora that endures against all odds, the high desert has a primal beauty that can impact you to your core. The sheer vastness of the landscape is intoxicating, a feeling that is only

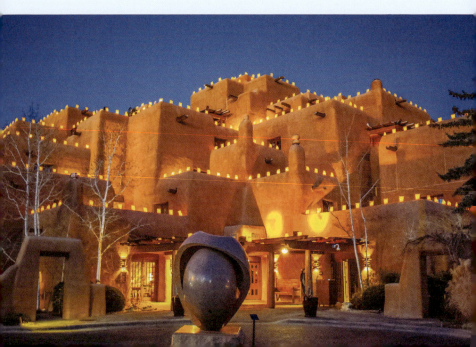

enhanced by relatively compact population centers. When you get out on a hiking trail, chances are you won't be fighting the crowds to do so.

GEOGRAPHY AND GEOLOGY

Much of New Mexico's landscape is the product of volcanic activity that ceased (at least for now) around the year AD 500. The main mountain ranges, which form part of the **Continental Divide,** are relatively young, pushed up in the Eocene era between 55 million and 34 million years ago, when shock waves from the collision of the North American plate and the Farallon plate caused the continent to heave.

Just a few million years later, the **Rio Grande Rift**—one of the biggest rift valleys in the world—formed, as eras' and eras' worth of accumulated rock was pulled apart by shifting faults, leaving the perfect path for the Rio Grande when it began to flow about three million years ago. The water carved deep canyons, such as the 800-foot-deep gorge west of Taos. These canyons are perfect slices of geologic time, layers of limestone, sandstone, clay, and lava neatly stacked up.

A million years ago, a volcano's violent eruption and subsequent collapse created the huge **Valles Caldera,** and the jagged edges of the crater have barely softened in the intervening time. Only 1,500 years ago, in the Tularosa basin, molten lava hardened into black badlands. One tangible benefit of the state's volcanic activity is the numerous hot springs, especially in the young Jemez Mountains (15 million years old).

Beneath all this is evidence of a more stable time. For some four billion years, the land was completely underwater, then spent hundreds of millions of years supporting prehistoric sealife—hence the marine fossils found at the top of the Sandia Mountains, 10,000 feet above the current sea level. Dinosaurs, too, flourished for a time. One of the first, the nimble meat-eater *Coelophysis,* lived during the Triassic period around Abiquiu, but all of them were apparently killed at once, perhaps by a flash flood. Another product of the dinosaur age (specifically, the Jurassic) was the lurid red, pink, and orange sandstone. It began as a vast desert, then petrified into the very symbol of the U.S. Southwest, and is visible around Abiquiu as well as Jemez Pueblo.

CLIMATE

For the most part, altitude determines the climate in New Mexico, where central Albuquerque, in the river valley, can be crisp and cloudless while Sandia Crest, 20 miles away and almost 5,000 feet up—it's the highest point in the Sandia Mountains—is caught in a blinding snowstorm. (Yes, it snows plenty in New Mexico.) Nowhere, though, is it a particularly gentle climate; expect sudden changes in weather and temperature extremes.

At the lower elevations, winter is cold—days usually between 40°F and 55°F—but rarely cloudy, with a few snowstorms that never add up to as much moisture as people hope. Come spring, which starts in late April or May, the number of wildflowers that dot the hills is a direct reflection of the previous winter's precipitation. The higher the elevation, the later the spring: At 8,500 feet, snow could still be on the ground in May. Little rain falls in May and June, typically the hottest and windiest months of the year, with temperatures climbing into the 90s—though it can still drop to the 50s at night.

By early or mid-July, the so-called monsoon season brings heavy, refreshing downpours and thunderstorms every afternoon for a couple of months. If you're out hiking in this season, steer clear of narrow canyons and arroyos during and after rains, as they can fill with powerful, deadly flash floods in a matter of minutes. Summer nights are rarely too warm.

Leave No Trace

So as not to upset the rather precarious environmental balance in much of New Mexico, you should internalize the ethic of "leave no trace"—even on a short stroll. Let the phrase first guide your trip in the **planning** stages, when you equip yourself with good maps and GPS tools or a compass, to avoid relying on rock cairns or blazes. Backpackers should repackage food and other items to minimize the waste to pack out. And everyone should try to keep group size under six people; pets should not go in wild areas.

On the trail, resist the urge to cut across switchbacks. Stick to the center of the trail, even if it has been widened by others trying to avoid mud. Be quiet, to avoid disturbing wildlife and other hikers. Leave what you find, whether plants, rocks, or potsherds.

Camp only where others have, in durable areas, at least 200 feet from water sources; dig cat holes 200 feet away, too. Pack out your toilet paper and other personal waste, and scatter dishwater and toothpaste. Safeguard food in "bear bags" hung at least 15 feet off the ground. Campfires are typically banned in New Mexico—please honor this policy, and keep a close eye on camp stoves. Pack out all cigarette butts.

Day hikers should also maintain a strict policy regarding litter. Tossing an orange peel, apple core, or other biodegradable item along the trail may not cause an environmental disaster, but it reminds other hikers that humans have been there and intrudes on the natural solitude of New Mexico's wilderness.

For more information, contact **Leave No Trace** (http://lnt.org).

September, October, and November are again dry, with the temperature dipping lower each month. Snow can often start falling in late October or November, although in recent years, overall winter precipitation has been quite low, so it takes months for a good base layer to build up at the ski areas.

ENVIRONMENTAL ISSUES

For thousands of years, New Mexicans have faced a water shortage. In prehistoric times, farming in the river valley was relatively easy, if subject to flooding. But at higher elevations, mountain streams had to be channeled into irrigation ditches. This system was perfected by Spanish settlers, who called their ditches "acequias," a word they'd learned from the Arabs (*as-saqiya*), who used the system to cultivate the Iberian Peninsula.

Today, as an ever-growing population demands more amenities, traditional ways of managing water have given way to more complex legal wranglings and outright hostility (No chingen con nuestra agua—don't f—k with our water—reads a bumper sticker

on some trucks in northern New Mexico). Some 49 billion gallons are pumped out of the middle Rio Grande aquifer every year, and only a portion of that is replenished through mountain runoff. Albuquerque started using filtered river water in late 2008. "Smart growth" gets lip service in city council meetings, although construction continues apace on Albuquerque's arid West Mesa. Neo-homesteaders install cisterns to catch rain, as well as systems to reuse gray water, but these features are still far from standard.

Years of relative drought can make tinderboxes of the forests. In a few weeks in the summer of 2012, for instance, the Whitewater-Baldy fire in the Gila National Forest burned almost 300,000 acres, the largest recorded fire in New Mexico history (almost double the scale of the previous record-setter, near Los Alamos the year before).

Visitors to New Mexico can help by following local environmental policies: Take scrupulous care with fire in the wilderness (no campfires, of course), and follow drought measures such as keeping showers short. Golfers may want to consider curtailing their play here. New courses, improbably, have been installed at every new casino resort and high-end residential development, despite the fact that they're intense draws on the water table.

Plants and Animals

Just as humans have managed to eke a life out of New Mexico, so have plants and animals—and a rather large variety of them. The state supports the fourth most diverse array of wildlife in the country.

PLANTS

Although much of the plant growth in New Mexico is nominally evergreen, the landscape skews toward brown, until you get up to the wetter alpine elevations.

Vegetation Zones

Below 4,500 feet, New Mexico's **Lower Sonoran** zone, in the river valleys in the southern part of the state, is dotted with cactus, yucca, and scrubby creosote bushes. The **Upper Sonoran** zone, covering the areas between 4,500 and 7,000 feet, is the largest vegetation zone in the state and includes the high plains in the northeast and most of Albuquerque and Santa Fe, where the Sandia and Sangre de Cristo foothills are covered with juniper and piñon trees. The **Transition** zone, 7,000-8,500 feet, sees a few more stately trees, such as ponderosa pine, and the state's more colorful wildflowers: orange Indian paintbrush, bright red penstemon, purple lupine. Above 8,500 feet, the **Mixed Conifer** zone harbors that sort of tree, along with clusters of aspens. The **Subalpine** zone, starting at 9,500 feet, is home to Engelmann spruce and bristlecone pine, while 11,500 feet marks the tree line in most places and the beginning of the **Alpine** zone, where almost no greenery survives. At 11,973 feet, the top of Sierra Blanca, near Ruidoso, is the southernmost example of this zone in the United States.

Trees and Grasses

Trees are the clearest marker of elevation. Along the Rio Grande and the Pecos River,

Indian paintbrush in the Manzano Mountains

thirsty **cottonwoods** provide dense shade; the biggest trees, with their gnarled, branching trunks, are centuries old. In spring, their cotton fills the air—hell for the allergic, but the source of a distinctive spicy fragrance—and in fall, their leaves turn pure yellow. Willow and olive are also common.

Everywhere in the foothills grows **piñon** (also spelled "pinyon"), the scrubby state tree that's slow-growing and drought-resistant, evolved to endure the New Mexican climate. When burned, its wood produces the scent of a New Mexico winter night, and its cones yield tasty nuts. Alongside piñon is **shaggy-bark juniper,** identifiable by its loose strips of bark, sprays of soft needles, and branches that look twisted by the wind. In season, it's studded with purple-gray berries—another treat for foraging humans and animals alike. At ground level in the foothills, also look for clumps of sagebrush and bear grass, which blooms in huge, creamy tufts at the ends of stalks up to six feet tall.

Up in the mountains, the trees are a bit taller. Here you'll find the towering **ponderosa pine,** with its thick, almost crusty chunks of reddish-black bark; the crevices smell distinctly of vanilla. At slightly higher elevations, dense stands of **aspens** provide a rare spot of fall color in the evergreen forests. The combination of their golden leaves and white bark creates a particularly magical glow, especially in the mountains near Santa Fe. The highest mountain areas are home to a number of dense-needled hardy pines, such as blue-green **Engelmann spruce, corkbark fir, bristlecone pines,** and **subalpine fir,** with its sleek, rounded pinecones. Hike your way up to stands of these, which are tall but with sparse branches, and you'll know you're close to the peak.

ANIMALS

As with plants, what you see depends on whether you're down in the desert or up on the mountain slopes. And you'll have to look carefully, because a lot of the animals that have survived here this long are the sort that blend in with their surroundings—which means there are a lot of brown critters.

Mammals

In the open, low-elevation areas on Albuquerque's fringes (and sometimes in the occasional vacant urban lot), look for **prairie dogs,** which live in huge underground warrens. When you're camping, the first creatures you'll meet are **squirrels** and **chipmunks**—at higher elevations, look out for Abert's squirrel, with its tufted ears and extra-fluffy tail. Long-haunched, clever, and highly adaptable, **coyotes** roam the lower elevations and are not shy about nosing around backyards; they make a barking yelp at night.

On the plains, you may see **pronghorns** (often called pronghorn antelope, though they are not related to true antelope) springing through the grasses, while long-eared **mule deer** flourish in mountain forests, such as the Pecos Wilderness. Herds of **elk** live in the high valleys; Rocky Mountain elk are common, thanks to an aggressive reintroduction effort in the early 20th century to make up for overhunting. A group of the largest variety, Roosevelt elk, whose fanlike antlers are the stuff of dreams for trophy hunters, roams in Valles Caldera. **Bighorn sheep** live in the mountains around Taos and in the Gila Wilderness.

Taos is also a hot spot for **North American river otters,** which were reintroduced in the rivers in Taos Pueblo starting in 2008—after their absence from the whole state for some 55 years. The small aquatic mammals seem to be flourishing and can now be spotted in the Rio Grande and tributaries, from the Colorado border to Cochiti Dam.

Black bears crash around the forests, though their name is misleading—at any given time, they can be brown, cinnamon-red, or even nearly blond. (Smokey Bear, the mascot of the National Forest Service, was from

1: chipmunk in the Taos Ski Valley **2:** snow geese at the Bosque del Apache **3:** young black bear at Valles Caldera National Preserve

New Mexico, a cub rescued from a forest fire in the southern town of Capitan.) Drought often drives the omnivorous beasts into suburban trash cans to forage, with tragic results for both people and the animals. Campers are strongly urged to pack food in bear-proof canisters.

And then there's the elusive **jackalope,** a jackrabbit sporting elaborate antlers. Alas, it seems now to appear only on postcards, although you may occasionally see a taxidermied head in a curio shop.

Birds

New Mexico's state bird is the impressive **roadrunner:** It grows up to two feet long, nests in the ground, feeds on insects and even rattlesnakes, and has feet specially adapted to racing on sandy ground. It can be spotted at lower desert elevations. Blue-and-black **Steller's jays** and raucous all-blue **piñon jays** are common in the foothills and farther up in the mountains, where you can also see **bluebirds, black-masked mountain chickadees,** and **Clark's nutcrackers,** which hoard great stashes of piñon nuts for winter. Also look around for **woodpeckers,** including the three-toed variety, which lives at higher elevations. On the highest peaks are **white-tailed ptarmigans,** which blend in with their snowy environment. But you can't miss the yellow-and-red **western tanager,** a vivid shot of tropical delight in the Transition zone forests.

In late summer, keep an eye out for tiny, red-throated **rufous hummingbirds** on their way to Mexico for the winter, along with hundreds of other birds that use the center of the state as a migratory corridor. The Sandia Mountains and the Las Vegas National Wildlife Refuge, among other spots, are on the flight path for **red-tailed hawks, eagles,** and other raptors, especially numerous in the springtime.

With more than 450 species spotted in New Mexico, this list is only scraping the surface. If you're a dedicated birder, first contact the **Randall Davey Audubon Center** in Santa Fe, which leads bird walks, or the **Rio Grande Nature Center** in Albuquerque. **Bosque del Apache National Wildlife Refuge,** south of Albuquerque, is a must in the winter when thousands of **sandhill cranes**—and even the occasional rare **whooping crane**—rest in the wetlands. Bill West of **WingsWest Birding** (505/989-3804; www.wingswestbirding.com) is a reputable guide who has been leading groups around New Mexico since 1996. Tours range from half-day options to multi-day outings.

Fish

Trout is the major endemic fish, found in the cold waters of the Rio Grande as well as the San Juan, Chama, and Pecos Rivers. The cutthroat is particularly beloved in New Mexico—the only variety of trout originally found on the eastern side of the Continental Divide. (The more aggressive rainbow and brown trout are interlopers.) The Rio Grande cutthroat, the official state fish, is now quite uncommon. Another local fish in jeopardy is the **Rio Grande silvery minnow,** listed as endangered since 1994. The last of the Rio Grande's five native fish, it's in such a dire state that biologists have scooped them out of the water individually during dry spells and taken them to the Albuquerque aquarium for safekeeping.

Reptiles

One can't step foot in the desert without thinking of **rattlesnakes,** and New Mexico has plenty of them, usually hidden away under rocks and brush, but very occasionally sunning themselves in full view. The predominant species in the Rio Grande Valley, the **Western diamondback,** can grow to be seven feet long. Although its venom is relatively weak, it has an impressive striking distance of almost three feet. Around Taos and Santa Fe, the main species is the **prairie rattlesnake,** which is only four feet long at most; the threatened **New Mexico ridgenose** is only about two feet long. The snakes you're more likely to encounter, however, are **bull snakes.** Though often mistaken for rattlesnakes due to similar size and colorings, they're not venomous.

More benign cold-blooded critters include **lizards,** such as the **short-horned lizard** (aka horny toad), a miniature dinosaur, in effect, about as big as your palm. Look for it in the desert and the scrubby foothills.

Insects and Arachnids

Because it's so dry, New Mexico isn't teeming with bugs. The ones that are there, however, can be off-putting, particularly if you chance upon the springtime **tarantula migration,** usually in May around Albuquerque. It's not a true seasonal relocation, just the time when males come out of their dens to prowl for mates. The fist-size spiders move hundreds

at a time, and occasionally back roads are closed to let them pass. If you'll be camping in the desert in the spring, ask the ranger's office about the status. Though they're big and hairy, they're not venomous.

Scorpions, though, can be more dangerous, if very rarely deadly. In the southern desert areas, the most common variety is the bark scorpion, which nestles in rock crevices and woodpiles and can find its way into your shoes or the bottom of your sleeping bag. Its sting can cause anything from severe pain to difficulty breathing and should be treated with antivenin as soon as possible. Hard-shelled, segmented **desert centipedes** are another local creepy-crawly; they're often out at night and can grow up to nine inches long.

History

The historical and cultural continuity in New Mexico is remarkable. The state has been transformed from ice-age hunting ground to home of the atom bomb, but many people claim roots that stretch back hundreds, even thousands, of years.

ANCIENT AND ARCHAIC CIVILIZATION

New Mexico was one of the first places to harbor humans after the end of the last **ice age.** Archaeological findings indicate that some 12,000 years ago, people were hunting mastodons and other big game across the state. Mammoth bones, arrowheads, and the remains of campfires have been found in the Sandia Mountains east of Albuquerque; Folsom, in northeastern New Mexico; and Clovis, in the south. Sometime between 8000 and 5000 BC, these bands of hunters formed a small temporary settlement just north of Albuquerque, but it was not enough to stave off the decline of that ancient culture, as climatic shifts caused the big game to die off. Nomadic hunter-gatherers, seeking out smaller animals as well as seeds and nuts, did

better in the new land, and by 1000 BC, they had established communities built around clusters of pit houses—sunken, log-covered rooms dug into the earth.

Along with this new form of shelter came an equally important advance in food: Mexican people gave corn kernels (maize) and lessons in agriculture to their neighbors, the **Mogollon,** who occupied southern New Mexico and Arizona. By AD 400, the Mogollon had begun growing squash and beans as well and had established concentrated communities all around the southern Rio Grande basin. This culture, dubbed the Basketmakers by archaeologists, also developed its own pottery, another skill learned from the Indigenous people of Mexico. So when the Mogollon made contact with the Ancestral Puebloans in the northern part of the state, they had plenty to share.

THE PUEBLOS

The year 700 marks the beginning of what archaeologists call the **Pueblo I** phase, when disparate groups began to form larger communities in the upland areas on either side of the northern Rio Grande. Pit houses were still in use, but aboveground buildings of clay and sticks were erected alongside them. Increasingly, the pit houses were sacred spaces, chambers in which religious ceremonies were carried out; these are now known as kivas and are still an integral part of pueblo life.

The **Pueblo II** era began in 850 and is distinguished by the rise of Pueblo Bonito in Chaco Canyon, northwest of Santa Fe, into a full-scale city and perhaps capital of a small state. It was home to an estimated 1,500 people ruled by a religious elite. But Chaco abruptly began to crumble around 1150, perhaps due to drought, famine, or warfare. This shift marked the **Pueblo III** period, when the people who were to become today's Puebloans began building their easily defended cliff dwellings—most famously in the Four Corners area, at Mesa Verde in present-day Colorado, but also farther south, on the Pajarito Plateau in what's now Bandelier National Monument, and in Puyé, on Santa Clara Pueblo land. A drought at the end of the 13th century cleared out the Four Corners at the start of the **Pueblo IV** era, provoking the population to consolidate along the Rio Grande in clusters of sometimes more than a thousand interconnected rooms. These communities dotted the riverbank, drawing their sustenance both from the river water and from the mountains behind them.

THE SPANISH ARRIVE

These settlements were what the Spanish explorer **Francisco Vásquez de Coronado** and his crew saw when they first ventured into the area in 1540. Their Spanish word for the villages, "pueblos," stuck and is still the name for both the places and the people who live in them. Coronado wasn't impressed, however, because the pueblos were made out of mud, not gold as he had been hoping. So after two years and a couple of skirmishes with the natives, the team turned around and headed back to Mexico City.

It took another 50 years for the Spanish to muster more interest in the area. This time, in 1598, **Don Juan de Oñate** led a small group of Spanish families to settle on the banks of the Rio Grande, at a place they called San Gabriel, near Ohkay Owingeh (which they called San Juan Pueblo). About a decade later, the settlers moved away from their American Indian neighbors, to the new village of Santa Fe. The territory's third governor, Don Pedro de Peralta, made it the official capital of the territory of Nuevo México, which in those days stretched far into what is now Colorado and Arizona.

This time the colonists, mostly farmers, were motivated not so much by hopes of striking it rich but simply of making a living. Moreover, they were inspired by Catholic zeal, and Franciscan missionaries accompanied them to promote the faith among the Puebloans. It was partly these missionaries and their ruthless oppression of the native religion that drove the Indians to organize the **Pueblo Revolt** of 1680. The Franciscans' "conversion" strategy involved public executions of the pueblos' medicine men, among other violent assaults on local traditions. But the Spanish colonists were no help either. In their desperation to squeeze wealth out of the hard land, they exploited the only resource they had, the enslaved labor of the Indians, who were either conscripts or stolen from their families. (The Indians did some poaching from Spanish families, too, creating a violent sort of cultural exchange program.)

The leader of the Pueblo Revolt was a man named Popé (also spelled Po'pay), from San Juan Pueblo. Using Taos Pueblo as his base, he traveled to the other communities, secretly meeting with leaders to plan a united insurrection. Historians theorize he may have used Spanish to communicate with other Puebloans who did not speak his native Tewa, and he distributed among the conspirators lengths of knotted rope with which to count down the days to the insurrection. Although the Spanish captured a few of the rope-bearing messengers (Isleta Pueblo may never have gotten the message, which could explain its being the only pueblo not to participate), they could not avert the bloodshed. The Puebloan warriors killed families and missionaries, burned crops, and toppled churches. Santa Fe was besieged, and its population of more than 1,000 finally evacuated in a pitiful retreat.

The Spanish stayed away for 12 years, but a new governor, **Diego de Vargas,** took it upon himself to reclaim the area. He managed to talk many pueblos into peaceful surrender, meeting resistance only in Taos and Santa Fe, where a two-day fight was required to oust the Indians from the Palace of the Governors; in Taos, violence ground on for an additional four years. The Spanish strategy in the post-revolt era was softer, with more compromise between the Franciscans and their intended flock, and a fair amount of cultural and economic exchange. The threat of raiding Comanche, Apache, and Navajo also forced both sides to cooperate. Banding together for defense, they were finally able to drive the Comanche away, culminating in a 1778 battle with Chief Cuerno Verde (Green Horn). The decisive victory is celebrated in the ritual dance called Los Comanches, still performed in small villages by Hispanos and Puebloans alike.

The other bonding force was trade. The Spanish maintained the **Camino Real de Tierra Adentro** (Royal Road of the Interior), which linked Santa Fe with central Mexico—the route follows roughly the line carved by I-25 today. Caravans came through only every year or two, but the profit from furs, pottery, textiles, and other local goods was enough to keep both cultures afloat, if utterly dependent on the Spanish government.

MEXICAN INDEPENDENCE AND THE FIRST ANGLOS

Spain carefully guarded all of its trade routes in the New World, even in a relatively unprofitable territory like Nuevo México. The only outside trade permitted was through the Comancheros, a ragtag band who traded with Comanche and other Plains Indians, working well into what would later be Oklahoma and even up to North Dakota. The Spanish governor encouraged them because their tight relationship with the Comanche helped protect New Mexico and Texas against intruders.

Interlopers were not welcome. Only a few enterprising fur trappers, lone mountain men in search of beaver pelts, slipped in. Spy-explorer **Zebulon Pike** and his crew were captured (perhaps intentionally, so Pike could get more inside information) and detained in Santa Fe for a spell in 1807. But in 1821, Mexico declared independence from Spain, liberating the territory of Nuevo México along with it. One of the first acts of the new government was to open the borders to trade. Initially just a trickle of curious traders came down the rough track from St. Louis, Missouri, but soon a flood of commerce flowed along the increasingly rutted and broad **Santa Fe Trail,** making the territory's capital city a meeting place between Mexicans and Americans swapping furs, gold, cloth, and more.

THE MEXICAN-AMERICAN WAR AND AFTER

Pike's expedition gave the U.S. government new details about the locations of Spanish forts. Just as important, Pike, who returned not long after Lewis and Clark completed their march across the Louisiana Purchase, helped fuel the country's expansionist fervor. In the next few decades, **"manifest destiny"** became the phrase on every American's lips, and the government was eyeing the Southwest. It annexed Texas in 1845, but New Mexico, with its small population and meager resources, didn't figure heavily in the short-lived war that followed. The Mexican governor surrendered peacefully to General Stephen Kearny when he arrived in Santa Fe in 1846. In Taos, the transition was not accepted so readily, as Hispano business leaders and Taos Pueblo Indians instigated a brief but violent uprising, in which the first U.S. governor, Charles Bent, was beheaded.

During the **Civil War,** New Mexico was in the way of a Texan Confederate strategy to secure the Southwest, but the rebels were thwarted in 1862 at the Battle of Glorieta Pass. The territory stayed in the hands of the Union until the end of the war, and people were more concerned with the local, increasingly brutal skirmishes caused by the arrival in Santa Fe of Bishop Jean-Baptiste Lamy, a tyrannical—or at least very thoughtless—Frenchman who tried to impose a European vision of the Catholic Church on a populace that had been beyond centralized control for centuries.

Even more significant to New Mexico's development was the arrival of the **railroad** in 1880, as it was laid through Raton Pass, near Santa Fe, and close to Albuquerque. Virtually overnight, strange goods and even stranger people came pouring into one of the remoter frontier outposts of the United States. Anglo influence was suddenly everywhere, in the form of new architecture (red brick was an Eastern affectation) and new business. Albuquerque, almost directly on the new railway tracks, boomed, while Santa Fe's fortunes slumped and Taos all but withered away, having peaked back in the late days of the Camino Real.

But while wheeler-dealers were setting up shop in central New Mexico, some more intrepid souls were poking around in the less-connected areas farther north. These tourists were artists who valued New Mexico not for its commercial potential but for its dramatic landscapes and exotic populace who seemed untouched by American ways. From the early 20th century on, Santa Fe and Taos were cultivated as art colonies, a function they still fulfill today.

FROM STATEHOOD TO WORLD WAR II

Based on its burgeoning economy, New Mexico became the 47th state in the union in 1912, effectively marking the end of the frontier period, a phase of violence, uncertainty, and isolation that lasted about 300 years, longer here than anywhere else in the United States. In addition to the painters and writers flocking to the new state, another group of migrants arrived: tuberculosis patients. Soon the state was known as a health retreat, and countless people did stints in its dry air to treat their ailing lungs.

One of these patients was J. Robert Oppenheimer, whose mild case of TB got him packed off to a camp near Pecos for a year after high school. He loved northern New Mexico and got to know some of its more hidden pockets. So when the U.S. Army asked him if he had an idea where it should establish a secret base for the **Manhattan Project,** he knew just the place: a little camp high on a plateau above Santa Fe, named Los Alamos. This was the birthplace of the atomic bomb, a weird, close-knit community of the country's greatest scientific minds (and biggest egos), working in utter secrecy. Only after the bomb was tested at White Sands, and Fat Man and Little Boy were dropped over Japan, was the mysterious camp's mission revealed.

CONTEMPORARY HISTORY

The A-bomb ushered New Mexico into the modern era. Not only was it world-changing technology, but it also boosted the local economy. High-paying support staff jobs at Los Alamos and Kirtland Air Force Base in Albuquerque pulled some of the population away from subsistence farming and into a life that involved cars and electricity. But even so, the character of the state remained conservative and closed, so when the 1960s rolled around and New Mexico's empty space looked like the promised land to hippies, the culture clash was fierce. Staunch Catholic farmers took potshots at their naked, hallucinogen-ingesting neighbors who fantasized about getting back to the land but had no clue how to do it. After a decade or so, though, only the hardiest of the commune-dwellers were left, and they'd mellowed a bit, while the locals had come to appreciate at least their enthusiasm. Even if the communes didn't last, hippie culture has proven remarkably persistent in

New Mexico. Even today, distinctly straight Hispanos can be heard saying things like, "I was tripping out on that band, man," and the state still welcomes Rainbow Gatherings, would-be Buddhists, and alternative healers.

The end of the 20th century saw unprecedented growth in both Albuquerque and Santa Fe. As usual, Albuquerque got the practical-minded development, such as the Intel chip-manufacturing plant and the services headquarters for Gap Inc., while Santa Fe was almost felled by its own artsiness, turned inside-out during a few frenzied years in the early 1990s when movie stars and other moneyed types bought up prime real estate. In just a matter of months, rents went up tenfold and houses started selling for more than $1 million. Santa Fe has yet to work out the imbalance between its creative forces, which did save the city from utter decline, and economic ones, though it implemented a living-wage law in 2009. The state's capital drew both praise and ire in 2017 for standing firm in its stance as a sanctuary city. In recent years, attention has shifted to Santa Fe's policies toward monuments venerating historical figures who played a role in the persecution of Native Americans.

Meanwhile, Taos has grown slowly but steadily, as have the pueblos, thanks to the legalization of gambling on their lands, but all of these communities still have an air of old New Mexico, where the frontier flavor and solitude can still be felt.

Government and Economy

New Mexico doesn't look so good on paper—in national rankings of income, education, and more, it often ranks 49th or 50th. "New Mexico is a third-world country" is a common quip, at least among an older generation that has seen a lifetime of nepotism and incompetence. But these issues have also inspired a good deal of activist sentiment, and politics are lively.

GOVERNMENT

New Mexico's political scene is as diverse as its population, though the cities tend to vote Democrat. Still, Republican Susana Martinez became New Mexico's first woman governor in 2010 (her opponent was also a woman, incidentally), and was reelected in 2014. It didn't take the state long to elect its second woman governor: Democrat Michelle Lujan Grisham began her term in 2019. In the 2020 presidential election, counties skewed extremely red or blue, but ultimately President Joe Biden won the state by a wide margin. Two years later, Lujan Grisham was elected to a second term, though not be as comfortably as initially expected.

New Mexico is notable for its equitable Hispanic representation in every level of government, including the state legislature, where it consistently matches the state Hispanic population, just under 50 percent. This has helped keep the immigration debate at a relatively polite pitch—unlike in neighboring Arizona and Texas, where the Hispanic population is underrepresented in the government.

Each American Indian pueblo (as well as Navajo, Zuni, and Apache lands elsewhere in the state) acts as a sovereign nation, with its own laws, tax regulations, police forces, and government. Indians vote in U.S. and state elections, while in the pueblos, most domestic issues are decided by a tribal governor, a war chief, and a few other officials elected by a consensus of men in the kiva.

The Navajo Nation, with more than 250,000 people to manage, as well as a substantial cache of natural resources, does practice direct democracy, open to both men and women. In its system, the reservation, which reaches into Arizona and Utah, is divided into "chapters," and their elected representatives participate in the Navajo Council, which convenes in the capital at Window Rock, Arizona. Since a reform in 1991, the Navajo system has had three branches, like the U.S. one. In 2006, Lynda Lovejoy was the first woman to run for nation president; she ran again in 2010, losing by a small margin. The 2014 election brought up a different issue, when one candidate was disqualified for failing to demonstrate fluency in the Navajo language, a legal requirement for holding the position.

Deb Haaland, of the Laguna Pueblo and former chair of the New Mexico Democratic Party, became one of the first Native Americans to serve in the United States Congress, when she was sworn into the House of Representatives in 2019.

ECONOMY

In New Mexico, roughly 20 percent of the population lives below the poverty level, compared with national averages around 15 percent. It's also near the bottom in the number of high school and college graduates per capita. Statistics in the pueblos and reservations have historically been grimmer, with up to 50 percent unemployment in some areas—but this has changed due to casino-fueled development. The Navajo Nation has extensive landholdings, but with an infrastructure that's more 19th than 21st century, businesses seldom invest. The same could in fact be said for many of the rural sections of the state, on Indian land or not.

The unemployment rate, however, is often lower than the national average, in part because Albuquerque continues to be a **manufacturing** center for computer chips, mattresses, specialty running shoes, and more. And the city where Microsoft was founded (Bill Gates and Paul Allen later moved back to Seattle to be close to their families) does foster **technology** development.

As well, the Sandia and Los Alamos **national laboratories** are the state's biggest employers—together they employ over 23,000 people. **Aerospace** manufacturing parks are growing outside Albuquerque and Las Cruces. Despite heady optimism, private spaceflights are, however, still some ways from taking off from Spaceport America near Truth or Consequences.

Outside the cities, significant profits from coal, copper, oil, and natural gas—most in the southern part of the state, as well as in the northwest—keep the economy afloat. Only Texas produces more oil than New Mexico and production continues to increase apace. That's the big money, but the **agricultural** sector, from dairy cows in the south to apple orchards along the Rio Grande to beef jerky from the numerous cattle ranches, contributes a decent amount to the pot. And Santa Fe's **arts** sector shouldn't be overlooked—galleries post sales of $200 million every year, though they're criticized for sending much of that money right back to artists who live and work out of state. Thanks to tax rebates, the **film industry,** nicknamed "Tamalewood," has flourished. Albuquerque Studios is one of the largest production facilities in the country and in the fall of 2018 was bought by Netflix, a deal which is expected to see a huge upturn in the studio's output. To the north, Santa Fe Studios has been the site of a number of film and TV productions in the relatively short time since it was founded.

Even if the economic situation isn't ideal, it's nothing New Mexicans aren't used to. Low income has been the norm for so long that a large segment of the population is, if not content with, at least adapted to eking out a living from very little (the median family income is only around $51,945, compared with the U.S. median of $68,703). In this respect, the state hasn't lost its frontier spirit at all.

Local Culture

New Mexico's 1.8 million people have typically been described as a tricultural mix of Indians, Spanish, and Anglos. That self-image has begun to expand as residents have delved deeper into history and seen that the story involves a few more threads.

DEMOGRAPHY

The labels of Indian, Spanish, and Anglo are used uniquely in New Mexico. First, **Indian:** This is still a common term, as "Native American" never fully caught on. You'll see "American Indian" in formal situations, but even the "American" part is a bit laughable, considering "America" wasn't so named until Christopher Columbus made his voyage west. "Indian" refers to a number of different peoples who do not share a common culture or language: Navajo on the west side of the state, Jicarilla and Mescalero Apache, and the Puebloans of the Rio Grande and west as far as Acoma and Zuni. "Pueblo" refers not to a particular tribe, but to a larger group of people who speak four distinct languages but are banded together by a common way of living. Typically, people will identify themselves by their particular tribe: Santa Clara, for instance, or Taos. With about 10.2 percent of the population claiming American Indian ancestry (nearly 10 times the national average, and second only to Alaska), traditions are still strong.

Spanish really means that: the people, primarily in northern New Mexico, whose ancestors were Spaniards, rather than the mestizos of Mexico. For many families, it's a point of pride similar to that of *Mayflower* descendants. Over the years, particularly during the 20th century, a steady influx of Mexican immigrants blurred racial distinctions a bit, but it also reinforced the use of Spanish as a daily language and inspired pride in the culture's music and other folkways. In some circles, the word **Hispano** is used to label New Mexico's distinct culture with centuries-old Iberian roots, which includes the **Basque** people, who came here both during the conquest (Don Juan de Oñate, the first Spanish governor, was Basque) and in the early 20th century as sheepherders. The discovery of families of **crypto-Jews** (Spanish Jews who nominally converted to Catholicism but fled here to avoid the Inquisition) has added another fascinating layer to the Spanish story, along with the knowledge that many of the first Spanish explorers likely had Arab blood as well.

Anglo is the most imprecise term, as it can mean anyone who's not Spanish or Indian. Originally used to talk about traders of European descent who came to hunt and sell furs and trade on the Santa Fe Trail, it still refers to people who can't trace their roots back to the conquistadors or farther. If you're a Vietnamese immigrant, a Tibetan refugee, or an African American whose family settled a farm here after the Civil War, you could be, at least in jest, Anglo. (As of 2014, about 38.9 percent of the population was non-Hispanic Caucasian; Asians were only 1.7 percent, and African Americans made up 2.5 percent.) But all Anglo culture is shot through with Spanish and Indian influence, whether among the organic garlic farmers from California who rely on their acequias for water or the New Age seekers who do sweat-lodge rituals.

Even with a liberal application of "Anglo," the tricultural arrangement is limiting, as it doesn't assign a place to contemporary immigrants from Mexico and other Latin American countries, and their numbers are growing steadily. It also doesn't acknowledge the strong Mexican American **Chicano** culture that's shared across the Southwest, from Los Angeles through Texas. The U.S. census form lumps both newer arrivals and old Spanish under "Hispanic"—a category (distinct from race) that made up 47.7 percent of the population in 2014, the highest in the country.

RELIGION

Four hundred years after the arrival of the Franciscan missionaries, New Mexico is still a heavily **Catholic** state—even KFC offers a Friday-night fish fry during Lent. But the relative isolation of the territory produced some variances that have disturbed the Vatican. In both Indian and Spanish churches, the pageantry of medieval Christianity is preserved. Las Posadas, the reenactment of Mary and Joseph's search for lodging in Bethlehem, is a festive torch-lit tradition every December, and during the annual Holy Week pilgrimage to Chimayó, devoted groups stage the stations of the cross, complete with 100-pound wood beams and lots of fake blood.

The Pueblo Indians play on church-as-theater, too: During Christmas Eve mass, for instance, the service may come to an abrupt end as the priest is hustled off the pulpit by face-painted clowns making way for the parade of ceremonial dancers down the aisle. In both cultures, the Mexican Virgin of Guadalupe is highly revered, and a number of saints are honored as intercessors for all manner of dilemmas, from failing crops to false imprisonment.

Eastern religions have a noticeable presence in New Mexico as well, and even a bit of political clout. A community of primarily U.S.-born converts to **Sikhism** in Española, for example, is a major donor to both parties. Santa Fe is home to a substantial number of **Buddhists,** both U.S. converts and native Tibetan refugees who have relocated to this different mountainous land. Stupas can be found up and down the Rio Grande.

LANGUAGE

English is the predominant language, but **Spanish** is very commonly used—about 30 percent of the population speaks it regularly.

Spanish-speakers in northern New Mexico were for centuries only the old Hispano families, communicating in a variant of Castilian with a distinct vocabulary that developed in isolation. This "Quixotic" dialect changed little until the early 1900s, when immigrants arrived from Mexico and elsewhere in Latin America. For much of the 20th century, English was the only permissible classroom language, although many school districts required Spanish as a foreign language. Since the 1990s, education policy has shifted to include bilingual classrooms.

Additionally, you'll occasionally hear Indians speaking their respective languages. Of the four main Pueblo tongues, **Tewa, Tiwa,** and **Towa** are part of the Tanoan family of languages, which are also spoken by Plains Indians. They are related but mutually unintelligible, roughly equivalent to, say, French, Spanish, and Italian. Tewa is the most widely spoken, used in all of the pueblos just north of Santa Fe: Ohkay Owingeh, San Ildefonso, Santa Clara, Pojoaque, Tesuque, and Nambé. Four pueblos speak Tiwa—Taos and Picurís share one dialect, while Isleta and Sandia, in an odd pocket near Albuquerque, speak a different dialect. Towa is now spoken only at Jemez Pueblo. Part of the greater Athabaskan family, the **Navajo** and **Apache** languages are related to, but distinct from, one another.

Keresan (spoken in Laguna, Acoma, Cochiti, Kewa, San Felipe, Santa Ana, and Zia) and **Zuni** (spoken only at that pueblo) are what linguists call "isolates." Like Basque, they are not connected to neighboring languages, nor to any other language. Additionally, each Keresan-speaking pueblo has developed its own dialect, so immediately adjacent communities can understand each other, but those farthest apart cannot.

One interesting characteristic of the Pueblo languages is that they have remained relatively pure. Tewa vocabulary, for instance, is still less than 5 percent loan words, despite centuries of Spanish and English influence.

New Mexico's Penitentes

Most Hispano villages in northern New Mexico have a modest one-story building called a **morada**—the meeting place of **Los Hermanos Penitentes** (The Penitent Brothers), a lay Catholic fraternity with deep roots in medieval Spain and a history that has often put it at odds with the church.

The Penitentes developed in New Mexico in the early colonial era and were at the height of their influence during the so-called Secular Period (1790-1850), when the Franciscans had been pushed out by church leaders in Mexico but no new priests were sent to the territory. Members of the brotherhood cared for the ill, conducted funerals, and settled petty disputes and even elections. They maintained the spiritual and political welfare of their villages when there were no priests or central government to do so.

The Penitentes are best known for their intense religious rituals, which are rumored to still include self-flagellation, bloodletting, and mock crucifixion—activities that took place in public processions for centuries but were driven underground in the late 19th century following official church condemnation. The secrecy, along with sensational journalism by visitors from the East Coast, fueled gruesome rumors. For their crucifixion reenactments, it was said Penitentes used real nails, and the man drawn by lot to be the Cristo had a good chance of dying—though no eyewitness ever recorded the practice on paper. One well-documented ritual involves pulling la carretera del muerte, an oxcart filled with rocks and a wooden figure of Doña Sebastiana, Lady Death. Morbid imagery bred morbid curiosity: Photos in a *Harper's* magazine story from the early 1900s show Anglos looking on agog as Penitentes clad in white pants and black hoods whip themselves.

In 1947, after years of concerted lobbying (but not an official renunciation of its rituals), the Penitentes were again accepted into the fold of the Catholic Church. The hermanos mayores (head brothers) from all of the moradas convene annually in Santa Fe, and the group, which has an estimated 3,000 members, functions as a political and public-service club.

The rituals do continue, most visibly during Holy Week, when the group's devotion to the physical suffering of the human Jesus is at its keenest. The Penitentes reenact the stations of the cross and the crucifixion, and although ketchup is more prevalent than real blood and statues often stand in for the major players, the scenes are solemn and affectingly tragic. On some days during Holy Week, the morada is open to non-Penitentes—a rare chance for outsiders to see the meeting place of this secretive group.

This is probably due to the way speakers have long been forced to compartmentalize, using Tewa for conversation at home and switching to English or Spanish for business and trade. For centuries, the Franciscan priests, then the U.S. government, attempted to stamp out Native American languages. Following the Civil War, Puebloan children were moved forcibly to boarding schools, where they were given Anglo names and permitted to speak only English, a policy that continued for decades.

Only in 1990, with the passage of the **Native American Languages Act,** were American Indian languages officially permitted in government-funded schools—indeed, they are now recognized as a unique element of this country's culture and encouraged. In Taos, where the Tiwa language is a ritual secret that outsiders are not permitted to learn, one public school has Tiwa classes for younger students, open only to tribe members and taught by approved teachers; as an added measure against the language being recorded, the classroom has no chalkboard. Less-formal instruction within the pueblos as well as on the Navajo Nation has also helped the Indian languages enjoy a renaissance.

The Arts

New Mexico is a hotbed of creativity, from Santa Fe's burgeoning contemporary art scene to traditional Spanish folk artists working in remote villages, using the same tools their great-grandfathers did, to whole American Indian villages, such as Acoma, devoted to the production of fine silverwork. Here's what to look for in the traditional arenas of pottery, weaving, jewelry, and wood carving.

POTTERY

New Mexico's pottery tradition thrives, drawing on millennia of craftsmanship. About 2,000 years ago, the **Mogollon** people in the southern part of the state began making simple pots of brown, coiled clay. A thousand years later, the craft had developed into the beautiful black-on-white symmetry of the **Mimbres** people. Later, each of the pueblos developed its own style.

By the 20th century, some traditions had died out, but almost all felt some kind of renaissance following the work of San Ildefonso potter **María Martinez** in the first half of the 20th century. Along with her husband, Julian, Martinez revived a long-lost style of lustrous black pottery with subtle matte decoration. The elegant pieces, which looked at once innovative and traditional, inspired Anglo collectors (who saw the couple's work at the 1934 Chicago World's Fair, among other places) as well as local potters. Today, many artists make their livings with clay.

The various tribal styles are distinguished by their base clay, the "slip" (the clay-and-water finish), and their shape. Taos and Picurís pueblos, for instance, are surrounded by beds of micaceous clay, which lends pots a subtle glitter. (It also helps them withstand heat well; they're renowned for cooking beans.) Acoma specializes in intricate black designs painted on thin white clay. Pottery from Ohkay Owingeh (formerly San Juan) is typically reddish-brown with incised

symbols. And Santa Clara developed the "wedding jar," a double-neck design with a handle. If a particular style catches your eye in city galleries, then you can visit the specific pueblo, where you may be able to buy directly from the artisan and perhaps see where the piece was made.

TEXTILES

After pottery, **weaving** is probably the state's most widespread craft. Historically, Indian and Spanish weaving styles were separate, but they have merged over the centuries to create some patterns and styles unique to the Rio Grande Valley. The first Spanish explorers marveled at the Navajo cotton blankets, woven in whole panels on wide looms; Spaniards had been working with narrow looms and stitching two panels together. Spanish weavers introduced the hardy Churro sheep, with its rough wool that was good for hand-spinning, as well as new dyes, such as indigo (although the blue-tinted rugs are often called **Moki** rugs, using a Navajo word).

In the early 1800s, in an attempt to make a better product for trade, the Spanish government sent Mexican artists north to work with local weavers. Out of this meeting came the distinctive **Saltillo** styles (named for the region the Mexican teachers came from), such as the running-leaf pattern, which Rio Grande weavers alternated with solid-color stripes. In the 1880s, New Mexican artisans first saw quilts from the eastern United States, and they adapted the eight-pointed star to their wool rugs. Another popular motif from the 19th century is a zigzag pattern that resembles lightning.

One item that shows up in antiques shops is the **Chimayó blanket,** an invention of the tourist age in the early 20th century, when Anglo traders encouraged local Hispano weavers to make an affordable souvenir to sell to visitors looking for "Indian" blankets.

Luminarias or Farolitos?

luminarias in Santa Fe … where most people would call them "farolitos"

The cultural differences between Santa Fe and Albuquerque don't apply just to the number of art galleries per square block and whether you eat posole or rice with your enchiladas. Every Christmas, a debate rears its head: What do you call a paper bag with a bit of sand in the bottom and a votive candle inside? These traditional holiday decorations, which line driveways and flat adobe rooftops in the last weeks of December, are commonly known as "luminarias" in Albuquerque and most towns to the south, and as "farolitos" in Santa Fe and all the villages to the north.

To complicate matters, another holiday tradition in Santa Fe and other northern towns is to light small bonfires of piñon logs in front of houses. Santa Feans call these little stacks of wood … luminarias. Farolitos, they argue, are literally "little lanterns," an accurate description of the glowing paper bags—and under this logic, use of the term "farolito" has spread a bit in Albuquerque, at least among people who weren't raised saying "luminaria" from birth.

Albuquerqueans do have Webster's on their side, however; the dictionary concurs that luminarias are paper-bag lanterns and notes the tradition comes from Mexico, where the bags are often colored and pricked with holes. Because this author's loyalties are to Santa Fe—and the city does have a hugely popular annual event named after them—the argument is settled, at least in these pages: Farolito it is.

They're handsome, single-width rugs with a strong central motif, perhaps the iconic Southwestern-look rug.

Also look for **colcha** work, a Spanish style in which a loose-weave rug is decorated with wool embroidery. It was revived in the 1930s by Mormons, and you will occasionally see beautiful examples from this period in collectors' shops. Contemporary weaving can draw on any and all of these innovations and is practiced just as often by a young Anglo as a Hispano grandmother. A strong small-batch wool industry in New Mexico helps the scene tremendously—expect to see vivid color-block contemporary pieces alongside the more traditional patterns.

JEWELRY

Despite a long native tradition, the familiar forms of jewelry seen today date only from the mid-19th century, when the Navajo of western New Mexico pioneered silversmithing (it's thought they learned it during their internment at Fort Sumner) and taught it to the Pueblo Indians. The most iconic piece of Southwestern jewelry, a signature Navajo design, is the turquoise-and-silver **squash-blossom necklace,** a large crescent pendant decorated with flowerlike silver beads. Actually derived from Spanish pomegranate decorations, rather than native plant imagery, it's seen in every Southwest jewelry store.

Look also for shell-shaped **concha belts** (also spelled "concho"), silver "shells" linked together or strung on a leather belt, and the San Felipe specialty, **heishi,** tiny disks made of shell and threaded to make a rope-like strand. The Zuni carve small animal **fetishes**—bears, birds, and more—often strung on necklaces with heishi. In addition to turquoise, opals are a popular decorative stone, along with brick-red coral, lapis lazuli, and black jet and marble. Whatever you buy, the gallery or artisan should supply you with a written receipt of its components—which stones, the grade of silver, and so forth.

Turquoise

Although New Mexico's turquoise is all mined out, the stone is still an essential part of local jewelry-making; most of it is imported from mines in China. It is available in shades from lime-green to pure sky-blue, and much of it has been subjected to various processes to make it more stable and versatile, which affects the price.

Rare gem-grade turquoise is the top of the line—a high-quality piece with complex spiderwebbing from now-empty mines like Lander or Lone Mountain can cost $350 per carat. "Gem-grade" applies only to **natural stones** (those that have not been chemically treated in any way) and is based on the piece's luster, hardness, and matrix, the term for the web of dark veins running through it, which you should be able to feel in any natural turquoise, regardless of grade. Highest-quality stones from still-functioning mines in China or Tibet will cost significantly less ($10-20 per carat) but will be of the same quality as some premium U.S. stones. Slightly less splendid natural stones are graded jewelry-quality,

high-quality, or investment-quality—but they are not quite hard enough to guarantee they will not change color over decades. They cost $2-5 per carat. For any natural stone, the seller must provide you with a written certificate of its status.

Because good natural turquoise is increasingly difficult to come by and turquoise is such an unreliable stone, various treatments are common and acceptable to make a great deal of the stuff usable. **Treated turquoise** refers to any stone that has added resins, waxes, or other foreign elements. A certain proprietary treatment, **enhanced turquoise,** also called "Zachary process turquoise," is usually applied to medium-grade or higher stones.

Turquoise that has been **stabilized,** or submerged in epoxy resin to harden it and deepen the color, makes up the bulk of the market. Because it's less expensive, it allows for a little waste in the carving process, and good-quality stabilized turquoise is often found in expensive jewelry with elaborate inlay. Average-quality stabilized stone, the next grade down, is used by perhaps 70 percent of American Indian artisans—it can stand up to being carved and is very well priced. Though it ranks relatively low in the range of turquoise available, it produces an attractive piece of jewelry—perhaps not with the elaborate spiderwebbing of a rare piece, but with an overall good color and luster.

Below this are low-quality stabilized stones that have been artificially colored (often called "color shot," or, more confusing, "color stabilized"). **"Synthetic"** stones are actually real turquoise—small chunks mixed with a binding powder of ground turquoise or pyrite, then pressed into shapes and cut. The result is surprisingly attractive, with natural spiderwebbing, but it should be clearly labeled as synthetic. And of course there is the turquoise that isn't at all—plastic stuff that can be quite convincing.

Aside from the synthetic stuff, don't worry too much about getting "bad" or "cheap" turquoise—because each stone is different, the more important thing is to find a piece that's attractive to you and is priced to reflect its quality. Just remember that the words "genuine," "authentic," or "pure" have no real meaning—only "natural" is legally defined. Likewise, the phrase **"authentic Indian handmade"** is a legal one—any variation on this wording (such as "Indian crafted") is likely some kind of ruse. Shopping in New Mexico provides many opportunities to buy direct from the artisan—under the portal at the Palace of the Governors in Santa Fe, for instance. Otherwise, just avoid shopping in too-good-to-be-true stores that are perpetually "going out of business" or "in liquidation."

WOOD AND TINWORK

When Spanish colonists arrived in New Mexico, they had few resources, little money, and only the most basic tools. A group of settlers would typically include one carpenter, whose skills helped fill everyone's houses with heavy wood **furniture** (still made today). But the carpenter also helped the group to worship—for chief among the wood-carvers was (and is) the santero or santera, who carves images of saints. These so-called **santos** can be either flat (retablos) or three-dimensional (bultos) and are typically painted in lively colors, though some outstanding work has been produced in plain, unpainted wood.

Santo styles have shown remarkable continuity over the centuries. The most notable break from tradition was by Patrocinio Barela, whose WPA-sponsored work in the 1930s was almost fluid, utilizing the natural curves and grains of the wood. His sons and grandsons practice the art today. For centuries, the piousness of the santero was valued at least as much as his skill in carving, though many contemporary carvers do their work for a large market of avid collectors. One popular figure is San Isidro, patron saint of farmers, from 12th-century Spain.

Look also for **straw marquetry,** another product of hard times in the colonial period, in which tiny fibers of "poor man's gold" replaced precious metals as inlay to make elaborate geometric designs on dark wood. Tinwork is another ubiquitous craft, found in inexpensive votive-candle holders as well as elaborately punched and engraved mirror frames and chandeliers.

Essentials

Transportation

GETTING THERE
Air

Albuquerque International Sunport (ABQ; 505/244-7700; www.abqsunport.com) is the main access point to the region. It's served by the three major U.S. air carriers, plus Southwest Airlines, JetBlue, Alaska Airlines, Allegiant Air, and Frontier. Fares fluctuate on the same schedule as the rest of the country, with higher rates in summer and over holidays; in the winter, it's wise to choose a connection through a more temperate hub, such as Dallas (American) or Salt Lake City (Delta).

Small **Santa Fe Municipal Airport** (SAF; 121 Aviation Dr.; 505/955-2900; http://flysantafe.com), west of the city, receives direct flights from Dallas and Phoenix with American Eagle, and from Denver with United.

Train

Amtrak (800/872-7245; www.amtrak.com) runs the *Southwest Chief* daily between Chicago and Los Angeles, stopping in **Raton, Las Vegas, Lamy** (18 miles from Santa Fe), **Albuquerque,** and **Gallup.**

Arriving in Albuquerque, you're in the middle of downtown, in a depot shared with Greyhound. There are lockers here (occasionally full), and city buses are available just up the block. Lamy (the stop nearest Santa Fe) is no more than a depot—though it is a dramatic and wild-feeling place to get off the train. Amtrak provides an awkwardly timed shuttle service to Santa Fe hotels (passengers arriving on eastbound trains must wait for passengers from the westbound train, an hour later). From Chicago, Amtrak pads its schedule heavily between Lamy and Albuquerque—so if the train is running behind, you'll be late arriving in Lamy but generally will still get to Albuquerque on schedule.

Bus

Greyhound (800/231-2222; www.greyhound.com) connects New Mexico with adjacent states and Mexico. Routes run roughly along I-40 and I-25, with little service to outlying areas. If you're coming from elsewhere in the Southwest, you may want to investigate **El Paso-Los Angeles Limousine Express** (866/691-9732; www.eplalimo.com), a long-established operator that originally served the Mexican immigrant population. Its route runs east-west from El Paso to Los Angeles, stopping in Las Cruces and Deming; it also connects Denver to Santa Fe and Albuquerque.

Car

Conveniently, New Mexico is crisscrossed by interstates: **I-40** and **I-10** run east-west, and **I-25** cuts roughly down the center, north-south. Denver, Colorado, to Santa Fe is 450 miles, about a six-hour drive; add another hour to reach Albuquerque. El Paso, Texas, to Albuquerque is 275 miles, about four hours. Coming from Flagstaff, Arizona, Albuquerque is 325 miles along I-40, about 4.5 hours; from Amarillo, Texas, it's just slightly less distance in the other direction.

Southwest road-trippers often combine New Mexico with southwestern Colorado, in which case **U.S. 550** makes a good route south from Durango. Other southern Colorado options to consider include **U.S. 84** from Pagosa Springs and **U.S. 285,** which runs from Alamosa to Carlsbad. From Tucson, Arizona, a nice route into New Mexico is to cut north off I-10 at Lordsburg, following Highway 90 to Silver City and winding through the mountains northeast to reach I-25 to Albuquerque.

GETTING AROUND

Practically speaking, you will need a car. Traveling between towns by bus or train is feasible, but it certainly limits what you can see. Within Albuquerque and Santa Fe, you can often get around by walking, biking, or public transport, but getting to or around anywhere smaller requires your own wheels.

Bus

Between Santa Fe and Taos (and communities around and in between, including the pueblos), the **North Central Regional Transit District** (866/206-0754; www.ncrtd.org) offers commuter bus service. It's not very frequent, but it's free on Saturdays and Sundays, and it covers a lot of area, making it an option for the hard-core no-car traveler.

Another option is the weekday **Park & Ride** (866/551-7433; http://dot.state.nm.us) service offered by the New Mexico Department of Transportation. It covers stops between Santa Fe, Los Alamos, and Española.

Greyhound (800/231-2222; www.greyhound.com) connects Albuquerque with Santa Fe and Las Cruces, as well as a few other midsize towns. Anything off the interstate in the southeast will require a transfer in Las Cruces. **El Paso-Los Angeles Limousine Express** (1611 Central Ave. SW, Albuquerque; 505/247-8036; www.eplalimo.com) offers good alternative service to Las Cruces from Albuquerque and Deming.

Train

The **Rail Runner** (866/795-7245; www.riometro.org) commuter train connects Belén, Albuquerque, and Santa Fe, with convenient downtown stations, making a car-free visit quite feasible, or even a day trip. The train passes through odd pockets of Albuquerque and stunning, untouched pueblo lands. Tickets are based on a zone system; the 90-minute ride between downtown Albuquerque and Santa Fe costs $10, or $11 for a day pass. (Kids: Listen for the "meep-meep!" warning as the doors close!)

Via **Amtrak** (800/872-7245; www.amtrak.com), Gallup, Raton, and Las Vegas are feasible destinations from Albuquerque.

Car

Driving New Mexico's scenic byways is definitely one of the pleasures of traveling here. On the other hand, parking in Santa Fe can be difficult, or at least expensive—and you can get around the center of town very easily on foot. So, ideally, you would rent a car only for the days you plan to go out of the city.

Central Taos is small, but sights are spread out on the fringes, and only the most dedicated can manage without a car. In Albuquerque, you can live without a car for a few days, but it requires planning and rules out a few of the sights. All of the major car-rental chains are at Albuquerque's airport, in a single building; see the respective city chapters for other rental companies and offices.

All but a few roads are passable year-round. You won't need four-wheel drive, but be prepared in winter for ice and snow anywhere other than central Albuquerque and the southernmost section of the state. Also check your car-rental agreement for restrictions on driving on dirt roads—a rare clause in the United States, but occasionally employed by smaller companies. Needless to say, this is a liability, as it's almost impossible to go anywhere interesting in New Mexico without winding up on a dirt road.

Bike

With beautiful vistas, often deserted roads, and a strong community of both road cyclists and mountain bikers, New Mexico can be a great place to get around on two wheels, as long as it's not your main form of transport. Whether you'll be riding your own bike or renting one here, always pack a patch kit, and consider installing tire liners. Goathead thorns and broken glass are particular scourges of New Mexican roads—and bear in mind that many roads don't have much of a shoulder at all.

Central Albuquerque and Santa Fe are both manageable by bicycle, with separate lanes. In Taos, traffic on the main road can be unpleasantly heavy and fast. But services such as the Rail Runner, Taos Express, and Park & Ride have space for bicycles, so it's possible to take your wheels with you from town to town.

Food

New Mexicans love their food so much, they have been known to enshrine it on lottery tickets, with scratch cards named Chile Cash, Chips and Salsa, and Sopaipilla Dough (promising "lots of honey and plenty of money"). The state cuisine is a distinctive culinary tradition that shouldn't be confused with Tex-Mex, Californian Mex, or south-of-the-border Mexican—even though most locals will say they're going out for "Mexican" when they mean they want a bowl of purely *New* Mexican green-chile stew. (But if you're eating mole or ceviche, that's "*Mexican* Mexican," and you can get more of it the farther south you drive.) New Mexican cuisine doesn't typically do bean-and-meat chili, certainly not mango-flavored anything, and only rarely guacamole—you can get it, but avocados are expensive here.

ALL CHILE, ALL THE TIME

The cuisine's distinguishing element is the **New Mexico chile pepper.** The best-known variety is the Hatch chile, named for the southern New Mexican town that's the center of the industry. In the north, Chimayó is another big chile-producing town, with its own heirloom strain, usually picked red.

When the chile is picked green, it is roasted and peeled, then used whole to make chiles rellenos (stuffed with cheese and fried in batter), or cut into chunks and cooked in sauces or used as the base of a meaty green-chile stew. In northern New Mexico, that sauce is pure chile, maybe thinned with chicken broth; in some towns in the southern part of the state, it's more like a green-chile cream gravy, often with a base of cream-of-mushroom soup.

When the New Mexico chile is left to ripen, then dried in the sun, it turns turn dark red and leathery. These dry red chiles are stored whole, in long chains called ristras, or ground into flakes (chile caribe) or finer powder to be the base of a sauce or marinade. The heartiest red-chile dish is carne adovada: chunks of pork shoulder stewed with pure red sauce.

Most other items—enchiladas, burritos, and eggs (huevos rancheros), to name a few—can be ordered with either variety of chile, so a standard query in restaurants (and now enshrined as the official state question) is "Red or green?" You can have both, splitting the plate half-and-half, a style many people call "Christmas," though old-timers still call it "Mexican flag."

The chile is often coupled with the traditional Native American triad of **corn, squash,** and **beans.** The beans are typically brown, meaty pintos, served whole in a stew or mashed up and "refried" (not actually fried twice—the term is a mistranslation of the Spanish "refrito," which means "really fried"). Corn takes the form of tortillas as well as hulled kernels of hominy, called posole here and often cooked into a stew with chile, oregano, and meat. Ground corn paste (masa) is whipped with lard (or Crisco, if you're "healthy") and wrapped around a meaty filling, then tied in a corn husk and steamed to make a **tamale.** Squash comes in a common side dish called **calabacitas,** sautéed with onions and a touch of green chile. Spanish settlers brought lamb, which finds its way into tacos and stews.

American Indian cuisine isn't so distinct from what everyone else eats—its one major element is **fry bread,** a round of deep-fried dough served with honey or filled with ground meat, cheese, and lettuce to make an "Indian taco"; a "Navajo taco" often uses shredded lamb or mutton in place of ground beef. Bread baked in a traditional domed adobe horno oven is also popular, and the Zuni make a distinctive sourdough this way. In pueblos and on the reservations, you'll see these mud ovens in most yards. Game meat, such as deer, is also a major component of

Red-Chile Sauce

Use only freshly ground New Mexico red chile for this sauce—not the "chile powder" sold in most grocery stores. The sauce will keep in the refrigerator for a month, and you can use it to top eggs or steaks, or devote the whole batch to a tray of enchiladas. (If you're doing the latter, you'll want to keep the sauce relatively thin, so you can easily coat the tortillas with sauce before filling them.) The flavor is best if it is prepared ahead and left to sit overnight.

Yield: 2 cups
½ c. New Mexico red chile powder
½ tsp. ground cumin (optional)
1 tsp. ground coriander (optional)
2 Tbsp. all-purpose flour
2 Tbsp. lard (or vegetable oil)
2 or 3 cloves garlic, crushed or minced
2 c. chicken stock or water
1 tsp. dried oregano (optional)

Measure the chile, cumin, coriander, and flour into a heavy-bottomed saucepan and place over medium-high heat. Stir continuously until the spices are just fragrant and the flour has darkened slightly. Remove the chile-flour mix to a small bowl. Heat the lard or oil in the pan, and add the garlic and stir until fragrant. Then stir the chile-flour mix into the oil-garlic mixture—you will have a very coarse paste. Stirring constantly, slowly add half of the stock or water. Continue stirring, and the mixture will thicken and become velvety. Add the remaining stock or water and the oregano, mix well, turn heat to low, and let sauce simmer for about 20 minutes, until it is somewhat reduced and thickened to your liking. If the mixture becomes too thick, simply add more water.

American Indian cooking, though you'll rarely see it in restaurants.

Green chile makes its way into standard American fare as well. It's a popular pizza topping (great with pepperoni or ham), and the **green-chile cheeseburger** is a top choice everywhere. Also look out for **breakfast burritos,** big flour tortillas filled with scrambled eggs, hash browns, and some kind of meat—bacon, crumbled sausage, or sometimes Mexican chorizo, a spicy pork sausage. Some places sell them as to-go food, wrapped in foil with green chile added to the mix. At sit-down places, you get the whole construction smothered in either red or green chile.

Sopaipillas are another New Mexican specialty. They're palm-sized pillows of deep-fried dough, used to mop up chile and beans during the main meal, then slathered with honey for dessert. In a disturbing trend, some restaurants now offer a honey-flavored corn syrup, because it's cheaper and doesn't crystallize—if you encounter this, complain at top volume.

Bizcochitos, little anise-laced cookies, are the state's official sweet treat. Wash it all down with a **margarita,** which purists insist should involve only lime, tequila, and triple sec and be served on the rocks in a salt-rimmed glass. (Restaurants with only a beer-and-wine license often offer an agave-wine margarita—decent flavor, but pretty weak.)

How to Take the Heat

When your server plunks down a heavy white ceramic plate covered in chile and melted cheese, the words "this plate is very hot" cover only half of the story. Every year the harvest varies a bit, and the chile can be mild or so spicy as to blister lips and produce a dizzying (and addictive) endorphin rush. Locals look back on particularly incendiary seasons with that mixture of awe, fear, and longing that junkies reserve for their best scores. In general, green chile tends to be hotter than red, but it's best to ask your server what to expect—some restaurants specialize in one or the other.

You can protect yourself against chile-heat by ordering a side of sour cream with your enchiladas or burrito—although be warned that many consider this a "Texan" affectation, and you may be derided by your fellow diners. Locals usually just reach for a **sopaipilla,** the starch from which can absorb some of the chile oils. Don't gulp down water, which only spreads the searing oils around your mouth. Beer is a marginal improvement, and margaritas are at least distracting.

FINE DINING AND WINE

While there are plenty of time-warp diners and mom-and-pop hole-in-the-wall joints in New Mexico, dining can also be very sophisticated, keeping pace with the national trend toward local and organic produce. This movement hasn't been such a huge leap here: Many small family farms didn't have to "go organic," because they were never very industrialized in the first place. At white-tablecloth places, Southwestern fusion is still common, with chile working its way into foie gras appetizers and even high-concept desserts.

The fine dining scene is enhanced by a burgeoning wine industry, initiated by Spanish settlers in the 17th century but enjoying a resurgence since the 1980s. Gruet Winery in Albuquerque is the best-known New Mexico producer, especially for its excellent sparkling wine. This makes for a nice little perk of New Mexico dining: You can get inexpensive bubbly by the glass almost everywhere. The **New Mexico Wine & Grape Growers Association** (www.nmwine.com) has information on more wineries, and you can read more about the high-end and organic food scene in the periodic *Edible New Mexico* guides (www.ediblenm.com).

VEGETARIAN FOOD

New Mexican food isn't meat-centric, but strict vegetarians will have to be vigilant, as many chile dishes are traditionally made with beef or chicken stock as well as lard for flavoring. The closer you get to Texas, the more likely it is that red chile sauce will contain bits of meat. Decades of hippie influence, though, have resulted in many menus stating clearly whether the chile is meatless. Some restaurants have an unreconstructed 1970s worldview, with alfalfa sprouts and squash casseroles galore.

the ubiquitous breakfast burrito

Accommodations

Throughout this guide, distinctive choices—bed-and-breakfasts, lodges, and small, independently owned hotels and motels—are emphasized over chain options as much as possible. Just because the chains are not listed doesn't mean they're not available—and in many small towns, they're the only solid option.

The prices listed are the official high-season rack rates—that is, what you'd pay if you just walked in off the street, with no discounts; tax is not included. Most often, the numbers are the least expensive room for one person in one bed (a single, abbreviated *s*) and two people in two beds (a double, abbreviated *d*). **High season** is usually June-August. **Ski season** is January-March; prices in Taos and Santa Fe don't completely bottom out—but they are still cheaper than summer. Expect higher rates in the week following Christmas and during special events, such as Indian Market in Santa Fe and Balloon Fiesta in Albuquerque, but overall you will be able to secure lower rates than those listed simply by looking online or calling the hotel directly.

Note that while many hotels tout their swimming pools, they are often forced to leave them empty due to water restrictions imposed during droughts. If you've booked at a hotel specifically for the pool, call to check the status before your trip, so you don't wind up paying a premium for a service you can't use. Santa Fe is the strictest area in the state; it limits hotels to changing towels and bed linens only every four days during your visit.

Travel Tips

WHAT TO PACK

The contents of your suitcase will be determined largely by the time of year, but be prepared for a **wide range of temperatures**—with a variety of layers—whenever you visit. Many people wrongly assume that New Mexico's desert setting means heat all day, all year round. In fact, due to the altitude in much of the state, you may encounter severe cold. Winter temperatures can dip well below freezing even in the relatively low elevations of central Albuquerque and farther south. If you think you'll attend pueblo ceremonial dances during the winter, pack mittens, long underwear, double-thick wool socks, and a hat with earflaps—there will be a lot of standing around outside.

Spring is mud season—if you hike or head to rural areas during this time, save a clean pair of shoes for around town. Summers are hot by day (July's average temperature is 92°F), but as soon as the sun dips below the horizon, the temperature can drop up to 30°F, especially outside of city centers; always keep a sweater on hand. Brief afternoon **"monsoons"** in July and August sometimes warrant an umbrella or rain slicker. In the strong sun, you'll be more comfortable if you cover up, in long-sleeve, light-colored shirts and pants in silk or cotton. In fact, you should guard against the sun any time of year, as the thin atmosphere at this altitude means you'll burn more quickly than you're used to. You should never be without **sunglasses,** heavy-duty **sunscreen,** and a **brimmed hat.**

As for style, anything goes. If you'll be hobnobbing with Santa Fe's upper echelon, you might want to pack something dressy—the local formalwear for men is clean jeans, shined cowboy boots, and a bolo tie. Otherwise, though, New Mexicans are very casual. But note that when visiting churches and pueblos, it's respectful not to show excessive skin—women should avoid obvious cleavage and super-short skirts.

TOURIST INFORMATION

For pre-trip inspiration, the New Mexico Tourism Board publishes the monthly *New Mexico* magazine (www.newmexicomagazine.org), which does an excellent job covering both mainstream attractions and more obscure corners of the state.

Many smaller towns' chambers of commerce can also be extremely helpful.

If you plan to do a lot of hiking, you can order detailed topographical maps from the Southwestern Region office of the **National Forest Service** (505/842-3292; www.fs.usda.gov) in Albuquerque or from the Bureau of Land Management's **Public Lands Interpretive Center** (301 Dinosaur Tr.; 505/954-2002; www.publiclands.org) in Santa Fe. Also, in Santa Fe, **Travel Bug** (839 Paseo de Peralta; 505/992-0418; 10am-6pm Mon.-Sat., noon-4pm Sun.) bookstore has an extensive selection of maps as do the **REI** stores in Santa Fe (500 Market St.; 505/982-3557; 10am-8pm Mon.-Fri., 10am-7pm Sat., 10am-6pm Sun.) and Albuquerque (1550 Mercantile Ave. NE; 505/247-1191; 10am-9pm Mon.-Fri., 9am-7pm Sat., 10am-6pm Sun.).

Telephone and Internet

Albuquerque, Santa Fe, Los Alamos, Gallup, and Farmington use the area code 505, while the rest of the state's numbers start with 575.

For mobile phone reception, the corridor between Albuquerque and Santa Fe is fine, but in rural areas, phones on the GSM network (AT&T, T-Mobile) get very poor or no reception. Data service is equally spotty. If you'll be spending a lot of time outside of the cities or counting on your phone for emergencies, you might consider a CDMA phone (Verizon is best). Likewise, don't count on data service on your smartphone.

Internet access is widespread, though DSL and other high-speed service is still not necessarily the norm, and thick adobe walls can be a hindrance for wireless signals. Rural areas still rely on satellite Internet, which can be poor in bad weather. In the cities, cafés often have hotspots, and the city of Albuquerque even maintains a few free ones in public spaces, such as the Old Town plaza.

Time Zone

New Mexico is in the **Mountain time zone,** one hour ahead of the West Coast of the United States and two hours behind the East Coast. It's -7 GMT (Greenwich Mean Time) during the winter and -6 GMT in summer, when Daylight Saving Time is followed statewide.

Note that neighboring Arizona does not follow Daylight Saving Time, which can lead to confusion around the border.

CONDUCT AND CUSTOMS

New Mexico is a part of the United States, but it can sometimes feel quite foreign, particularly in the high mountain Spanish villages and in the Indian pueblos. Regardless, basic courtesy rules and, in smaller communities, modest dress are appreciated, especially at the older Catholic churches.

Some Pueblo Indians, as well as Navajo, find loud voices, direct eye contact, and firm handshakes off-putting and, by the same token, may not express themselves in the forthright way a lot of visitors are used to. Similarly, a subdued reaction doesn't necessarily mean a lack of enthusiasm.

New Mexico is not a wealthy state, and the gap between rich and poor can be wide. In general, people don't appreciate conspicuous displays of wealth, and it's doubly rude to flash cash, fancy gadgets, and jewelry in tiny villages and pueblos (and public cell-phone use is still considered tacky most places). Be thoughtful when taking photos, particularly of people's homes—always ask permission, and consider that some of the more "scenic" elements of New Mexico are also the products of poverty, which some people may not be proud to have captured on film.

You can help the local economy by favoring New Mexican-owned businesses, rather than chain operations, and buying directly from artisans wherever possible. In these situations, don't get too bent on bargaining. The item you're buying represents not just raw materials and hours of work, but a person's particular talent, skill, and heritage. Insisting on an extra-low price belittles not just the item, but the artisan as well.

Pueblo and Reservation Etiquette

When visiting pueblos and reservations, remember that you are not at a tourist attraction—you are walking around someone's neighborhood. So peeking in windows and wandering off the suggested route isn't polite. If you want to take photos, you'll usually need a camera permit, for an additional fee. Always ask permission before taking photos of people, and ask parents, rather than children, for their consent. All pueblos ban alcohol.

Some pueblos are more welcoming than others. San Ildefonso, for instance, is open year-round, whereas Jemez is completely closed except for some feast days. So it's flawed logic to seek out the less-visited places or go in the off times in order to have a less "touristy" experience. In fact, the most rewarding time to visit *is* on a big feast day—you may not be the only tourist there, but you have a better chance of being invited into a local's home.

CLASSES AND VOLUNTEERING

From afternoon cooking workshops to intensives on adobe building techniques, the opportunities to learn in New Mexico are broad.

General Education

Look first into the art, music, and outdoors programs at **Ghost Ranch** (877/804-4678; www.ghostranch.org), the beautiful property in Abiquiu. Santa Fe and Albuquerque are both home to renowned alternative healing, herbal medicine, and massage schools, more than can be listed here; visit **Natural Healers** (www.naturalhealers.com) for a list.

Arts and Crafts

Taos in particular is a hotbed for art classes. **Fechin Art Workshops** (575/751-0647; www.fineartservices.info) are five-day live-in retreats that have been running for more than two decades; they are based in Taos Ski Valley. The equally long-established **Taos Art School** (575/758-0350; www.taosartschool. org) focuses on landscape techniques, in six-day painting or photo workshops that include hiking and rafting options. Taos is also home to the **Taos School of Metalsmithing and Lapidary Design** (575/758-0207; www. taosjewelryschool.com), which covers a range of jewelry-making topics, starting with half-day sessions.

Almost on the border with Colorado, in the town of Chama, the long-running **Tierra Wools** (575/588-7231; www.handweavers. com) offers five-day weaving workshops and three-day natural dye classes, among other classes.

The excellent **Santa Fe Photographic Workshops** (505/983-1400; www. santafeworkshops.com) offers nationally recognized photography classes in its campus in the Sangre de Cristo Mountains, just outside the city. Workshops range from three days on-site to longer field programs around New Mexico. On the southern outskirts of the city, the **Santa Fe Community College** (505/428-1000; www.sfcc.edu) has a wide selection of classes focused on arts and crafts, including woodcarving, landscape drawing, and tinwork.

In Albuquerque, **Casa Flamenca** (505/247-0622; www.casaflamenca.org) offers classes in flamenco dance and classical Spanish guitar.

Music

Throughout the year, the highly regarded **New Mexico Jazz Workshop** (nmjazz.org) in Albuquerque offers a variety of jazz-focused courses, from improvisation to singing.

Cooking

Santa Fe School of Cooking (125 N. Guadalupe St.; 505/983-4511; www.santafeschoolofcooking.com) offers day classes in contemporary Southwestern cuisine, as well as traditional Native American cooking and New Mexican standards; nice farmers market trips and restaurant walking tours are offered, too.

In Arroyo Seco, **Cooking Studio Taos** (575/776-2665; www.cookingstudiotaos.com) offers intimate classes led by a James Beard-recognized chef and focusing on a variety of cuisines, including New Mexican, Greek, and Moroccan.

Permaculture and Alternative Construction

In Albuquerque, **The Old School** (505/926-1280; www.abqoldschool.com) offers instruction on winter gardening, permaculture, and building solar panels. If you're interested in New Mexico's solar architecture movement, you can enroll in the monthlong intensive **Earthship Academy** (575/751-0462; www.earthshipglobal.com), a crash course in building the off-the-grid rammed-earth houses that have their roots in Taos. The Earthship Biotecture organization also accepts volunteers. For more on local building styles, look into the semester-long classes in adobe construction at **Northern New Mexico College** (575/747-2100; www.nnmc.edu).

INTERNATIONAL TRAVELERS

As for any destination in the United States, check before departure whether you'll need a **visa** to enter; most European nationals do not need one.

New Mexico uses the **United States dollar,** and currency exchange is available at most banks as well as in better hotels, though the rates in the latter case will not be as good. For the best rates and convenience, withdraw cash from your home account through **automatic teller machines** (ATMs); check first, though, what fee your home bank and the ATM's bank will charge you for the transaction, including any fee for a foreign-currency transaction.

Tipping is similar to elsewhere in the country: 15 percent to cab drivers, and 15-20 percent on restaurant bills. For larger groups, often restaurants will add 18 percent or so to the bill; this is suggested, and you may refuse it or write in a lower amount if service was poor. Add $1 or so per drink when ordered at the bar; $1 or $2 to staff who handle your luggage in hotels; and $3-5 per day to housekeeping in hotels—envelopes are often left in rooms for this purpose. **Bargaining** is acceptable only if you're dealing directly with an artisan, and even then, it is often politely deflected. But it doesn't hurt to ask, nicely, if the quoted price is the best possible one.

Electricity is 120 volts, with a two-prong, flat-head plug, the same as Canada and Mexico.

ACCESS FOR TRAVELERS WITH DISABILITIES

Wheelchair access can be frustrating in some historic properties and on the narrower sidewalks of Santa Fe and Taos, but in most other respects, travelers with disabilities should find no more problems in New Mexico than elsewhere in the United States. Public buses are wheelchair accessible, an increasing number of hotels have ADA-compliant rooms, and you can even get out in nature a bit on paved trails such as the Santa Fe Canyon Preserve loop and the Paseo del Bosque in Albuquerque.

If you'll be visiting a number of wilderness areas, consider the National Park Service's **Access Pass** (888/467-2757; www.nps.gov), a free lifetime pass that grants admission for the pass-holder and three adults to all national parks, national forests, and the like, as well as discounts on interpretive services, camping fees, fishing licenses, and more. Apply in person at any federally managed park or wilderness area; you must show medical documentation of blindness or permanent disability.

TRAVELING WITH CHILDREN

Though the specific prices are not listed in this guide, admission at major attractions is almost always lower for children than for adults. Your little ones will be welcome in most environments, the only exceptions being a few of the more formal restaurants in Santa Fe and Albuquerque. Kids are sure to be fascinated by ceremonial dances at the pueblos, but be prepared with distractions, because long waits are the norm. Prep children with information about American Indian culture, and brief them on the basic etiquette at dances, which applies to them as well. Kids will also enjoy river rafting (relaxing "floats" along placid sections of the Rio Grande and Rio Chama are good for younger ones). For skiing, Taos Ski Valley has a very strong program of classes for youngsters.

SENIOR TRAVELERS

Senior discounts are available at most museums and other attractions. If you'll be visiting a number of wilderness areas, look into a **Senior Pass** ($80), a lifetime pass for people 62 and older that grants free admission for the pass-holder and three additional adults to national parks, National Forest Service lands, and many other areas, as well as discounts on activities such as camping and boat-launching. The pass can be purchased in person at any federally managed wilderness area, or online with an additional $10 processing fee; for more information, contact the **National Park Service** (888/467-2757; www.nps.gov).

Road Scholar (800/454-5768; www.roadscholar.org) runs more than 15 reasonably priced group trips in New Mexico, from a five-day general introduction to Santa Fe history and a week-long exploration of top draws in southern New Mexico to more focused tours on the history of crypto-Jews, for instance, and ancestral Puebloan culture.

PEOPLE OF COLOR

The influence of Hispanics, Latinos, and Native Americans remains strong, and that is reflected in the wealth of activities that honor and celebrate their various cultures and traditions across New Mexico, from Taos in the north to Las Cruces in the south and at the 23 Indian tribes throughout the state. As a result, Hispanic, Latino, and Native American travelers to New Mexico will have many opportunities to connect with vibrant communities and cultural institutions—such as the **Natural Hispanic Cultural Center** and the **Indian Pueblo Cultural Center,** both in Albuquerque—that bring these traditions to life.

As the state's biggest city, Albuquerque is also its most diverse. It's home to New Mexico's largest Black population and hosts several annual events honoring the community, such as the **Martin Luther King Day Parade** in January and **Black History Month** activities in February. **NMBLACK.COM** (http://nmblack.com) serves as an online resource for African Americans in the state and offers a wide range of content. The Duke City is also home to several Asian American communities, predominantly Vietnamese, Chinese, Japanese, Korean, and Filipino.

SHARE NM (https://sharenm.org) is a fantastic resource on a broad range of communities across the state including people of color and has an up-to-date events calendar.

GAY AND LESBIAN TRAVELERS

Gay marriage was legalized in New Mexico in late 2013, but Santa Fe has been one of the major gay capitals in the United States for decades, second only to San Francisco in the per-capita rates of same-sex coupledom. There are no designated "gay-borhoods" (unless you count RainbowVision Santa Fe, a retirement community) or even particular bar scenes; gay men and lesbian women are well integrated, running businesses and serving on the city council. The city's Pride parade is usually in late June, and is preceded by several big events. Another big event is the annual **Zia Regional Rodeo,** sponsored by the **New Mexico Gay Rodeo Association** (505/720-3749; www.nmgra.org). It takes place every summer in Santa Fe, with all the standard rodeo events, plus goat dressing and a wild drag race.

Albuquerque also has a decent gay scene, especially if you want to go clubbing, which is not an option in quieter Santa Fe.

As for smaller towns and pueblos, they're still significantly more conservative.

Health and Safety

CORONAVIRUS

At the time of writing in 2023, the United States had declared an end to the COVID public health emergency. While life had largely returned to normal in New Mexico and face masks were not required indoors or in public spaces outdoors, all Native American pueblos covered in this guide were closed to the general public.

Now more than ever, Moon encourages its readers to be courteous and ethical in their travel. We ask travelers to be respectful to residents, and mindful of requests in their chosen destination when planning their trip. The New Mexico Department of Health (http://cv.nmhealth.org) has the latest coronavirus updates for the state, including current public health orders, pandemic guidelines, and tracking figures.

OUTDOOR HEALTH HAZARDS

Visitors to New Mexico face several unique health concerns. First and foremost are the environmental hazards of **dehydration, sunburn,** and **altitude sickness.** The desert climate, glaring sun, and thinner atmosphere conspire to fry your skin and drain you of all moisture. (On the plus side, sweat evaporates immediately.) Apply SPF 30 sunscreen daily, even in winter, and try to drink at least a liter of water a day, whether you feel thirsty or not. (Request water in restaurants—it's usually brought only on demand, to cut down on waste.) By the time you start feeling thirsty,

you're already seriously dehydrated and at risk of further bad effects: headaches, nausea, and dizziness, all of which can become full-blown, life-threatening **heatstroke** if left untreated. Heatstroke can happen even without serious exertion—just lack of water and very hot sun. So if you're feeling at all woozy or cranky (another common symptom), head for shade and sip a Gatorade or similar electrolyte-replacement drink.

Staying hydrated also staves off the effects of the high elevation, to which most visitors will not be acclimated. The mildest reaction to being 7,000 feet or more above sea level is lethargy or light-headedness—you will probably sleep long and soundly on your first night in New Mexico. Some people do have more severe reactions, such as a piercing headache or intense nausea, especially if they engage in strenuous physical activity. Unfortunately, there's no good way to judge how your body will react, so give yourself a few days to adjust, with a light schedule and plenty of time to sleep.

Flash floods are a real threat in New Mexico and, given their sudden and intense nature, have the potential to catch you off guard and create a life-threatening situation. They're most common during the "monsoon season"—July and August—when thunderstorms produce heavy rains over a short period of time. If the rains have been preceded by a long dry spell, flash floods become more likely, as the ground simply can't absorb the rain. Areas that are prone to flash flooding are generally marked by signs, but don't rely upon signage alone; if you're hiking in an arroyo or canyon during the height of summer, be especially mindful of your surroundings, as rain can collect and flow in these channels at an alarming rate.

More obscure hazards include **West Nile virus** (wear a DEET-based insect repellent if you're down along the river in the summer); **hantavirus,** an extremely rare pulmonary ailment transmitted by rodents; and the even rarer **bubonic plague** (aka the Black Death), the very same disease that killed millions of Europeans in the Middle Ages. Luckily, only a case or two of the plague crops up every year, and it's easily treated if diagnosed early. **Lyme disease** is almost as rare, as deer ticks do not flourish in the mountains.

If you'll be spending a lot of time hiking or camping, take precautions against **giardiasis** and other waterborne ailments by boiling your water or treating it with iodine or a SteriPen (www.steripen.com), as even the clearest mountain waterways may have been tainted by cows upstream. **Snake bites** are also a hazard in the wild, so wear boots that cover your ankles, stay on trails, and keep your hands and feet out of odd holes and cracks between rocks. Only the Western diamondback rattlesnake can be aggressive when disturbed; if you spot one or hear the telltale rattle (take note also that they don't always rattle), exit the area with extreme caution. Other snakes typically will not bite if you simply back away quietly.

General **outdoor safety rules** apply: Don't hike by yourself, always register with the ranger station when heading out overnight, and let friends know where you're going and when you'll be back. Pack a good topographical map and a compass or GPS device; people manage to get lost even when hiking in the foothills, and if you're at all dehydrated or dizzy from the altitude, any disorientation can be magnified to a disastrous degree. Also pack layers of clothing, and be prepared for cold snaps and snow at higher elevations, even in the summer.

CRIME AND DRUGS

Recreational drug use is not uncommon in New Mexico—generally in a relatively benign form, with marijuana fairly widespread. (Former governor and Republican presidential candidate Gary Johnson, though no longer a user himself, has been a strenuous advocate for its legalization.) But as in much of the rural United States, crystal methamphetamine is an epidemic, and some villages in northern New Mexico have also been devastated by heroin use, with overdose deaths at a rate several hundred times higher than the national average. None of this affects travelers, except that petty theft, especially in isolated areas such as trailheads, can be an issue. Always lock your car doors, and secure any valuables in the trunk. Don't leave anything enticing in view.

Drinking and driving is unfortunately still common, especially in rural areas; be particularly alert when driving at night. A distressing number of crosses along the roadside (descansos) mark the sites of fatal car accidents, many of which involved alcohol.

Resources

Glossary

abierto: Spanish for "open"

acequia: irrigation ditch, specifically one regulated by the traditional Spanish method, maintained by a mayordomo, or "ditch boss," who oversees how much water each shareholder receives

adobe: building material of sun-dried bricks made of a mix of mud, sand, clay, and straw

arroyo: stream or dry gully where mountain runoff occasionally flows

asado: stew (usually pork) with red-chile sauce

atrio: churchyard between the boundary wall and the church entrance, usually used as a cemetery

bizcochito: anise-laced shortbread, traditionally made with lard

bosque: Spanish for "forest," specifically the cottonwoods and trees along a river

bulto: three-dimensional wood carving, typically of a saint

caldera: basin or crater formed by a collapsed volcano

canal: water drain from a flat roof; pl. canales

carne adovada: pork chunks marinated in red chile, then braised; meatier and drier than asado

cerrado: Spanish for "closed"

chicharrón: fried pork skin, usually with a layer of meat still attached

chile: not to be confused with Texas chili, Cincinnati chili, or any other U.S. concoction; refers to the fruit of the chile plant itself, eaten green (picked unripe and then roasted) or red (ripened and dried)

chimichanga: deep-fried burrito; allegedly invented in Arizona

colcha: style of blanket, in which loom-woven wool is embellished with long strands of wool embroidery

concha belt: belt made of stamped, carved silver medallions; concha is Spanish for "shell"; also concho

convento: residential compound adjoining a mission church

enchilada: corn tortilla dipped in chile sauce, filled with cheese or meat, and topped with more chile; can be served either rolled or flat (stacked in layers)

farolito: in Santa Fe and Taos, a luminaria

GCCB: common abbreviation for green-chile cheeseburger

genízaro: during Spanish colonial times, a detribalized Indian (usually due to having been enslaved) who lived with Spaniards and followed Catholic tradition

gordita: a variation on the taco, with a thicker tortilla-like shell, sometimes deep-fried; these are a more traditionally Mexican dish (though in that case rarely fried) and are available only in the southern part of the state

heishi: fine disk-shaped beads carved from shells

horno: traditional dome-shaped adobe oven

jerga: Spanish-style wool blanket or rug, loosely woven and barely decorated, meant for daily use

kachina: ancestral spirit of the Pueblo people as well as the carved figurine representing the spirit; also spelled "katsina"

kiva: sacred ceremonial space in a pueblo, at least partially underground and entered by a hole in the ceiling

latillas: thin saplings cut and laid across vigas to make a solid ceiling

lowrider: elaborately painted and customized car with hydraulic lifts

luminaria: in Albuquerque, lantern made of a sand-filled paper bag with a votive candle set inside; in Santa Fe and Taos, refers to small bonfires lit during the Christmas season

menudo: tripe soup, said to be good for curing a hangover

morada: meeting space of the Penitente brotherhood

nicho: small niche in an adobe wall, usually meant to hold a santo

Penitente: member of a long-established Catholic brotherhood in northern New Mexico

petroglyph: rock carving

pictograph: painting on a rock surface

piñon: any of several fragrant varieties of pine tree that grow in New Mexico

portal: the covered sidewalk area in front of a traditional adobe structure; pl. portales

posole: stew of hulled corn (hominy), pork, and a little chile, either green or red

pueblo: Spanish for "village," referring to the various communities of American Indians settled in the Rio Grande Valley, as well as the larger land area owned by the community (preferable to the term "reservation"); also, capitalized, the people themselves, though they speak several different languages

rajas: rough-hewn slats laid over vigas to form a ceiling; also, strips of roasted chile

ramada: simple structure built of four sapling posts and topped with additional saplings laid flat to form a shade structure and a place to hang things to dry

reredos: altar screen, usually elaborately painted or carved with various portraits of Christ and the saints

retablo: flat portrait of a saint, painted or carved in low relief, usually on wood

ristra: string of dried red chiles

santero/santera: craftsperson who produces santos

santo: portrait of a saint, either flat (a retablo) or three-dimensional (a bulto)

sipapu: hole in the floor of a kiva, signifying the passage to the spirit world

sopaipilla: square of puffed fried dough, served with the main meal for wiping up sauces and with honey for dessert

tamale: corn husk filled with masa (hominy paste) and a dab of meat, vegetables, or cheese, then steamed; usually made in large quantities for holidays

terrón: building material of bricks cut out of sod and dried in the sun, similar to adobe, but less common

Tewa: language spoken by the majority of Pueblo Indians; others in the Rio Grande Valley speak Tiwa, Towa, and Keresan

torreón: round defensive tower built in Spanish colonial times

vato: cool Chicano, usually driving a lowrider

viga: ceiling beam made of a single tree trunk

zaguán: long central hallway

Suggested Reading

ART AND CULTURE

Clark, Willard. *Remembering Santa Fe*. Layton, UT: Gibbs Smith, 2004. A small hardback edition of selections from the Boston artist who stopped off in Santa Fe in 1928. He stayed to learn printmaking and produce this series of etchings depicting city life.

Eaton, Robert. *The Lightning Field*. Boulder, CO: Johnson Books, 1995. Eaton served as a forest ranger in Chaco Canyon for five years, so his eye is for the empty and the starkly beautiful destinations around the state, including the art installation of the title (in Quemado, in western New Mexico). His essays, each focusing on a different destination, combine history and strong description. Seek this title out if you want to get well off the usual track.

Lamadrid, Enrique. *Hermanitos Comanchitos: Indo-Hispano Rituals of Captivity and Redemption.* Albuquerque: University of New Mexico Press, 2003. Fascinating documentation, in descriptive prose and rich black-and-white photos, of the traditional Spanish dances of northern New Mexico, such as Los Comanches and Los Matachines.

Lummis, Charles F. *A Tramp Across the Continent.* Lincoln, NE: University of Nebraska Press, 1982. In 1884, fledgling journalist Lummis decided to walk from Cincinnati to his new job in Los Angeles; this book chronicles his trip. The sections on New Mexico shine, and Lummis was so entranced that he later moved to the territory. He was the first to write stories about the Penitente brotherhood in the national press.

Myers, Joan. *Pie Town Woman: The Hard Life and Good Times of a New Mexico Homesteader.* Albuquerque: University of New Mexico Press, 2001. The biography of a woman captured in famous Farm Security Administration photos from 1940, this book also muses on the power of memory and photography.

Padilla, Carmella, and Juan Estevan Arellano. *Low 'n Slow: Lowriding in New Mexico.* Santa Fe, NM: Museum of New Mexico Press, 2005. Lovingly lurid color photographs by Jack Parsons are the centerpiece of this book, which pays tribute to New Mexico's Latino car culture—an art form that has even landed a Chimayó lowrider in the Smithsonian.

Parhad, Elisa. *New Mexico: A Guide for the Eyes.* Los Angeles: EyeMuse Books, 2009. Informative short essays on the distinctive things you see in New Mexico and then wonder what the backstory is: concha belts, beat-up pickup trucks, blue sky. The richly illustrated book makes good pre-trip reading or a souvenir when you return.

Price, Roberta. *Across the Great Divide: A Photo Chronicle of the Counterculture.* Albuquerque: University of New Mexico Press, 2010. Documentary photographer Price "went native" with a Colorado commune in the 1960s and visited several groups in New Mexico. She also wrote the narrative *Huerfano: A Memoir of Life in the Counterculture* (Amherst: University of Massachusetts Press, 2004).

Price, V. B. *Albuquerque: A City at the End of the World.* Albuquerque: University of New Mexico Press, 2003. Journalist and poet Price writes a travel guide to New Mexico's biggest metropolis but disguises it as a discourse on urban theory, recommending his favorite spots in the context of the city's unique position and growth processes. Black-and-white photographs by Kirk Gittings highlight the stark landscape.

Robinson, Roxana. *Georgia O'Keeffe: A Life.* Lebanon, NH: University Press of New England, 1998. A strong and intimate biography, focusing on the celebrated painter's role as a protofeminist and her difficult relationships.

FOOD

Feucht, Andrea. *Food Lovers' Guide to Santa Fe, Albuquerque & Taos.* Guilford, CT: Globe Pequot, 2012. A good companion for adventurous eaters, with especially good coverage of Albuquerque's more obscure ethnic restaurants.

Frank, Lois Ellen. *Foods of the Southwest Indian Nations.* Berkeley, CA: Ten Speed Press, 2002. Beautiful photographs are a highlight of this thorough documentation of a little-covered cuisine. They help make an ancient culinary tradition accessible and modern without subjecting it to a heavy-handed fusion treatment. For good reason, it earned a James Beard Award.

Jamison, Cheryl and Bill. *Rancho de Chimayo Cookbook: The Traditional Cooking of New Mexico.* Guilford, CT: Lyons Press, 2014. Like the famous namesake restaurant in a village north of Santa Fe, this engaging cookbook expertly captures the essence of New Mexican cuisine.

Kagel, Katharine. *Cooking with Café Pasqual's: Recipes from Santa Fe's Renowned Corner Cafe.* Berkeley, CA: Ten Speed Press, 2006. Re-create your best meals from the legendary restaurant that set the standard for Santa Fe fusion cooking. Chef Kagel is a charming contrarian, too, which makes for great reading.

HISTORY

Childs, Craig. *House of Rain: Tracking a Vanished Civilization Across the American Southwest.* New York: Little, Brown, 2007. The story of the Ancestral Puebloans, as told by a curious naturalist, becomes less a solution to an archaeological puzzle than a meditation of why we romanticize "lost" civilizations. His more recent book, *Finders Keepers: A Tale of Archaeological Plunder and Possession* (Little, Brown, 2010), takes the drama to the academy, with tales of scholarly intrigue.

Egan, Timothy. *The Worst Hard Time: The Untold Story of Those Who Survived the Great American Dust Bowl.* New York: Mariner Books, 2006. The town of Clayton features a bit in the pages of this highly readable history that conveys the misery and environmental folly of the period.

Held, E. B. *A Spy's Guide to Santa Fe and Albuquerque.* Albuquerque: University of New Mexico Press, 2011. A former CIA agent reveals nefarious Cold War intrigue—fascinating details, if not so grippingly told.

Hordes, Stanley. *To the End of the Earth: A History of the Crypto-Jews of New Mexico.* New York: Columbia University Press, 2008. An exhaustive but intriguing account of the Jewish families who fled the Inquisition and lived in the Southwest as Catholic converts. The communities, some still practicing distinctly Jewish rituals, came to light only a few decades ago.

Horgan, Paul. *Great River.* Middletown, CT: Wesleyan University Press, 1991. Two enormous tomes (*Vol. 1: The Indians and Spain* and *Vol. 2: Mexico and the United States*) won the Pulitzer Prize for history. They're packed with drama, on a base of meticulous analysis of primary sources.

Martinez, Esther. *My Life in San Juan Pueblo.* Champaign, IL: University of Illinois Press, 2004. Born in 1912, Martinez has a lot of stories to tell. This free-flowing book incorporates her memories with larger pueblo folklore, and a CD with recordings of some of her stories is included.

Poling-Kempes, Lesley. *Valley of Shining Stone: The Story of Abiquiu.* Tucson, AZ: University of Arizona Press, 1997. Georgia O'Keeffe fans will like the personal stories of those in her circle in the 1930s, while historians will appreciate the detailed, linear second half of the book, about the transformation of this remote valley into an artists' haven.

Sides, Hampton. *Blood and Thunder: An Epic of the American West.* New York: Doubleday, 2006. Working from the story of Kit Carson and the campaign against the Navajo, including the Long Walk, Sides tells the gripping story of the entire U.S. West. He's an excellent storyteller, and the 480 pages flow by in a rush of land grabs, battles on horseback, and brutality on all sides.

Simmons, Marc. *New Mexico: An Interpretive History.* Albuquerque: University of New

Mexico Press, 1988. The state's historian laureate presents an easy, concise overview of the major historical events. Also look into his more specialized titles, such as *The Last Conquistador: Juan de Oñate and the Settling of the Far Southwest* (Norman: University of Oklahoma Press, 1993).

Smith, Mike. *Towns of the Sandia Mountains.* Charleston, SC: Arcadia, 2006. This slim volume of vintage photographs and juicy stories in extended captions is about a very specific region, but it could tell the story of much of New Mexico in its shift to modernity.

Usner, Donald J. *Sabino's Map: Life in Chimayó's Old Plaza.* Santa Fe, NM: Museum of New Mexico Press, 1995. This balanced and gracefully written history of the author's hometown is illustrated with fond photos of all the craggy-faced characters involved.

LITERATURE AND MEMOIR

Anaya, Rudolfo. *Bless Me, Ultima.* New York: Warner, 1994. Anaya's story of a young boy coming of age in New Mexico in the 1940s is beautifully told. The book, first published in 1973, launched Anaya into his role as Chicano literary hero; his later books, such as *Alburquerque* (1992), are not quite so touching, but they have a lot of historical and ethnic detail.

Blume, Judy. *Tiger Eyes.* New York: Delacorte, 2010. A young girl with family troubles relocates to Los Alamos, giving a great teen's-eye view on the landscape of New Mexico.

Connors, Philip. *Fire Season: Field Notes from a Wilderness Lookout.* New York: Ecco, 2012. In the tradition of Edward Abbey, this memoir recounts life in a remote fire tower in the Gila Wilderness.

Evans, Max. *Hi-Lo to Hollywood: A Max Evans Reader.* Lubbock, TX: Texas Tech

University Press, 1998. Prolific Western author Evans coined the term "Hi-Lo Country" for the "high lonesome" eastern plains of New Mexico, and all of his works, whether essay or fiction, somehow reflect the rolling expanse and the particular dilemmas of the modern cowboys who work on them. A ranch kid himself, he has an eye for detail and a direct and affectionate tone; this reader includes many of his own favorite pieces.

Goodman, Tanya Ward. *Leaving Tinkertown.* Albuquerque: University of New Mexico Press, 2013. A poignant memoir of growing up in the wondrous folk-art assemblage outside Albuquerque. The author's father, Ross Ward, died of early-onset Alzheimer's disease, and this book logs that medical tale, unflinchingly, alongside the larger-than-life artist's own story.

Hillerman, Tony. *Skinwalkers.* New York: HarperTorch, 1990. Hillerman's breakout detective novel, set on the Navajo Nation, weaves a fascinating amount of lore into the plot—which comes in handy when Tribal Affairs police Joe Leaphorn and Jim Chee investigate homicides. Hillerman spun Leaphorn and Chee into a successful franchise, and all of the books show the same cultural depth.

Nichols, John. *The Milagro Beanfield War.* New York: Owl Books, 2005. A comic novel about water rights, set in a northern New Mexico village. Nichols's visionary environmental nonfiction in *On the Mesa* (Layton, UT: Gibbs Smith, 2005) is also stunning.

Pillsbury, Dorothy. *Roots in Adobe.* Santa Fe, NM: Lightning Tree Press, 1983. Pillsbury's charming stories capture the strangeness and warmth of Santa Fe culture in the 1940s. The author tells hilarious stories of settling into her little home and the characters she meets.

Quade, Kirstin Valdez. *Night at the Fiestas.* New York: W. W. Norton, 2015. Quade, who grew up in New Mexico, sets many of the short stories in this collection in tiny Hispano towns, amid the most intense belief and ritual. A great mix of cultural detail and poignant characters.

Silko, Leslie Marmon. *Ceremony.* New York: Penguin, 1988. Silko's classic novel about the impact of the atomic bomb on Native Americans' worldview (and that of all Americans) is brutal, beautiful, and bleak.

NATURE AND THE ENVIRONMENT

Coltrin, Mike. *Sandia Mountain Hiking Guide.* Albuquerque: University of New Mexico Press, 2019. A meticulously compiled guide with thorough trail descriptions, GPS coordinates, color photos, and a foldout map of the east and west slopes of the mountain.

Julyan, Robert, and Mary Stuever, eds. *Field Guide to the Sandia Mountains.* Albuquerque: University of New Mexico Press, 2005. A thorough guide illustrated with color photographs, detailing birds, animals, plants, even insects of the Sandias. Most of it applies to the Santa Fe area, too.

Kavanagh, James. *New Mexico Nature Set: Field Guides to Wildlife, Birds, Trees & Wildflowers of New Mexico.* Dunedin, FL: Waterford Press, 2017. This collection of three pocket guides provides a handy means to identify and better understand what you're likely to see out in the wild on hikes across the state.

Kricher, John. *A Field Guide to Rocky Mountain and Southwest Forests.* New York: Houghton Mifflin Harcourt, 2003. A Peterson Field Guide, covering both flora and fauna: trees, birds, mammals, you name it.

It's illustrated with both color photos and drawings. It's not encyclopedic, but it's a great basic reference. Peterson guides are also available for narrower categories such as reptiles and amphibians or butterflies.

McFarland, Casey, and S. David Scott. *Bird Feathers: A Guide to North American Species.* Mechanicsburg, PA: Stackpole Books, 2010. While not New Mexico-specific, it is the only guide of its kind, and its authors grew up in the state and know the birdlife well. Great for serious birders and curious hikers, with detailed photographs.

Price, V. B. *The Orphaned Land: New Mexico's Environment Since the Manhattan Project.* Albuquerque: University of New Mexico Press, 2011. Journalist Price examines New Mexico's droughts and other trials—in the same vein as Reisner's *Cadillac Desert.*

Reisner, Marc. *Cadillac Desert: The American West and Its Disappearing Water.* New York: Penguin, 1993. Not specifically about New Mexico, but an excellent analysis of the Southwest's water shortage and how the U.S. government's dam-building projects exacerbated it. Apocalyptic, sarcastic, and totally compelling.

Sibley, David Allen. *The Sibley Field Guide to Birds of Western North America.* New York: Knopf, 2003. The New Mexican birder's book of choice, with 810 species listed, about 4,600 color illustrations, and a handy compact format. Generally beats out Peterson's otherwise respectable series.

Tekiela, Stan. *Birds of New Mexico: Field Guide.* Cambridge, MN: Adventure Publications, 2003. A great book for beginning birders or curious visitors, with 140 of the state's most common species listed, many illustrated with photographs.

Happy Trails!

See northern New Mexico through a focused lens, with these specialized guides to the state.

- **Brewery Trail** (www.nmbeer.org): Features a downloadable map to breweries across the state.
- **Green Chile Cheeseburger Trail** (www.newmexico.org): Between this and a breakfast burrito trail (same site), you'll never go hungry again.
- **Film Trails** (www.newmexico.org): Takes visitors to filming locations for more than a dozen films, plus *Breaking Bad*.
- **Trails in New Mexico State Parks** (www.emnrd.state.nm.us): Offers an alphabetized list and summaries of some of the best hikes in state parks.
- **On the Trail of Ghost Towns** (www.newmexico.org): Includes an interactive map of ghost towns throughout the state, including several in northern New Mexico.

Internet Resources

TRAVEL INFORMATION

Visit Albuquerque
www.visitalbuquerque.org
The official intro to the city and surrounding areas provides events listings as well as hotel-booking services.

ExploreNM
http://explorenm.com
This site includes an extensive, if barebones, repository of user reviews of hikes and campgrounds around New Mexico.

New Mexico Tourism Department
www.newmexico.org
The best of the official sites, this one has thorough maps and suggested itineraries.

Public Lands Information Center
www.publiclands.org
Buy USGS, Forest Service, and other topographical maps online from the Bureau of Land Management's well-organized website. There's a good stock of nature guides and other travel books, too.

Sangres.com
www.sangres.com
Scores of travel details about the mountain communities, culture, and history of northern New Mexico, as well as southern Colorado are available, though the site is not updated regularly.

Taos Vacation Guide
www.taos.org
This thorough directory includes events listings.

Tourism Santa Fe
www.santafe.org
Near-exhaustive listings of tourist attractions and services are on this slickly produced site.

Visit Los Alamos
www.visitlosalamos.org
This site is colorful and helpfully arranged, with suggestions based on the time you have available.

NEWS AND CULTURE

Albuquerque Journal
www.abqjournal.com

The state's largest newspaper is available free online after answering survey questions.

Chasing Santa Fe
www.chasingsantafe.blogspot.com

The glamorous Santa Fe lifestyle is lovingly documented: local chefs, events, new shops, and fashion spotting.

New Mexico Political Report
http://nmpoliticalreport.com

This nonprofit news site covers New Mexico politics thoroughly and unearths stories you're not likely to find anywhere else.

New Mexico Politics with Joe Monahan
www.joemonahansnewmexico. blogspot.com

Political analyst Joe Monahan's obsessive, snarky blog charts the circus that is state politics.

The Paper
http://abq.news

The Paper, formerly the long-running *Alibi,* has an extensive events calendar.

Santa Fe New Mexican
www.santafenewmexican.com

Santa Fe's main newspaper includes the gossip column "El Mitote," which documents celebs in Santa Fe, and the "Roundhouse Roundup" does roughly the same—but with politicians.

Santa Fe Reporter
www.sfreporter.com

Santa Fe's free weekly is politically sharp and often funny. Get opinionated reviews and news analysis here.

Smithsonian Folkways
https://folkways.si.edu

Prep for your road trip at this enormous online music archive, which has a number of traditional treasures from the state, including the excellent *Music of New Mexico: Hispanic Traditions* and *New Mexico: Native American Traditions.*

Taos News
www.taosnews.com

The town paper is a weekly, but its website has daily updates and an events calendar.

Index

A

List of Maps

Photo Credits

MOON

ACADIA
NATIONAL PARK

SEASIDE TOWNS · FALL FOLIAGE
CYCLING & PADDLING

HILARY NANGLE

MOON

ARCHES &
CANYONLANDS
NATIONAL PARKS

HIKING · BIKING
SCENIC DRIVES

JUDY JEWELL & W. C. McRAE

MOON

BANFF
NATIONAL PARK

HIKE · CAMP
SEE WILDLIFE

ANDREW HEMPSTEAD

MOON

DEATH VALLEY
NATIONAL PARK

HIKING · SCENIC DRIVES
DESERT SPRINGS & HIDDEN OASES

JENNA BLOUGH

MOON

GLACIER
NATIONAL PARK

HIKING · CAMPING
LAKES & PEAKS

BECKY LOMAX

MOON

GRAND
CANYON

HIKE · CAMP
RAFT THE
COLORADO RIVER

TIM HULL

MOON

GREAT SMOKY
MOUNTAINS
NATIONAL PARK

HIKING · CAMPING
SCENIC DRIVES

JASON FRYE

MOON

JOSHUA TREE
& PALM SPRINGS

HIKING · SCENIC DRIVES
DESERT GETAWAYS

JENNA BLOUGH

MOON

ROCKY
MOUNTAIN
NATIONAL PARK

HIKE · CAMP
SEE WILDLIFE

ERIN ENGLISH

MOON

CANADIAN
ROCKIES
WITH BANFF & JASPER NATIONAL PARKS

SCENIC DRIVES · WILDLIFE
HIKING & SKIING

ANDREW HEMPSTEAD

MOON

YELLOWSTONE
& GRAND TETON

HIKE · CAMP
SEE WILDLIFE

BECKY LOMAX

MOON

YOSEMITE
SEQUOIA &
KINGS CANYON

HIKING · CAMPING
WATERFALLS & BIG TREES

ANN MARIE BROWN

MOON

ZION &
BRYCE
WITH ARCHES, CANYONLANDS, CAPITOL REEF,
GRAND STAIRCASE-ESCALANTE & MOAB

HIKING & BIKING
STARGAZING · SCENIC DRIVES

MAYA SILVER

Spending
only a few
days in a
park?

Try our Best
Of guides.

MOON

- BEST OF -

ACADIA
MAKE THE MOST OF
ONE TO THREE DAYS
IN THE PARK

TOP SIGHTS, TOP HIKES,
TOP SCENIC DRIVES

HILARY NANGLE

MOON

- BEST OF -

GLACIER, BANFF,
& JASPER
MAKE THE MOST OF
ONE TO THREE DAYS
IN THE PARKS

TOP SIGHTS, TOP HIKES,
TOP SCENIC DRIVES

BECKY LOMAX & ANDREW HEMPSTEAD

MOON

Plan your parks adventure!

Get inspired for your next adventure

Follow **@moonguides** on Instagram or subscribe to our newsletter at **moon.com**

#TravelWithMoon

MAP SYMBOLS

——— Expressway	○ City/Town	🛈 Information Center	♠ Park
——— Primary Road	◉ State Capital	🅿 Parking Area	⚑ Golf Course
⋯⋯ Secondary Road	⊛ National Capital	⚑ Church	✦ Unique Feature
⋯⋯ Unpaved Road	★ Highlight	🍷 Winery/Vineyard	➘ Waterfall
---------- Trail	★ Point of Interest	🔲 Trailhead	△ Camping
⋯⋯⋯ Ferry	• Accommodation	🚉 Train Station	▲ Mountain
◆-◆-◆ Railroad	▼ Restaurant/Bar	✈ Airport	⛷ Ski Area
⬛⬛ Pedestrian Walkway	■ Other Location	✈ Airfield	◠ Glacier
⬛⬛⬛ Stairs			

CONVERSION TABLES

°C = (°F - 32) / 1.8
°F = (°C x 1.8) + 32
1 inch = 2.54 centimeters (cm)
1 foot = 0.304 meters (m)
1 yard = 0.914 meters
1 mile = 1.6093 kilometers (km)
1 km = 0.6214 miles
1 fathom = 1.8288 m
1 chain = 20.1168 m
1 furlong = 201.168 m
1 acre = 0.4047 hectares
1 sq km = 100 hectares
1 sq mile = 2.59 square km
1 ounce = 28.35 grams
1 pound = 0.4536 kilograms
1 short ton = 0.90718 metric ton
1 short ton = 2,000 pounds
1 long ton = 1.016 metric tons
1 long ton = 2,240 pounds
1 metric ton = 1,000 kilograms
1 quart = 0.94635 liters
1 US gallon = 3.7854 liters
1 Imperial gallon = 4.5459 liters
1 nautical mile = 1.852 km

MOON SANTA FE, TAOS & ALBUQUERQUE

Avalon Travel
Hachette Book Group
1700 Fourth Street
Berkeley, CA 94710, USA
www.moon.com

Editor: Rachael Sablik
Managing Editor: Hannah Brezack
Copy Editor: Barbara Schultz
Graphics and Production Coordinator:
  Lucie Ericksen
Cover Design: Toni Tajima
Interior Design: Avalon Travel
Map Editor: Kat Bennett
Cartographers: Abby Whelan and Karin Dahl
Proofreader: Callie Stoker-Graham
Indexer: Greg Jewett

ISBN-13: 979-8-88647-038-3

Printing History
1st Edition — 2006
7th Edition — May 2024
5 4 3 2 1

Front cover photo: adobe house, animal skull and hanging chili peppers ristra in Santa Fe © ivanastar / Getty Images
Back cover photo: San Geronimo Church at Taos Pueblo © Rinus Baak | Dreamstime.com

Printed in Thailand